WARRIOR DIPLOMAT

WARRIOR

DIPLOMAT

A Green Beret's Battles from
Washington to Afghanistan

MICHAEL G. WALTZ

Foreword by Peter Bergen

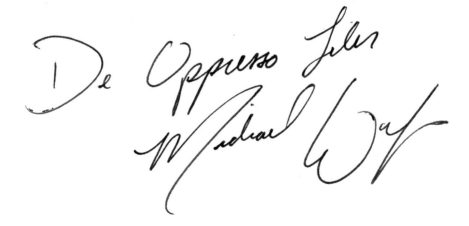

Potomac Books
An imprint of the University of Nebraska Press

Potomac Books is an imprint of the University
of Nebraska Press. Manufactured in the United
States of America. ∞

Library of Congress Control Number:
2014944961

Set in Chaparral Pro by Renni Johnson.
Designed by A. Shahan.

Dedicated to the families of our fallen soldiers. They bear the greatest burden of our wars.

All net proceeds from this writing will be donated to veterans' charities.

CONTENTS

ILLUSTRATIONS

MAPS

FOREWORD

With the Afghan war ostensibly coming to an end after thirteen long years, many who were involved with the American adventure in South Asia have written a postmortem on America's longest war. Journalists, policymakers, and soldiers have all provided their perspectives on what went right and what went wrong. What distinguishes Waltz's book from the rest is that he experienced Afghanistan both at a senior policy level and on front lines around the country.

Serving first in the Office of the Deputy Assistant Secretary of Defense for Counternarcotics, where he helped establish the Defense Department's funding, programs, and strategy for counternarcotics activities in Afghanistan, and then as Vice President Richard B. Cheney's special advisor for South Asia and counterterrorism, Waltz brings readers into the Pentagon and the Eisenhower Executive Office Building where the sausage of policy is made. It is not a pretty process.

Having been the commander of a U.S. Army Special Forces unit, making multiple deployments to Afghanistan and the Middle East, Waltz also illustrates how these policies affected the war fighters on the ground as they tried to work with their coalition partners, Afghan security forces, and the local populace.

A well-trained operator, Waltz notes that from the very beginning, there didn't seem to be a strategic vision for Afghanistan, causing coalition efforts to be primarily reactive in nature. This was only compounded by the U.S. decision to invade Iraq in 2003, diverting key resources and expertise from Afghanistan. It's a theme he repeats throughout the book: that the men and women on the ground didn't have the tools they needed to make effective changes. One can't help but wonder where Afghanistan would be now if they had.

With his years of service, Waltz is one of the most qualified people to bring these two sides of the Afghan war together, and the story he tells is one of seemingly good intentions but confused, uncoordinated, and stifling bureaucracy. While he is not afraid to criticize his former employers—a refreshing trait in Washington—he also shows how completely unprepared NATO was for the mission in Afghanistan. Having worked alongside a variety of coalition countries in a number of Afghan provinces, from Herat in the west to Kandahar in the south, Waltz saw firsthand how much Europe's war fighting abilities had atrophied since World War II. Expecting a peacekeeping mission similar to that in Bosnia, NATO was not prepared for the devastation decades of war had wreaked on the country. On top of that, each international partner came with its own chain of command and national "caveats," which dictated how and when they could conduct security missions and interact with the locals. Though some resourceful officers were able to think up workarounds for these limitations, Waltz details how these different units chafed at the restrictions and were embarrassed that they couldn't do more to help. The frustration at countless missed opportunities is palpable.

But while many of NATO's problems stemmed from its inability to operate under a unified command, the U.S. military suffered from the opposite problem. At one point in the text Waltz details how he had to process a mission request through a chain of twelve different commanders. As he notes, a more stringent approval process for U.S. operations had been put into place in 2005 by Lt. Gen. Karl Eikenberry, then-commander of U.S. forces in Afghanistan, after President Hamid Karzai of Afghanistan complained about the night raids that were being conducted. Four years later the situation on the ground had changed, but the rule—which required all missions to be approved by Eikenberry and his successors—had not. The result was a system that required mission packages to be submitted at least a week in advance and could not react quickly enough to the rapidly changing conflict.

Though Waltz highlights a number of different issues in the book, from NATO partners not having compatible equipment to the drawbacks of an all-volunteer force, he argues that President Barack Obama's 2009 announcement of both a surge in U.S. forces in Afghanistan and a timetable for their withdrawal was a critical mistake in the war effort. In his view, "just as he [Obama] announced he was sending our military and civilians the resources they had so long deserved, he pulled the rug out from under the effect they would have before they even arrived." The entire region began preparing for a post-U.S. Afghanistan, often in ways that ran counter to U.S. interests, and NATO partners and civilian agencies began heading for the exits. Instead of talking about how to win in Afghanistan, Washington's focus was on simply ending "the good war." All Afghans heard was that they were being abandoned by the United States yet again, and the Taliban knew that they only had to outlast the surge.

What makes all of this worse, in Waltz's opinion, is that years after making the same mistakes over and over again, the United States finally seems to have the makings of a winning formula. Special Operations forces are working alongside key tribes in strategic areas, the Afghan security forces are taking over the fight against the insurgency, and multinational corporations are investing in Afghanistan's economy. What is missing is a positive and consistent message that lets Afghans know the United States will be with them for the long haul and explains to the American public why our troops are still in Afghanistan, three years after Osama bin Laden was killed in Pakistan.

As Waltz notes, Afghanistan is a place where time is measured in centuries, not decades. America once took the long view with regard to its strategic priorities—stationing thousands of troops in South Korea, where they remain today—and a similar commitment is needed in Afghanistan. It may not be a politically attractive argument to make to voters, especially in today's hyperpartisan environment, but instead of repeatedly telling the public that fighting in Afghanistan is hard and that the United States should leave, policymakers should clearly indicate why the country needs to stay engaged.

With *Warrior Diplomat*, Waltz makes it painfully clear that all of the U.S. soldiers, coalition fighters, and Afghan civilians who have supported this war effort deserved far better than they received. As both a policymaker and an operator, Waltz illustrates how the decisions made behind a desk thousands of miles away from the front have very real and sometimes deadly consequences.

Peter Bergen

PREFACE

Just a few months after I had been sitting in the White House Situation Room, I found myself staring into North Waziristan, Pakistan, the heartland of international terrorism and ground zero for the insurgency raging across eastern Afghanistan. It was 2009, and I was in command of a reserve U.S. Army Special Forces unit on the Afghan border. Only then did I fully appreciate how few people have a hand in crafting U.S. policy for a war and then also have to go to the war zone to personally execute the strategies they advocated. Fewer still have the opportunity to then return to Washington multiple times to attempt to address the major disconnects between the intent of the policies and what actually occurs in the field.

My goal in writing this book is to explain the errors we've made in how the war in Afghanistan has been executed. Despite the best of intentions, our military's and government's management of this war has been deeply flawed. Frankly, the effectiveness of our policies has not been worthy of the sacrifices of men like Brian Woods, Matt Pucino, and thousands like them who are no longer with us. I firmly believe that historians will point to five key mistakes as they examine the effort in Afghanistan to explain why we have had such difficulty there: (1) the chronic lack of resources to stabilize the country (NATO's shortcomings and the Iraq War were important subsets); (2) an ill-defined overall strategy for success; (3) risk aversion in the execution of operations; (4) our inability to deal with the Taliban sanctuary in Pakistan; and (5) declaring the 2014 withdrawal years in advance. These errors must be discussed and documented by a direct participant at multiple levels.

I have sought to reveal these policy points through my personal experiences in the field. Each chapter illustrates a theme, such as the key mistakes previously listed and the issues of civilian casualties and our disjointed development efforts. I do not address many important issues that also had an enormous impact on the war, such as the actions of President Hamid Karzai, the impact of Iran, and the widespread corruption from multiple quarters throughout the war. Their omission is more a reflection of my lack of personal involvement during my combat tours than their importance. I also realize that significant fault lies with the Afghans themselves for the problems they continue to face. However, that topic alone could be an entirely separate book. Unfortunately, just as we finally seemed to be getting things right with the "surge" in 2010, the Obama administration undercut its positive effects by announcing the withdrawal of U.S. troops by the end of 2014. Several chapters highlight the immediate damage this announcement had on our efforts in the field to secure the support of Afghan tribes and continues to have on the psyche of the region's people.

Though my focus is primarily on our faulty polices and inadequate execution, there is an inherent friction in the book as I also try to emphasize why the war was, and still is, worth fighting. The last thing I want is for readers to close this book with validation that the war in Afghanistan was simply too hard and therefore not worth pursuing. Despite its massive difficulties, stabilizing Afghanistan is absolutely still in our national interest. Preventing Afghanistan from descending back into chaos is essential to the long-term defeat of al Qaeda and the ideological extremism of the Taliban, just as shoring up Germany, Japan, and Korea were essential to defeating the ideology of communism after World War II. I fear that in the wake of an American withdrawal we will see an Afghanistan in civil war; an unstable, nuclear-armed Pakistan; and a resurgent al Qaeda. Long-term engagement is a difficult case to make, but for our children's sake, it is one our policymakers must have the courage to make despite our blunders over the past decade.

To be sure, there will be folks who will not appreciate some of the criticisms I level and will dislike and disagree with what they read. I initially resisted writing, knowing there are those in the Special Operations community of "silent professionals" who will see this project as self-serving or making excuses for personal failings. It was not my intention to assign individual blame. In fact our difficulties in Afghanistan have been much bigger than any one person and are the result of fundamental flaws in how our government is organized and underlying incentives to avoid risk. In the end a mentor convincingly scolded me, "It is this type of firsthand account historians will reference as they look back on this war. You have a duty to capture your truly unique perspective as a warrior diplomat."

It is important for me to note that I sought to protect the identities of those who will continue to find themselves overseas and in harm's way doing the nation's business. I have used only the first names of all still serving. These men know who they are, what they have done, and that they have my enduring admiration and respect.

I describe events as I remember them, augmented by dozens of little black notebooks I kept with me in Washington and the field. These notebooks cover everything from meetings in the White House to *shuras* (meetings) with Afghan elders over cups of tea. A number of colleagues and participants in those events reviewed drafts of the manuscript to ensure its accuracy. The actual dialogue may not be exact, but it conveys the essence of what was said. My story is admittedly only one perspective, one man's journey from one end of the spear to the other in fighting our nation's longest war.

The Department of Defense Office of Pre-publication and Security Review, the White House Office of Access Management, and the State Department have cleared this book for publication.

ACKNOWLEDGMENTS

No one writes a book, makes policy, or fights a war alone. I am so grateful to the following people who had a direct and lasting impact on those three aspects of my life.

Dr. Marin Strmecki encouraged me to capture my experiences and frustrations with the war in writing. My editors, Hilary Clagget and Alicia Christensen, and publisher, Potomac Books, took a chance on a first-time author. Dr. Joe Blady, Sgt. First Class (Ret.) Brian Duffy, and Bailey Cahail of the New America Foundation offered tireless, patient, and detailed reviews of the manuscript that greatly improved my writing. Peter Bergen was kind enough to craft a foreword that captured the book's essence.

Mary Beth Long tirelessly pushed for better policies toward Afghanistan from the Pentagon and NATO. John Hannah and Samantha Ravich honored me with the opportunity to serve in the White House in what may turn out to be the best job of my life.

My daughter, Anderson, dealt with many nights and weekends with Daddy on the computer. My mother created limitless opportunities for a poor kid from Jacksonville, Florida, and provided me a living example of the American Dream. My ex-wife, Kellie, cared for our daughter during my tours in Afghanistan and bore the burden of my service. Without spouses on the home front, the volunteer army could not exist.

The soldiers and the people of Afghanistan will always have my admiration; we stood by them and shared their sacrifices as they struggled to create a future free of extremism. I'm utterly convinced that the futures of both countries will be inextricably linked for at least the next generation. Special thanks to the men of the United Arab Emirates Special Operations Command's Task Force 6 and 7. They stood tall as examples of tolerance and a brighter future for the region. Most of all, I am grateful to my fellow Green Berets depicted in this book. It was the honor of my life to serve our country alongside such great Americans.

Finally, I thank God that I am still alive. I will do my very best to never take it for granted and fulfill His purpose for me.

ABBREVIATIONS

ANA: Afghan National Army

ANP: Afghan National Police

ATVs: all-terrain vehicles

CDI: Community Defense Initiative

CJSOTF: Combined Joint Special Operations Task Force

CJTF: Combined Joint Task Force

CSTC-A: Combined Security Transition Command–Afghanistan

ETTs: embedded training teams

FATA: Federally Administered Tribal Areas

FOB: Forward Operating Base

GMV: ground mobility vehicle

HIG: Hezb-e-Islami Gulbuddin

IED: improvised explosive device

INL: Bureau for International Narcotics and Law Enforcement, U.S. State Department

ISAF: International Security Assistance Force

ISI: Inter-Services Intelligence

JTAC: joint tactical air controller

M-ATV: MRAP all-terrain vehicle

MBITR: type of radio

MRAP: mine-resistant ambush-protected vehicle

NATO: North Atlantic Treaty Organization

NCO: noncommissioned officer

NSC: National Security Council

ODA: Operational Detachment Alpha

ODB: Operational Detachment Bravo

OSD-Policy: Office of the Secretary of Defense–Policy

PRT: provincial reconstruction team

QRF: quick-reaction force

RPG: rocket-propelled grenade

SAS: Special Air Service

SATCOM: satellite communications

SOTF: Special Operations Task Force

TIC: troops in contact

UAE: United Arab Emirates

USAID: U.S. Agency for International Development

VSO: Village Stability Operations

WIA: wounded in action

WARRIOR DIPLOMAT

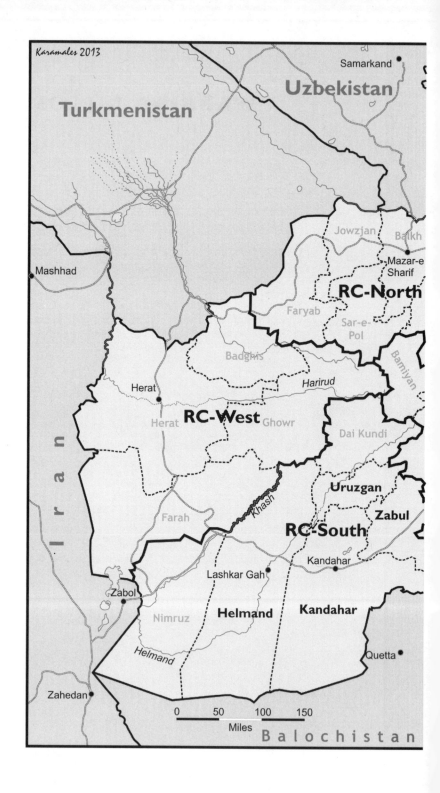

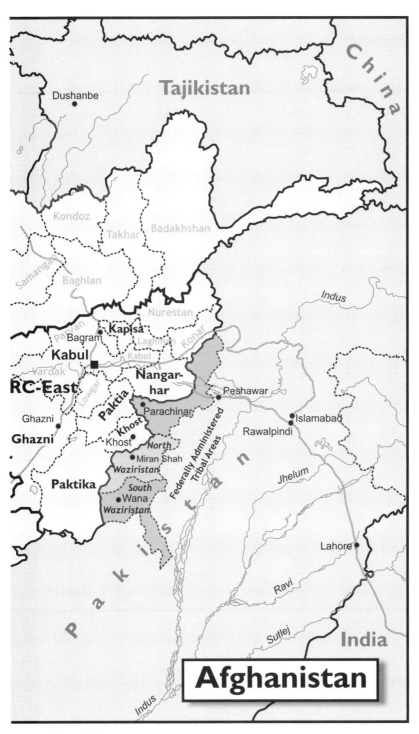

Map 1. Afghanistan.

Introduction
A Little Girl in Ghazni

No one dared make a sound. We were in the heart of Taliban country, infiltrating quietly on foot, several kilometers from our vehicles and their heavy weapons. We were even farther from the nearest coalition base or any type of reinforcements. Twenty-foot-high mud brick walls loomed above us as the long line of U.S. Special Forces operators, Afghan police, and Afghan commandos silently snaked through the narrow alleys and dirt pathways of Mangur village in Ghazni Province. Many of the thick walls were anchored with castle-like turrets and slit windows. Some windows had glass; most did not, and I waited for the black silhouette of an AK-47 rifle to slide out from one of them and begin firing.

Through my night-vision goggles I could see dozens of green lasers flickering from window to window and scanning the tops of every wall and doorway. The lasers and spotlights were visible only through goggles and shone from attachments aligned perfectly with the barrel of each man's weapon. Where the laser hit, the bullet would hit.

That night the target was Mullah Hasmani. Mangur had special meaning to me and the men of Special Forces Operational Detachment Alpha (ODA) 21, one of six teams under my command in the summer of 2009. It was the site of my unit's first soldier killed in action, Staff Sergeant Brian Woods, as well as the death of Afzali, the deputy commander of the Afghan National Police (ANP) unit that was partnered with ODA 21. The village was relatively large and located in the heart of the volatile Andar District, Ghazni Province, in Eastern Afghanistan and was mainly inhabited by the Andar tribe. The Andar was one of the earliest tribes to support a resurgent Taliban and oppose the local government in Ghazni City, which it viewed as corrupt and ineffective.

Map 2. Mangur ambush, Ghazni Province.

My men really wanted Mullah Hasmani. He was a midlevel commander known to have brutally mutilated the Andar district police chief as well as several Andar tribal elders who had opposed him as the Taliban steadily took over most of Ghazni Province, district by district, in 2009. Hasmani had led the ambush that resulted in the deaths of Brian and Afzali as well as the wounding of several other Afghan policemen. The team's intelligence cell had tracked him for months, and a source in the village had tipped us off that he was due to arrive back from Pakistan that night. The potential for a serious firefight was high, so I had flown in an additional team, ODA 23, and their partnered Afghan National Army commandos, as well as a small command and control cell from my headquarters in eastern Afghanistan. By having my command cell present, the leadership of the ODAs could focus on tactically employing their teams and Afghan partners while we took care of coordinating any required support, such as aircraft, reinforcements, or medical evacuation (medevac).

The plan was for each ODA and their partners to split in two sections. We planned to hit Hasmani's house and three other compounds simultaneously. One of them belonged to his lieutenant, one was a school that reportedly doubled as an ammunition storage site, and one belonged to a relative of Hasmani and doubled as an alternate place for Hasmani to sleep. Most insurgent commanders regularly rotated where they slept in order to avoid night raids—that is, when they were not resting or refitting in the neighboring lawless tribal areas of Pakistan. Hitting all four compounds simultaneously took an extra level of coordination and complexity but would hopefully prevent Hasmani from escaping if he had switched houses since our source last saw him. It would also prevent one of his lieutenants or relatives from counterattacking once we initiated the raid. ODA 21 and the police had Hasmani's house as their primary target, as well as his relative's compound. ODA 23 and the commandos had Hasmani's lieutenant and the weapons cache at the school.

Our higher headquarters did not have helicopters permanently assigned to it, which meant we had to request them from the U.S. conventional command for each mission. As was typical, the helicopter support was denied. Driving our vehicles down the only road into the village would surely have given us away to the Taliban. Instead we used a tactic called vehicle offset. We drove our armored Humvees at night, completely blacked out, to a spot far enough away to prevent the engine noise from

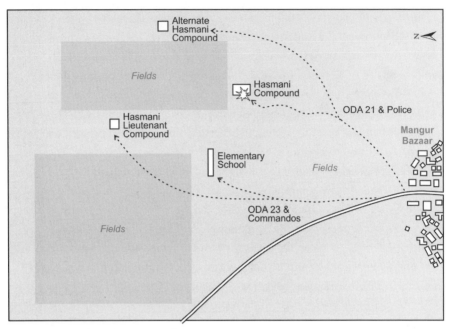

Map 3. Plan of Mangur raid.

tipping off the Taliban but close enough to walk to the target. We had an Afghan informant with us who was from the neighboring village and was supposed to lead us on a safe route to the target. We originally intended to skirt the edge of Mangur village but had somehow ended up walking right through the heart of it. As we stumbled down the main road through the village, exactly where we didn't want to go, I was beginning to wonder if the informant was double-crossing us and leading us into a trap.

I listened to my radio headset. Grant, the team leader for ODA 21 at the front of the line, reminded everyone to be extra vigilant as we slowly made our way past the shops of the village bazaar. Grant was an experienced West Point graduate on his second tour as a team leader in Afghanistan. He rarely got excited, even under the most difficult circumstances, such as taking a wrong turn in a Taliban-controlled village.

We were particularly on edge because many villages paid a night watchman, who was sometimes armed, to keep an eye on their closed shops. If we stumbled upon him, at best he would tip off everyone to our presence; at worst he would open fire. We spotted the night watchman asleep on a wood-and-rope cot just above us on the roof of one of the mud hut shops. We could see the outline of his AK-47 leaning against his bunk. A dozen infrared lasers flickered on his body as the operators with night vision kept their rifles trained on him while the rest of the group quietly slid by. I prayed that he didn't wake up, hear us, and reach for that rifle. Not only would it be a very bad night for him if he did, but it would compromise the entire mission.

We reached the edge of town without incident, and I saw the black silhouettes of several large compounds looming in the distance across a number of plowed fields. This was the point where the teams were to split off toward their various targets. Behind me, Jason, the team leader for ODA 23, whispered into his microphone for his team and their Afghan Army commandos to halt. Jason was a stocky, gregarious officer with a quick wit. His relaxed demeanor made it easy to underestimate him, but he was incredibly smart and a very good tactical planner. The infrared strobe light on his helmet flickered as he walked down the line of the Afghans, counting them off and making sure they went with the right group on the correct trail to the correct target. I chuckled to myself as I saw Jason's short, bulky outline gesturing in frustration as he ran back down the trail to retrieve two Afghan commandos who had inexplicably stopped in the middle of the trail while the rest of the group walked away. The commandos were the best of the best of the Afghan Army. They had more training, better equipment, and an ODA dedicated to their ongoing training. But they still regularly made mistakes and had to be closely managed.

In general Afghan National Army soldiers tended to be better trained, more capable, and far less corrupt than the ANP. However, 21's partnered police were the Afghan equivalent of a SWAT team and had been conducting operations alongside Special Forces teams since 9/11. They were known for their discipline, and I would put them toe to toe with the Afghan commandos any day. The commandos were an ethnic mix of Tajiks, Uzbeks, Hazaras, and Pashtuns (the Pashtuns were the ethnic group in southern and eastern Afghanistan that formed the Taliban movement) in order to ensure no one major ethnic group dominated the Army. The ANP unit, however, was nearly completely Hazara, an ethnic group that had been brutally repressed during the Taliban's reign. The police unit was good, but its members had scores to settle with the Pashtun-dominated Taliban and could be very aggressive when conducting these types of missions in Taliban-leaning villages. ODA 21 knew they had to watch them closely, particularly in Mangur, where their second in command had been killed.

I joined the tail end of ODA 23's second split team heading toward the compound of Hasmani's lieutenant. This compound was centrally located on a small hill roughly in the middle of the four targets, and I wanted to position myself there as it would be the best place to maintain radio contact should we get into a firefight.

As we navigated across the fields toward our target, I couldn't help but think about the last time I had spoken with Brian Woods, months before the deployment, during our premission training at Camp Guernsey in Wyoming.

"Hey, sir, let me show you something," Brian said, waving me into his barracks room. He proudly showed me a new "upper" for an M4 rifle he had purchased. "Has a floating barrel," he grinned.

"Nice," I said, and proceeded to ask him a dozen questions about the weapon. My guys were truly experts in their fields, and I loved learning from them.

Brian relished walking me through every detail of his new toy and why that particular barrel was far superior to the plethora of other gun parts the team had scattered about the room and were now instantly obsolete as far as Brian was concerned. Even though he was the team's medic, trained to the level of a trauma physician's assistant, his real passion was guns. Regardless of their specialties, every Special Forces operator loved the latest gear, from the newest type of magazine pouch attached to their body armor to that year's selection of Patagonia fleeces. Some guys, like Brian, took the gear obsession to whole new levels.

Months after our chat in his barracks room, Brian's ODA was on a mission to reopen a bazaar that had been ordered closed by a Taliban commander allied with Hasmani. The ODA had attempted to raid the commander's house the night before, but their lumbering twenty-ton mine-resistant ambush-protected (MRAP) armored vehicles had become stuck several times in the drainage ditches and irrigation canals that crisscrossed the province. It took all night to recover the heavy vehicles, and the ODA ran out of time to conduct the raid. They decided to press on to the village bazaar during the day, despite the hugely increased danger of getting hit by an improvised explosive device (IED). They were determined to chip away at the Taliban's stranglehold on the area, even though it meant traversing Andar District, a hotbed of tribal rivalry and insurgent activity in the increasingly volatile Ghazni Province.

As the team passed through the town of Mangur, the lead vehicle with Brian and the team's senior communications sergeant, Tony, received some sporadic fire from across a field. The ODA's partnered ANP charged toward the fire in their Humvees, with Tony and Brian having no choice but to follow them in their much larger and heavier MRAP. The MRAP again became stuck as the trails narrowed in a series of orchards and the harassing fire continued. Eventually Tony ordered Brian and the police to get out of their vehicles and continue the pursuit on foot. Tony was the senior sergeant in the lead vehicle of the convoy and a veteran of multiple Afghanistan rotations. He later told me, "Looking back, the only time I ever saw Brian hesitate under fire, for just an instant, was when I told everyone to leave the vehicles. Somehow his voice was different when he responded. Then he took a deep breath, grabbed his medical bag, and hopped out the back door." The squad of ANP with Brian and Tony moved toward a group of men they saw about a hundred yards away. Suddenly a barrage of automatic fire erupted from a line of trees to their left. Later Tony explained what happened: "We were standing right in the middle of an open field, with no cover, no place to run, and bullets flying everywhere around us. We could hear the rounds fly by our heads with that distinctive crack and whizzing sound. Several ANP hit the ground and curled up into a ball. I was thinking, 'What the Hell! Why isn't anyone shooting, what am I doing wrong?'

"I shouted at the police to return fire as I took a knee and raised my weapon. Bullets were hitting the dirt in front of me. Brian turned and moved to the Afghan a few feet away that was curled up like a baby and bent over him so they were face to face. Brian yelled, 'What the hell are you doing? Let's go!' Suddenly, the back of Brian's head exploded. The force of the blow flipped him onto his back and he slammed into the ground very hard. I saw his face and instantly knew Brian was gone. My heart broke at the loss.

"I instinctively grabbed a few Afghan policemen and shoved them forward. It was either stay exposed in the middle of this field and die or charge the ambush. I moved forward at a fast walk with my rifle raised and emptied my magazine into the tree line as I advanced. As I dropped to a knee and looked back at my friend lying in the field, I saw him move. Brian was alive! I yelled at the interpreter to tell the police to clear the tree line of any remaining Taliban and then went back to Brian, determined to save his life."

Tony spent the next hour trying to keep Brian alive. At the same time he tried to talk the remainder of his team to his location and coordinate calling for a medevac helicopter. He tore into Brian's medical kit, stuffing gauze into the head wound and desperately trying to remember everything Brian had taught him during their medical training. Brian was breathing, but with great difficulty. His mouth was foaming blood and mucus through clenched teeth.

"I knew I needed to open an airway, quickly, to help him breathe," Tony recounted. "I needed to insert a six-inch hose into his nostril, so I used a trick he taught me long ago; use the casualty's own blood and mucus to lubricate the tube. The technique worked. With the airway open, breathing became easier for him. I then focused on improving the small security perimeter to prevent a counterattack. Here I was, alone in one of the most dangerous districts in all of Afghanistan, cut off from the rest of my ODA, with our team's only medic dying, and a dozen very shaken Afghan police almost in a state of panic. I used the hand and arm signals I'd taught the ANP during training to direct them into position and assign sectors of fire. I tried to push the perimeter farther out, but the Afghans refused to leave each other's side. The more I signaled them to new positions, the less they moved. When I instructed one young policeman to move twenty-five meters to the west, he moved only two steps in that direction."

Tony was also trying in vain to talk his team to his location using landmarks. He hadn't brought smoke grenades because this was originally supposed to be a night mission. Fortunately Brian had planned ahead. Tony ripped a green smoke grenade off his body armor and threw it into the open field so his team could find them. Brian started to go into shock, and Tony loosened his clothes and started rubbing his belly to comfort him. As the green smoke billowed for the whole area to see, he sat there, cradling Brian's head and waiting to die from another ambush if his team didn't arrive. The ODA arrived minutes later and guided in the medevac helicopter. As the helicopter landed in a billow of dust, Tony kissed Brian on the forehead and yelled to the flight medic, "Take care of him!" They were the same last words Brian's wife said to Tony when they got together for dinner before shipping out to Afghanistan. "Take care of him."

Brian's survival was a testament to his insistence on training and retraining his teammates on medical skills. Cross-training specialized skills was an essential element of Special Forces doctrine. With small, twelve-man teams operating in some of the most remote places in the world, it was essential that the members be able to back each other up.

Tony told me later that when the team grumbled during their medical training, Brian said, "Hey guys, this isn't for you, this is for me. As your team's only medic, if I'm hit, I'm totally dependent on you guys to take care of me. So I'm going to damn well make sure you guys know what you're doing!"

Despite the severity of the wound, Tony managed to stabilize Brian long enough to get him to the medevac, and he was eventually evacuated to the massive military hospital in Landstuhl, Germany. There, though, the doctors declared Brian brain dead. He was kept alive long enough for his wife to be notified and flown to Germany. She was able to spend a final night with her husband before the doctors took him off life support the next day. It was August 16, 2009.

Back in their vehicles, the ODA had to fight their way back to their base. As they left Mangur, volleys of rocket-propelled grenades (RPGs) and machine gun fire began flying across wide open fields at the convoy from two directions. Spotting the machine gun in a walled compound several hundred meters to their right, Tony ordered the gunner in his MRAP to begin firing on the compound with the vehicle's heavy machine gun.

An RPG hit one of the Afghan police Humvees just in front of the MRAP. It struck the back right window and decapitated the police unit's deputy commander, Afzali. The blast flew through the vehicle and fragments took a chunk out of the neck of the driver. The rest of the police frantically tried to extricate their friends from the Humvee before it started burning. Tony couldn't leave their partnered police behind and knew he was stuck smack in the middle of the kill zone until they could evacuate the wounded. He told his driver to pull the MRAP up beside the police Humvee so he could shield the Afghans from the most intense fire.

"The .50 cal. from my MRAP was barking and I could see its rounds splashing all over the mud walls of a Taliban compound," Tony said. "But the damn thing was built like a fort. We could see the muzzle flashes belching back at us from the windows and roof, and we could hear the impact of the rounds on our vehicle. We knew we would have a hard time getting approval to call in air support to bomb the compound because headquarters would demand we confirm there were no civilians in it before authorizing the pilot to drop. Crossing the open field in the face of machine gun fire to confirm no civilians were present kind of defeated the point. I radioed back to Grant that we were pinned down as more and more enemy rounds slammed into the side of the MRAP."

The ODA had been in similar situations before and were repeatedly denied permission to bomb compounds because there might be civilians inside with the Taliban. The higher headquarters' excessive caution stemmed from the "tactical directives" issued the previous month by the new four-star commander of the International Security Assistance Force (ISAF), Gen. Stanley McChrystal. He directed every soldier in Afghanistan to take every measure possible to avoid causing civilian casualties on the battlefield. The directive had particularly focused on the use of artillery and air power.

We all understood the need for restraint in an irregular warfare environment and for doing our best to avoid harming the very civilians we were trying to win over to our side. It was a fundamental tenet of counterinsurgency. But another fundamental aspect was allowing small units the flexibility to deal with complex tactical situations on the ground. Unfortunately, the directives resulted in a number of subordinate commands second-guessing nearly any use of close air support going forward. The questions and hand-wringing often had the effect of making its use impractical. Taking that tool out of our tool bag severely limited a unit's options in situations like the one ODA 21 found itself in that terrible afternoon outside of Mangur. Their leadership had no choice but to order the operators and ANP in the rear vehicles of the convoy to assault the fortified compound on foot. Fortunately they outflanked the Taliban machine gun position and destroyed it without taking more losses. But the overzealous enforcement of the civilian casualties directive would come to plague our efforts to beat back the Taliban for the rest of the tour.

A barking dog snapped me back to the present, my mind quickly refocusing. Through my night vision goggles I could see a dog's black silhouette coming straight at us. Everyone knew it would quickly give away our presence. One of the operators in front of me triggered his infrared laser directly into the dog's eyes, hoping to irritate it and force it to turn around. But the dog kept coming, running across the field, barking louder and louder as it closed the distance.

I heard the whumpf of an M4 rifle firing with a silencer. The dog stumbled and rolled forward as its momentum carried it several more feet in a ball of fur and dust. Then it didn't move. Our line halted for a moment and listened for the occupants of the compound or any other sign of compromise.

We picked up the pace as we started moving again, climbing over low walls and lifting ourselves in and out of ditches. The more I thought about Brian and the daughters he left behind, the more I wanted Hasmani dead. The fact that Brian was killed on his way to help Afghan villagers reopen their shops made me that much angrier. I had been preaching the tenets of counterinsurgency to my men for the past several years. Coming out of the Pentagon and the White House, I knew we had to shift our focus from targeting Taliban commanders to protecting the populace from insurgent intimidation and winning over sympathetic tribes. But tonight I just wanted Hasmani dead, and I found myself hoping I would be the one to pull the trigger.

We slid along the outer concrete wall of our target compound, awkwardly ducking under several windows, each of us with sixty pounds of gear pulling at our shoulders. I could see up the line of Afghan and American soldiers to a heavy black metal gate. I took a quick look at the GPS mounted on my wrist and saw that we were in the right place.

The team leaders from ODA 21 and 23 called in over the radio.

"Arrowhead 2-0, this is Arrowhead 2-1, set at my objective," Grant said.

"Roger," I whispered. Standing just a few feet from the window of a Taliban lieutenant's compound, my muffled whispers sounded like yells. I cupped my hand over my mouth to muffle the sound further.

"Arrowhead 2-3 not set," Jason whispered over the net.

The teams were poised outside their respective targets with their door charges ready to blow. They were potential sitting ducks as they waited for me to give the go-ahead so that we all hit our targets at once.

"Let's go!" I whispered in my microphone to the lead man in our cell. I saw one of the commandos struggling to hand up some bolt cutters to cut the lock on the gate. The chain was slid out of the way and we eased into the courtyard while one operator quickly ran up to the door with an explosive charge. Two Afghans stayed behind us at the gate to maintain rear security.

"Arrowhead 2-3 Set," Jason called up as soon as the charge was placed on the heavy wooden door leading to the actual home.

"On my mark. 5, 4, 3, 2, 1, Mark!" I called over the net.

The shock wave of the door charge cracked and hit me squarely in the chest a lot harder than usual. The line of soldiers, known as a "stack," paused. The charge was too big and had too much explosive in it. Everyone stood there stunned for a second and then surged into the compound.

"Damn, P for plenty on the charge jackass," someone said dryly over the net, referring to the excessive amount of explosives that were apparently in the charge.

Inside was another large courtyard with a series of low, squat rooms on the far side. As the operators and commandos sprinted across the courtyard to clear the rooms while stepping around goats and sheep, I heard automatic weapons fire belching in the distance in the direction of Hasmani's compound.

I immediately started running with Zeke, the joint tactical air controller (JTAC), over to the stairs leading to the roof so that we could get the best reception for our satellite radios and Zeke could get hold of any needed air support or medevac. JTACs were airmen from the Air Force's Special Tactics Squadron specially trained to control all types of aircraft to make sure they accurately placed the right types of ordnance in the right place at the right time. Zeke was a big, strapping Irishman, cocky, and very good at his job. In the isolated mountains of Afghanistan, where a small team could easily find itself surrounded and hours away from the nearest friendly unit, the JTAC was the lifeline to medevac and reinforcements and therefore critical to the survival of the team.

By the time we got to the roof the fire in the distance had subsided. "That was a shitload of fire," I said to Zeke.

"Yeah, want me to call up a TIC?" he replied. TIC stands for *troops in contact*, and once it was called up on the satellite communications net, all other units were pushed to an alternate channel. The unit in contact received priority treatment across the theater when it came to surveillance aircraft such as the Predator drone as well as close air support from the Air Force. Every unit in Afghanistan fought constantly for these scarce assets to be dedicated to its mission and was often not able to get them. All of that changed once a TIC was called because the unit was instantly bumped to the top of the list.

"Yep. Call it up," I said. "This area is bad news, and I want some support ready in case Hasmani's fighters start pouring out of their compounds against us."

Jason, the team leader for 23, called up on the local FM radio net that fed into my right ear that the school was clear. They had found a small cache of RPG rounds as well as several boxes of machine gun ammunition. It was a typical tactic for the Taliban to attack us from schools and clinics and then blame us with their propaganda machine when we returned fire and damaged these buildings or, worse, injured Afghan civilians.

Moments later Jason called up that the compound I was located in had been fully searched and was a "dry hole," meaning the target wasn't there. "Nothing but women and children," Jason said. "But one of the kids blurted out that his dad was in Pakistan." The boy's father was Hasmani's lieutenant.

Zeke and I stood on the roof, looking in the direction of the gunfire we had heard earlier, near Hasmani's compound, waiting on ODA 21 to call in their status. As we stood there shivering in the cold, clear night, we could hear what sounded like a long, high-pitched wail wafting across the fields. We took off our headsets to try to make out the sound. It was the unmistakable wail of an Afghan woman.

"That's not good, sir," Zeke said, stating the obvious. My first thought was that the woman had been wounded in the crossfire.

"Sir," Grant called up from Hasmani's compound, "we have jackpot, but I need you to come down here to my location." *Jackpot* was the code word used to communicate that we had killed or captured our target.

I knew something was wrong as I carefully stepped down the narrow mud brick stairway to the courtyard, grabbed an interpreter and two commandos, and began jogging down a trail toward Hasmani's compound. As I neared his compound, the wailing became louder. It sounded as though someone had ripped out the woman's soul. Grant walked up the trail to meet me, and I found out that someone was us.

"We killed a kid, a little girl," Grant said as we came face to face. We both just stood there. Grant had two young children, and I immediately thought of my own little girl.

"Dammit, damn, damn, damn!" I muttered, looking down at the ground. "What the hell happened?"

"We aren't 100 percent sure," Grant replied. "The stack of ANP went in first, and before we could even follow them inside, Hasmani opened up from the far side of the compound. He missed and the ANP just friggin' unloaded on him. It looks like the girl was standing right next to him. What kind of asshole opens fire with his AK while his daughter is standing next to him?"

"What the hell happened to all of that training we've given the police on well-placed, aimed fire?" I asked in frustration.

"Come on, Mike," Grant replied. "We've trained these guys until we're blue in the face. They're not your average police. You know that. Hell, I'd put them up against the commandos any day. But they still have a very long way to go until they're accurate shooters. There is also the fact that they're all Hazara and how upset they were about Afzali. So here's the Taliban commander that's responsible for Afzali's death shooting at them. Hell, they probably were taking out years of Hazara oppression from the Taliban on his ass."

"Believe me, I get it," I said, "but we have to keep telling these guys that the spray-and-pray approach to returning fire isn't acceptable. Okay, I'm going to go get on the satellite phone and call the SOTF and give them a heads up."

The Special Operations Task Force (SOTF) was my higher headquarters, consisting of our Special Forces battalion staff and support elements. It was located at the massive Bagram Airfield, the main U.S. base in Afghanistan just northeast of Kabul. Also located at Bagram was our next level higher headquarters, the Combined Joint Special Operations Task Force (CJSOTF), led by an Army Special Forces colonel who had responsibility for all of the Army Special Forces teams, Navy SEALs, Marine Special Operations Forces, and coalition Special Operations Forces from a half dozen allied countries. I didn't want to announce bad news over the satellite communications, as every unit and headquarters monitored the net. Instead I called my headquarters directly on the satellite phone.

"Go back and finish the site exploitation on Hasmani and have the ANP or the interpreters try to talk to the family. Get as much information as you can. Eventually we are going to have to look at some way to make this right by them—if that's even possible," I said to Grant. He was clearly dreading going back into the compound to face the family.

Since General McChrystal had issued his tactical directive on avoiding civilian casualties, he had put a finger in the chest of any subordinate general officer whose soldiers harmed a civilian, particularly if those generals did not provide a thorough explanation to him within hours of an incident. The multiple layers of staff officers between him and me would be demanding a series of reports on a very tight timeline. The rationale behind these myriad reports was to get the facts to the ISAF headquarters so that they could contact the local and international media as soon as possible. In previous years we had found ourselves in reaction mode and constantly falling behind the news cycle when it came to civilian casualties. And the Taliban consistently beat us to the punch in spinning their version of events to the media. We were losing the information war as we took time to investigate each incident. I agreed completely that we had to minimize civilian casualties as part of our counterinsurgency campaign and get the facts pushed up as fast as possible to help in the war of ideas fought in the international media. Plus, I knew firsthand from my time in Washington that General McChrystal would also have President Karzai to deal with. But as I witnessed multiple layers of headquarters overreact to McChrystal's directives by questioning operations to the point of paralysis, I wondered if we had taken the notion too far. We couldn't afford to continue to alienate the Afghan populace and President Karzai, but we couldn't completely cede the battlefield to the Taliban either.

Almost a year before, in September 2008, I sat in the White House Situation Room as Vice President Dick Cheney's senior advisor for South Asia during a videoconference between President George W. Bush and President Karzai. The call was held in the aftermath of an incident in which nearly ninety civilians were killed in Farah Province in southwestern Afghanistan.

"Good morning, your Excellency," President Bush said as he sat down in the chair at the head of the table. The table ran the length of the narrow room, with flat-screen monitors covering the far wall. The remaining walls were bare except for a large presidential seal on the wall behind the president. Running parallel to the large leather chairs at the conference table was a single row of smaller chairs with their backs to the wall on both sides of the room.

At the table to the the president's left was his national security advisor, Stephen Hadley, and to the president's right was his chief of staff, John Bolton. Bolton was sitting where Vice President Cheney typically sat during National Security Council meetings, and I sat directly behind him in the chair typically reserved for Cheney's "plus one." On the other side of the room sat the president's "war czar," Lt. Gen. Doug Lute, and his senior director for Afghanistan, Col. John Wood. Both men had pushed for the president to have the videoconference to cool down the situation. They both knew that relationships were critical in the Middle East and South Asia and sought to use the goodwill between the two presidents and hopefully convince Karzai to tone down his rhetoric against the United States in the international media.

"Good morning, Mr. President. I see the hurricane did not stop your speech to the convention," Karzai replied, mentioning the president's satellite address to the 2008 Republican convention in Minnesota.

"You look upset, Hamid," Bush said.

"I am indeed very upset, Mr. President. I am angry," Karzai replied with his brow furrowed.

"Are you upset with me?" Bush asked.

"I'm very, very upset. I'm upset that these innocent people keep getting killed in these incidents, and I am upset with your military. I am not angry with you, my friend. But if it were not for you I would be even angrier!"

"Well, if it were not for me, you would probably be dead!" the president retorted.

Both men laughed.

I thought to myself, "Wow, now that sets the tone!"

"Yes, yes, you are right, Mr. President. You know you are like a brother," Karzai said. "These bombing incidents in Shindand, these types of things are going to cost us the support of the Afghan people. I know we do not agree on the numbers, but there were definitely fifty children and fourteen women who are dead. Our partnership must be truthful. I want to go to the Afghan people. I will go to where the incident happened in Shindand tomorrow, and I would like to offer the condolences of the

American president. These people normally would forget over time, but now we are disputing whether the deaths happened."

I could see Bush's jaw tighten. "Any time there is innocent loss of life, it hurts," he said after a long pause. "You know there was no intent to do this," he continued. "Unlike with the Taliban, when these things happen with us, it's an accident. You know that, my friend. Please do send my condolences when talking to your people. I demand truth like you. I'm not second-guessing you or the U.S. military. It's just two views. But we need you to help us publicly. I understand what pressures you are under, but you can't say you love the Americans but then say to your people that Americans are killing us," the president pressed.

"Exactly!" I thought. I had hoped Bush was going to press Karzai on this point. It astounded me that Karzai said little as the Taliban regularly killed civilians with roadside bombs, set off car bombs in crowded markets, and even threw acid on little girls trying to attend school. In contrast, a single accident on the coalition's part, and Karzai would denounce the United States all over Afghan national television and radio. I knew he was playing to domestic politics and that we should be held to a higher standard, but the Taliban committed those offenses on purpose and we did not. Unfortunately, really sticking it to Karzai was not Bush's style. He greatly respected Karzai's position as a sovereign head of state and also believed they had to maintain a strong relationship as two leaders of nations fighting a war together. Bush knew that if they could not have conversations such as these to air differences candidly, then the entire relationship between the two countries would suffer. There was too much at stake, and he was only going to push Karzai so hard.

"The Afghan people don't want America to leave," Karzai replied. "People strongly back the United States, but they do want a change in behavior. We must offer change. If we fail, Afghanistan will go back down the drain. We must not waste the love for America. But the number of these incidents makes a heavy burden."

"Agreed. The irony is our soldiers and your soldiers are forces for good. The Taliban in these kinds of things are not viewed as bad. We must win the propaganda war," Bush responded, subtly pushing the public rhetoric theme again. "We must continue our strategy for victory," the president continued. "You need more U.S. troops—to help you protect your highways and clear insurgents so your Army can hold. We need to help you increase the Afghan National Army. They're good, but you need more of them. We will get the current situation to where you are comfortable that your people can handle it. That spooks our coalition partners, but we will handle them. Europe defaults in their thinking to the notion that people are dying because we are there."

I was pleasantly surprised. More U.S. troops, more Afghan National Army troops, realization that the Europeans weren't going to get the job done. It was the fall of 2008, and after years of banging my head against the wall for these changes, it sounded like President Bush had just outlined a shift in strategy.

"If I can make one more point, Mr. President," Karzai said. "The nighttime raids by your Special Forces into individual homes are a serious problem. Recently a player from the Afghan cricket team was killed in a raid. There is also some dispute here, and I would be most appreciative if you could look into it. I'm also worried about Pakistan. They continue to aid our enemies."

Bush said he was encouraged by some of the tribal uprisings against the brutality of the Taliban in Pakistan's tribal areas and hoped we could foster the same in Afghanistan.

Both men ended the call with niceties. Then Bush angrily turned to Lieutenant General Lute. "Karzai has a right to be pissed. I'm pissed. I don't understand this discrepancy and why we keep killing civilians. Why are we sending Special Operations Forces to kill a cricket player? Over there, that's like killing Cal Ripken. Plus, he truly believes ninety people are dead. I want the Pentagon to get a handle on this, like now," the president said, jabbing his finger toward the ground.

Lute reminded the president that Defense Secretary Robert Gates had ordered a review of rules of engagement for using close air support. I knew that General McChrystal, then on the Joint Staff, was leading the review.

"It's undermining everything we are trying to do over there. And Karzai is right, things need to change," the president snapped before walking out of the situation room.

I stood at the outside gate of Hasmani's compound listening and watching the commotion inside the courtyard of the main house. I decided to stay at a distance from the fray and let Grant and his team sergeant handle the situation. Grant was a competent and intelligent officer who had been in Special Forces just as long as I had. He didn't need me coming in and taking charge just because I could. A Special Forces unit full of smart, independent operators, who are trained to be autonomous and all of whom secretly (and in many cases not so secretly) believe they should be in charge, could not be led with a heavy hand. In a bottom-up culture that prides itself on solving the toughest problems in the murky gray areas of third world guerrilla warfare, I tried to give general guidance and priorities, and then plenty of rope for my teams to accomplish their mission.

I could see Grant, the interpreter, and the police commander standing with an older man, trying to have a conversation with him. The old man was waving his hands wildly and eventually spit on the ground at the group's feet and walked off. The team sergeant was walking the perimeter, making sure everyone else pulled security while two operators dropped a pile of AK-47s and ammunition boxes they had found in the house in the center of the courtyard. Off to my right a group of Afghan policemen seemed to be arguing. I could tell by the way they were pointing and gesturing that they were reenacting what happened. Above it all I could hear the sobbing and wailing of three women in black and white shawls kneeling over a small body in the courtyard just outside a large broken window. Bullet holes pockmarked the wall behind her. I could see the legs of the girl's father in the doorway to the room.

One of 21's interpreters approached me. "I am from Ghazni City. This will not turn the Andar against us," he said.

"The Andar tribe is already against us," I replied. "Even though Hasmani was a known Taliban commander, this can't help. The Taliban will spin this against us by tomorrow morning and say that the police and the Americans came here to assassinate his family."

"You are right," the interpreter replied. "The Andar will never support the government or you. But they will not support the Taliban either. If you compensate this family it will be a big help. You must do it so that the whole village knows you did it. You notice they are not crying for Hasmani. The women are not even looking at his body. Maybe he treated them badly. Now, with him gone, there might be a chance to help them stand up to the *dushman* [the local name for the Taliban]. I know these people. If you give them some support, some weapons, some organization, some money, they will fight the Talibs. Everyone is tired of them. But without support, some other Taliban commander will rise up and take over here."

We spent the next week at ODA 21's base dealing with the aftermath of the little girl's death. I had sent the initial incident report directly from the scene at Mangur via satellite phone to our headquarters at the Special Operations Forces Task Force at Bagram. As soon as we returned to 21's base south of Ghazni City, I began filling out the myriad follow-on reports describing in detail everything that happened.

Meanwhile Grant was on the phone with the provincial governor Mohammed Osmani to let him know what happened and to craft a plan to deal with the elders of Mangur. Grant had developed a close working relationship with Osmani, particularly since the Polish brigade with overall responsibility for operations in Ghazni Province had not really engaged him or established a personal relationship. Osmani was typical of many governors we had seen over the years since 9/11: happy to work with U.S. and coalition forces to further reconstruction and development projects as well as hunt down insurgent commanders, but truly interested only in furthering their business interests and those of their tribe.

"I will invite the Andar elders to my house for chai. Can you talk reparations, my friend?" the governor asked Grant.

"Yes, sir," Grant replied. "We will have to get it approved through our chain of command, but we can pay them."

Osmani worried that our military bureaucracy would be too slow to approve the payments. "If we immediately show the family that we are willing to compensate for the girl's death and take that message to the village, this will be forgotten. We cannot let this wait," Osmani said. "It will be very embarrassing for me to call the *shura* and then have nothing to offer."

We discussed the fact that we were certain the money would go back to Hasmani's group of Taliban fighters. "Yes, but Hasmani is gone now," the governor responded. "If you want to have any chance of ever dealing with Mangur village or the Andar tribe, you must provide something to his family. You must show them compassion. In Afghanistan a daughter can bring thousands of dollars for a dowry. A girl cannot work the fields or get work to support the family, so having some form of payment is survival for the rest of the family. You must provide something, even though he was a Talib commander. It is our way."

We decided to try to get the payment approved but became caught in a maddening bureaucratic loop for the rest of the week. On the one hand, our headquarters, who wanted to stay out of trouble with General McChrystal, was telling the ISAF staff there was no need for a formal investigation into the incident because it was the Afghan police who actually shot the girl, not us. However, that caused us problems in getting the reparations payment approved because we only paid reparations for civilians killed by U.S. soldiers, not Afghan policemen.

Finally, over the course of several days of phone calls and emails, I managed to get my commander, a commonsense, pragmatic officer with a long history in Special Forces, to talk some sense into the lawyers up in Kabul. My executive officer, a former White House attorney and federal prosecutor, also authored the equivalent of a legal brief on the various precedents and policies behind reparations payments that put the lawyers on their heels.

At the same time we were fighting for the reparations payment, we were also answering a barrage of questions about what happened and why. Once we made it clear that it was our partnered Afghan National Police and not us who shot the girl, the intensity of the questioning slackened considerably. Several hours later the emails and calls picked up again, but now from Combined Joint Task Force (CJTF), the conventional command for eastern Afghanistan, questioning why we were sending Afghan police into homes first. I spent hours recounting the emphasis that had been placed over the years on putting an Afghan face to our operations, of building their capacity by letting them lead, and how Karzai himself had insisted that Afghans lead any searches of Afghan homes. "We can't have it both ways," I said, concluding the final note. "If our policy is to place the Afghans in the lead whenever possible, then we have to accept the consequences of that policy when the Afghans make mistakes."

Despite our best efforts to get our story up to the higher headquarters so that we could get it out to the media, we watched via a Predator video feed as a huge protest gathered outside Hasmani's home in Mangur. The local police chief, who we thought was afraid to even go into the village, was quoted in the local press as saying he had not authorized the operation and that the ANP who participated would be punished. He hinted that the killing of the little girl was a revenge mission. Not helpful. Grant called Osmani, but the governor replied that he had not seen or heard from that police chief in months and that he wasn't surprised at the remarks since he and Hasmani were from the same clan.

Next we saw the incident being described on CNN's ticker on the television in the ODA's operations center. Grant had authorized the team's civil affairs sergeant to play an account of the incident on a local radio station that we ran out of the base. All new content was supposed to be approved through the strategic communications cell in Bagram, but we knew the approval process would be too slow to be effective and told him to just do it.

Grant attended the *shura* at Governor Osmani's house that night. He listened as the Andar elders complained about the invasion of their homes and stated that no Talibs were present. Osmani stepped in and reminded the elders of the ambush that happened from those same homes only a few months earlier as the Americans were trying to aid the villages to the south of Mangur. The elders replied that those Talibs that day were outsiders. Grant bit his lip as he listened to the elders lie. We had signals intercepts of Hasmani coordinating the attack that day from his lieutenant's home—the very home that I was in just two nights before.

Eventually, after every elder had his say, Grant offered to initiate a reconstruction project directly in Mangur, to repair and refurbish the school. The elders refused. Grant eventually produced $3,000 as reparations to the Hasmani family for the death of the girl. We found out later that Hasmani's lieutenant had instructed the elders not to come back unless they had cash. Half of it was to go to Hasmani's family and half to the lieutenant. Eventually the elders accepted the promise of the payment, the promised refurbishment of the school, and some additional money to repair the Hasmani home. I was surprised at the lack of emotion among the elders. The whole thing smacked of a business negotiation. I was always stunned at how cheap life could be in a country that had known nothing but war for the past three decades.

I was also a bit surprised that the death of the little girl didn't seem to sway the elders one way or the other in terms of their loyalties or feelings about the coalition and Afghan government. Frankly, I think the men of ODA 21 and I were more upset than they were. The muted reaction was certainly less than I had come to expect given the high level of attention the issue received in Kabul and Washington. Nor did their reactions seem to warrant the blanket orders that effectively tied the hands of operational commanders and made our Air Force so difficult to employ. Surprisingly the death of Hasmani's daughter also seemed to have less effect than we expected on the broader dynamics of Mangur and the area. The backlash was minimal. It could have been that she was the daughter of a known Taliban commander, or it could have been that a relatively low value is placed on life in such a harsh place in the world, particularly a female life.

We had caught only a few hours of sleep since kicking off the mission two days before, and I was delirious. But it was time for my weekly attempt to Skype with my daughter. My mother often kept her on Sundays to give my wife a break before the week began. It was always the best part of my week, but this time I was dreading seeing her. I knew it was going to be very tough for me emotionally.

"Hi Daddy!" she beamed as the screen came up. "Hi baby!" I said, trying not to choke up at her angelic little face.

"Why are you sad, Daddy?" she asked, intuitively knowing something was wrong even though she was five years old and thousands of miles away.

"We accidentally hurt someone today when we didn't mean to," I said, starting to choke up again. "A little girl just like you."

"It's okay, Daddy. Can't you say 'I'm sorry' to her mommy and daddy?" she asked.

"It's going to be really hard, honey, but I will try my best," I told her. I could see my mother's face contort for a second.

"Your beard is getting really big, Daddy. I bet it itches!" She scratched her face, seeming to know instinctively when to change the subject.

We continued to make small talk, but this time all I could think about was that mother's wailing in Mangur. I was there to create a better life for the children of Afghanistan and by extension create a safer future for my daughter. But now one was dead as a result of a mission I led. I didn't know what type of future she would have had under the Taliban-led society her father espoused, but for the first time I could remember I started to wonder what impact we were really having.

On balance, Mullah Hasmani, the Taliban commander who led the attack on ODA 21 and the ANP as they were trying to open a village bazaar, was dead. His message to the people of Mangur that the Afghan government and the Americans were weak, ineffective, and unable to touch him was shown to be a lie. In the relative calm after the mission, the local government was able to make some headway, and the ODA was able to further undermine the insurgency.

Just after the mission the ODA started a whisper campaign that the lieutenant we missed that night was the person who informed us that Hasmani was in Mangur. Another of Hasmani's deputies traveled back to Mangur from Pakistan three weeks later and killed the lieutenant, causing a factional war inside the insurgent group. The infighting became so vicious that Hasmani's group dissolved for a while. To take advantage of the vacuum, Governor Osmani fired the police chief of Mangur and accompanied his replacement to a large *shura* with the elders of the Andar tribe from the area. It was the first time an Afghan government official had dared to go to Mangur in at least eighteen months.

But unfortunately, as I had seen so many times in previous years, we lacked the resources and the will to take full advantage of the situation. The Polish Army brigade with security responsibility for Ghazni refused to permanently send forces to Mangur to establish a presence and prevent insurgent influence from returning. The Poles' unofficial rules from their government for operating in Afghanistan essentially limited them to patrolling the Ring Road, the single highway traversing the province.

The Afghan National Army brigade a dozen kilometers away claimed to be decisively engaged in other areas. We knew better but had no authority to order the Afghans to place troops in the village.

With only ten operators, ODA 21 lacked the manpower to leave its current base and transplant to a new base in Andar. The province of Ghazni had become so infested with Taliban that the team spent more and more of its time playing whack-a-mole against the growing number of insurgent cells taking over the districts surrounding the provincial capital, Ghazni City. It was all they could do to keep up with the intelligence from their informant network and continue to beat back the insurgent leadership as they tried to recruit and multiply. Eventually a rival Hasmani lieutenant consolidated power and announced his return to the area by dragging a man who worked on the coalition base out of his home near Mangur, holding a trial, and executing him in front of the entire village. The Taliban were back in charge.

In the end, the inability of the coalition and Afghan security forces to protect the people of Mangur had far greater impact on which side they supported in the war than accidentally causing the death of a civilian. Everyone on the team was deeply emotionally affected by the incident, but this experience and others like it proved to us that the best way forward to counter the insurgency was to find a way to allow villages like Mangur to protect themselves.

Soon after Brian's death I visited the team to check on how the men were handling the loss of one of their key leaders and personalities. I discovered that Brian had apparently had distinct premonitions of his death. These were so clear that he had had several long conversations with one of his closest friends just before he deployed. He also wrote several lengthy letters to his wife discussing her life after his death.

"He even went so far as to write letters to his teammates and divvied up his most prized gear," Grant said, shaking his head.

I was astonished. Many people have a bad feeling that something is going to happen to them, and nothing ever does. Yet here was a man who was so convinced he was going to die on our tour, after multiple previous tours to Iraq and Afghanistan, that he went to extraordinary lengths to prepare for it. Rather than try to avoid his fate, he faced it head-on. He always volunteered for every mission, no matter how dangerous. And when he suddenly found himself in one of the worst ambushes of his life, he didn't sit in his heavily armored vehicle; he didn't send the Afghans out front; and he didn't hang back as the medic in case someone was hurt, even though all of those actions would have been acceptable. Despite his belief that he was not going to make it back, Brian charged in the face of the enemy. It was an amazing testament to him as a soldier and a man.

Nine months later, on Memorial Day 2010, at the headquarters for Army Special Operations Command in Fort Bragg, North Carolina, I sat in a crowd while Brian's name was read aloud during a memorial wall dedication. When I looked over at his two beautiful little girls, the older girl glared back at me as though to say, "You took my Daddy." I would rather have been shot than to have received that look. I couldn't stop staring at them and feeling a tremendous sense of guilt that my daughter still had her father.

It was truly the civilians, on the battlefield and at home, who suffered in these wars. Everyone thanked us for our sacrifices and showered us with gratitude when we returned. But we had all volunteered and were overseas doing what we had trained our entire lives for and what we believed in. Our families bore the real burdens of the war on terror. They had no choice but to wait and worry and then live with the consequences of our service. They deserved the focus of our nation's gratitude, not us. I also thought of Hasmani's daughter. She suffered because of his decision to support the Taliban. Her family would suffer the consequences of his decision for the rest of their lives.

As I sat at Fort Bragg that day, the weight of all the years I had devoted to Afghanistan and the war, in the field and in Washington, seemed to weigh on me as it never had before.

1 State of the War
Office of the Secretary of Defense

I stood in the middle of my living room in shock as the second plane flew into the South Tower of the World Trade Center on September 11, 2001. I had just hung up the phone with a childhood friend who worked there but, by the grace of God, happened to be out of the building at breakfast that morning. We had agreed that there was no way the first strike was an accident. Like so many millions around the world, that moment launched my life on a completely different trajectory. In my case it was toward Washington DC and Afghanistan.

A year later I found myself back in the Army that I had left before 9/11 as part of Bravo Company, 2nd Battalion, 20th Special Forces Group (Airborne), one of two Army Special Forces groups in the National Guard. The unit mobilized in early 2003 for Operation Enduring Freedom in Afghanistan, and a small group of us proceeded to Fort Bragg, North Carolina, where we completed the required training to deploy as full-fledged Green Berets.

Based in Uzbekistan, my unit conducted operations in every region of Afghanistan, from Herat in the west to Kandahar in the south. Despite the early military successes in the months after 9/11, they witnessed early signs of the Taliban laying the groundwork for an insurgency. In the political arena Afghanistan was making historic strides, including establishing an interim government that was moving toward presidential elections and the nation's first constitution. However, increasing attacks from across the Pakistani border, including targeted assassinations of pro-government officials, elders, and mullahs, and the security vacuum created by a nonexistent Afghan army made those early successes extremely fragile.

To make matters worse, opium cultivation and a burgeoning drug trade were exploding in Afghanistan, flooding the nascent economy with millions in illicit funds and having corruptive effects on the new government. The Pentagon, however, was resisting taking on narcotics as a military issue, pointing instead to the State Department and the U.S. Agency for International Development (USAID) to take the matter on. In response some influential staffers in Congress wrote $70 million into the Pentagon's counternarcotics budget to force the Pentagon to set up programs in Afghanistan to fight the opium trade.

Weeks later I met the new deputy assistant secretary of defense for counternarcotics, Mary Beth Long. Her predecessor, Andre Hollis, made the introductions. Upon demobilizing and becoming a civilian again in 2004, I had been looking for a way to remain engaged in creating a better future for Afghanistan and, by extension, a safer future for the United States. Andre, an intense and dynamic lawyer devoted to the ethos of public service, looked me in the eye over the dinner table one evening and said, "Mike, she is going to need someone who can represent the Defense Department at meetings at the White House one day and then to go to the mountains of Afghanistan the next day to oversee programs the office is funding. My gut tells me you're that rare guy who can do both."

Mary Beth smiled as she sat down, looking at my résumé. "Well, at least you can spell Afghanistan correctly! Most of this building can only spell Iraq right now, and I'm concerned we've taken our eye off the ball," she said. Her office was part of the Office of the Secretary of Defense–Policy, commonly called OSD-Policy. Essentially it was the defense secretary's civilian staff who advised him on the formulation of strategic plans and policies and the resources needed to implement them. They worked closely with their uniformed colleagues on the Joint Staff to run the Defense Department. The official charged with leading OSD-Policy was an undersecretary who, in turn, had assistant and deputy assistant secretaries who divided up the world and reported to him. The counternarcotics office was under the assistant secretary of defense for special operations and low-intensity conflict. As deputy assistant secretary, Mary Beth had responsibility for Defense's support to domestic and global counternarcotics efforts. Congress had just appropriated money to force the Department to pay attention to the exploding opium trade in Afghanistan. To do that she needed someone immediately.

"I have $70 million to spend by the end of September, or I'm going to have the Hill breathing down my neck," she continued. "You would be standing up programs to support the State Department and Drug Enforcement Administration in theater. Hopefully we will eventually be able to convince Central Command and folks in this building to provide our troops with the authority they need to go after drug kingpins and their labs. The intel community doesn't agree yet, but in this office we are convinced drug money threatens to undermine Karzai's government and could finance a Taliban comeback. I want to be clear, though, that you are not going to be operational. This isn't a door-kicking job. This is a policy office—but a unique one in that we have the ability to directly establish programs to implement our policies. What we really need is someone who can navigate the interagency here in Washington with the State Department, USAID, the National Security Council, and the military in this building."

The meeting had unexpectedly turned into an interview. Over the next hour I explained to her as well as her deputy that I thought the military had become overly focused on direct action raids, and the Army Special Forces community in particular needed to get back to its roots of operating by, with, and through the Afghans. I told them that I was certain we could win in Afghanistan if we approached it as we had in Colombia, where Special Forces ODAs were used to advise, train, and equip the Colombian Army. "We will never have enough troops in Afghanistan to protect every village, and we aren't going to be able to hunt insurgents forever. We have to start addressing the underlying causes of instability, like the exploding drug economy. It will undermine everything we are trying to do there."

She smiled before asking me when I could start. She quickly cautioned that the U.S. government was in the midst of developing a strategy for combating the drug trade in Afghanistan and that many in the Pentagon didn't think it was the military's job to be involved at all. "They think the counternarcotics mission is a distraction and that, to the extent it should be done, it's the civilian agencies' job," she said. "Problem is, our civilian agencies can't operate in a place like Afghanistan in the midst of a low-level war. So, with that in mind, you will have a key role in helping finalize the broader interagency strategy. I've only been here a few months, so we will all figure it out together. Sound good?"

"Absolutely," I replied. That was the start of my career inside the policy apparatus of Washington.

In the fall of 2004 Afghanistan continued to enjoy political successes. Hamid Karzai became the first freely elected president of the Islamic Republic of Afghanistan, a seminal moment in Afghanistan's history. A constitutional grand council, called a Loya Jirga, had formally adopted Afghanistan's first constitution earlier in the year. In 2005 the fledgling democracy formed a bicameral Parliament and, as a tangible sign of reconciliation with the Taliban regime, elected several former Taliban ministers to both houses. Vice President Cheney attended the opening session with the former king Zahir Shah and President Karzai presiding.

"This assembly is a sign of us regaining our honor," Karzai said in his speech to the 351 members of the upper and lower houses, cabinet members, and guests. "This—dear Afghanistan—has risen again from the ashes," he added, pausing to gain control of his emotions.[1] After nearly a generation of the devastating Soviet occupation, a brutal civil war, and the repressive Taliban regime, it did indeed seem to be a new dawn for the forlorn country.

International donors and countries interested in rebuilding Afghanistan adopted a strategy that assigned international partners to take the lead in various aspects of reconstruction. Known as the "lead nation" strategy, the effort divided reconstruction efforts and funding into various priority sectors. The United Kingdom became the lead nation for counternarcotics, the United States the lead for rebuilding the Afghan National Army; the Germans took the lead for training the Afghan National Police, the Japanese for disarming the existing militias, and the Italians for the Justice sector. Many of us found the individual national assignments puzzling, and all of us working Afghan policy found the idea of the notoriously corrupt Italian judiciary reforming Afghanistan's court system quite ironic.

Nevertheless, the strategy itself appeared sound to the extent the goal was to spread the burden of rebuilding such a devastated and impoverished country, to focus key participants on certain sectors, and to assign priority lead roles to specific countries. Moreover, it fit into the U.S. desire to share the burden in Afghanistan and avoid getting bogged down with long-term nation building. In reality, however, the strategy turned out to be a disaster. Some nations devoted substantial resources to the effort, while others did little. For example, well into 2004 the Germans had slightly more than a dozen people working to train the entire Afghan police capability, and the Italians had difficulty deploying judges and staff for over a year. The approach also created independent, uncoordinated efforts that, far from being mutually supporting, sometimes were in conflict. It proved nearly impossible to move forward with police reform while Italian efforts lagged and a judicial system was nonexistent. In turn British efforts to successfully arrest and punish narcotics traffickers on behalf of the new Afghan government depended on anemic police and judicial capabilities.

With no one entity to take charge, allocate resources, and synchronize efforts, progress was slow and sporadic. Further, by the time the United States realized certain sectors were lagging, it was very difficult to reassert leadership due to our allies' political sensitivities. As the lead nation effort floundered, the Afghan people grew frustrated and warlords filled the void. I would see the effects of this disappointment firsthand during future deployments as the Afghan people increasingly grew disillusioned with the lack of basic services provided by the coalition and the Afghan government.

Leading efforts on the ground in the fall of 2004 were Lt. Gen. David Barno, in command of the Combined Joint Task Force 180, and Ambassador Zalmay Khalilzad. Early on, they attempted to slowly move the national security apparatus in Washington away from the "light footprint" approach that had dominated our policy since the fall of the Taliban in December 2001. One of the biggest advocates of that strategy was Gen. Tommy Franks, the U.S. Central Command commander responsible for Afghanistan and all of the Middle East. He argued that in the post-Taliban era "our footprint had to be small, for both military and geopolitical reasons. I envisioned a total of about 10,000 American soldiers, airmen, special operators, and helicopter assault crews, along with robust in-country air support."[2] Lt. Gen. Dan McNeill, Barno's predecessor as U.S. commander in Afghanistan, also advocated the light footprint and even went so far as to publicly suggest that U.S. forces could be completely out of Afghanistan by the summer of 2004.[3] The prevailing thinking in the military and the Pentagon was that the United States should avoid the mistakes of the Soviets, who sent large numbers of conventional soldiers into some of the most difficult terrain on earth in an attempt to occupy every town and village. I always thought this rationale was flawed. The fundamental issue with the Soviet occupation was their attempt to radically change Afghanistan's culture and literally depopulate swaths of the countryside with bombings and land mines. We were not the Soviets, and larger numbers of American soldiers providing protection for development programs would not have met the same type of resistance.

Nonetheless the mission of the relatively small U.S. military presence was counterterrorism, focused on tracking down the remnants of the Taliban regime still hiding out in Afghanistan and killing or capturing al Qaeda's senior leadership. The secondary mission was to rebuild the Afghan National Army and to support civilian efforts to provide the Afghan people with basic humanitarian assistance. Upon arriving in Uzbekistan in early 2003 to prepare for missions into Afghanistan, my Special Forces unit received a brief that specifically forbade the use of the term *counterinsurgency*. Terrorists who remained in-country, warlords who still represented a security threat, and other opponents of the government could not be labeled insurgents.[4] This view stemmed from our senior leaders in the Pentagon. Defense Secretary Donald Rumsfeld, Undersecretary for Policy Douglas Feith, and many others were interested in continuing counterterrorism operations in Afghanistan only to the extent of hunting remaining al Qaeda and Taliban leadership; they did not believe the Defense Department should be responsible for nation building, reconstruction, or development efforts.

By the fall of 2004 U.S. troop numbers hovered around twenty thousand.[5] The size of the force paled in comparison with the 130,000 troops in Iraq at the time but was intended to provide enough security to allow for the political gains from crafting the Afghan constitution, the presidential elections, and the parliamentary elections. In addition it was viewed as a sizable enough force to intimidate some notorious warlords, such as Ismail Khan in the western city of Herat, the Uzbek strongman Abdul Rashid Dostum in the north, and Pacha Khan Zadran in the east. These warlords were the subject of a complementary political effort known as the "Warlord Strategy," led by State, to persuade them to relinquish their heavy weapons and come peacefully into the fold of the new government.

Unfortunately, despite these early successes, the negative ramifications of the light footprint approach slowly began to surface. The fundamental flaw in the strategy was in not realizing how devastated Afghan state institutions had become after thirty years of warfare, leaving little capacity to protect the Afghan people or provide them basic services. In a postconflict environment, it is essential to provide a basic level of security for society to begin to function again; the light footprint was insufficient for this task. The reasoning behind the strategy was understandable in wanting to avoid an Afghan popular backlash similar to that faced by the Soviets. As I would not come to appreciate until years later, while sitting in dozens of *shuras*, the Afghan people wanted just the opposite: they wanted us heavily engaged in improving their future. Initially buoyed by the intervention of the world's only superpower and dozens of other nations, Afghans had very high expectations of the improvements they would see in their lives. Coupled with the failings of the lead nation strategy, the light footprint left many Afghans disillusioned and open to intimidation and exploitation. Slowly but surely individuals and tribes, particularly those that were marginalized and felt left out in this new environment, began shifting back to the insurgency, either due to pressure from the insurgents or by choice.

As they regrouped in their sanctuaries in Pakistan, the Taliban and its affiliated insurgent groups, the Haqqani network and Gulbuddin Hekmatyar's Hezb-e-Islami, slowly began inserting themselves into the security void. Operating from their bases in Pakistan's tribal areas, they aligned with alienated and underserved Afghan tribes, threatened individuals who supported the Karzai government, and interrupted development efforts whenever and wherever they could. Drug traffickers, criminal gangs, and predatory local officials and their militias joined the insurgents in using the lack of trained Afghan Army and police to their advantage. By the summer of 2005 nearly every province in the south and the east experienced an alarming increase in the use of improvised explosive devices targeting Afghan and coalition security forces. That summer also saw a spike in the use of suicide bombers in Afghanistan, something that had been far more prevalent in Iraq and the Palestinian territories and, at least according to Afghans, was heretofore relatively unknown in Afghan culture.[6]

Seeing this dynamic unfolding, Khalilzad and Barno, bolstered by key thinkers in Washington such as the increasingly alarmed Marin Strmecki in the Office of the Secretary of Defense, had embarked on efforts starting in 2003 to shift away from the light footprint approach and begin building Afghan capacity. Strmecki, the bookish and brilliant graduate of Yale Law with a PhD in Afghan politics from Georgetown, authored a white paper and a series of briefings that established a framework for accelerating U.S. assistance to Afghanistan. The accelerated training of the Afghan National Security Forces was key to the new framework. The briefings, approved by the Cabinet-level Principals Committee and the president in mid-2003, tackled disarming warlords and building Afghan infrastructure and advocated programs for improving governance. While he was still at the White House, before taking on his ambassadorship, Khalilzad chipped away at the anti-nation-building policies prevalent in the Bush administration by helping to push through a package that effectively doubled the amount of assistance from the previous year. As ambassador he focused on working with Karzai to remove, or at least to relocate away from their strongholds, the most notorious Afghan warlords, such as Gul Agha Sherzai in Kandahar and Ismail Khan in Herat. He also championed major development projects, such as the Ring Road, as symbols of international investment in Afghanistan's future. The road was important because it circled Afghanistan and passed through the four major Afghan cities in each of the four geographical regions and, in doing so, linked all of Afghanistan's varied ethnic groups.

Meanwhile Lieutenant General Barno slowly began to shift U.S. forces and NATO's ISAF away from a purely counterterrorism mission and toward counterinsurgency operations. He organized brigade headquarters in the south and east and began establishing provincial reconstruction teams, focused on delivering development aid at the local level in the volatile south and east. Barno assigned units geographic areas of responsibility and population protection as part of their mission. He also began the important work of accelerating the training and equipping of the Afghan National Army.

Though Khalilzad and Barno began putting the organizational building blocks in place for a long-term counterinsurgency and nation-building campaign, resources remained limited; in retrospect they were a drop in the bucket compared to what was really needed. We lost critical time when the Karzai government had momentum, the Taliban were on their heels, and the Afghan people were supportive. In hindsight it's disheartening to think what a little more investment back then could have saved in blood and treasure years later.

My role in these early days was to participate in finalizing the U.S. government's counternarcotics strategy for Afghanistan and to help to stand up a number of programs for the Pentagon to support our civilian partners and the Afghans. From supporting the Drug Enforcement Administration's interdiction teams and training the Counternarcotics Police of Afghanistan to seeking congressional support for building a helicopter fleet for the Afghan Ministry of Interior, the office's unique counternarcotics authorities made it one of the most interesting and operational policy shops in Washington. The office had oversight of a nearly billion-dollar account and could provide training and equipment to almost any foreign entity that was involved in combating illicit trafficking—border police, paramilitary entities, military intelligence services, and so forth.

Although the mission of the office was to counter illicit narcotics, Andre Hollis and then Mary Beth Long championed a more strategic approach to focus resources on countering any type of illicit trafficking that supported terrorists and insurgencies related to the global war on terror. We strove to make others in the Pentagon understand that an illicit pipeline run by criminals could move all kinds of things that could harm America's interests: a pipeline that moves drugs can just as easily move weapons, explosives, terrorists, money, and even weapons of mass destruction. This expansive view of our mission allowed us to quietly provide assistance and equipment to foreign security forces in the form of everything from intelligence fusion centers to night-vision goggles and helicopters. The authority and money allowed us to accomplish a lot over the course of 2004 and 2005 while staying under the radar of senior leaders who wanted the Defense Department to do less in Afghanistan, not more.

Our operational efforts were part of a broader, five-pillar strategy for combating opium trafficking in Afghanistan that was intended to be a comprehensive strategy designed to attack the rapidly growing cancer of the narcotics trade in Afghanistan. The five pillars were public diplomacy, interdiction, law enforcement, alternative livelihoods, and eradication.[7] I came to the interagency working group just as the strategy was taking shape. In many ways it was a good strategy that struck at the multiple aspects of a narco-economy. However, for a number of reasons, it was never effectively executed. The main reason was that each element of the strategy was led by a different agency in the U.S. government that applied different timelines and uneven resources to each pillar. Thus, the interdiction and law enforcement efforts were led by the Drug Enforcement Administration, the alternative livelihoods pillar led by US-AID, and the public diplomacy and eradication pillars led by the State Department's Bureau of International Narcotics and Law Enforcement (INL). As a result the pillars were often underresourced, uncoordinated, and poorly synchronized. My office provided support to all of the pillars on behalf of the Defense Department because we were the most able to move people and supplies around a place like Afghanistan.

The U.S. strategy may have been holistic in design, but in execution one pillar quickly became the primary focus: eradication. State INL, led by Assistant Secretary Robert Charles, wanted to employ the tactics that had enjoyed some limited success in Colombia. Charles was particularly determined to use crop duster–type airplanes to spray chemicals over vast swaths of Afghan farmland in an effort to wipe out large tracts of opium cultivation. When I heard of the idea, I had a mental image of a U.S. military patrol entering an Afghan village as planes flew overhead, spraying droplets of chemicals on the locals working their fields. I also had mental pictures of al Qaeda and Taliban recruiting videos showing deformed babies and poisoned wells as a result of the spraying.

In one of my first meetings with the Afghan Interagency Operations Group, I sat aghast as operational plans to implement chemical spraying were discussed. This was a weekly working group with representatives from the Pentagon, State, USAID, and other parts of our government that tackled policy issues before elevating them to the leading officials in each agency for decision in higher level meetings known as Deputies and Principals Committees. Charles briefed State's plan to deploy armored crop dusters from Colombia to the heaviest poppy-producing provinces in southern Afghanistan. The planes would be flown by contractors and focus initially on Helmand and Kandahar provinces. The military representative from the Joint Staff respectfully, but assert-ively, began peppering Charles and his team with questions about their plan for rescuing downed pilots if they were shot down deep in Taliban-dominated areas and asked for specifics on INL's mechanisms for coor-dinating and de-conflicting the spraying with military operations such as ground patrols. Charles gave strong assurances that the operations would be thoroughly coordinated with military operations. Both the Drug Enforcement Administration and USAID representatives then in-dicated they did not have the resources to deploy interdiction teams or alternative livelihoods programs where the spraying was to take place, deep in the heart of Helmand and Kandahar, where both poppies and hostile insurgents were plentiful. Both the military officer and the US-AID representative pressed the importance of having alternatives for farmers who had just had their livelihoods destroyed.

I asked about the strategic communications plan to inform local resi-dents through media networks like al Jazeera and local Afghan radio to counter the inevitable Taliban propaganda campaign that would accom-pany the spraying. I pointed out that it was inevitable that the effort would be misunderstood and very likely that people would accuse the co-alition of conducting Soviet-style chemical warfare. Another uniformed officer asked how we would explain to the world that we were there to win hearts and minds while wiping out farmers' only means of making a living.

After several more questions, Charles, red-faced, slammed his hand on the table and said, "These farmers are criminals, period. They are breaking Afghan law. We are not there to win the hearts and minds of criminals. We are there to restore stability and rule of law to Afghanistan and not let it become a narco-state!" He then stalked out of the room.[8]

The aerial spray effort was further complicated by the "lead nation" agreement that made the United Kingdom the lead for counternarcot-ics in Afghanistan. The UK had its own strategy for combating the drug trade and wanted (rightly, in my view) to emphasize interdicting and arresting high-profile traffickers rather than focusing on the very farm-ers our military efforts were trying to win over. Our British counter-parts were absolutely not in favor of eradication and certainly not aerial eradication; in fact, during one of our monthly videoconferences they asserted bluntly that we would threaten European popular support for the war effort if we proceeded with chemical spraying.

The irony of the long-running debate between State INL and Defense was that our counternarcotics office in the Pentagon agreed with State about the destabilizing and corrosive effects of narcotics on Afghanistan's ability to create a viable government. However, we differed greatly with them on how to deal with the opium trade and tended to agree with the Brits that interdiction should be emphasized. The arrest of some high-profile traffickers or corrupt government officials would have sent a strong signal about the growth of the fledgling Afghan justice sector, would have made a powerful statement against corruption, and would have had the fewest negative effects on the folks we wanted on our side: the average rural Afghan farmer.

It became apparent to us in the counternarcotics office that neither Gen. John Abizaid, who succeeded General Franks at Central Command, nor Secretary Rumsfeld had any intention of allowing aerial chemical spraying while American soldiers were patrolling the Afghan countryside. More important, neither did President Karzai, who eventually put the final nail in the coffin of the idea. We found it unfortunate, however, that our leadership in the Pentagon also had no intention of changing the rules of engagement to allow our soldiers to target drug labs, caches, or major traffickers. The counternarcotics issue in general was simply seen as mission creep for the war in Afghanistan, an effort many in the building were looking to draw down, not escalate. Thus as the 2005 summer fighting season wore on, we felt as though we were fighting a two-front bureaucratic war, trying to stop State from instituting a disastrous policy of aerial eradication while trying to get the military engaged on interdicting trafficking.

In the meantime we continued to quietly put programs in place to support the Drug Enforcement Administration's growing presence and put some basic controls on the wide-open Afghan border. Most important, the office put resources into training and equipping the fledgling Afghan National Police with radios, helicopters, training, buildings, and weapons at a time when relatively little was going to them from the rest of the Pentagon and the State Department.

I experienced these policy failures directly the next time my unit was mobilized to deploy to southern Afghanistan. During a briefing on rules of engagement, I questioned a lawyer from Central Command on why we were not allowed to target criminals if we could demonstrate their activities were supporting the Taliban. He replied a little heatedly, clearly not appreciating being questioned by a lowly captain, "Counterdrug is not something for the military to be involved in. It's the civilians' job. Bottom line, we don't do drugs, we break things and destroy our nation's enemies!"

"Sir, we also protect things," I responded. "And to the extent that we are protecting Afghanistan from being destabilized, we should take on the drug trade to prevent it from financing a Taliban comeback and completely corrupting the new government. Otherwise, we risk having another mid-1990s Colombia." I thought it was a fantastically short-sighted statement and evidence of how myopically many people in the military viewed their role in this new type of warfare. The intelligence officer giving us our briefing chimed in that they had no evidence of drug proceeds directly supporting the Taliban and that their puritan ideology would not accept drug money anyway. I remember thinking that the assessment was almost laughable and showed how little under-standing we had of the root causes and motivations of the insurgency. Throughout my deployment in 2006 I would see indisputable evidence of the insurgency's benefiting from the estimated $600 million in local proceeds from narcotics.[9] I also experienced the fact that our eradication operations were not only poorly coordinated but had a negative effect on my attempts to win local support. Eventually the evidence that the drug trade was supporting the Taliban grew to the point where it was undeniable, and coalition units were finally allowed to actively target drug labs, caches of opium, and traffickers with ties to the insurgency. By that time, though, the tide of drugs and money flowing to criminal groups, corrupt officials, and the Taliban had done its damage.

Our long-term strategy to deal with Afghanistan's security challenges was growing and training the fledgling Afghan National Security Forces, consisting of its army, police, and intelligence service. Though building these forces was how we planned to eventually leave, we devoted rela-tively few resources to the effort in those early days, particularly given the challenges involved. The United States had never rebuilt an entire army and police force from scratch, much less in a landlocked, conserva-tive Muslim country that was still at war. Even more challenging was try-ing to build a force made up of men who were largely illiterate, had ethnic and tribal divisions, and had been devastated by a decade of civil war.

Reconstructing the national army in Afghanistan was a herculean task. Actually *reconstruction* was the wrong word to describe that process because there was nothing left to construct. In the decade between the disintegration of the communist-backed Afghan Army in 1992 and 9/11, the Army's facilities, equipment, and infrastructure had been destroyed or had slowly disintegrated. The disarmament process backed by the international community was relatively successful in repurposing heavy weapons such as anti-aircraft guns and tanks from regional militias that had sprung up over the 1990s to the new Afghan National Army. However, critical internal Army functions such as recruiting, logistics, training, maintenance, and procurement of new items were nonexistent and had to be started from scratch. The biggest challenge was the lack of trained, or even literate, Afghans with whom the United States could work to try to get these basic systems established. Just getting Afghan soldiers paid on a regular basis was a monumental hurdle that would take the new Army and its American advisors years to put into place.

For a number of reasons the police were most afflicted by these issues. Many police officers could not read or write their name, much less understand the concept of the rule of law. In fact, to many, having a position with the police was seen as a way to protect one's family and gain some additional income through tolls and bribes. Further, trying to develop and grow a force while simultaneously using it in continuous combat operations proved to be a fantastically difficult undertaking. In retrospect, many of us across the U.S. government grossly underestimated the magnitude of these issues in 2004 and 2005.

The problems were difficult enough, but we were poorly organized as a government and within the international community to address them. We effectively lost the years from 2002 to 2005 due to the lead nation construct because the Germans adopted a slow, methodical approach to improving the quality of the police. In a country ravaged by war for thirty years and populated by a largely illiterate, feudal society, the Germans focused on passive, European-style, rule of law training. They implemented this training in a five-year process at a training academy in Kabul that produced only a few hundred officers at the end of the program. While the Germans focused on small classes and quality, the Afghan police out on the nation's borders and in remote rural provinces were either predatory toward the populace or underequipped and overwhelmed by a growing insurgency. This lapse in getting the Afghan police back on their feet would prove critical to the Taliban's resurgence in later years.

Over a series of videoconferences Lieutenant General Barno and Ambassador Khalilzad highlighted to both Rumsfeld and Secretary of State Colin Powell the paucity of resources the Europeans were providing to build Afghan capacity. A few weeks later Powell, Rumsfeld, and National Security Advisor Condoleezza Rice decided during a small group lunch that the United States would take on a greater role in training police and the justice sector and that, within that effort, the Defense Department would play a more significant part.

The decision was viewed as long overdue by many of us working the issues, but once again our government was not organized properly for the effort. The underlying problem with how we handled the issue of the Afghan police, as well as many other issues we would face in trying to do nation building in Iraq and Afghanistan, was that our expertise was housed in our civilian agencies, such as the State Department, Customs and Border Patrol, and law enforcement, where one could find police trainers, border and customs experts, and investigators. Unfortunately, these agencies and their civilian employees lacked the ability to operate in a combat zone, and the leaders of these agencies didn't want to give up control or funding for those missions, so they often ended up hiring contractors to fill the gaps.

Conversely, the military had the ability to move people and things to operate in difficult, hostile places but lacked the type of specialized expertise found within the other agencies. I consistently found mixed views within the Pentagon on this dichotomy in those early days of dealing with the wars in Iraq and Afghanistan. There were those who thought that taking on softer tasks such as counternarcotics and police training distracted soldiers from pure military missions and let our civilian agencies off the hook. Others, including me, believed the military had to learn to do what the civilians couldn't.

During one meeting between OSD-Policy and colleagues on the Joint Staff over how to implement the decision for Defense to take a greater role in police training, a colonel lamented, "We don't have nearly enough military policemen to take on rebuilding a national police force, and the average infantry officer in the 82nd Airborne Division isn't trained for it. This is why State INL exists. They need to step up and do their job."

A lieutenant colonel at the end of the conference table who had just returned from a tour in Afghanistan replied, "Sir, we had better start getting our soldiers ready for this mission fast, because the Afghan police are out there doing more harm than good, and they are turning the people against the government and against us. We don't have any choice but to turn them around. State's contractors are doing the basic police training, but once the Afghans leave the training center to report back to their districts, we don't have a clue what's going on with them. We have to provide mentors to be with them on the job, like we do with the Afghan Army."[10] (As a sad aside, I would later think of this conversation when I saw desperately needed military police handing out tickets for speeding and improper uniforms on Bagram Airbase rather than using their precious expertise to train the Afghan police.)

The result was often an odd mix of government civilians, contractors, and military personnel out in the field trying to accomplish what they could. They had to deal with a convoluted mix of authorities and reporting chains among State Department civilians in Washington, the embassy in Kabul, their contracting companies, and the military headquarters in Afghanistan responsible for building, training, equipping, and mentoring both the Army and the police during combat missions.

Despite the frustration over the lack of progress in the police and judiciary, the alarming growth in the drug trade, and the mounting levels of Taliban intimidation, the rapidly declining situation in Iraq came to overshadow and influence all aspects of our policies in Afghanistan. It also created a massive sucking sound as resources were drawn away from Afghanistan. With the Iraqi insurgency worsening, senior U.S. policymakers decided to hand off more and more responsibility in Afghanistan to NATO, thus freeing up American forces to go to Iraq. During a series of videoconferences with Central Command, the Joint Staff, and Lieutenant General Barno, Secretary Rumsfeld argued that the United States needed to "reduce the amount of money it is spending in Afghanistan and the amount of troops deployed there." With losses mounting in Iraq, Rumsfeld said, current levels of spending were not sustainable. At the time the United States was spending between $600 million and $1 billion per month on the war effort.[11] The issues that Barno and Khalilzad were highlighting—growing insecurity, rebuilding the Afghan National Security Forces, the poppy trade, and a corrupt Afghan government—would simply have to be addressed by NATO. The secretary's desire to minimize the U.S. commitment in Afghanistan would have long-lasting effects.

In my office in the Pentagon I was copied every month on briefing slides from Central Command to the Joint Staff that highlighted the troop numbers in Afghanistan and the fact that they remained under a cap. At one point Central Command produced a briefing with a longer-term drawdown strategy that took the total commitment of U.S. forces in Afghanistan from six battalions down to two in the east plus one battalion of Special Operations Forces by 2007. The plan left fewer than six thousand troops on the ground, including the support personnel for those units. I regularly spoke with the staff down at Central Command working Afghanistan, and they confided in me that they were constantly under pressure to figure out ways to keep the footprint as small as possible in Afghanistan in order to have as many forces as possible available for Iraq.[12]

I had mixed feelings about the Iraq invasion. I was certain that the war would require far greater numbers of soldiers to occupy the country than what we dedicated to the invasion. I feared we were underestimating the huge, centuries-old sectarian and ethnic rifts among Shia, Sunni, and Kurds that Saddam Hussein's dictatorship had suppressed for years. But I had no moral objections to the invasion. The U.S. intelligence community and our allies' intelligence services were certain Saddam had biological weapons and was actively pursuing a nuclear capability. In fact, in the waning days of the Bush administration, while at the Office of the Vice President, I would come across some of those reports as I helped organize files to send to the National Archives. They were unequivocal that Saddam had weapons of mass destruction. In the wake of 9/11, we simply could not sit back and risk his providing that capability to a terrorist organization.

My objection to the invasion was the timing. Our job was far from finished in Afghanistan. Osama bin Laden, Ayman al-Zawahiri, and scores of other al Qaeda senior leaders were still on the loose. In addition, the key leaders of the former Taliban regime were still active in Pakistan and were reasserting themselves in Afghanistan. The same underlying causes of instability—warlordism, ethnic strife, lack of governance, extreme poverty, no border controls—that had allowed the Taliban to rise to power in the 1990s were still present. Yet resource after resource, from helicopters to scarce Predator drones, from police trainers to billions in reconstruction dollars, were diverted away from the theater from which our homeland had been attacked to a theater from which it might have been attacked. It was enormously frustrating as we watched our golden window from 2002–5 close and popular frustrations in Afghanistan grow, along with ever increasing levels of violence.

At the same time that U.S. resources were diverting to Iraq, the new commander of the U.S. 3-Star Headquarters called Combined Forces Command–Afghanistan, Lt. Gen. Karl Eikenberry, was advocating reducing the number of Afghan National Army soldiers from seventy-two thousand to fifty thousand. Eikenberry had previously served as the head of the small training command in Kabul charged with beginning the process of rebuilding the Afghan Army, and he had since replaced Lieutenant General Barno as the head of U.S. forces.

I repeatedly asked my colleagues if we were seeing the same data: the signs of steadily rising violence in the midst of declining U.S. resources. Though I disagreed with doing so, I could understand the logic behind backfilling U.S. forces with NATO forces. However, I could not understand the logic behind reducing the number of Afghan National Army soldiers we planned to train, equip, and field. That Army was America's ticket out of Afghanistan.

I sat in on a number of meetings with Eikenberry as he made the rounds of various policy offices in Washington, making the case that we should focus our efforts on producing quality Afghan soldiers and institutions rather then numbers. "We simply do not have the numbers of troops we need to simultaneously conduct combat operations and build a quality Afghan Army up to seventy-two thousand," he insisted to a room full of OSD-Policy officials and Joint Staff general officers in 2005. He pressed the idea that we were moving too quickly in building and training the Army with the limited resources he had on hand and, by doing so, risked fielding a force of very poor quality that could not sustain itself.

"Moving too quickly?" I wrote in my notes. I was one of the junior people in the room, but I was dying to yell out, "Then ask for more resources!"[13] It was a theme we would see consistently for the next five years when it came to troop numbers and resources in Afghanistan. From various offices in the Pentagon, I observed multiple four- and three-star commanders ask for what each thought he could get from the Pentagon in the shadow of Iraq rather than making the case for what he needed to be successful while also making clear the risks to the mission in Afghanistan that not providing those forces presented.

For the first few years of the war the umbrella authorization for the coalition in Afghanistan was the International Security Assistance Force, while U.S. Forces operated under Operation Enduring Freedom. In early 2004 Gen. James Jones, the square-jawed former commandant of the Marine Corps and U.S. general commanding NATO, presented a four-phase plan to transfer overall security responsibility for the country from the United States to the NATO-led coalition. The first phase started in the north, moving counterclockwise around the country to the west, south, and east along the Pakistan border. The plan called for the United States to place its conventional units under ISAF command but keep its Special Operations Forces and Afghan National Army trainers separate and under the less restrictive rules of engagement found under Operation Enduring Freedom. The security forces in each region of the country would be led by an ally commanding a Regional Command.

A number of us in the intelligence and policy community working Afghanistan closely had serious concerns about transitioning the entire theater to the control of the International Security Assistance Force. It was difficult to understand how, in good conscience, we could give more responsibility to NATO when we had witnessed the lead nation approach fail so miserably. By late 2004 the Italians had sent only one technical team to help build the Afghan judiciary, and the Germans had fewer than twenty instructors at their police academy in Kabul.[14] And yet, under the NATO transition plan, Italy was slated to take the lead for security in western Afghanistan along the Iranian border and Germany was to take the lead in the north. It made little sense that the very same European allies that had failed to provide resources to the judicial and police sectors were now entrusted with security responsibility for half the country. Regardless, the move to hand off the effort to the Europeans seemed to take on a life of its own, and the plan moved forward.

Each NATO member nation participating in the campaign had pledged certain numbers of troops, funds for building bases and infrastructure, and other critical support items such as helicopters, transport aircraft, and communications gear. However, with Phase I of the transition to the north and Phase II to the west, NATO charged ahead with the plan while these pledges remained unfulfilled. The provinces involved were relatively peaceful and dominated by Tajiks and Uzbeks who had opposed the Taliban regime, but we knew Phases III and IV in the Pashtun-dominated south and east, where the Taliban enjoyed most of its support, would be infinitely more difficult.

I raised these concerns during a meeting with a visiting group of NATO colonels in mid-2005, and a Dutch officer remarked with some bravado, "Before my unit deployed to Bosnia in the 1990s we were not as ready as we should have been, but we made the mission work and eventually brought peace to that nation. Sometimes one cannot wait until every single vehicle and helicopter is perfectly in place and must just move forward and tackle the mission."

A salty Marine who had served in the invasion of southern Afghanistan replied, "Sir, I don't think you will find fighting the Taliban in Tarin Kowt or Kandahar to be anything like peacekeeping in Sarajevo."[15] It was a prescient statement. This and numerous other meetings confirmed our suspicions that the Europeans were preparing for a peacekeeping operation à la Bosnia, not for a complex counterinsurgency campaign in one of the most hostile climates in the world.

In the Pentagon we were receiving back-channel reports from American officers in Kabul that the Germans and Italians were grossly short-staffed and without key support items. In some sense it was understandable. NATO was originally formed to defend its members' home territories against a Soviet invasion; their primary mission was static defense. It was now being asked to operate thousands of miles away, in some of the most difficult terrain in the world, with virtually no infrastructure, in a very hostile environment. They were finding it very difficult to be expeditionary, which required forward deployment of key capabilities like maintenance facilities, air traffic control terminals, and supply depots. They also found themselves in a counterinsurgency mission that was very different from the peacekeeping mission their governments had signed up for.

To make matters worse, each country, including Spain, the Netherlands, and Turkey, deployed its soldiers with a series of restrictions or caveats on what types of combat operations each could do. Though they nominally worked for the ISAF commanding general in Kabul, each country also had a national representative with its forces, who had a parallel chain back to his national capital and could overrule the commander's orders. However, these shortcomings were overlooked during a series of meetings of NATO defense ministers in 2004 and 2005, where the United States pushed for continuing to hand over the regional commands to the ISAF despite the lack of progress on meeting the troop milestones.

In December 2005, in the midst of the security transition from the United States to NATO, the Pentagon announced that it would not back-fill one of its battalions currently deployed to southern Afghanistan, thereby reducing the numbers of overall U.S. forces from nineteen thousand to sixteen thousand. It was a relatively benign announcement and in keeping with Secretary Rumsfeld's stated desire to draw down our presence in Afghanistan.

In the announcement, made on the heels of the good news story about the seating of the Afghan Parliament, the Defense Department spokesman Bryan Whitman told Reuters news service, "The American troop reduction has been anticipated since NATO agreed to assume control of an American command in southern Afghanistan next year. The Atlantic alliance is looking to raise its 9,000-strong [International Security Assistance Force] to about 15,000 troops from early next year. Secretary Rumsfeld gave the Afghan order on a recommendation from the senior U.S. Commander there, Army Lt. Gen. Karl Eikenberry, because Afghanistan's own Army and police forces are growing and NATO is increasing its international security assistance peacekeeping force . . . in the country."[16]

In my view, this was a seminal moment in the Afghan war effort. The announcement barely made the news in the United States, but, coupled with the announcement that NATO would assume full security responsibility for the country, the signal was loud and clear to everyone in the region: "The Americans are leaving us again."

The Taliban heard it as a signal that the United States was leaving and that they could take advantage of less aggressive, less capable NATO forces. For the Pakistani Army, the announcement confirmed that it would be left with an unstable Afghanistan on its border that was ripe for Indian influence and that Pakistan should maintain its influence in Afghanistan through support for the Taliban. For the many Afghans I spoke with in the government and Army, it confirmed their worst fears about being abandoned before they were ready. And most important, for the Afghan people, the announcement told them that they had better hedge their bets, as they were making daily life-and-death decisions in their villages about which side to take.

In March 2006 Condoleezza Rice, who was now secretary of state, met with Dr. Abdullah Abdullah, Afghanistan's foreign minister and future presidential candidate. He warned her not to continue to let Afghanistan slip into conflict. "I am deeply worried about the rising insurgency," he said. "People are beginning to lose hope in their government. We are losing the support of the population."[17]

Together, the lead nation strategy, the light U.S. footprint, the aversion to nation building, the unchecked drug trade, the hand off to NATO, and the diversion of resources to Iraq contributed to Afghanistan's backsliding from the post-9/11 heyday. For me personally, it meant that as I mobilized with my Special Forces unit, we would face one hell of a fighting season the following spring of 2006 and a sharp turning point in the war.

2 Arabs, Afghans, and Americans
The War of Ideas

"My friends, my brothers, look what the Americans have done for Germany and Japan," our Afghan interpreter Muhammad bellowed out to the crowd of men sitting around the walls, leaning against large pillows or rolled-up carpets. Muhammad was not your average interpreter, who learned a little English in secondary school before moving on to the high salaries of interpreters who worked for the U.S. military. He was a former teacher with a master's degree in Arabic and had lived abroad before coming back to the "new," liberated Afghanistan. He spoke Afghanistan's two national languages, Dari and Pashto, and was fluent in Arabic and English. His ability to communicate a positive strategic message while translating almost simultaneously in four languages was worth more than having a platoon of infantry with me.

"The Americans rebuilt entire cities from the rubble of World War II," Muhammad continued, grandly gesturing to mimic buildings rising from the ashes. "They have built thousands of roads like the one that now takes us from Kabul to Kandahar in a day instead of a week. Even after millions of Americans died there at the hands of the Nazis, they rebuilt Germany. They are a good people. They are here to help us rebuild our country. They are not here to destroy it, like the Russians. We must work with them."

We were in one of the most remote locales in the world, Uruzgan Province, smack in the center of Afghanistan. Uruzgan sits at the southern tip of the Hindu Kush Mountains and is often overshadowed in terms of media attention and political clout by its larger provincial neighbors to the south, Kandahar and Helmand. But, as I was coming to learn, Uruzgan was the heart of the Pashtun tribal structure of southern Afghanistan. This was one of the primary reasons President Karzai, as the son

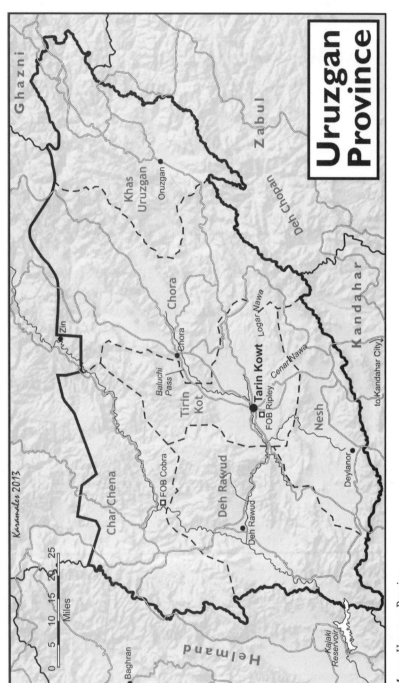

Map 4. Uruzgan Province.

of a prominent Pashtun leader who fled to Pakistan when the Taliban regime took power, chose Uruzgan of all places to insert himself in the aftermath of 9/11 and foment an anti-Taliban revolt. It was here that I came to fight the war on terror. What I quickly discovered was that the real fight was the war of ideas and that our strategic messaging to the Afghan people was more important than killing the remaining Taliban loyalists. It was also in Uruzgan that I would experience firsthand some of the consequences of our policies, such as the light footprint, and the slow start in rebuilding the Afghan National Army.

It was the winter of 2005–6. My U.S. Army Special Forces Operation Detachment Alpha was on patrol in the heart of Taliban country. I had left my civilian position in the Pentagon the previous fall and had mobilized as the leader of ODA 53, part of 20th Special Forces Group in the Army National Guard.

All of my men had the same two years of training in unconventional warfare as our active-duty counterparts, but once the training was over, mine went back to their civilian careers, devoting one weekend a month and two weeks a year to continued military training, similar to other reserve component units. It was our unit's second mobilization since 9/11 and second deployment to Afghanistan. We faced the typical skepticism from our active-duty brothers, who questioned how we could possibly shoot, move, and communicate as well as they could while training only once a month. They were right to be skeptical, particularly when it came to familiarization with the latest gear and gizmos that seemed to be changing every six months since the Department of Defense began pumping money into the Special Operations Command after 9/11. But the active-duty units soon learned that we brought a myriad of other civilian skills that played a critical role in an irregular warfare environment. Many of my men were police officers or federal agents in their civilian careers and understood the art of running informants, dealing with organized criminal elements, and recognizing corruption. Importantly, they understood the challenges and gray areas associated with separating and protecting an intimidated civilian populace from elements opposed to rule of law. Other skill sets from our civilian professions stemmed from our careers as intelligence analysts, business owners, bond traders, lawyers, and engineers, to name just a few. I would argue that in many ways our men were likely even more qualified to operate in unconventional, irregular environments than active-duty Green Berets who had known only a regular army unit before coming to Special Forces. For example, on my team alone, we had a medic that was also a physician's assistant at a trauma center, a vice president of a major telecommunications company, and analysts from our intelligence services. Plus, my own background was in the Office of the Secretary of Defense.

My team was tasked to embed with and provide support to the United Arab Emirates (UAE) Special Operations Task Force 6. This meant we gave tactical advice to their platoons when necessary and provided the ability for the Task Group to plug into coalition artillery, close air support, medical evacuation, and quick-reaction forces in case of a firefight. The UAE was one of the earliest participants in the U.S.-led coalition in Afghanistan and had had a presence in theater since 2002. The commander of their Special Operations Command, Maj. Gen. Juma Ahmed al Bawardi al Falasi, had apparently expressed a desire for his Task Forces to be "bloodied," which meant he wanted them sent to the more dangerous Pashtun areas of southern Afghanistan where the Taliban were staging a comeback. Initially, my entire team was dedicated to supporting the UAE, but as the transition to the International Security Assistance Force progressed through 2006, I was ordered to divide my team into three- and four-man cells and to embed with Czech, French, Polish, Dutch, and other nations' Special Forces scattered throughout theater.

Naturally, we would rather have stayed together for the tour, but splitting a team into smaller, autonomous elements is a key part of Green Beret doctrine. An ODA consists of twelve men with duplicative skill sets. There are two officers, a captain and a warrant officer, as team leaders, and two senior sergeants, or NCOs, one who runs the team as the "team sergeant" and the other charged with intelligence analysis. The rest of the team consists of two weapons specialists, two engineers, two communications specialists, and two medics who are trained in everything from combat to trauma care. Thus, we can easily divide into a split-team configuration of two groups of six, or even further down to groups of four or even groups of two.

The very essence of the Green Beret is to operate by, with, and through local security forces. Unlike the Navy SEALs or any other Special Operations Force around the world, we emphasize cultural and language ability in our training, on top of advanced tactics and specialty skills. Special Forces Green Berets are then assigned to operate in specific regions of the world. The wars in Iraq and Afghanistan threw much of the regional assignments model up in the air. (My unit was habitually assigned to South or Central America, and most of my men were Spanish speakers.) But the fundamental aspects of being able to identify the needs and motivations of local power brokers and align them with U.S. national security interests are the same across any culture. Thus, in Special Forces doctrine a relatively junior sergeant can find himself the senior—or only—American in a murky environment, with little guidance, representing U.S. interests with strategic consequences. With that in mind, our selection and training included a heavy psychological element that specifically sought out the type of individual who thrived on that kind of autonomy. For me as an officer, it also made leading such strong personalities quite the challenge.

The remoteness and famously difficult terrain of Afghanistan made our ability to operate independently with indigenous units even more critical. We often scoffed at our Special Operations Forces brethren in Iraq, who typically were never more than a few kilometers or even a few blocks from another American unit that could provide support if they needed it. By contrast, I found myself with only three other Americans embedded with two platoons of Emiratis out on a joint patrol with a platoon of Afghan National Army soldiers. We were hours by helicopter from the nearest coalition base. To boot, we were a several days' drive into a portion of Afghanistan dominated by the Noorzai tribe, which was in a century's old feud with President Karzai's Popalzai tribe. We had set out to patrol the Cenar Lawa Valley, running east and southeast from Tarin Kowt, the provincial capital of Uruzgan. The valley was the stomping ground of tribes that had supported the Taliban during their reign, but these tribes had since been marginalized, and even preyed upon, by the strongman provincial governor Jan Mohammad Khan, whom Karzai had put in place upon coming to power. In short, we were deep in Taliban country. I couldn't have been happier.

After Muhammad finished speaking to the crowd, Yousef, the UAE Special Forces captain in command of the patrol, stood up and announced in Arabic, "The way of the Taliban and al Qaeda is not the way." Muhammad translated into Pashto for the group and then whispered in English to me.

"The Taliban do not have properly trained mullahs," Yousef continued. "They call themselves mullahs, but they do not have the proper Islamic education and credentials. Many of them can barely read Arabic and are just guessing at the words of the Holy Quran!" The men laughed. "You should not listen to them. They are not authorities on Islam. Look at us. We are Arabs. We have authority in these things." Yousef spoke with conviction. Normally a quiet and somewhat reserved man from the desert oasis town of Al Ain in the UAE, he came alive in these *shuras*. He would tell me stories of his father taking him to the markets in Dubai and how they all looked admiringly on the Afghan businessmen and traders in the bazaars. "Now a bunch of idiots calling themselves religious students"—the literal meaning of Talib—"have led this proud people astray," he would say to me in frustration.

I kept a low profile in the back corner of the large room in the community center that doubled as a classroom, meeting center, and mosque. I was the only Westerner inside with the captain, an Afghan Army lieutenant, and over a hundred Afghan men sitting around the edge of the room covered in red, black, and tan carpets. My three other operators manned the radios and heavy machine guns on our two Humvees outside and generally kept an eye on things in the village while groups of kids gathered around, giggling and asking for candy. We deliberately wore the same brown and tan desert-patterned camouflage uniform as the UAE soldiers in order to avoid standing out as the potentially lucrative American targets in the crowd. As had become the norm since the early days of the Afghan conflict, Green Berets were authorized to grow beards out of respect for the Pashtun culture and to further blend in, at least from a distance. In this case, the more we could blend in, stand back, and project this patrol as a joint Arab-Afghan effort, the better.

"You can develop your cities and deal with the rest of the world and still be Muslims of good faith," Yousef continued. "Look at Dubai. Look at Abu Dhabi. Look at the great Muslim cities of Cairo, Beirut, and Jakarta. Your children can have better lives. Your sons and daughters can be educated and still live as proper Muslims. Afghanistan must move forward, not backward. The Taliban want to keep you backward so they can control you."

The hardened faces, particularly of the young men in the black turbans and eyeliner often associated with Taliban fighters, began to soften. Some even nodded. The captain spoke for several more minutes. It was a powerful speech.

From a strategic messaging standpoint, it was a gold mine. To have Arab and Afghan military officers in sync, communicating the upside of the coalition presence in Afghanistan and the downside of the Taliban extremist ideology, was strong indeed. Their questioning of the Taliban's ideological credibility in the Islamic world was a strategic cruise missile and worth more than thousands of coalition soldiers. Obviously a Westerner could never credibly get away with it, so I just sat quietly, wearing my Arab-style turban and beard, trying to fade as far into the background as possible.

I had read about it but had never fully appreciated the extent to which non-Arab Muslims looked up to Arabs from the Gulf region. Now I was seeing it firsthand. The Arabs held both ideological and financial authority. From an ethnic and ideological standpoint, they were the custodians of Islam's most holy sites in Arabia. From a financial standpoint, the Arabs were the proverbial distant cousins who had made it big. Dubai, one of the new financial, commercial, and transportation hubs of the world, was really only a decade old as a major metropolis. The Emiratis had brilliantly created a magnet for multinational businesses out of a desert town by effectively leveraging their oil wealth, enacting clever deregulation, and maximizing their centralized geography. It was fascinating to see the deference with which the Afghans treated them, particularly when they didn't know a Westerner was present.

A year later, when I was back in the Pentagon as a civilian in the Office of the Secretary of Defense Policy, I tried to lead an effort for the Pentagon to approach the UAE and other Gulf countries about leading an all-Arab provincial reconstruction team (PRT). The PRTs were the coalition entities in each province charged with leading reconstruction and development initiatives. The UAE Task Force had a very active civil affairs component that was engaged in projects ranging from a hospital in Zabul Province to a University in Khost, as well as dozens of mosque restorations. I felt strongly that a PRT led by the UAE and supported by other Arab countries that had also sent troops to Afghanistan, such as Bahrain, Egypt, and Jordan, could have been a powerful reconstruction and strategic communications tool. Unfortunately, as soon as I floated the idea in a series of meetings in 2007, I met bureaucratic resistance, and the effort died. The Middle East directorate in OSD-Policy and the Joint Staff were adamant that such an effort would be a distraction from other high-priority efforts, such as the Iraq War, Iran, and the Gulf Cooperation Council. In the end, in my view, we failed to leverage the full potential of the participation of Arab Muslim states in Afghanistan.

We patrolled the hills and valleys of Uruzgan that winter in our special operations version of the Humvee known as the ground mobility vehicle (GMV). The GMV was built on a Humvee chassis but, rather than the typical hatch-back version found on most armored Humvees, the GMV was open in the back, allowing for the stacking of extra supplies, extra soldiers on the flat bench seats, and, typically, a rear-facing machine gunner. It also had a more powerful engine and stronger suspension. In addition to the turret-mounted .50 caliber heavy machine gun or Mark-19 automatic grenade launcher, some ODAs would also outfit the right front passenger side of the vehicle with a light machine gun on a swing arm for additional forward-facing firepower. Most ODAs also took out the two rear passenger seats to allow more room for water, food, and, most important, ammunition. Before the massive uptick in roadside bombs, an ODA was much more likely to face a Taliban ambush and wanted to be able to respond with as much firepower as possible in all directions. We also used all-terrain vehicles, commonly called ATVs, to scout in front of patrols. The single rider on the ATV was much closer to the ground and could more easily see tell-tale disturbances in the ground or wires that may give away an IED. They were also fantastic for driving ahead of a convoy to find paths through maze-like villages or suitable trails. The UAE platoons used a mix of armored Humvees and the French-made Panhard light armored vehicle. The three-man Panhard was considerably smaller and narrower than the Humvee and could therefore go places the Humvee couldn't fit. But it severely limited the Emiratis' ability to conduct dismounted operations with only one extra crewman outside of the driver and gunner. The Afghan Army, for their part, used Ford Ranger pickup trucks with a steel roll bar over the crew cab that mounted a machine gun. We were amazed at how many Afghan soldiers could be packed into the back of those trucks, usually with their legs dangling over the sides.

As we patrolled up and down the Noorzai valleys in central Uruzgan in our hodgepodge of vehicle types that composed our combined Afghan-Arab-American convoys we repeated the same engagement speeches again and again. In some cases they had great effect. In one village in the Nesh District of southern Uruzgan, an elder stood up after Captain Yousef completed his talk and announced, "As a true and faithful Muslim, I am renouncing poppy. I will no longer grow it on my land. It is un-Islamic, bad for my family, and bad for my village, Deylanor. We may go hungry, but we will be pure and we will hold our heads up high." He then ceremoniously snapped the wooden handle of a scythe, often used to score poppy bulbs, over his knee. He handed it to the Emirati captain to the great applause of the rest of the elders sitting in the shade of two large trees where we were meeting.

"Thank you for your courageous stand for all of Deylanor," I said, standing up and deciding this should be one of the rare times I would speak. The crowd was jolted at hearing English, clearly not realizing until then a Westerner was in their midst. "I will do everything in my power to request seeds and other types of aid from the PRT in Tarin Kowt and from the NGOs to help you. I make this as a personal pledge to you," I said, looking at the elder. "I am honored to be in the presence of your courage and leadership."

Unfortunately, I ended up having a hell of a time getting help for the elder and Deylanor. The spring poppy harvest was already complete, and planting would start again in the fall. But on returning to base I discovered the USAID officer had left, and her replacement would not be assigned there for several months. The civil affairs team had obligated their funds to other projects. The district government was pretty much nonexistent, and the higher level provincial minister for agriculture lived in the relative safety of Kandahar and only periodically visited his office in Tarin Kowt. The UAE commander and I agreed to go back to Deylanor in the coming weeks and just give the elder cash.

Weeks later, when we returned to Deylanor, the elder who had ceremoniously broken his scythe refused to speak to us. After multiple requests he finally came to meet with us after a messenger went to his compound and told him the Arabs wanted to give him money for his village to buy wheat and barley seed. Muhammad, walking over after chatting with a group of men, whispered in my ear, "The drug lord for this area visited after we left. When the elder told him Deylanor was no longer growing poppy, the drug lord threatened to kill him and his family. He also threatened to bring the Taliban to close the schools."

Most farmers took loans in the fall from opium traffickers to buy seed and equipment. The following spring their harvest paid off this debt and hopefully left them with enough to buy food and supplies for the year. Horror stories abounded of families having to give their daughters as payment should the harvest fail. It was one of the reasons I was so opposed to putting eradication first in our counternarcotics strategy. It was the traffickers driving the trade, not the farmers.

The elder finally came out and sat with us, but only for about ten minutes. He was polite and very grateful for the money. Muhammad leaned over again and whispered, "Sir, this man is very scared." Before walking away the elder said, "I want a better future for my people. But we must have security. Please send some Afghan soldiers here. Not police. Soldiers."

Sadly, there were nowhere near enough Afghan National Army soldiers in Uruzgan to station them in Deylanor. We heard later that the villagers stuck to their word and refused to plant poppy and that several men were beaten when they refused to take a loan for that year's harvest. An interpreter from the village later brought me a letter from the Taliban (commonly known as "night letters" because they were left on people's doors in the night) that threatened the village school principal and warned him to no longer speak with the infidel Americans. Eventually the elder moved to the relative safety of Kandahar City.

This episode strengthened my conviction that getting rid of the traffickers would have far greater impact on the trade than cutting down farmers' crops. The erroneous assumption behind eradication was that farmers could freely choose to stop planting poppy. They could not. When it became evident that the poppy trade was directly supporting the Taliban insurgency, the U.S. military was authorized to begin targeting these traffickers. But the shift in authorities didn't happen until 2008.

I thought back to the strategic communications pillar of our counternarcotics strategy and how it had largely failed. I also thought about the broader debate, sometimes called the war of ideas, about our engagement with the Muslim world. The war on terror was being painted by al Qaeda, the Taliban, the Muslim Brotherhood, and a host of other groups as America's war on Islam and the Muslim people. Fundamental Western ideals such as free markets and religious tolerance were overshadowed on international airwaves and at the neighborhood mosque by criticism of U.S. support for Israel, the Iraq War, and the U.S. prison at Guantánamo. It quickly became clear to me during these patrols that we had to get better at communicating those ideals if we hoped to be successful in the long term.

At an operational level in Afghanistan, every time an errant bomb resulted in a civilian casualty or a wayward soldier offended Islamic sensibilities, our enemies were beating us to the punch and painting America as an occupier in the tradition of the ancient Crusaders. As soon as an incident happened, Taliban spokesmen would be on the phone to and emailing the international media to spin their side of the story, often just making things up. My interpreters would bring me DVDs from local bazaars showing women and children in front of destroyed mud compounds claiming they were a result of deliberate bombings of civilians by the U.S. Air Force. Recordings of mullahs in local mosques told tales of American soldiers raping Afghan women and torturing prisoners. While these mullahs had no proof, of course, incidents like the Abu Ghraib photos were proof enough for the average person in South Asia and were like steroids for the insurgent propaganda campaign.

The bottom line was that both tactically and strategically, we used information operations or strategic messaging as a response mechanism to explain incidents or operations when things went wrong. We definitely got better over time, but too often communications were an afterthought. By contrast, the Taliban used information operations and their propaganda campaign to drive operations. They figured out what message they wanted to send and then tailored their tactical operations and their overall campaign plan to fit the message. That was the opposite of our approach. For example, the Taliban would decide they wanted to show their strength in a certain area, so they would seize a government district center or attack a ministry in Kabul, knowing they would eventually be expelled and defeated. They were perfectly willing to trade tactical defeats to get their strategic message out.

In other villages and valleys our Afghan-Arab-U.S. engagement created some heated exchanges, and I began to fully realize our level of ignorance regarding the complicated tribal dynamics at play across Afghanistan. I also came to appreciate the Taliban's efforts to lay the groundwork for an insurgency and the extent to which the poor governance and warlordism of those placed in charge in the aftermath of the Taliban's defeat were driving people back into the Taliban's arms. In *shura* after *shura* I heard the frustrations of the Afghan people and the doubts they had about America's willingness to do what it would take to truly see Afghanistan prosper.

As we progressed deeper into the Cenar Nawa and Logar Nawa valleys toward the eastern border of Uruzgan with Zabul Province and the notorious De Chopan region, we detected more and more evidence of insurgent influence and activity—particularly in the behaviors of the children. De Chopan was a hotbed of al Qaeda and Taliban activity and the site of a multiday firefight for my ODA in 2003. In most villages the kids, alerted by their early warning network of other kids, would be waiting at the edge of town to mob us and the vehicles if we stopped. Small bags of hard candy became one of my favorite giveaways, along with pens and pencils. For most kids who attended schools with few books or supplies, having a writing utensil was a badge of honor. Seeing these kids standing barefoot in frozen mud, grinning from ear to ear just because we had given them a pen, truly touched our hearts.

We pressed down the valleys over several days, and the meetings became more tense and challenging. "How do we know you will not abandon us?" a bespectacled young man asked as he looked past the Afghan lieutenant and Emirati captain and directed his question squarely at me, obviously recognizing me as the American in the room. He clearly was educated, and we later found out he was visiting his family in Uruzgan while on break from Kabul University. He spoke in broken but understandable English.

"Well, I am standing here with you now, thousands of miles away from my home and my family, and the men who are with me will continue to stand with you," I replied. "I cannot promise what will happen in the future, but America is standing with you now."

"But the United States has announced it is withdrawing and turning the security over to the Europeans. America only cares about Iraq now and thinks the Talibs are defeated. The Talibs are not defeated!" he said, slapping his hand down on the carpet. "They are regaining their strength, and Pakistan will help them because they want to control Afghanistan and you have told the world you are leaving. Everyone knows that Europe will not fight. They will not last long here." Grumblings from the group grew as Muhammad translated. All eyes were on me.

"America's future and Afghanistan's future are like this," I said, holding up my hand and pressing my two fingers together. "Our destiny is the same now. If Afghanistan fails, al Qaeda and other groups will take advantage of Afghanistan again to kill innocent people. Al Qaeda and the Taliban do not want to work for a better Afghanistan. They continue killing because they want back into power. The Taliban want to keep Afghanistan backward so that they can control it. Our goal is to make Afghanistan strong so it can chart its own path in the world." I said this despite the fact that just months earlier the Pentagon had announced a further drawdown of the already meager number of U.S. forces.

"We thought America was going to change Afghanistan," the young man rejoined. "We thought America would lift us from this very poor state. You have now left us with a government that is just as bad as the Talibs." It was a common theme: unmet expectations and severe disappointment with the new government. In 2001 the world's only remaining superpower committed itself in a historic way to Afghanistan with a coalition of other nations. From the Afghan perspective, the world's richest nations had come to its rescue. But five years later Afghan lives had changed little. In fact, depending on what tribe you were from, some had become worse.

The UAE captain sought to change the subject. "If you want your situation to change, we must have development. If you want development, we must have NGOs. For there to be NGOs, we must have security. The NGOs are too scared to come to Uruzgan. They have all left. Every man is responsible for security. This is your home. Just as you would defend your family, you must defend your village. We cannot be everywhere. You must take responsibility for the village security, and the NGOs will come back."

A grizzled elder with a white beard stood up and pointed in the direction of Tarin Kowt. "But you will leave us tonight," he said. "The Talibs do not leave here and we have nothing to stop them. Give us some weapons and some training, and we will not allow them to pass through this valley. You should stay here with us and help us, or you should not come visit here. Even talking to you is dangerous. People talk," he said, pointing outside as he looked over his shoulder at the group of young men and boys milling about. It was a point that was made often in our *shuras* out in the villages. Just by interacting with us, the elders were putting their lives on the line. Someone sympathetic to the Taliban or holding a grudge against one of the elders would inform a Talib commander that the elder was working with the Americans; the result was a severe beating at best or a gruesome death at worst. In one case, a day after we left the village of Kalatak in eastern Uruzgan, Muhammad received a call from one of the men who secretly worked on our base. Fifteen men on motorcycles rode into Kalatak the next morning and lined up all the men in the village. They pulled out two elders who had hosted us for lunch to discuss a development project and publicly beat them. They then hanged a man when they discovered he worked on our base.

I often debated whether the patrols to various rural villages to spread our message was doing more harm than good. On the one hand we would never have enough coalition or Afghan National Army soldiers to protect them. On the other hand, we couldn't just cede the countryside to the Taliban and allow them to dominate the narrative on the coalition. The notion that the Afghans were xenophobic or reflexively hated outsiders just didn't ring true in my experience. In fact, I found time and again that the opposite was true. The angriest Afghans I came across were the ones who were upset we were not there more often. They were disappointed we hadn't done more for them, but, in general, they wanted us there. I came to be convinced that what the Afghans most needed was just basic security, and we would have to find a local security framework to allow them to provide it for themselves. Security was the oxygen that development and other initiatives needed to breathe, and the country could not move forward without it.

One elder summed it up perfectly: "You can build all the schools, roads, and clinics you want. We are deeply thankful, as we have many needs. But when the Taliban has a gun to my family's head, what do you expect me to do?"

These series of *shuras* and meetings in Uruzgan, Kandahar, and Helmand in the winter and spring of 2006 profoundly affected my thinking about what policy we needed to implement in the war. I came away convinced that, four years into the war, we did not have our strategic messaging right. We had not effectively explained to the Afghan people, the government, or the international community why we were there.

Nor had we sent the signal that we would stand with the Afghans until they could stand on their own feet. Out in the valleys and villages of southern Afghanistan I also came to realize that, given the devastation of infrastructure and human capacity, the United States had to face the fact that our involvement in Afghanistan would be a generational effort. In a country physically larger than Iraq, with exponentially more difficult mountainous terrain, with no real infrastructure, little human talent, a 75 percent illiteracy rate, fledgling security forces, and an insurgency enjoying sanctuary where they could rest and regroup unscathed, the United States needed a security presence exponentially larger than what it had on the ground until we could establish this local security framework and build up the Afghan Army and police.

Two generations of Afghans had been decimated by the Soviet intervention in the 1980s and the civil wars between the victorious mujahideen groups, followed by the Taliban in the 1990s. It would take two generations to recover. The sooner we started planning and resourcing an enduring effort, the less time we would need to be engaged in the long run.

3 The Tagab Valley
Patrolling to Ambush

As we bumped along pockmarked dirt roads in our convoy heading toward the Tagab Valley in Kapisa Province, I looked out across the storied Shomali Plain north of Kabul and marveled at its history. Stretching across Afghanistan along the route of the ancient Silk Road, the Shomali Plain has been the scene of countless wars of conquest over thousands of years, fought by foot soldiers of Alexander the Great, armies of the British Empire, and armored divisions from the Soviet Union. As we stopped to allow several herds of goats cross the road in front of us, I stepped out of my ground mobility vehicle and kicked at the gray, rocky dirt. I had read about those wars my entire life and couldn't believe I was yet another foot soldier from a foreign army traversing the same ground. But unlike all of those armies that had invaded before us, ours was the only one whose homeland had been attacked by an enemy that had based itself in Afghanistan. This was not a war of choice nor of conquest. We were ostensibly there to rid the country of an insurgency that previously harbored a group that had directly attacked the United States. Yet, as I looked around at the villages dotting the countryside, I was seized by how little I really knew about the people here and what we were getting ourselves into.

We were on a "presence patrol" to the Tagab Valley, a hotbed of insurgent activity, in order to project a sense of security to the area and gather information. The valley ran north to south and was about sixty kilometers east of Bagram Airfield, just over a small mountain range from the Shomali Plain. It served as a final staging ground for insurgents who were traversing into Afghanistan from Pakistan to carry out attacks on the capital, Kabul. The main insurgent group in Tagab was Hezb-e-Islami Gulbuddin (HIG), a group loosely affiliated with the Tal-

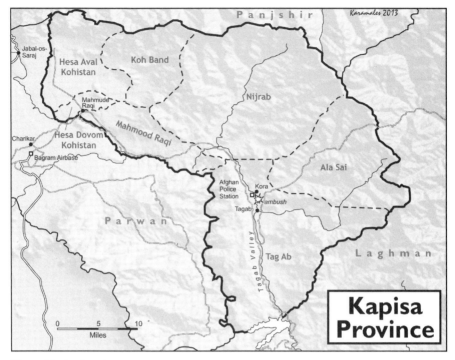

Map 5. Kapisa Province.

iban and led by the mercurial Gulbuddin Hekmatyar. In Afghanistan's previous three decades of war, Hekmatyar had served in various capacities; he was one of the key mujahideen warlords during the Soviet resistance; he was a prime minister; and he was a militia leader responsible for shelling his rivals in Kabul during Afghanistan's civil war. He now led the HIG resistance to both the "American occupiers" and the Karzai government from his base outside of Peshawar, Pakistan. The HIG was largely considered the weakest of the three insurgent groups primarily because it was believed to be the least supported by Pakistan and the least ideological because of Hekmatyar's opportunist reputation. Nonetheless the group was still quite dangerous, reputedly with some of the most experienced midlevel commanders of the insurgency.

Though we had information about the HIG broadly as an organization and about some of their commanders in the area, I was bothered by our lack of knowledge about Tagab and the people in the valley. We knew little beyond the very basics about the local government, the police, or the local economy. We also knew little to nothing about the tribal makeup of the area or which tribes had aligned with the HIG. Most important, we had no idea why certain locals were supporting them. Was it ideological? Tribal rivalry? Abuse from local officials? I hoped our patrol to the valley would answer these questions, but I was astonished that we didn't know more about an area so close to our main base in Afghanistan. Four years into the war, in 2005, we were going into the area partially blind because of our lack of meaningful intelligence.

After several hours of heading east from Bagram on roads so rutted and bumpy that we felt like our guts were in a blender, we crested a line of low brown and gray hills running north to south. Stretching off to the south was Tagab, a lush green valley flanked by cliffs on both sides. In the distance to the north the snow-capped peaks of the Hindu Kush Mountains dominated the skyline. The single unpaved road through the valley stretched out before us, nestled against the cliffs on the western side of the valley. Clusters of tan, mud-walled compounds dotted the green landscape, or "green zone," as we called it. The homes and villages looked beautiful, even idyllic, but from my vantage point they were operational nightmares.

The villages in Tagab and across Afghanistan had existed for hundreds, even thousands of years and certainly were not built with motorized wheeled vehicles in mind, much less seven-foot-wide armored Humvees or GMVs. Relatively few Afghans owned vehicles, so most paths were still only wide enough for walking. The vehicles that were owned were invariably Toyota Corolla sedans or small pickup trucks. The green zones were mazes of trails, irrigation ditches, small fields, and retaining walls. Dry riverbeds, called wadis, often cut through these hamlets and could be anywhere from three to thirty feet deep. When dry, the wadis often served as a veritable highway that heavy trucks could easily navigate, but during a hard rain they could quickly turn into raging rivers or mud quagmires. Further, our mobility, fields of fire, and even our ability to see across villages were cut by the thick, mud-brick walls that surrounded every Afghan home. Thus, every village contained dozens of natural defensive positions and ambush sites. Every fort-like home had thick outer walls that provided cover and protection for insurgent fighters. Every farm field was surrounded by irrigation ditches and stone walls that formed natural trench lines and prevented our vehicles from crossing them. During our patrols we would sometimes see suspicious groups of men or vehicles on the other side of a village, and it would take us hours to get to them by foot.

This difficult terrain caused a superficial level of engagement by the coalition and contributed to our ignorance of the people. Many units, particularly coalition units, stayed out of the green zones and conducted what I called "drive-by counterinsurgency." Often they would drive up to the Afghan government district centers and police stations that were mostly accessible by some form of road and limit their patrols to inviting the local officials or elders to meetings right there. It was understandable that few wanted to leave the relative safety of the heavy weapons, radios, and supplies in their vehicles for the unknown mazes of the Afghan green zones. To make matters worse, it was often brutally exhausting to try to traverse these areas on foot. This was particularly the case for the conventional units that were required to wear significantly more equipment than Special Operations units in the form of body armor, helmets, mandatory loads of ammunition and other equipment. The result was a strong disincentive to get into the villages and really engage with the Afghans. Our lack of engagement in turn severely limited our understanding of the complex sociopolitical dynamic that was unique to every province and district in Afghanistan.

The village of Kora was about a third of the way down from the north end of the valley. An abandoned girls' school sat on its western edge and was occupied by local Afghan National Police. Just off the road, the school was a low, squat one-story rectangular building made of gray stone and whitewashed interior walls. All of the window glass was either missing or broken, and every room was devoid of furniture except a small blackboard on the wall. The place reeked of feces emanating from a small stone outhouse built on two overflowing holes in the ground.

The school was perched on a small bluff that overlooked Kora. With its ample courtyard surrounded by a six-foot-high stone wall, the school was a perfect place to create a patrol base for our vehicles. As soon as we parked, I climbed to the roof of the school and looked out over Kora. It was the typical labyrinth of farm fields surrounded by walls, trails, and ditches, interspersed with scores of homes with their ubiquitous, fort-like walls. The village sprawled across the valley to the south and east and had a deep wadi running north to south. It was late April, and the fields were full of poppies in full bloom that gave the place an air of serenity.

I wanted to get a foot patrol out into the village to get a sense of the area and how the villagers interacted with us. Previous Emirati Task Forces had come here several times to check on some small development projects they had inherited from the Red Crescent Society (the Muslim version of the Red Cross). What little history I could gather before we left Bagram indicated that nearly every patrol to Kora had resulted in an attack of some kind. The numerous bullet holes and the half dozen black smears of burned explosives from RPG rounds confirmed the information. I wasn't going to sit there and passively wait for the attack to come.

I headed over to the police commander and the UAE platoon leader, Captain Hussein, who I could see were already engaged in conversation and sipping the ubiquitous Afghan green tea known as chai on the front porch of the school. I wanted to get a sense of the police commander and his men and their perspective on what was going on in the valley. The commander, short and stocky, with an oversized mustache typical of many Tajiks, lounged on the bottom half of a bunk bed that had been moved outside to serve as a couch.

"There are no problems in Kora, my friend," the police commander was saying as I walked up. He introduced himself as Captain Fahim and gripped both of my hands warmly. One of his men pulled up an upside-down bucket for me to sit on while the commander's servant, commonly called a "chai boy," leaned forward with a tray of chai in glasses dark with tea stains. I could tell the glasses hadn't been washed in a while, if ever. I grabbed one and took a sip. "Tashakur," I thanked him in Dari.

In Afghanistan it's considered rude to dive straight into business without spending at least some time discussing family, village, and other personal issues. After a respectable amount of small talk, I pointed to the bullet holes over Fahim's shoulder and asked, "Why is this school in such bad condition if there are no problems?"

"The Koreans and Americans built this school in 2003, but the government has not taken care of it. I take care of it as best I can, with what little money I can spare," Fahim said, positioning himself as the good guy. A rusting old metal sign adorned with U.S. and Afghan flags and symbols of their aid agencies stood outside. The sign read, "This Primary

School is dedicated to the girls of the Tagab Valley, Kapisa Province. A joint project of the U.S. Agency for International Development and the Afghan Ministry of Rural Reconstruction and Development, 2003." The sign seemed to be a symbol of the great intentions but lack of follow-through from the international community in Afghanistan to this point.

"I meant problems with security in the village," I said, glancing over to our new interpreter, Sami, as he began translating. "If there are no problems in Kora, then why so many attacks on this beautiful school? I am sure Kora is proud to have one of the newest primary schools in the valley."

Captain Fahim stared at me for a moment as Sami translated my questions. Sami, a young man on his first mission as an interpreter, was not pleased about coming to the infamous Tagab Valley and was clearly nervous. "The Talibs have attacked this school in the past. You can see this," Fahim replied. "They do not think it is right for girls to have an education. The villagers stopped sending their girls here and the attacks stopped. Just the boys come here. The only time the Talibs attack this school now is when you arrive."

The implication was clear: he had cut a deal with the local insurgents. If he didn't bother them, they wouldn't bother his police. Only when the Americans or coalition forces came did things get stirred up. Obviously Fahim was willing to sacrifice the education of the girls of Kora to keep the peace. Unfortunately, the Afghan police, and sometimes even the Army, established local deals with insurgent commanders. Motivations ranged from both sides being from the same tribe to marriages of convenience that allowed the police to maintain relative calm while the insurgents pursued other goals. Regardless, coalition forces were often blind to what was really going on because we commuted to the battlefield from our heavily fortified bases and only received a snapshot over several days.

"We would like to take a walk through Kora. Will you allow some of your men to accompany us?" I asked.

As Sami translated, the commander waved over one of his men and barked some orders. "Six of my ten men here today will patrol with you."

We continued to chat for another thirty minutes or so. As the conversation continued, I grew more and more frustrated at my lack of knowledge of the area. I knew nothing about this police chief, though he told me he had been in his position for nearly two years. I had no idea of the tribal makeup of this village, nor did I know why the HIG held such sway here. In my research before leaving Bagram for the patrol, I couldn't even determine the last time a U.S. unit or NGO had been to the valley, much less what occurred or whom they dealt with. All I could determine after locating some intelligence reports about the area was that a local HIG commander, Qari Barial, regularly slept in his father-in-law's compound in Kora. Apparently another ODA had tried to get an informant to pinpoint the compound for them or notify them when Barial was present so that they could put together a raid to capture him. Beyond the small bit of information on Barial, I had no idea what was going on in the village or the Tagab Valley.

Before leaving for the mission I had tried to at least locate some history on the reasoning behind building the school in that particular village in Tagab. However, when I approached our higher headquarters at the Combined Joint Special Operations Task Force there was little information to be found.

I spoke to the captain in charge of intelligence analysis. "The UAE Task Force told me that their patrols from previous rotations typically stopped at a school in a village named Kora. Do we know why a new school was built in that particular village? Was there a tribe or elder we were trying to influence for some reason? Do we have any information on the elders or who we have dealt with in the past?" He shrugged and said he would try to find any after-action reports he could from previous patrols, but he warned me that every rotation organized its files differently and then archived them before the next rotation fell in. "We know the development projects in that valley were mainly USAID efforts implemented in 2002 or 2003. But we don't have access to a database of AID's projects. Honestly, I don't even know if one exists. And if it was built by a coalition partner like Korea or Germany, I have no idea how to find out for you. What I can give you are some files on the HIG commanders that we know operate in Tagab."

Neither the division command's intelligence shop nor the provincial reconstruction team at the other end of Bagram airfield had much information on development projects or past operations beyond those initiated by their units during their tours. All they could tell me was that whoever went into the valley usually got attacked and where the attacks occurred. I was astonished at the lack of depth in our information and analysis of what it meant. No one knew who was doing the attacking—criminal groups, insurgents, or disgruntled tribes who associated us with their rivals. In short, we had become very good at providing information on *what* had happened but had very little analysis on *why* it happened.

In the absence of information several of my men began sarcastically calling our presence patrols "patrols to ambush." In theory the patrols were intended to keep the enemy off guard, provide a sense of security to the populace, and collect intelligence on the area. Patrolling was a basic component of counterinsurgency and needed to occur. However, we were not cumulatively building our base of knowledge with each mission. Instead we patrolled into areas while relatively blind about the local situation, expecting the Taliban to eventually make contact through an ambush. We would then rely on our superior tactics, firepower, and sometimes air support to get us out of the situation. Needless to say, I wasn't a fan of this approach.

The reasons for our ignorance were multiple. One was the fact that we were prioritizing meager intelligence collection capabilities on targeting insurgent commanders; another was our shallow engagement of Afghans. Mostly we did a terrible job of sharing between the international actors in Afghanistan and then building on that knowledge over time. At that point in the war our military intelligence apparatus was almost singularly focused on tracking, locating, and executing kill/capture missions; it didn't surprise me that the only help our intelligence shop could provide was a target profile on an insurgent commander. It wasn't the fault of our military intelligence community. Rather it was a lack of resources in Afghanistan at the time and how the few remaining resources were prioritized. With a majority of our intelligence collection platforms and personnel in Iraq, what relatively few assets we did have in Afghanistan were focused on kill/capture missions. These missions were critical to counterinsurgency in that they pressured the leadership of the insurgency by putting it under constant threat. The key was conducting them with surgical precision so that no civilians or property were damaged. Prioritizing them, however, meant that little was left over for collecting information on the broader political, tribal, and economic causes of instability in rural Afghanistan that were also vital to defeating an insurgency. I often debated whether we were in a negative spiral in our intelligence collection, whereby ignoring these softer sociopolitical objectives actually created more insurgent commanders, which in turn required even more intelligence work to be focused on kill/capture missions. The answer I always came to was that it could not be an either/or proposition: if we were serious about counterinsurgency in Afghanistan, we had to get enough resources to do both.

What I could not understand, however, was why we did not have a searchable database available to at least build on the efforts of the intelligence collection and combat patrols accumulated over the previous years. As a tactical leader with the technology available in 2005 I should have been able to type in "Tagab Valley" and have access to every patrol, raid, and development project that had occurred in the previous four years. I should have been able to read the reporting on past units' dealings with individual Afghans and what they promised. Inexplicably, such a database simply didn't exist. In the end, we just had to get out into the countryside, find out what was going on, and positively influence the situation as best we could.

I wasn't particularly concerned about the patrol that afternoon in Kora, despite reports of both HIG fighters and Qari Barial's base of operations in the village. Many of the typical positive signs were present: kids were clustered at the front gate, farmers were out in their fields, women could be seen scurrying about their daily business in their dusty blue burqas. If there was going to be a fight, the villagers would have known.

I looked over at the gate where the men going out on the patrol had gathered. They were a mishmash of uniforms, with the Afghan National Police in solid grayish blue, the Afghan National Army (ANA) in green and brown camouflage nearly identical to the old U.S. Army woodland pattern, and the U.S. soldiers in tan and brown camouflage. Captain Hussein preferred to keep his men in their vehicles on the bluff, and we had a brief and tense discussion about his unwillingness to send his men on patrol with us. I could tell that several of his men wanted to go, but I had no formal authority over the platoon leader and finally let the issue pass.

Most of the men waiting to begin the patrol checked their equipment. The technology behind basic infantry gear stagnated between

1970 and 2000. During my active duty days before 9/11, the average U.S. soldier was wearing nearly identical equipment as during the Vietnam War. Since 9/11, however, a revolution in infantry equipment occurred, the biggest change being the use of body armor vests covered in straps so that an operator could arrange any number and type of modular pouches into an infinite number of combinations. In fact adjusting the configuration of one's load nearly became an addiction for most men in the unit. No Special Forces operator ever seemed to be completely satisfied with the arrangement of his equipment. There was always a way to slightly improve the feel and arrangement of the load, with an eye toward shaving fractions of a second off the time it took to retrieve an extra magazine, flashlight, tourniquet, or some other piece of kit that could save your life.

Unlike conventional infantry, we could vary our load and what we carried, though some items were mandatory: basic body armor with armored plates front and back, M4 rifle, pistol, first aid kit, handheld GPS, an individual radio called an MBITR (em-bit-er), and, of course, extra magazines. Pretty much everything else was optional, or "shooter's choice."

Despite technological advances, particularly in lowering the weight of our gear, everyone seemed to simply carry more of it, making a standard rig about forty to sixty pounds. I opted for a lighter rig with minimal equipment, as the village looked like an absolute maze of walls, goat trails, and wadis. My rig held only four extra magazines for my M4 rifle (the standard infantry basic load was seven), a GPS, an MBITR radio, and my night-vision goggles since it was getting late in the day. The most important factor in my decision to go light that day, including leaving my helmet behind, was my intent to engage the villagers in Kora and look as nonthreatening as possible. My beard was coming into full growth by this time, so I donned a traditional Afghan *pakol* hat and draped a scarf over my shoulders to cover up much of the gear. From a distance I hoped to look little different from an Afghan Army soldier.

After a quick briefing, we left the school in two parallel files and walked through the center of the village from west to east. Each file consisted of three U.S. soldiers, three Afghan Army soldiers, and three policemen. As we reached the east side, we split into two groups, one led by my senior sergeant or noncommissioned officer, Eric, and the other by me. Eric was built like a linebacker and towered over the Afghans following him down a trail heading north into the village. I took the other group south and looped around back to the base in a classic cloverleaf patrol pattern. This allowed us to be seen in a greater portion of the village and still stay close enough to support each other if something happened. Importantly, it ensured that we would be back-to-back and firing away from each other should we get ambushed.

As our patrol weaved through town, I greeted the local men as we walked by and often stopped to engage them in conversation. As often as possible I let the Afghan lieutenant take the lead in the discussions. He took some prodding, but after a while he was engaging people on his own. After a full day of patrolling and several meetings with the local elders back at the school, I wondered why we didn't have a permanent presence in the valley. The elders' complaints were typical of those we had heard in Uruzgan Province earlier that year and across Afghanistan. They didn't want a return of the Taliban but often felt powerless to resist them when groups of armed men came through Kora or one of the men in the village came back from Pakistan with wads of cash and weapons and set up a local cell. Often the local police and government was powerless or inept or both. Most of all, villagers were disappointed that their lives hadn't changed with the coming of the Americans. I reminded them that the school on the edge of town was built by the American people, but they complained that the teachers were rarely paid, the children had no supplies, and the police and HIG took turns extracting taxes from the locals.

The elders indicated things would be different if the Americans would put a base in Tagab, checked on the police, and helped stimulate the local economy so the local men could work in the valley rather than travel to Kabul. I sensed we could make a difference with some good intelligence on local personalities, key influencers, and some labor-intensive projects. Yet the Pentagon's plans were for fewer U.S. soldiers in Afghanistan in the long run, not more.

The next afternoon, as the sun dropped behind the mountains, we saw a series of flashing lights signaling across the valley from one ridgeline to the other. To my surprise, the Afghan reconnaissance platoon's head NCO, a sergeant major, suggested to me that we send a patrol up the steep hills bordering the western part of the valley to where one of the lights was emanating. This was a first. In keeping with the armies of many second and third world countries, most Afghan platoons were led by an officer with an iron fist. He was typically the only member with any sort of education, institutional knowledge, and motivation to get things done. To have a sergeant proactively suggest we embark on a tough climb to a place where insurgents seemed to be operating was rare indeed—and I wasn't about to say no.

I had come to know the sergeant major, Sumar, on previous missions, before his platoon was attached to us for the patrol to Tagab. My team all agreed he was a rare breed who was far sharper and more proactive than his lieutenant. He was from the Pashtun Shinwari tribe, which had traditionally supported the government and had more moderate views on social issues. Plus, at over six feet tall and at least two hundred pounds, he towered over his men.

He was from Jalalabad and had six children. I was always curious about what motivated Pashtun men to side with the government and risk their lives as well as the lives of their family members to join the Army. For Tajik, Uzbek, and Hazara men, the reason was obvious: ethnic differences with the Pashtun-dominated Taliban and the severe repression of minorities under their reign. But for fellow Pashtuns to side with the government against the Taliban was often much more complicated and frequently boiled down to long-standing tribal rivalries. In my view the motivations of Pashtun men who opposed the Taliban were the keys to unlocking popular resistance. Sumar was a living example of what could be accomplished, but he and those like him were little understood by the U.S. intelligence community.

Sumar told me about his father and the emphasis he had placed on education. His father was convinced that education was the mechanism to lift his family out of poverty and into a better life. Unfortunately Sumar grew up in the midst of the Afghan civil war in the 1990s and the Taliban regime, when there wasn't much opportunity for his father to send his children abroad to be educated. Sumar told me that a group of Talibs came to his village one day in four pickup trucks and ordered the local girls' school closed. The villagers continued to educate the girls secretly in various homes under the threat of Taliban reprisals.

He told me that a rival tribe still supported the local Taliban in Nangarhar and were funneling men and weapons through the Tora Bora Mountains for operations against the government. Sumar wanted to complete his Army obligation and return to his village to lead his Shin-wari tribal militia in carving the Taliban problem out from his home. He made a carving motion with his knife in the ground as he explained. Sami, our interpreter, seemed to hesitate for a moment as he translated. "He wants to know if you will come back home with him," Sami continued. "He says that with just a few 'bearded ones'"—referring to the beards grown by Green Berets—"that could help them organize and call for support, they could eliminate the Talibs in all of southern Nangarhar."

"But America will have to stand with us," Sumar said.

"America will stand with you," I replied. "Our future is your future. I would love to come with you, Sumar. You are a leader, and I would be proud to support you in protecting your village from the Taliban."

I sat there thinking of how I could present this concept to the Combined Joint Special Operations Task Force in Bagram, or even back in Washington. I couldn't imagine our leadership allowing just a few Green Berets to live with the Afghans in their village rather than on large, well-protected bases. The risk would be deemed too great. Plus, Lieutenant General Eikenberry, the commander of U.S. Forces in Afghanistan in 2006, was in the process of demobilizing all legacy militias from the early years of the war. He and others saw them as competitive with the fledgling Afghan Army and police. I agreed in theory but thought we were standing them down too soon. The Afghan Army was nowhere near ready to take on securing the rural countryside, and removing the local militias too quickly would create a security vacuum for the Taliban to easily fill.

But that conversation with Sumar helped me realize the direction that we needed to take this war. We could create tribal militias overseen by cadres of ANA leaders, an Afghan National Guard of sorts that could complement rather than compete with the Afghan Army. This war was going to be won one valley and one village at a time, and it had to be done by leveraging the tribes. But before we could even attempt such a program we had to become much smarter on the local dynamics. We could not continue to be as ignorant as I felt throughout our patrol in the Tagab Valley.

That day, as we ascended the steep hillside, sometimes on hands and knees, we watched Sumar lead his men, cajoling and sometimes getting behind and pushing them up the hill. He looked back at me with a grin as I panted my way from boulder to boulder while we ascended in altitude. Even though I had my light rig on, it still weighed over thirty pounds, while Sumar's gear consisted of his AK-47 rifle slung over his back and two spare magazines stuffed in his cargo pocket. He smiled and bounded back up to the front of the line. In the U.S. Army, officers who shared risk with their men were respected. Officers made plans and sergeants executed them. By contrast, in the Afghan Army greater rank meant greater stature and less risk. Most Afghan officers and sergeant majors stayed behind in their offices; preserving strength and assets was the path to survival in Afghanistan. Sumar led by example as we patrolled the ridgeline, and we were happy to let him take charge.

We ended up finding a goat trail with multiple sets of tire tracks that looked fairly fresh on the top of the ridge line. At one location overlooking the valley we found two empty boxes of ammunition for a Russian-made PKM machine gun.

The next morning Kora was eerily quiet. The kids at the gate were gone. My sergeants, Frank, Eric, Brian, and Graham, up on the roof of the school with binoculars, could barely count a dozen men tending to their fields, while the day before the fields had been full of workers. Captain Hussein called one of the Kora elders on his mobile phone, who said that many men had gone to the markets in Kabul that day. Hussein was becoming increasingly nervous that some type of attack was imminent and began to wonder aloud if we should go back to Bagram early. Some of the other UAE officers and I were able to convince him that leaving would send exactly the wrong message. We spent the morning accompanying a UAE civil affairs detachment as it checked on several small development projects in the area and then preparing for another patrol into Kora in the afternoon. Graham, a former all-state wrestler from Alabama and our team's junior communications sergeant, cracked jokes as he walked to each vehicle to ensure the various radios had fresh batteries. Easygoing and funny, Graham was constantly quoting movie lines from *Wedding Crashers* and *The 40-Year-Old Virgin* as he went about his work. Brian, our senior medic, was nearly twice Graham's age and had a serious, thoughtful demeanor. He smiled at Graham's jokes as he silently packed extra medical supplies into his trauma bag. Brian was a physician's assistant as a civilian and one of the best medics in the unit. I made a point to always keep him near me.

By the time we were ready to leave the school for the patrol, most of the police seemed to have melted away, including Fahim, the Afghan police commander. I asked the most senior police sergeant remaining if he could send some men with us on patrol. He replied that the commander had urgent business in Kabul and that he did not have the authority to send anyone with us.

To fill in for the missing police, I brought along an American sergeant from a psychological operations (psyop) detachment that had joined us at the school and wanted to go on a patrol with us, despite his inexperience. That left two sergeants from the embedded training team that accompanied the Afghan Army recon platoon as the only Americans back at the school. The patrol consisted of two sections of ten, with six Afghan and four American soldiers per section.

I specifically briefed Captain Hussein that, should a firefight break out in the village, both of my patrol elements would immediately fire red flares into the air so that the UAE vehicles, with their .50 caliber heavy machine guns and MK19 automatic grenade launchers, would know where we were and where not to shoot. My fear was that insurgents would start shooting from the village at our vehicles at the school and that the return fire from the UAE vehicles would inadvertently catch us in a crossfire.

Just before we departed, one of the UAE snipers spotted a cluster of tents on the far ridge line. We set out to cross through Kora to the other side of the valley to check them out. I thought about leaving behind my pistol to lighten my load even further, but my team sergeant had beat into me during our premission training the need for good pistol skills, particularly in tight places. I used to joke with him that if we had to rely on pistols in a firefight rather than the heavy machine guns on our vehicles, close air support, and our M4 rifles, then it would be time to turn and run anyway. But his training stuck with me, and I just couldn't leave it behind. My last pouch was now filled with an extra pistol magazine, so I left behind the two frag grenades I normally carried on my standard rig.

When I looked back, Sumar was checking his men's weapons and inspecting their magazines to be sure they were bringing enough of the ammunition and other basics, such as water, that Afghan soldiers often forgot. He jogged to the front of the line and led my section. The recon platoon's lieutenant accompanied us this time, and he elected to follow

Sumar as number two in the line. I always wanted to be near him so that we could command our men together in case of potential action. I put our interpreter, Sami, between him and me.

As we made our way through the village, no kids approached us this time with requests for candy or "do-lars." We slowly worked our way through the village, greeting the few old men still standing around until Eric's element split off to the north, as we had done in the days prior. After several hours we took a break at the foot of the mountains bordering the eastern side of the valley. We could see the cluster of tents at the top but could not make out any movement. Getting there had taken a lot longer than we planned, and we knew from the previous night's climb that getting to the top of the ridge line would take us until after sundown. The lieutenant was convinced the tents belonged to nomadic Afghan herders called Kuchis, but I suspected he really did not want to climb up the steep hillside to check them and then have to return to the school at night. The Afghan soldiers did not have night-vision equipment, and patrolling through a village in the pitch-black night made them nervous.

I decided not to press the issue. Frankly, I knew they were exhausted. The lieutenant and I soon fell into a heated discussion on which way to patrol back to the school. He wanted to go back the way we had come, as it was the fastest route. I objected. Sami looked at me pleadingly as he interpreted. He too just wanted to get back. I was tempted for a split second and then said, "No." Going back along the same path was a cardinal sin in basic infantry tactics. It was too predictable, and I wasn't about to risk the patrol because the Afghans were tired. I suggested a compromise: we would head back by a different direction but would walk down a wide, shallow wadi that would be much easier than weaving in and out of the narrow alleys and walking across the farmers' fields.

Sumar led the patrol as point man, with the lieutenant close behind, followed by Sami and me. One Afghan soldier carrying the squad's shoulder-fired RPG and another Afghan were behind me, while Graham, a few more Afghan soldiers, the psyop sergeant, and Brian pulled up the rear of the line. We were heading west-southwest, and the sun had set behind the western ridgeline, casting a huge shadow over the valley. It was getting to that awkward time of day when it was still too light for our night-vision devices but getting dark enough that we had trouble seeing.

The wadi ended up being deeper and longer than I had bargained for. Six- to ten-foot walls loomed over us on either side, and I started getting an uneasy feeling. Worse, there was not a single villager in sight. The silence was eerie and disconcerting. There were fields occasionally interspersed among homes, but they all had stone retaining walls that, at best, would be difficult to climb over if we had to exit, and, at worst, were fantastic close-range firing positions for an insurgent ambush. We would be fish in a barrel. I quickly radioed for my guys to be sure they had their night-vision goggles at the ready when I noticed a gap developing between me and Sami in front of me and an even bigger gap between him and the lieutenant. They were starting to act like horses smelling the barn and were not conducting basic patrolling techniques. Instead of walking slowly, maintaining proper spacing, and vigilantly looking around, they were nearly sprinting, bunching up, and looking straight ahead. I turn around and the RPG being carried by the ANA soldier behind me practically smacked me in the nose, he was so close.

"Get back!" I hissed, motioning for him to back off and maintain his spacing.

I remember thinking that Sumar knew better than to rush back and drop his guard. They were hungry, tired, ready to return to the school before dark, and as a result they were no longer alert. It was my responsibility to make sure that they kept their discipline. If their lieutenant wouldn't step in, I would. I ran up to Sami, grabbed him by the back of his shirt, and told him to tell the lieutenant to slow down immediately. Sami trotted up to the lieutenant and tapped him on the shoulder. As he began speaking, I saw Sumar stop and look back at us.

The sound of the bolt slamming forward in the stillness of the evening was loud and unmistakable. Sumar simultaneously turned and raised his weapon as a burst of machine gun fire no more than ten feet to his left raked across him, Sami, and the lieutenant. All three dropped to the ground. I stepped to my left to ensure they were clear of my field of fire, brought my rifle up to my shoulder, and began firing. A second burst from the machine gun raked the wadi, kicking up dirt, hitting the wall to my front right, and rolling past me. Growing up reading military history I had read of these moments when time suddenly slowed, and here I was smack in the middle of one. I could see the air moving and the bullets flying by me like yellow lasers. The whiz-crack of the rounds breaking the air was distinct. Thirty feet to my front on the left side of the wadi I could see the bipod legs of the PKM machine gun hanging over the wall, belching flames as it fired. It was shockingly loud.

Another, smaller burst, likely from an AK-47, let loose just to the left of the machine gun. I was completely exposed. Any sane person would have instinctively dived to the ground or looked for cover. Years earlier I would have too. Instead I was now a product of post-9/11 Special Forces training that focused on clearing urban structures. During this training we squared our body with the enemy because our body armor covered our vital organs to the front. So rather than diving for cover during this close ambush, I instinctively squared up my body armor to the enemy and began putting as many rounds back on him as possible. I absolutely, positively should have been shot at this point. I was standing in the middle of a six-foot-deep, ten-foot-wide ditch toe-to-toe with a machine gun firing from behind a wall. I shifted my weight and began firing at the second muzzle flash when I suddenly felt my rifle bolt slam forward. Instinctively I canted my M4 to the left to be able to see into the chamber. I saw the bolt only three quarters of the way forward. I slapped the bottom of the magazine and pulled the charging handle back to eject the errant round and load a new one. I tried to pull the trigger again. It was the slap, rack, and pull malfunction clearance procedure every sergeant I had known since I was a cadet had beaten into me while on the firing range.

The trigger wouldn't squeeze. Another burst from the PKM raked the wadi high over my head.

Without thinking, I dropped my rifle and swept it to the left so that it dangled from its sling on my left side. Simultaneously I reached for my pistol with my right hand. I had often grumbled as we practiced drawing our pistols a thousand times on the range, thinking there were better uses of our time. Yet here I was, drawing my pistol when every second mattered.

As I drew my pistol, I saw the barrel of the machine gun slide toward me. For some reason it did not open up. I saw a head pop up and shifted my weight to my left leg to line my sights up with the silhouette. I pressed the gun forward and squeezed off two rounds. The head dropped. I didn't know if I hit him or if he ducked, so I kept firing on the ambushers as fast as possible to make them keep their heads down.

I will never forget the sight of my pistol locking to the rear, indicating the magazine was empty. I seemed to stare at it for ten seconds. It was probably less than one.

Another lengthy burst from a third position on the wall flew past my left ear in a long yellow stream of bullets. At that moment everything instantly sped up. It was as though God had taken his finger off the slow-motion button. The insanity of standing toe-to-toe with a Taliban machine gun protected by a stone wall while I stood in the open in the middle of a wadi, pistol in hand, came crashing down on me. I was so damned angry, furious really, that someone was trying to kill me and my guys. In an instant that anger turned to cold fear and a certainty that I was going to die if I was still standing there when the the next burst came.

Without thinking, I took a few steps to my right and dove over a break in a low wall of an orchard on the opposite side of the wadi from the ambushers. My goggles flew off my head. With my body armor on, I landed like a bag of bricks and rolled over on my back with my feet pointed toward the machine gun position. I felt someone slide to my right and saw Graham on his knee firing his rifle in two-round bursts toward the ambushers. As I lay on my back, I slammed another magazine into my pistol. I spread my legs and fired between my feet. Then all hell came crashing overhead as I looked up and saw green tracers clipping the treetops. I heard the rapid thud, thud, thud of rounds firing from the automatic grenade launchers on the UAE vehicles on overwatch landing behind the insurgent position. The tracers weren't coming from the ambush but from our rear.

As soon as the insurgent machine gun started raking our patrol in the wadi, Graham had immediately launched a red flare into the air. He then maneuvered directly toward the machine gun fire until he found me. I had specifically briefed Captain Hussein to avoid firing near where he saw the flares, but it looked like the flares had the exact opposite effect and were attracting fire.

To say we were in a seriously bad situation was an understatement. Still firing my pistol whenever I saw a muzzle flash, I cursed myself for not bringing grenades and yelled at Graham to throw one. He ripped one out of a pouch and fumbled with a ring of black tape holding the safety pin down as an extra precaution. "Son of a bitch," Graham cussed in his southern drawl. He flinched as another burst of heavy machine gun fire came from the school, fortunately at least ten feet over our heads. Graham chucked the grenade in a high arc. It exploded with a thud just behind the HIG position. The firing stopped.

I had emptied another pistol magazine. Graham tossed me one of his. From a thicket of trees, Brian yelled at us to come to him. He had begun to gather the psyop sergeant and the ANA into the orchard on a small knoll twenty feet behind our current position. As I scrambled up there, I found Sami, the interpreter, curled in a fetal position and crying. I picked him up by his shirt, slapped him on the side of the head to get his attention, and told him to find the lieutenant.

The psyop sergeant appeared to be in shock. He sat in the middle of our perimeter with his rifle in his lap, rocking back and forth. I asked him if he was hurt, and he shook his head. I grabbed his night-vision goggles out of his gear—he should have been wearing them and scanning the perimeter—so that I could go back down into the wadi and find my own. Leaving my goggles behind for the enemy to find was a definite no-go. I wasn't about to be responsible for giving that advantage up to the enemy, even if it meant going back into the kill zone. By this time the sun had set completely and the moon had yet to rise. It was pitch black. As I scrambled over the low walls and down into the wadi, my biggest fear was getting shot while returning to the perimeter by a very nervous Afghan soldier hearing my movement.

By the grace of God I found my goggles and made it back to our makeshift perimeter. I tried to assess the situation. I had heard groaning and movement in the vicinity of the machine gun as I made my way back, but I wasn't sure what was going on. I had no idea if the insurgents were dragging away their wounded or massing for another attack. For all I knew, multiple groups could have been surrounding us, and we still had a kilometer of Kora's alleys, wadis, and walled compounds between us and the school.

I radioed one of the embedded trainers back at the school. I instructed him to send a report to our headquarters back at Bagram and to alert them we had casualties and might need reinforcement. I told Graham to radio the other patrol to ask if they had also been hit and to determine their status.

My biggest concern at this point was accounting for everyone, especially Sumar, whom I had seen go down. I had no idea if the lieutenant was alive or if we had any other ANA casualties. For all I knew, they could

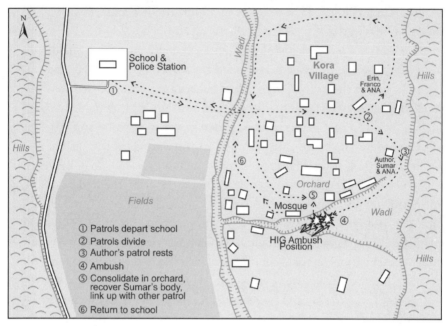

Map 6. Ambush in Kora.

have been down in the wadi, wounded and dying. Sami whispered to me that he had found the lieutenant. We walked over to him.

"Do you have all of your men?" I asked.

"Yes," the lieutenant replied.

I felt a surge of excitement that perhaps Sumar had miraculously survived. "Where is the sergeant major?" I asked. "Is he wounded?"

"He is still down in the wadi," Sami translated with a shaky voice.

Bending over to get my face nose-to-nose with the lieutenant, who was squatting, I whispered, "Then what the hell are you doing up here? Why aren't you looking for the sergeant major?"

"The lieutenant says we should get back to the school, right now. His soldiers are very upset," Sami whispered.

"You tell the lieutenant we are not going anywhere without the sergeant major and every one of our men. We do not leave people behind. We will all leave together, or we will all die together right here. Period. Tell him exactly what I just said, Sami." I walked back to Brian and Graham, who were on the perimeter facing the wadi in the direction of the machine gun.

"The sergeant major is still out there," I whispered to Brian. "I'm going to get him."

"Mike, I'm hearing a lot of movement across the wadi, but I can't see anything," Brian said. "I'm worried they're maneuvering on us while we sit here."

"That's why I'm not waiting on the lieutenant to find him and going myself."

I tried to clear my jammed rifle for a few seconds but could feel that the two rounds forming the double feed were so jammed in the barrel that it would take a while to get them out. I had left my Leatherman tool with its pliers in my other rig. I felt like a complete idiot.

I didn't have a lot of options but to go myself. I couldn't risk Brian, our only medic. We could take more casualties, and the patrol would need him. It was a similar calculus with Graham, our communications sergeant and a critical asset for contacting any help we might receive, such as medevac or close air support. In short, as the officer, I was the most expendable member of our team. Frankly, I also felt better risking my own life going to get Sumar than ordering Brian or Graham to go back into a point-blank kill zone.

"You want me to coordinate a link-up with Eric and his patrol?" Graham whispered as I climbed over the low wall at the edge of the orchard.

"Yes, but very carefully," I replied. "If their ANA are half as freaked out as ours, it could be a total nightmare as soon as one of them steps on a twig." Coordinating a link-up at night was always difficult, but doing so in a hostile village, with scared Afghan Army soldiers lacking night vision, coupled with roving bands of HIG fighters and trigger-happy gunners at the school, had colossal disaster written all over it.

I crept forward along the wadi toward where I thought Sumar might be. I looked up to my left and could see in the green glow of my night vision the wall where a few minutes before the PKM machine gun had rested. Suddenly fire erupted from the orchard, and I flattened on my stomach until it subsided. Graham had either seen or heard something across the wadi and opened fire on it. I crawled on my hands and knees until my outstretched hand touched Sumar's head. Putting my face next to his, cheek to cheek, I thought I heard him breathing. I ran my hand down his chest until it hit a large, warm, wet mess across his abdomen. I tried to feel his neck for a pulse, but couldn't feel it. I couldn't tell if he was dead, or if I just wasn't checking the right spot. If he was going to have any chance at all, I knew I had to get him back to where Brian could work on him. I stood up, grabbed his web gear by the straps at his shoulders, and yanked as hard as I could. I flew backward onto my back with the straps in my hands and landed with a loud thud. The cheap Afghan gear had simply ripped off. I cursed all of those briefings the U.S. training command in Kabul had given us back at the Pentagon about the quality gear they were providing the ANA.

Another exchange of fire erupted from the wall and the orchard. "I'm going to die right here with him," I thought. For an instant I considered running back to the orchard and organizing the men to get out of there. But the Ranger Creed that we recited every day in that hellish school was burned into my head: "I will never leave a fallen comrade to fall into the hands of the enemy."

I clambered back up to Sumar, lifted him into a sitting position, slid my arms under his armpits, and began dragging him backward up the wadi. I've never felt more exposed and vulnerable in my life before or since. For the third time that night I was just waiting on the bullets to slam into me. As I struggled to get Sumar up and over a wall, I felt and heard a long slow exhale. It was his dying breath. I knew I had been too slow and hadn't moved fast enough to save him.

Graham came down from the perimeter and grabbed Sumar's legs to help me move him up the hill.

"The good news is that Eric, Frank, and the boys from the other patrol are almost here," Graham told me as we stopped, referring to the other American-Afghan patrol. Both of us were breathing hard after hoisting Sumar over two low walls. "The bad news is that I've lost contact with the guys at the school."

The satellite radios on the vehicles back at the school were our lifeline to support: medical evacuation, Predator support, close air support, or any other type of backup. My hair stood up as I realized we were totally cut off.

When the other patrol arrived we quickly crafted a plan to make our way back to the school. I walked over to where I had left Sumar's body with the lieutenant and found the Afghans in chaos. I had instructed them to carry Sumar's body, but they refused to touch him. I had no idea why, but I wasn't about to stand around to figure it out. I was livid and pulled Sami and the lieutenant to where our faces were almost touching. In a low but firm voice I said, "Get your men moving right now."

Brian called over our internal radio and said he thought he heard movement in the field next to us. In an effort to get us out of there, Frank and Graham offered to carry Sumar out. I told them absolutely not. I needed them to be able to use their rifles in case we had to fight our way out, and I was determined to have the Afghans carry their own man. They were bickering louder and louder about what to do with Sumar.

After several more minutes trying to assert some degree of control, I lost my temper. I pulled out my pistol and fired two shots into the air. Everyone hit the dirt. Sami started crying again.

"Sami, get your ass up here and tell these guys we are all going to die here before we leave Sumar behind."

It seemed to work. Two Afghan soldiers walked up with a ladder they had taken from a nearby compound and loaded his body on it as a makeshift stretcher. As we made our way through the village, every alley, trail, and compound was a potential ambush site. The Afghans cursed and fumbled their way in the dark under the load of the ladder, their weapons and gear noisily banging against their bodies. All the HIG fighters had to do to find us was stand still and listen. I was absolutely certain we were going to get hit again. At various points we all took turns carrying the ladder to give each other a break. Frank and Eric led the way, their rifles constantly at their shoulders as they scanned windows, doorways, and corners with their infrared lasers.

The logs framing the outside of the ladder were too thick to grip, so we had to wrap our forearms around them and hunch over as we walked. After just a few minutes everyone's arms burned with fatigue. I almost laughed in the middle of it all as I thought back to the infamous "downed pilot" scenario in the Special Forces selection course, a training event in which the candidates must determine how to move in a tactically sound manner while carrying two very heavy duffle bags full of sand. The bags represented how it felt to move several hundred pounds of dead weight over difficult terrain. I remembered the instructors saying over and over again, "Every scenario you will ever face in combat you will have faced here first, so pay attention."

As we neared the school I became very nervous about getting fired upon by the UAE gunners manning the heavy machine guns on their vehicles. From a healthy distance we signaled with an infrared light visible only through night-vision goggles. I breathed a sigh of relief when they signaled back. A UAE Humvee and a Panhard surged forward across an open field to the edge of the main wadi in the center of the valley to cover us as we struggled to lower Sumar down the thirty-foot drop. We had to tie him down to the ladder and rig a pulley system to pull him up the other side. When we finally made it to the top, exhausted and soaked with sweat, we laid him across the hood of the Humvee. One of the UAE sergeants, Hamad, who had been educated in Britain and was a very well-trained sniper from the elite UAE counterterrorism company, rushed up to me and said that we needed to move out. He had been watching several groups of insurgents in his long-range night-vision scope as they tried to surround us for the past several hours. At one point one group of insurgents passed just a few compounds away from us. Hamad and some other sergeants took the initiative and came out to meet us in their vehicles. I am eternally grateful to them. They took both a personal and professional risk coming to our aid.

The after-action review involved some heated exchanges but provided a useful learning perspective. There is no replacement for experience, and we all learned things that night that would make us better soldiers and leaders. In the end relationships were strengthened, and to this day I remain in contact with my brothers in arms from the UAE.

We continued to work closely with the UAE Task Force, and when a new commander arrived a few weeks later, we built on the trust we had established. The new UAE commander was a magnificent officer who would later rise to command the UAE's equivalent of the U.S. Secret Service.

A few hours after we returned to the school the sun came up, and the Afghan soldiers solemnly loaded Sumar's body on the back of their truck to take him back to his base. I took up a collection for his family of around $500. It was equivalent to about three months' pay. I walked up to the lieutenant talking to the American embedded trainers. He was complaining that Sumar was dead because I didn't allow him to go back through the village the way we had entered. He was also very upset that we did not call a helicopter to retrieve the body. I let him go on for a moment before speaking up.

"Sumar is not dead because of a route we chose," I said finally. The lieutenant spun around. "He is dead because people attacked us who oppose progress for Afghanistan and want it to return to a time when they had power."

I reminded him that we were on this patrol to check on development projects sponsored by the Red Crescent. I pointed to the Emiratis. "They are risking their lives to rebuild Afghanistan and so is America," I said. I also knew Sumar was dead because of our ignorance regarding what was really going on in the Tagab Valley.

After the change in leadership in the UAE Task Force, we returned to the valley and to Kora a number of times. I worked hard to do my part in documenting every *shura* with the elders and to begin building profiles on the tribal dynamics of the area as well as personality dossiers on key influencers. I personally took copies to every command I thought would be interested so that future units patrolling to Tagab would be able to learn from our experiences. Many of the staffs were very receptive and appreciative of our extensive reports. However, I had little confidence that future rotations would be able to access them because the United States lacked a centralized database of operations in Afghanistan.

The new UAE Task Force commander decided to shift his focus away from Tagab and back to Uruzgan and Helmand. Later in 2006 a sister team, ODA 51, and their partnered ANA were successful in establishing a permanent presence in the Tagab Valley in one of the largest sustained operations by the Afghan National Army to that point in the war, dubbed Operation Triple Crown. ODA 51 was in nearly continuous contact the first weeks of the operation, but once it became apparent that the ANA was not leaving, the valley quieted down to the point where several NGOs were brought back in for development work. Unfortunately, the ANA struggled to logistically sustain itself away from its main base and were eventually recalled to Kabul. ODA 51 and our headquarters tried mightily to convince the division command at Bagram to replace the Afghan brigade with U.S. or coalition units, to no avail. By mid-2006 only one brigade of U.S. infantry was committed to all of eastern Afghanistan, compared with fifteen brigades in Iraq. There were simply not nearly enough soldiers for the task. Qari Barial eventually decided that things were getting a little too hot for him and returned to Pakistan. But I knew bringing security and stability to the area would require us to permanently stay out there rather than commute back and forth from Bagram and Kabul in order to truly understand what was going on and have a lasting impact.

Weeks after the ambush in Kora our primary interpreter, Muhammad, returned from a trip to Jalalabad and brought me an update on Sumar's family. Things were bleak for them. The Afghan National Army offered no survivors' benefits for the families of soldiers killed in the line of duty. In contrast, if I had been killed that night, my family would have received $400,000 from the U.S. government, and my wife could have gone to work to support herself and our daughter. Sumar's family had lost not only a husband and father but also their only source of income. A woman working outside the home in rural Pashtun society was virtually unheard of and culturally taboo. Muhammad told me that two of Sumar's boys were going to be sent to a madrassa in the fall, and the rest of the family would be split up among relatives in the village.

Madrassas are Muslim religious schools that many poor Afghans used as a mechanism to provide their children some sort of food, shelter, and basic education. Since the time of the mujahideen resistance to the Soviet Union in the 1980s, many madrassas had been radicalized and served as a fertile recruiting ground for impressionable and isolated young Afghan boys. The Taliban, the HIG, and the Haqqani network used the madrassas to provide an almost unlimited pool of fighters and suicide bombers. I was determined not to let this happen to Sumar's family.

After returning home from Afghanistan in the fall of 2006, I made arrangements to support Sumar's family by matching his salary from the Army out of my own funds. It wasn't a simple process, as Afghanistan lacks a postal system and has an incredibly corrupt banking system. A single widow of a former Afghan Army soldier would be easy prey. It took me a while, but I was eventually recommended to a small bank in Jalalabad that was trustworthy.

I also put some protections in place for Sumar's wife. To prevent the men in her village from taking advantage of her situation, I authorized only his widow to withdraw funds from the account and only up to the amount of Sumar's salary once per month. During a later visit to Afghanistan I was able to listen in as an interpreter called her to check on how she was doing. She said she was scraping by but she had enough to send her two boys and three of her girls to a secular school.

Sumar's dream of using education to lift his children out of poverty would have a chance to come true. I have never attempted to visit her, as my presence would only endanger her and her family. All she knows is that an American who was with her husband when he died is sending the money. She told the interpreter that her boys planned to join the Army like their father and her daughters were studying to be teachers. I couldn't have been happier and knew then that I was going to care for them the rest of my life.

I believed more than ever that we were going to have to stabilize Afghanistan one family and one village at a time. But I was also convinced that doing so was going to take an enormous investment from the coalition to exponentially increase our understanding of the Afghan people. Finding bad guys would remain important, but it would not be enough. Most of all it was going to take an investment of time to understand what was causing the Afghans to support, or at least tolerate, the insurgency at a local level. Since the reasons were different in every valley and village in Afghanistan, the time investment was going to be considerable.

4 The Clinic in Achin
Development Dilemmas

Our armored Toyota Land Cruiser sat in a line of cars backed up behind a police checkpoint on the famed Kabul-to-Jalalabad road. Jalalabad, the fifth largest city in Afghanistan, is the only significant urban center due east of Kabul on the road to Pakistan. For two thousand years the thoroughfare has served as a key segment of the Silk Road from Europe to China. Canyon-like cliffs loomed on either side of us hundreds of feet above the winding road that was carved out of the mountain and barely wide enough for two vehicles to pass abreast. As each car in front of us pulled up to the police checkpoint (almost all of them the ubiquitous Toyota Corolla), we saw each driver handing a small wad of red Afghanis over to a policeman before he waved them through. The checkpoint must have collected tens of thousands of Afghanis in "tolls" every day.

"Salam Aleikum," said Todd as we pulled up. Surprise was noticeable on the police sergeant's face as he looked into our truck and saw four bearded Amerikis in civilian clothes, our M4 rifles between our legs. "Aleikum Salam," the policeman replied, recovering.

There was a pregnant pause. We didn't have our interpreter with us, but the message was clear as Todd gave him a look that said, "You aren't getting a fucking bribe, so don't even bother to ask." The police sergeant stepped back with a scowl on his face and waved us by. We laughed about how much more confused the Afghan policeman was going to be when he stopped the matching SUV behind us, full of Arabs and also with guns in their laps.

"That guy is going to think, 'Oh Shit, al Qaeda's working with the Americans now!'" Todd joked. Todd was the team's junior engineer sergeant and was very sharp and very sharp-witted. He kept all of us amused on our long drives with his perpetual sarcasm.

We were escorting a UAE civil affairs team from Bagram Airbase to Achin District in Jalalabad Province. Achin was south of Jalalabad City and bordered the Tora Bora Mountains to its south. Tora Bora was the mountain range that Osama bin Laden used as his hideout in December 2001 before eventually escaping south into Pakistan. The district was the home of the Pashtun Shinwari tribe and a major center of resistance for the mujahideen during the Soviet occupation. The Shinwari were one of Afghanistan's largest and most prominent tribes, consisting primarily of farmers and traders. They inhabited many of the districts in eastern Nangarhar Province that straddled the border with Pakistan.

Our mission that day was to proceed to Jalalabad's airfield, the airbase outside the city, and greet two planeloads of medical equipment. The UAE Task Force had committed to completing a clinic started by the Red Crescent Society the previous year. Apparently the security situation in Jalalabad and Achin had deteriorated to the point where the Red Crescent no longer felt comfortable sending its personnel to complete the clinic. Most NGOs monitored the United Nations' security reports and warnings. The UN Assistance Mission–Afghanistan had reported three hundred security incidents in March 2006 perpetrated by insurgent or criminal elements, increasing to nearly five hundred per month by September.[1]

Together with the UAE civil affairs team, we decided to take a low-profile approach while taking the roads to the remote clinic site, as they were increasingly laced with improvised explosive devices. By 2006 IEDs were becoming more prevalent in Afghanistan, primarily because of the success insurgents had with them in Iraq. The big difference between Iraq and Afghanistan was that Iraq had paved roads. Because most Iraqi roads were covered with asphalt, the insurgents were forced to hide the bombs along the sides of the roads. Accordingly, passing vehicles were attacked by blasts from the side. In Afghanistan, where nearly all the roads were dirt, the insurgents could bury the bombs in the middle of roads so that they exploded directly underneath vehicles. While there were significantly fewer IEDs in Afghanistan compared to Iraq in 2006, they tended to be much deadlier when they struck because the blasts came through the soft underbelly of the Humvees rather than the armored sides. To make matters worse, our electronic countermeasures were making us victims of our own success. The most common tactic for insurgents detonating IEDs was to remotely detonate the bombs with a cell phone or garage door opener. Just as a coalition vehicle lined up with a visual marker like a pile of rocks or specially marked tree, the insurgent, hidden some distance away, would enter a code in the remote device to set off the explosives. However, by 2006 we were successfully deploying jammers that blocked the transmission of signals as the vehicles passed. In response the insurgents, often illiterate but ever ingenious, began creating victim-initiated IEDs. The most common was triggered by a pressure plate. The insurgents would bury the explosives in the road and place two saw blades on top of each other just beneath the sand. As a vehicle rolled over the saw blades, the upper blade touched the lower blade, completing an electrical loop that blew the explosives directly underneath and straight up into the vehicle, with devastating effect. The pressure plates took the guesswork out of IED attacks for the Taliban. In later years our countermeasure for the pressure plate was to put mine rollers in front of the lead vehicle in a convoy so that the bomb was set off underneath the roller rather than the vehicle. The insurgent's simple and cheap response: offset the explosives from the saw blades the same distance that the vehicle was offset from the mine roller so that the charge still exploded underneath the vehicle when the mine roller hit the pressure switch. This tit for tat was costing us billions as we threw money and technology at the IED problem; we spent $3.5 billion on IED countermeasures, while the Taliban spent pennies.

Despite the danger, we decided to go to Jalalabad in civilian SUVs rather than armored Humvees or GMVs bristling with machine guns. Though the SUVs were armored, I knew that, if we were hit by an IED, the results would be catastrophic for all inside. Moreover, if we were hit by an ambush, there was no way to fight from inside the vehicles and we had no heavy machine guns—only our rifles and pistols. Yet, for the most part, I actually felt safer in the SUVs. These were not the shiny white or black Suburbans used by foreign dignitaries traveling around Kabul. They were scratched and dented like the average Afghan vehicle, had the side windows tinted, and had the ubiquitous photo of the Tajik national hero Ahmad Shah Massoud pasted across the back windows.

With our beards and Afghan *shalwar kameez* shirts, native to Southern Asia, we could easily pass for personnel from an NGO or some other type of aid organization. We also had low-profile body armor hidden un-

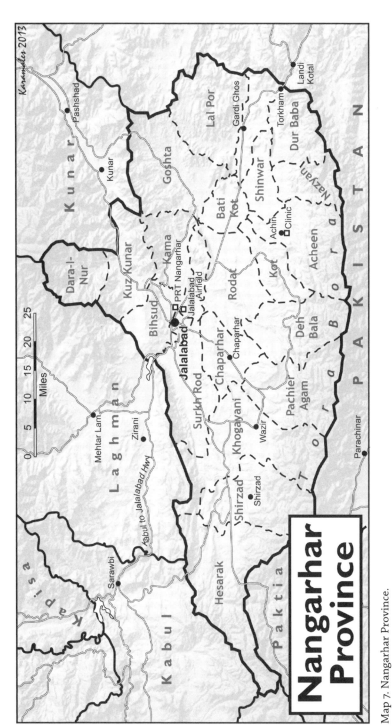

Map 7. Nangarhar Province.

der the shirts. Traveling while mixed in with Arabs made us confident that we would create enough confusion in a potential attacker to avoid an incident. It was unlikely that the Taliban would waste one of their precious IEDs on a couple of beat-up SUVs. They were much more likely to focus on a convoy of large tan armored vehicles that would bring the insurgents praise from their superiors, displayed in videotaped evidence of the attack. In short, we blended in with the local Afghans, which, in my view, was by far the best form of security.

Sadly, our ability and inclination to decide when to take a low-profile rather than a more traditional approach steadily diminished as violence worsened over the years. By my 2009 tour, any ODA wishing to take a more clandestine approach to an operation had to submit the mission plan for approval a week in advance to the theater Special Forces commander in the Combined Joint Special Operations Task Force. The commander's reasoning was simple: with the spike in IEDs, he wanted to personally ensure that every ODA was taking the proper precautions before going on a mission in a soft-skinned vehicle. The reality was that teams needed the flexibility to conduct these types of missions with less than a week's notice and did not have the personnel to answer the deluge of questions coming from layers of staff who had to brief the commander. Unfortunately, most teams just stopped traveling clandestinely, which I believe exposed them to greater risk in the long run. In 2006 we still had the freedom as local commanders to make these decisions, and it paid off. As we entered Jalalabad City proper on the way to the airfield, we listened on the satellite communications as a convoy of Humvees and trucks were ambushed about an hour's drive behind us near the police checkpoint where Todd had refused to pay a bribe. Two vehicles were destroyed and several men wounded.

Before going to the airfield we had arranged for two visits. The first was to the provincial reconstruction team; it was charged with managing development activities in the province and working with the local government. The second was to pay homage to the provincial governor, the storied Gul Agha Sherzai.

Before leaving our base at Bagram Airfield, I had asked Captain Assad, the UAE Civil Affairs team leader, if he or his team had coordinated his effort to equip the clinic with the provincial reconstruction team. He had not, but he wondered aloud if the Red Crescent had done so the previous year. We checked with the Red Crescent office in Kabul, but the representative with whom the previous UAE Task Force had made the arrangements to take over the clinic project had left theater. The office had few records regarding the clinic except for receipts from the Afghan construction company charged with building it. There was no information at all on why they had chosen to build a clinic or the reasoning behind its location. There was some indication of the effort being coordinated with the Afghan district government in Achin or the Ministry of Health office in Jalalabad, but when we tried to call the numbers and points of contact listed, the lines were no longer in service. This was important, as the office manager informed us that he had not included in his budget for the next year sustainment funds to run the clinic. He had assumed that the Afghans would cover those costs once the clinic was constructed or that the clinic would be able to sustain itself through patient fees. We weren't upset or surprised that the Red Crescent staff had not maintained records on the clinic project. Afghanistan had such tremendous needs and the lack of continuity that went with turnover in staff was all too common. The situation was typical of many development projects we had seen and a microcosm of why the international community had invested so much in Afghanistan and had so little to show for it. I encouraged Assad and his team to keep the most detailed records possible for future UAE Task Forces and to share them with both the Afghan government and the coalition headquarters.

Assad was very sharp and spoke nearly perfect English with a slight British accent. A thorough planner, his civil affairs team had reconnoitered Achin the previous month and had confirmed the location and condition of the clinic. His team discovered that it still had no equipment or physicians working in it. Fortunately, the clinic still stood empty; that meant neither the local police nor any other government agency had decided to squat there. An empty building was a valuable commodity. Many unfinished projects became a winter refuge for a village's goats and sheep or would be occupied by a returning refugee family.

On the long road from Kabul to Jalalabad, littered with the rusted hulks of destroyed Soviet vehicles, I bored Todd and the guys with policy wonk talk about the evolution of the provincial reconstruction team, how it fit into the broader concept of how we delivered aid in Afghanistan, and the problems with implementing the concept. The first PRT was established by a civil affairs team and Special Forces ODA in Gardez in 2003.[2] The original intent of the concept was twofold. The first was to pool resources from both military and civilian agencies to provide a mechanism for the delivery of aid projects beyond the capital of Kabul and into Afghanistan's rural provinces and districts. The second was to help to both advise and mentor the new provincial governments. The United States was hoping to transition control of the rural areas from local strongmen to elected local government officials. The PRT was instrumental in advising them how to govern.

In Washington the idea briefed well and was enthusiastically supported conceptually, but there were serious problems in the implementation of the PRTs because of difficulty in establishing the right balance of assigned civilian experts and military personnel. The original intent was for the PRTs to be established by military civil affairs teams and then transitioned to be fully led and staffed by civilian reconstruction experts with augmentation by the military for support such as airlift and security. By 2004 there was mounting frustration in the Pentagon because of the small numbers of civilians being assigned to the PRTs. The State Department and USAID maintained that they simply didn't have the required numbers of people in their organizations. This was partly true, but the real answer was more complicated. Part of the reason the civilian agencies could not get officers and experts out to the PRTs was that it was not good for their careers. Assignment to the embassy in backwater Kabul was bad enough, but assignment to a provincial PRT was far off the normal promotion track for Foreign Service officers and about as far from traditional diplomacy as one could get. Moreover, officers had to deploy to Afghanistan without their families. Individual positions at hardship posts were always difficult for the State Department to fill, much less filling whole units with civilian experts. In fairness, the State Department and USAID had shrunk substantially in the decades since Vietnam, when USAID and State were able to deploy nearly a thousand civilians in the provinces and districts of Vietnam as part of the pacification program. As Defense Secretary Gates stated in a speech in 2009 calling on Congress to provide more resources to State and USAID, "When I left the government they had about 16,000 employees—dedicated experts who were deployed, who were accustomed to working in insecure conditions in developing countries, and all the specialties: agronomy, rule of law, education. When I came back into government in 2006, [USAID] had 3,000 employees and mainly was a contracting agency."[3]

In addition, Iraq again came into play. To the extent that State and USAID were able to fill hardship posts, the vast majority went to Iraq instead of Afghanistan. Still my colleagues in the Office of the Secretary of Defense and the Joint Staff argued that they certainly could have provided more than the single individual per PRT that they pledged.

In the vacuum of civilian expertise, the military eventually embraced the mission. PRTs ballooned to sixty to a hundred military personnel and were typically commanded by a lieutenant colonel or Navy commander. The commanders were originally Army Civil Affairs officers, steeped in the art of providing local development in difficult places. However, in a strange bureaucratic twist, command of these organizations migrated to the Navy and Air Force. In 2004 Defense Secretary Rumsfeld sent a directive to the Joint Staff in the Pentagon to find ways to get Navy and Air Force personnel more involved in the wars in Iraq and Afghanistan to relieve pressure on the Army and Marine Corps. In the subsequent scrubs of personnel billets, someone in the Pentagon turned over PRT command and many support posts from Army Civil Affairs to joint positions. The action was taken under the premise that less combat-oriented PRT slots could be filled by any military service. It was a classic example of something that made sense in Washington but executed poorly on the ground. In 2006 I was surprised to be introduced to a Navy fighter pilot who was commander of the PRT in the volatile and tribally complex Uruzgan Province. These commanders were good people, but the notion that a fighter pilot or submarine driver was appropriately trained and experienced to handle the complex interagency, tribal, and development dynamics required to command a PRT was foolish. It made about as much sense as tasking me, an Army Special Forces officer, trained in the nuances of irregular warfare in third world cultures, to command a submarine in the Pacific Ocean.

Adding to the problems of limited resources and expertise were short rotations, limited predeployment training, and separate chains of command between the civilian and military leaders within the PRTs. Most PRTs typically had no more than one officer from the State Department and one from USAID, and a few would also have a representative from the Agriculture Department. Before 2006 there was no training program within the State Department that familiarized the officers with the complex dynamics of their assigned provinces or how to best work with the military. Well-meaning individuals would often show up with no other guidance than, "Go out to the PRT." Since the civilian agencies could not force their employees into hardship posts, they began enticing people to leave the relative safety of Kabul by limiting their tours in the provinces to only ninety or 120 days. While the short tours helped fill the vacancies, nearly everyone who served in Afghanistan agreed that it took at least six months to understand the complicated local Afghan power structures in any given location, much less to build strong relationships with the locals. The lack of predeployment training and short rotations greatly limited PRT effectiveness and meaningful engagement with the Afghans.

Compounding the problem was the fact that constant rotation of personnel, once the appropriate talent was in place, resulted in a constant loss of institutional memory and relationships with the Afghans. There was no single repository either in the Pentagon or at U.S. Central Command, USAID, or the headquarters in theater that could inform a senior leader of where aid money was spent or PRT projects instituted over time. Though PRTs and other entities spending reconstruction money diligently tracked their projects, the accumulated data were often lost over the years as individuals and units rotated. In 2009 the deputy commander of the PRT in Khost confided in me that when he took charge, he could not identify all of the projects his predecessors had implemented just in Khost Province since the PRT was established in 2003. He shook his head as he told me of a poor lieutenant whose sole job was to travel the province with a camera and GPS to locate and photograph rumored previous projects to ascertain their current status. He was almost killed twice by IEDs trying to figure out where the PRT had spent its money over the previous years. As late as 2008 Lt. Gen. Doug Lute, the "war czar" under President Bush, began holding monthly resources reviews at the White House, trying to determine where defense and aid dollars were being spent in Afghanistan and what returns the United States had realized for its massive expenditures. One of the outcomes of Bush's strategic review of the Afghan war led by Lute was to direct each agency to develop a single database to capture all of the reconstruction projects begun to date.

Another significant contributor to the very busy but inefficient aid effort was the divided chain of command among civilians and military members of the PRTs. The civilians reported directly to their superiors in the embassy, while the military reported to the regional International Security Assistance Force commander. The lack of coordination inherent in separate chains of command was often overcome by cooperative personalities that made things work. But sometimes it led to significant disagreements on PRT priorities and sent mixed messages to Afghan government counterparts. Further, because the military provided the vast majority of personnel and life support and all the security assets, the PRT commander had unusual sway in reconstruction issues. On several occasions I observed friction between PRT commanders and the State Department political advisor regarding who had primacy in dealing with the Afghan provincial leadership. In Uruzgan, for example, the PRT commander was not supportive of pressing President Karzai to remove the province's notorious governor, Jan Mohammad Khan. The commander's reluctance was understandable, as Khan ruled the province with an iron fist, provided a relatively secure area for NGOs to flourish, and aggressively repulsed attempted Taliban incursions. However, the political advisor stressed that Khan's brutal repression of tribes that he viewed as allied with the Taliban helped foster the insurgency's return. He argued that, while pressing Karzai to remove Khan may result in a decline in security in the short run, the improvement of decent governance would be a long-term win for the province and for U.S. interests. The disagreement sent mixed signals to Kabul and delayed Khan's removal.

The scarcity of civilians in the provinces again highlighted a fundamental flaw in the U.S. ability to conduct nation building in the midst of an ongoing conflict. The underlying issues involved a strategic misalignment of authorities, resources, and expertise. In short, the expertise to conduct nation building (agriculture, water, electricity, rule of law, etc.) lay within our civilian agencies. However, those same agencies didn't have the manpower or funding to operate in a place like Afghanistan. They just weren't designed, nor did they have the ability, to be expeditionary and operate in the midst of a war zone that also needed reconstruction activities. Our military could operate in such a place, of course, but lacked such specialized nation-building expertise. Your typical sergeant or captain from the 82nd Airborne was not trained in urban management, agribusiness, animal husbandry, or hydrology. We were often left with the least bad choice among having too few civilians to do the job, having a poorly trained soldier try to figure it out, or turning to contractors, an alternative that was often very costly.

Examples of this fundamental disconnect abounded in areas such as police training, border control, and justice system reform. The State Department had the authorities provided by Congress and the in-house expertise to train foreign police forces worldwide. However, they could not possibly provide and deploy the numbers of police trainers and volumes of equipment needed to stand up a police force of the scale needed in Afghanistan—much less do it while trying to do the same thing in Iraq. As a result much of the effort had to be contracted out at significant expense and with little government oversight. Eventually bureaucratic tinkering and ingenuity allowed the Department of Defense to conduct this mission in Iraq and Afghanistan, but it usually took a backseat to training the Afghan Army and combat operations. Similarly we needed to provide the Afghan government with experts to help them begin the process of controlling their porous borders, which would lead to realizing more income. Tariffs collected at border crossings represented the Afghan government's largest source of revenue, but only a fraction of it actually reached central government coffers. Our border control expertise and ability to maximize tariff revenue resided within the Department of Homeland Security and Customs and Border Protection. The Homeland Security leadership wanted to help in Afghanistan, but preventing another attack on the U.S. homeland and post-9/11 border control issues were understandably higher priorities. Likewise, the Department of Justice and State Department retained the ability to train and mentor Afghan judges and prosecutors and pledged to provide trainers through its Senior Federal Prosecutors Program. In reality, however, most Justice Department employees hadn't exactly signed up for long deployments to a combat zone, so getting the needed numbers of qualified trainers was nearly impossible. Each agency, including the FBI and U.S. Marshals Service, contributed what it could. In the end, sergeants and lieutenants trained as artillerymen or infantry officers found themselves in remote districts grappling with these issues as best as they could.

This dichotomy of having the needed expertise residing in our civilian agencies and the ability to operate in a combat zone residing in our military was larger than all of us. The solution lay in massive reform legislation similar to Congress's Goldwater-Nichols Act in the 1980s, which forced the Army, Navy, Air Force, and Marines to work jointly. A similar effort was needed to force the military and various civilian agencies to work for each other, not just with each other. We had done it before, with the Civil Operations and Revolutionary Development Support program in Vietnam. Under that program, the military, State Department, and USAID officers reported to each other from the districts to the theater command in carrying out a unified effort to good effect. Unfortunately the program wasn't fully implemented until the war was lost at home politically. We desperately needed a similar system of unity of command in addition to unity of effort in Afghanistan before it also lost domestic support.

The lack of data and the disjointed civil-military command chain reflected a much bigger issue: the lack of an overall coalition development strategy. Local NGOs, large international development organizations such as the World Bank and the Red Crescent, and military units with quick-impact development funds made enormous and well-meaning efforts to make an impact on improving Afghan lives. But the sum of the parts came nowhere near a meaningful whole. The transition from a U.S. to a NATO lead in 2006 resulted in over a dozen countries leading PRTs.[4] Volunteering to lead a PRT was a much easier sell for European defense ministers to make to their skeptical parliaments and constituencies than contributing more traditional combat forces. In the eagerness of the U.S. and Afghan governments to gain any contributions they could for the nation-building effort, they accepted nearly any contribution that was offered and did not try to shape them into an overarching strategy for fear of either appearing to dictate the nature of the contributions or turning off donors. In the absence of a strategy, each contributor charged ahead with its own well-intentioned projects, with no overarching authority or guiding plan to coordinate or synchronize the efforts.

For many in these organizations, just getting the projects completed meant success. Having served on the ground and experienced firsthand how difficult things could be in Afghanistan, I understood their perspective. The broader strategy aside, even getting the individual projects completed and working was incredibly challenging. There was a saying in the development community: "Everything in Afghanistan was twice as hard, cost twice as much, and took twice as long as one planned." You would build a school, and it would have no teachers. Find the teachers, and they would have no materials. Get the teachers, books, supplies, and facility in place, and the students would be too intimidated by Taliban sympathizers to come. Convince local elders and families to send the students, and the next week the Taliban would burn the whole thing down, intimidate and sometimes beat the teachers, and threaten the villagers so that you had to start all over.

Still, from a broader, strategic perspective, we had an obligation as policymakers in Washington to drive some type of geographic or sectoral focus across our development efforts. Senior officials from across the interagency consistently came to the meetings in the White House with lists of programs they had funded. These lists typically included percentages of monies spent or a project's completion status as the measurement of success: constructed seventeen women's resource centers; constructed 931 schools and clinics; paved 1,830 kilometers of roads.[5] These accomplishments were important, but they were only inputs. I knew from being in the field that the effects of these projects were often much different: women's centers and clinics attacked by extremists; schools without teachers; policemen who deserted their posts; roads that the government couldn't afford to maintain. I made these points to my Pentagon superiors, but they felt there was little they could do to impose a strategy or more accurate metrics on the international development community.

Such questions were debated at the interagency working groups, and even at the more staid White House meetings. Were the projects being built in line with the military's security focus? Was there coordination between programs? How was the Afghan government going to sustain the projects? Was the new court construction in the justice sector program coordinated with locations where prosecutors were being trained? Were those efforts coordinated with the deployment of newly trained police units so that we had a holistic rule of law approach? Typically all would agree on the need for better coordination and a clearer strategic direction, but little seemed to change before the next meeting.

By 2007 both State and USAID officers in Kabul tackled the herculean task of helping their Afghan counterparts across several ministries come up with the Afghan National Development Strategy. It was long overdue and, again, more of a list of needs than a strategy. But it was an essential start and, importantly, it was Afghan-led. By my later tour in 2009 some provincial development councils, working with PRTs, were referencing the Afghan National Development Strategy as they attempted to prioritize their meager budgets and their requests from the international community. It was a step in the right direction, at least.

The clinic in Achin was a microcosm of the challenges and problems associated with trying to rebuild a country as devastated and difficult as Afghanistan. The clinic building had apparently been completed but had been sitting vacant for over a year. It lacked electricity, medical equipment, supplies, and, of course, doctors, nurses, and staff. We had no idea why it had been built or why that particular location was chosen. We also had no idea of how it was going to be sustained once it was equipped and staffed. None of the parties involved with the clinic could be contacted. Missions like ours to outfit the clinic in Achin were going on all over Afghanistan with great intentions but at enormous expenditure of blood and treasure. Unfortunately, they were not coordinated to move Afghanistan in a particular strategic direction. Yet we charged ahead, determined to make a difference in our little portion of the war.

PRT Jalalabad was located in an old hotel that had served as a vacation spot for Russian soldiers in the 1980s. The hotel was on an Afghan military compound just up the road from the Jalalabad airport, surrounded by courtyards of magnificent flowers and plants that created an almost surreal scene of greenery and color compared to the brown canyons surrounding the Kabul-to-Jalalabad road and the dirty bustle of Jalalabad City.

"I've never heard of a clinic project in Achin, and I've been here nine months," Major Davis, the PRT Jalalabad Operations officer, said as he sat across the table in his operations center. Captain Assad explained where it was located and what he knew of the Red Crescent–sponsored effort.

"Do you have any record of Red Crescent projects in the province?" I asked. "Anything that would indicate why it was placed in Achin, or who was behind building it there? Also, do you know if the provincial health director has funding to support it, or if there are enough local doctors or nurses in Jalalabad willing to travel to Achin to work there?"

"The local Red Crescent office has deliberately kept an arm's length from us in order to maintain their neutrality. We really have nothing to do with their projects, and they want it that way," Davis answered. It wasn't his fault. That was the mentality shared by most of the NGOs. Their culture, and in many cases their charter, dictated that they not give even the perception of taking sides in a conflict. They feared being seen as cooperating with coalition efforts and therefore becoming a target for the Taliban. From the NGOs' perspective, they were in Afghanistan to help improve the lives of the Afghan people, not take sides in a war.

"I really don't have any good information for you guys," Davis continued. "The provincial government has over eighty NGOs registered to operate just in this province, and some of them will talk to us, but many won't. Plus the major international organizations like World Bank and the Asian Development Bank are really active down at the border crossing at Torkham. We regularly meet with them and have some visibility on their efforts but have no authority to shape them or point them in a different direction. Of course the Afghans also have projects they are doing with donor funding pumped through their ministries. We have a good relationship with USAID; our new representative is really aggressive and coordinates well with the Afghans. This is huge, as our last rep from USAID was only here ninety days and didn't do a damn thing. Both our State and Agriculture officers are on leave right now. Must be nice to get R and R every three or four months!

"In addition to all of that, we are trying to get our arms around the various smaller projects the infantry unit and the Special Forces ODAs have been doing," Davis said. "It's a mess, with everyone working hard but doing their own things. But the PRT does have oversight of all coalition projects in the province, and my commander will want to have some consultations before you guys proceed. He gets back from Kabul in two days. Plus the main road to Achin that supports Humvees is starting to get nasty. There were recently two IED strikes on some engineers trying to pave part of the road, so you guys should wait for us to organize a security package before you go down to Achin. I don't think the commander will object to you moving ahead with the project, but our security platoon is rotating back home, so we won't have any missions going out for a few weeks until the new guys get up and running."

I could see Assad bristling at both the suggestion that he needed clearance from the PRT and that he would have to wait. I spoke up. "I don't think that's going to work for us, sir. These guys have instructions from their higher headquarters to get that medical equipment deployed in the next week and get back to their base in Bagram. We can get three more projects done in the weeks you are telling us we need to wait for a security platoon."

"Look," Davis responded, "I'm not trying to get in your way. But we are trying to bring some coherence to all of the aid work going on, and we will be responsible from a force protection standpoint. It will either be us or the infantry battalion at Jalalabad Airfield that will have to come bail you out if you get in trouble down there. We will have to have all the PowerPoint slides developed and approved through the chain of command back at Bagram for the quick-reaction force before you go. I'm just telling you my boss is going to object to the command at CJTF [Combined Joint Task Force] that you guys are out there without his approval."

I could completely sympathize with his desire to bring some type of order to the hundreds of development projects floating around the province. Here I was contributing to the very thing that I lamented back in Washington: coalition countries implementing their own development agendas, independent of an overarching plan. But I also knew the Emiratis were not going to wait. Assad had his orders from his chain of command and wasn't going to be told no by the PRT or their bosses, CJTF at Bagram. I didn't sympathize at all with Davis's force protection argument, however. Such conventional thinking was making the problem worse, in my view, and endangering his soldiers' lives by making their routes predictable and easy to attack.

"We are going to take back roads in SUVs and try to travel at night," I said. The major's eyes went wide at the suggestion that we were not only traveling without a security platoon but were traveling in civilian SUVs.

Seeing his reaction, I said, "Sir, there is only one road that supports Humvees in and out of Achin District, and we are not going to run up and down it until we get ambushed or hit with an IED. By traveling in SUVs we can take a different trail or wadi each time and can blend in with local Afghan traffic. Your security platoon will only announce to the world we are coming and make us a target. It will also raise the profile of the clinic and anybody associated with it to any Taliban in the area. I'm not trying to be a jerk, but I'm guessing your civil affairs teams have been making the same point as they try to oversee their projects. I've dealt with two other PRTs so far this tour, and they are all very frustrated with all the rules that are preventing them from doing their job."

"Yeah, actually they have," the major relented. "No one goes out of the wire unless it's a four-Humvee convoy with a quick-reaction force on standby. Not my rules."

"Sir, here's the bottom line," I insisted. "These guys are going to deliver several truckloads of medical equipment to that clinic in Achin and get the thing up and running. It's my job to go with them and help them as best I can. We will call the ODA at the airfield if we need help."

Captain Assad was grinning from ear to ear. I later found out the story of my "standing up" to the major on behalf of the Emiratis made its way back to the UAE Task Force. Even though the story was a bit of an exaggeration, I let it go. It did wonders for our rapport.

The next stop was the compound of the provincial governor, Gul Agha Sherzai. One of his assistants led us out to a beautifully manicured garden surrounding the largest fountain, about fifty yards long, I saw in Afghanistan. The Sherzais were powerful figures in the Barakzai tribe, which was most prevalent in southern Afghanistan in Kandahar Province. Gul Agha Sherzai and his family had become very close to the Karzai family during their exile in Pakistan, which lasted throughout the Taliban's reign. He led a militia to fight the Taliban shortly after Karzai's infiltration into southern Afghanistan with a team of Green Berets and CIA officers in the aftermath of 9/11. Karzai appointed him governor of Kandahar Province, where he kept the peace, but, like Jan Mohammad Khan in Uruzgan, it was reportedly at the expense of tribes such as the Noorzai and other tribes that had supported the Taliban during their reign. Sherzai's heavy-handed tactics, coupled with widespread allegations of his involvement in opium smuggling, led to extensive pressure from the United States and the coalition to have him removed as governor. However, rather than firing him and having a potential Pashtun rival floating around Kandahar, in 2005 Karzai made him governor of Nangarhar. Once there, Sherzai reportedly cleaned up his act and began cracking down on opium farmers and producers, though back at the Pentagon, as counternarcotics policy officers, we took the reports with a grain of salt. Other reports indicated he was receiving large kickbacks from nearly every construction project in the province, as well as tariffs from the major border-crossing site with Pakistan at Torkham Gate.

As Sherzai strolled up to our group, I thought he was right out of Hollywood casting. Stocky, with a thick but neatly trimmed beard on large jowls, he was dressed in a more formal version of the traditional *shalwar kameez*. As he tugged at his crisp suit vest worn over his knee-length shirt, I caught a glimpse of a bright gold watch. He sat down at the head of the wrought-iron table in his garden. His chief of staff had warned us that he was about to depart for a trip abroad but had delayed his departure for a few minutes to be sure to greet us. I soon understood why.

"We are very pleased to have our esteemed brothers from the UAE conducting projects in our province," Sherzai opened in a low monotone as Muhammad translated.

"Thank you, your Excellency," Captain Assad replied as he proceeded to introduce each one of us.

"Unfortunately, I must leave very soon, but I wanted to let you know how important your visit to Nangarhar is to me and my people and leave you with some points to consider." Sherzai paused to let Muhammad catch up with the translation. "I am familiar with this clinic down in Achin Province. As I am sure you know, the Shinwari are an important and ancient tribe in this part of Afghanistan, and it is good to help them. But I am concerned at the quality of the construction of this clinic. I must be honest with you. I do not trust the construction company that the NGO used to build this clinic. I know the family that owns it, and they are known for the poor quality of the concrete and materials they use. The NGO did not use a competitive bidding process. You have insisted on using competitive bidding to fight against corruption yes?" Sherzai asked, looking directly at me.

I nodded yes.

"My chief of staff will give you a list of companies we have approved to participate in bidding. We should have the proposals handled through my government departments. I am very frustrated with all of these NGOs spending money outside of the control of the Afghan government. This includes your PRT," he said, again looking at me. "We often cannot support all of these efforts once the projects are completed, and you must imagine my embarrassment in not knowing what is going on in my own province. I don't like to be embarrassed," he added with a scowl, looking every part the warlord.

After a pause Sherzai then broke out in a smile and waved his servant over to pour more chai. "But we will fix these problems in time. Today we should celebrate the presence of our honored Arab brothers. I very much admire the UAE. My wife keeps bothering me to take her shopping in Dubai. But I am using the tactics I learned while fighting the Russians to resist her!" he said laughing. We all laughed with him, of course.

"I must depart, my friends," Sherzai said. "Please excuse me and do not find me rude. You are in good hands with my staff. They will ensure you have only the best Afghan companies as your partners, and a representative from the local Ministry of Health will contact you very soon."

Sherzai's point was valid. The dilemma of how best to funnel our development money was a constant debate in Washington. On one side of the debate were those who pointed to the endemic corruption found at every level of the Afghan government. (I was quite sure the "vetted" construction companies were partially owned by, or at least providing kickbacks to, Sherzai in some way.) They also pointed out the lack of qualified staff in the Afghan government to efficiently execute the billions of dollars flowing into the country, and pressed that only pennies of each dollar would actually make it to the Afghan people who needed it. Furthermore, moving money through Afghan government institutions, all of which were centralized in Kabul, would be prohibitively slow and not meet our shorter term counterinsurgency needs in the rural countryside. The other side of the debate argued along the lines of Sherzai's point that the Afghan government was sovereign and should have more input into how the funds were spent. They highlighted the coalition's relative ignorance of the Afghan people's real needs and that spending funds in the wrong way could actually be destabilizing. In the fractured Afghan society, building a well or awarding a contract on one side of a tribal rivalry and not the other could incite violence and cost the government support. It was a type of mistake that happened often and a dilemma that we never really resolved.

The next day we pulled up to the outer gate of the clinic after several hours of bouncing down a rocky and bumpy wadi. After Major Davis's warning, I wasn't up for taking chances, so we agreed to take the wadi. I regretted the decision after several jarring hours of bouncing along the riverbed. My spine felt like someone had beaten on it with a hammer.

As we entered Achin village, a mob of children chased behind us.

"So much for a low-key entrance," Todd said with his usual sarcasm.

My guys took up security on the roof of the clinic, where they had both clear visibility of the area around us and good fields of fire. It was a miserable, cold, rainy day, and a low ceiling of clouds hung halfway down the Tora Bora Mountains to our south. Within twenty minutes of our arrival, several village elders approached us and insisted we allow them to welcome us with a meal. As the trucks unloaded the medical equipment, Assad, our interpreter, Mohammad, the elders, and I sat down for a large meal spread on a rug on the front porch of the clinic. We were joined by Dr. Afridi, a local man who had a clinic just outside of Jalalabad in the neighboring district of Rodat. How he knew we were there or had made it down to us from the neighboring district so quickly was a mystery to me. The spread of food was a typical heartfelt example of Afghan hospitality. Bowl after bowl of vegetables, nuts, dried fruits, and meats had been laid on a large red and black wool carpet. A large flat plate sat in the center containing an enormous mound of rice. Known as *kabuli pilao* in Pashtu, the white and yellow rice was mixed with sweet grapes, carrots, and cashews. One of the elders smiled as he scooped a huge mound onto my plate with a flat wooden spoon.

We had passed dozens of children with bare feet and dingy clothes on our way through the village to the clinic. Mohammad, who was originally from Jalalabad, told us how poor the area was, particularly after a recent drought. Yet here we were, invited to a feast that could have fed the entire village for days. Seated around the edge of the carpet, the village elders insisted on our eating first. I deftly tried to avoid the bowl of cubed goat meat sitting in front of me. I remembered passing several butcher shops on the way there that had slabs of meat hanging from hooks in the open-air shops by the road. Groups of small boys stood by the slabs steadily swatting away flies and pouring water over the meat to wash off the dust.

"They will be offended if you do not eat the meat. They probably slaughtered a goat to celebrate our arrival," Mohammad whispered to me. I accepted the meat with a smile as one of the elders directed a small boy to serve me several cubes of goat on top of my rice. Brian, our medic, smiled through his enormous black beard as I grabbed a cube with my fingers, threw it into my mouth, and started chewing.

"I am honored to be in such a beautiful part of Afghanistan and that you would share this special meal with me and my men," I said, trying to look at the elder rather than the interpreter as I spoke.

"We are most grateful to the UAE and the United States for this clinic," Dr. Afridi said. It was the opening line of a long diatribe highlighting his personal biography, his medical training, and the status of his clinic. He continued with the history of the Shinwari tribe and its support for past monarchies and the current Karzai government. The doctor's English had a heavy Indian accent but was understandable. Fortunately, Captain Assad's English was very good, so Mohammad did not have to try to translate every sentence into Pashtu, English, and Arabic. Dr. Afridi's account of the Shinwari was fascinating, from their attacks against their British occupiers in the nineteenth century to their rebellion against King Amanullah in the 1920s. As is the Afghan way, he wound his way to his main point after about an hour.

"We are wondering why you do not deliver this modern and much needed equipment to a clinic that could better use it to serve the people of Nangarhar Province," he finally said. "Please do not misunderstand me; this clinic here is a fine building. Indeed the good people of the District of Achin are poor and need good medicine. But we must be realistic. No doctors will come here. It is too dangerous. The *dushman*—the Dari term for *enemy*—come through the mountains from Pakistan and make trouble for educated people," he said, pointing toward the Tora Bora Mountains that formed the border between Afghanistan and Pakistan.

"Sir, where do you suggest we put the equipment?" Assad asked politely.

"I understand you are bringing equipment to treat women. My clinic has women doctors," Afridi responded. "It is near the main Jalalabad road, and educated women doctors are not afraid to come there. Most of this equipment you are unloading looks to be intended to help women with childbirth and women's physical problems. It will never be used here because no women doctors will come here."

Dr. Afridi, not afraid of hearing his own voice, went on to tell the story of another clinic sponsored by an NGO that had been built and burned down in the neighboring district of Dih Bala. "The men who burned the clinic later burned a girls' school in the same district. Fortunately two of the perpetrators were later arrested by the police. The men were questioned before a large *shura* in Dih Bala district that was formed to hear the men out about why they had done such things. One of the criminals stood up and said, 'The doctors in the clinic were un-Islamic. They were touching women with their own hands. Men, even if they are doctors, should not do such things. We cannot allow it in the name of Allah.'"

"The men were also questioned about why they attacked and set fire to a girls' school," Afridi said. He recounted the second man standing up and saying, "The school was built by the Americans, infidels, and was teaching our girls their ways. Our girls belong in the home, caring for their fathers and brothers. They should not learn such things, and in the name of Allah, we cannot allow it. It is my duty as a Muslim man to stop it."

"I was there at this *shura*," said Afridi. "I then stood and asked those two men, 'Do you believe your mothers, sisters, and daughters deserve help and medicine when they are sick?' 'Yes,' the men replied. 'And your mothers, sisters, and daughters should only be treated by women doctors when they are sick, correct?' 'Yes,' the men replied. 'But never by men.' 'Well, if you will not allow a clinic to provide for our women because they do not have any women doctors, and you will not allow schools to educate our women so that they can become doctors, how will our women ever receive medicines and treatment?' The two stupid Talibs had no answer. They just looked at me. They finally saw their ignorance and were ashamed," Afridi said disgustedly.

"This is the ignorance you are dealing with. This is how the Talibs and their Pakistani masters manipulate people to send Afghanistan backward!" the doctor said, throwing his bread down to the ground. "And they will attack this clinic too if you are treating women here." He thrust his thumb over his shoulder in the direction of the clinic.

I excused myself to get up and stretch my legs. The Afghans and Arabs could sit for hours on rugs with their feet tucked up under their legs. As a Westerner used to sitting on furniture, the position killed my knees, and my feet were completely asleep. Assad and Dr. Afridi were discussing the idea of moving the clinic's equipment to Afridi's small hospital as I walked around the corner. I looked up to see the chai boy across the courtyard preparing the post-meal tea. He was spitting in each of the teacups and cleaning the dust out of them with his finger.

"Geez," I thought as I waved Brian over. "Cipro, please." He grinned and pulled a small plastic bag out of his cargo pocket, containing antibiotics. I thought about the pamphlet I had read indicating that tuberculosis epidemics still afflicted some of the least developed countries in the world. "After that meal and the chai boy spitting in my glass, I'm going to need it." After taking the pills, I walked back to the gathering and, of course, gladly accepted my cup of tea from the chai boy.

Ironically it was Graham, our junior communications sergeant, who was in a world of hurt the next day. He had used security duty as an excuse to deliberately skip the meal, so we found it pretty amusing that his face was four shades of green as he alternated between vomiting and shitting. We called the food poisoning that eventually attacked nearly everyone the "Intestinal Jihad," the Taliban's secret weapon on American stomachs. In a later tour I would lose six pounds in four days after contracting it. It was 100 percent pure misery. The next morning, after spending the night in a disgusting bathroom, pale and with cold sweats, Graham insisted on riding around with us for a full day as we escorted some of the medical technicians into Jalalabad City to purchase supplies. Despite his misery, he was even more afraid that he would miss a firefight if he stayed back at the base on the airfield. So we spent the day stopping at the side of the road while Graham repeatedly tried to relieve himself. Within seconds of our stopping, we would be mobbed by kids. Graham was constantly shooing them away as they peered down into the wadi, around the building, or wherever he was trying to hide. At one stop I gave the kids some candy, pointed to some rocks, and made a throwing motion. The next thing Graham knew, he had a slew of pebbles raining down on him as he squatted in a ditch outside of Jalalabad. All we heard was "Assholes!" coming out of the wadi over the giggles of the kids.

The next morning the provincial health director from the Ministry of Public Health and a member of Governor Sherzai's staff arrived to speak to Captain Assad and me. After several minutes it became clear that they completely disagreed with Dr. Afridi about where the medical equipment should be installed. Both men thought the equipment and clinic should stay in Achin. They argued that many of the poorer people in the southern districts around Achin did not have vehicles and therefore found it difficult and expensive to travel to Jalalabad, where Dr. Afridi's clinic was located. They pressed that this clinic would have a good effect on popular support among the Shinwari and that the Shinwari elders would be insulted if we provided the equipment to another area. They also informed us that, in their opinion, Dr. Afridi was empire building. He apparently was contemplating a run for Parliament and was not on Governor Sherzai's team. Having a clinic stocked with hundreds of thousands of dollars of new, modern equipment from the UAE would serve to increase his standing in the area. Both men assured us they would get doctors to the clinic and would supplement their salaries with government funds. They also assured us that they would have a few policemen live in an abandoned government building next door to keep an eye on the place.

Captain Assad and I looked at each other. Who knew what to believe? Both men also pressed us separately that they should have the keys until the clinic could be staffed with doctors.

Once again I found myself reflecting back to the Army Special Forces Qualification Course, where we faced these types of dilemma all the time. It was why Green Beret training was truly unique in the global Special Operations community. Others—the British SAS, the Polish Grom, the Navy SEALS—focused on being the most physically fit, most accurate shooters, and overall the most elite operators in the world. Green Berets, by contrast, also focused on being warrior diplomats and thinking their way through problems. We strove to be just as comfortable dealing with a foreign minister of defense, training a foreign commando unit, negotiating with a provincial health official, or advising a tribal chief in his native tongue as we were shooting and breaking things. Our training taught us to thrive in gray areas, like the problem we faced in Achin. It was the everyday life of developing countries.

Both Dr. Afridi and the provincial health director had made some valid points. Ultimately it was Captain Assad's decision where to install the medical equipment. I was there to facilitate U.S. external support if needed and to provide advice when wanted. Assad asked for my advice after a second long meeting with the health director. I suggested we take a hard look at our priorities and really ask ourselves why we were outfitting the clinic. Providing the Afghans basic health care was important in and of itself. But we were not an NGO doing development work simply for the sake of it; our projects needed to support our counterinsurgency objectives. Keeping the support of the Shinwari tribe was more important to those objectives, even if it meant pursuing a less than perfect development solution.

Fortunately, most of the gynecological equipment had not yet arrived, so we were not yet fully committed to equipping the clinic in Achin. I worked with Assad to present a compromise. We gave the health officials two months to locate a female physician willing to work in Achin. If they did, the second tranche of equipment would go to the clinic in Achin. If not, it would be diverted to Dr. Afridi's clinic, which we had already inspected. Additionally we got a commitment from the health officials to send a part-time physician and nurse to Achin until it could be fully staffed.

After many more cups of chai and discussions, Assad provided the keys of the clinic to the provincial health director as the most credible and "legitimate" government representative in the area. The technicians finished the installation of an X-ray room, a rudimentary operating room for minor surgeries, a pharmacy, and several other patient areas. We even had the generators working so that the place had electricity (although it was unclear who would pay for generator fuel in the future; nor was there a plan to maintain the equipment if it needed repairs). Days later we had a celebratory meal and ribbon-cutting ceremony, where we discussed the arrangements between Dr. Afridi and the Health Ministry with a dozen Shinwari elders, each of whom gave lengthy speeches on behalf of his village and subtribe.

Graham pulled me aside to let me know that the ODA that normally operated in the area had informed us that they had picked up an intercept of a midlevel Taliban commander complaining that a group of Arabs and Americans were running around on his turf in SUVs. They assumed we were CIA. Luckily he had not associated us with the clinic, but he did have a description of one of our vehicles. Our cover had been blown, and I didn't want to endanger our lightly armed team or the clinic. It was time to leave. We rented different SUVs and a van for the trip back to Bagram and arranged for some Afghans to drive our current vehicles back at a later date.

We gave a full report to Major Davis at the PRT on our way out of the province, complete with photos, a copy of the keys, and the same equipment inventory we had provided the Afghan officials. Fortunately, his team had worked constructively with Dr. Afridi and confirmed that he was a political rival of Governor Sherzai rather than a bad actor. Davis assured us he would do his best to incorporate the clinic into their overall development strategy for the province, would raise it in his meetings with the provincial officials, and maybe send a patrol to check on it when he could.

Back at Bagram several weeks later Assad informed me that the Afghan health officials in Jalalabad had produced a female physician. He then proudly showed me pictures of the new infant delivery room equipment that was installed in the clinic. Apparently, however, the provincial health officials were complaining they did not have the budget to provide clean water to the clinic. Assad had also heard that Major Davis had rotated home early to the United States. We could only hope that he passed along our report to his successor. I knew that without the PRT prodding the local government to budget for the staff and maintenance of the clinic, it would not be sustained over time and would likely end up as yet another abandoned project. I wondered if we had made a mistake in threatening to divert equipment to Dr. Afridi's clinic, thereby risking Sherzai's long-term support. It was just one of a thousand examples of why it was so hard to effectively implement development projects in Afghanistan, much less weave them into a broader strategy. But I was determined to keep trying to get it right as the militancy and distorted ideology of the Taliban and al Qaeda crept back into Afghan society, abetted by the coalition's failed attempts to deliver better lives for the Afghan people.

5 The Road to Musa Qala
The Taliban Are Back

"We are deeply honored to have you in Helmand, Colonel," Governor Mohammad Daoud said warmly as he motioned to the long row of couches in his office. Colonel Bishooh, Major Musa, several other officers from the UAE Special Operations Task Force 7, and I sat in a circle of couches in the governor's office.

"I understand you are interested in building a base in the Baghran Valley, north of the Kajaki Dam, near Musa Qala," the governor continued.

"Yes," Colonel Bishooh replied. "We are interested in conducting operations in northern Helmand and in possibly building an airstrip. With your permission, we are here to survey and verify the site. I will take with me a survey team from our Air Force. It has been approved by the commander of the Special Operations Command in my country and the American command," he continued. "Should this effort move forward, I can assure you that we will bring many development projects with our presence and help you turn Helmand Province into a better place for Afghanistan."

"Please have your team tell me anything they need," the governor responded eagerly. "From the authority of my office, it is done. I will be sure the land you need for the base is made available to you with no problems. The people of Helmand will be very pleased to have the United Arab Emirates in their province. We are not getting the support we need from Kabul, and the Americans have left us to NATO and the Europeans. But we know that our Arab brothers will stand with us. With your help, and the help of your government, we will have the next Dubai in Afghanistan!" the governor exclaimed with a huge grin.

"This is very good. My planners will meet with your staff when we return from the survey. We will also take a list of your most pressing development needs," Colonel Bishooh said before sipping his chai.

"Colonel, I must ask one thing of you to take back to the American headquarters immediately. It is of the highest importance and can be very bad for everything we are trying to do. This matter will hurt your efforts too," the governor added.

"Governor, we have an American officer right here. But you cannot see his face through his beard!" Everyone laughed as the governor's eyes went wide as he looked across the room more closely at me. I was wearing the same desert tan uniform as the Emiratis and the Arab equivalent of a turban. As always, I was trying to fade into the background, and he obviously did not notice my sunburned cheeks on top of my beard or the subdued American flag on my right arm facing away from him.

The heretofore jovial governor stopped laughing. The Emirati officers and the governor had been chatting for nearly an hour in a very positive meeting. Now it suddenly turned dour.

"Sir," the governor began, "you must tell your government to stop this eradication campaign in the poppy fields. I must stand against it. It is turning the people against us. You are taking their livelihoods and you are leaving them in debt to the drug mafia. Many of them are forced to settle their debts with the traffickers by giving them their daughters. These are proud Pashtun men. They are left with nothing but their guns to seek their revenge." The governor was clearly getting emotional. "I have raised this issue many times with Kabul, including with the president. The idiots around Karzai only remind me that my predecessor supported the campaign. You should know, my predecessor was the biggest drug baron of them all! He would send his thugs out with the drug police to cut down the poppy crop. But he was sending them to cut down his competitor's crop!" the governor said, slapping his knee.

His predecessor was the notorious Sher Mohammad Akhundzada. I knew exactly what he was talking about from the intelligence reporting I regularly received in my civilian position back in the Pentagon's counternarcotics office. A raid by the Afghan National Interdiction Unit supported by agents from the U.S. Drug Enforcement Administration on one of the governor's compounds the previous year had discovered over ten tons of raw opium waiting to be shipped to processing laboratories across the border in Pakistan, where the opium would have been refined into heroin. From refinery labs along the lawless border region, the heroin would move through routes in Iran and Central Asia to its final destination in Western Europe. I was quite familiar with the National Interdiction Unit, as my office in the Defense Department had funded their training program as well as the program to train the U.S. Drug Enforcement agents on how to operate in a combat zone. Despite our nascent interdiction efforts, the poppy crop was exploding year after year in Afghanistan and by 2006 accounted for nearly 90 percent of the world's opium supply. Helmand Province alone was accounting for half of what was coming out of Afghanistan, according to the UN's annual report on the opium harvest.

The U.S. government's five-pillar plan—strategic communication, law enforcement, interdiction, eradication, and alternative livelihoods—intended to combat the destabilizing effect of the drug trade had in reality become a one-pillar plan: eradication. The Drug Enforcement Administration was working with the Afghans to create specialized counternarcotics police, and USAID had a number of alternative livelihood programs, but they were isolated efforts that were taking a long time to gain traction. On the other hand, the State Department's Bureau of International Narcotics and Law Enforcement was moving full steam ahead with the Afghan Ministry of the Interior to create a several-hundred-man eradication force. Called the Counternarcotics Poppy Eradication Force, they literally lined men up with long sticks and moved through fields whacking the stems of the poppy plants while their bulbous heads oozed the paste that was processed to produce the drug. Additional teams employed tractors with drag bars to simply flatten the rows of poppy. The farmers often responded with a form of passive resistance by mixing their poppy crop with legitimate crops like wheat and barley and flooding their fields to cause the tractors to bog down. Other farmers resisted more aggressively, planting old land mines in the fields or actively siding with local Taliban commanders to ambush the teams.

In the spring of 2006 the Bureau for International Narcotics and Law Enforcement and the Ministry of Interior had begun their most concerted ground eradication campaign yet, called Operation Riverdance. The Counternarcotics Poppy Eradication Force was steadily working up the Helmand River Valley. However, it wasn't consistently moving from poppy field to poppy field. Instead the Force was selectively targeting fields owned by the Ishakzai tribe, a historical rival of Governor Sher Mohammad's Alozai tribe. The local police commanders and district leaders were incentivized by State's Good Governors Program, which provided the officials with cash and development projects as rewards for the number of hectares eradicated. It made sense on paper, but in reality the officials would bypass the poppy fields of their political allies or anyone who could afford a bribe. The American contractors accompanying the teams began complaining off the record to the press and to anyone who would listen that the program was driving farmers either deeper into poverty or into the arms of the Taliban. I had heard of Operation Riverdance and certainly knew of the eradication program, but I had no idea the program had commenced in earnest the week before my mission to Helmand. The poorly executed program served to throw fuel on the fire of tribal tensions, the security vacuum caused by the departure of U.S. military forces that spring, and an increasingly disillusioned populace. I had a sinking feeling as I thought about all of this hours before heading into one of the toughest areas in all of Afghanistan to recon the base at Musa Qala.

"I will take this message back to my command," I calmly replied to the governor, knowing that my higher headquarters could do nothing about it. It was State Department's program.

"I am also hearing rumors and am reading the newspapers that your government plans to use chemicals from airplanes to attack the poppy farms. If you do this, the people will rise against you as they did the Russians. You must not do this here," Governor Daoud implored. His eyes were watering with emotion as he made his point.

"Your point is very reasonable, Your Excellency, and I personally share your concern." I wanted so badly to tell him how much I agreed and how many months I had spent arguing the same point in Washington. But I bit my tongue, remembering that, in the eyes of the governor and the UAE colonel, I was representing the U.S. government.

"Sir, I must make one request of you, if it is acceptable to Colonel Bishooh," I said. The colonel nodded. "Sir, I feel it is very important to also have an Afghan National Army presence at this new base. Will you support a request to the Ministry of Defense to station some ANA alongside the UAE Task Force?" I asked.

"Yes, of course," the governor quickly agreed. "You are absolutely correct. You know that everyone wants soldiers stationed in their towns. We cannot have enough of them. There are currently some soldiers try-

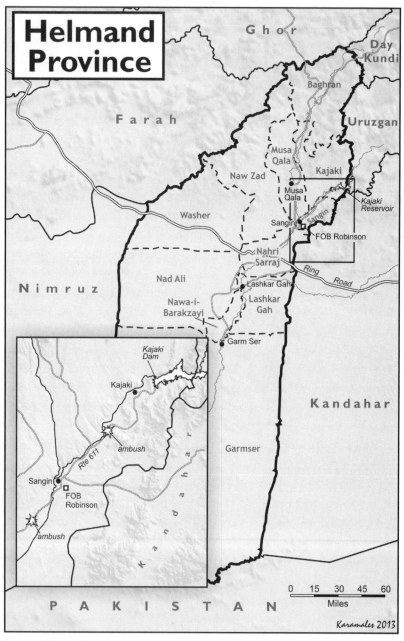

Map 8. Helmand Province.

ing to handle the insecurity in the town of Sangin. They are transferred from Herat and I will request that they move to this new base."

Months earlier I had recommended to the UAE Task Force commander that he propose to the Combined Joint Special Operations Task Force and his headquarters in Abu Dhabi that the UAE assume responsibility for the northern third of Helmand province. The area, formerly code-named Area of Operations Orca, had recently been vacated by Norwegian Special Forces when they redeployed back to Norway. The area was a hotbed of tribal support for the Taliban and was considered an internal sanctuary for them. The Emiratis had consistently told me that their crown prince, Sheikh Mohammed bin Zayed, had wanted his men to get into the fight. I intended to help them do just that. Having worked with the Emiratis for several months in Uruzgan and the Tagab Valley, I was convinced they would have a fantastically positive effect. They were ready to fight when necessary, but they could also approach development and strategic messaging with a level of credibility that we could not match. Plus we desperately needed the help in Helmand. In the spring of 2006 there were fewer than a hundred American soldiers in all of Helmand Province. By contrast, at the height of the U.S. military's surge in 2011 there were over twenty thousand.[1] U.S. forces left Helmand in early 2006, and the British were due to send replacements by the spring of 2006 as part of NATO's expansion into Regional Command South. However, the British delayed their deployment until the late summer, leaving just two Special Forces teams in the central part of the province and a small PRT in the capital of Lashkar Gah through the height of the fighting season in Afghanistan.

Throughout the spring I had built support in my headquarters for the UAE to move into the volatile northern Helmand region. The Task Force commander was supportive, as was the UAE military headquarters in Abu Dhabi. I had taken the UAE commanders on several reconnaissance flights over possible sites for the bases, and my men were now accompanying several UAE Task Force officers to meet with Governor Daoud and seek his support. We then planned to escort several UAE Air Force officers to survey a tract of land east of the town of Musa Qala to examine the possibility of building an airstrip capable of supporting cargo planes and several helicopters. The survey and selecting the site for the base were the final steps. I was very excited about the possibility of inserting a new base with an airstrip into one of the more unstable parts of the country. I thought we could really make a difference. We had patrolled the area over the winter with little enemy contact. Unbeknownst to us, things had dramatically changed for the worse over the spring.

We headed north from the capital of Lashkar Gah toward the Kajaki Dam, the seminal project of U.S. involvement in Afghanistan in the 1950s whose barely functioning turbines still provided most of southern Afghanistan's electricity. Not long after we crossed the Ring Road heading down a bumpy, pockmarked dirt road known as Highway 611, our rear element reported that they were taking RPG rounds. We had split the convoy into two platoons with several kilometers between them so that if one element was hit, the other could maneuver and hopefully flank the attackers. Each platoon, called a *falah* in Arabic, consisted of three UAE Panhard armored cars and one Humvee, plus one of my GMVs. I was with the lead platoon, Falah 1, listening to my guys embedded with Falah 2 report that they were receiving sporadic machine gun and RPG fire. I was absolutely sick of getting ambushed and then having to fight our way out to break contact. As I discussed with the UAE platoon commander when we were planning for the mission, these Taliban ambushes usually consisted of a few pickup trucks full of guys with an RPG and perhaps a light machine gun. We, on the other hand, had ten armored vehicles with a heavy machine gun or grenade launcher on each.

"I'm sick of running from these attacks," I said to the group of UAE officers at our mission briefing. "It sends the wrong message to the local people and to the Taliban. We need to send a message that if they attack the UAE Task Force they are going to get punched right back. After that happens a few times, I guarantee you word will spread to the other Taliban groups and you won't be attacked."

Major Musa loved it. He was a respected officer in the UAE Special Operations Command and had just arrived from Abu Dhabi with the Air Force survey team. Short, stocky, and aggressive, he took charge of this particular mission. "If they mess with us, we will bloody them." Musa stated. "I will send them a message taped to a bullet."

Graham, our junior communications sergeant, was up in the turret manning our .50 caliber machine gun that day. This was the same Graham who ran up the wadi with grenade in hand in the face of the PKM machine gun in the Tagab valley. Our senior communications sergeant, Sean, was driving. At six feet five inches, with a linebacker's build, long black beard, and Alabama drawl, Sean was unflappable and a steady hand on every mission. On the bench in the back of the GMV was my junior team medic, Gordo. Normally he would have also had a machine gun on a swing arm to cover the rear arc and sides of the vehicle, but we had to borrow this vehicle after our regular one broke down. Gordo, an executive with a telecommunications firm in his civilian career, had been detailed to help the Czech Special Forces build a new compound in Kandahar. When we made a stopover at Kandahar airfield on our way to Helmand for this mission, I asked him to come along. The Czechs were delayed in their deployment, and I was happy to have another operator and experienced medic.

The night we passed through Kandahar Airfield I stopped in the headquarters of the Special Operations Task Force for southern Afghanistan to see an old friend and VMI classmate, Josh, who was serving at the headquarters as the assistant operations officer. Josh was a talented and cerebral officer who had steeped himself in the theory of counterinsurgency well before the topic was fashionable in military circles, and I was looking forward to his input on why the Taliban seemed to be so rapidly gaining momentum in the south. As we talked I began to realize how much the security dynamic in the south had worsened since we patrolled Uruzgan and parts of Helmand over the previous winter.

"The Taliban flood gates have opened in Helmand's southern border with Pakistan," he said, spanning his arms like a gate opening. "We are seeing hundreds of fighters flowing over the border and right up the Helmand River Valley. With our troops pulling out over this past winter and the Brits delaying their move south from their base up north in Mazar-e-Sharif to Helmand until midsummer, there has been nothing to stop them. I'm sure you've heard that the two ODAs out there are getting hammered. They aren't doing any tribal engagement, they aren't training the ANA, and they aren't doing medical clinics in villages," he said, shaking his head. "They are just in daily dogfights for their lives."

I replied that I thought it was a combination of all those things plus a number of other factors that had led to such a sharp decline in security. "First, it's this big push on eradication coupled with the removal of Sher Mohammad Akhundzada as governor and his police chief that has various tribes enraged for different reasons," I said. "Second, it's the gap between us leaving and the Brits coming, combined with the hordes suddenly coming across the southern desert from Pakistan. Third, we've sent the message to the world that Afghanistan isn't important to us anymore, so we are handing it to NATO. And finally, we know that the Taliban leadership, including Mullah Omar himself, wants to cause the Europeans to take casualties and make their populations question why they are here. I think we are just beginning to see the Taliban's big push and this summer is going to be bad."

We discussed all of the indicators that we had seen in the past two years of the Taliban setting the stage for their comeback. "Assassinations of pro-government elders and mullahs. Reconnecting with their tribal support and recruiting disaffected tribes—especially those that Jan Mohammed Khan and Sher Mohammad have been kicking. Learning TTPs"—tactics, techniques, and procedures—"from the bad guys in Iraq with IEDs and suicide bombers. Massive disappointment with Karzai's government." I ticked them off on my fingers one by one.

"Yeah, the people are either starting to ride the fence or are outright switching sides because they have had it with these thug-like officials running the provinces. What really has me worried is that the ODAs are finding caches of brand new weapons right out of the box. Heavy weapons too. Much of it Chinese-made. We don't know yet if it's coming through Pakistan, Iran, or both. But the days of the old rusted guns left over from the Soviet resistance are over. You need to take this back to Washington, buddy," Josh continued, slapping me on the back. "This war is going south real fast with all of these things working against us. The first thing we need is just to provide a blanket of security, especially in Kandahar City. We need at least another infantry brigade down here—American infantry. The Canadians that just moved into Kandahar seem good, but there aren't many of them and they aren't planning to put anybody in Kandahar City proper! Isn't a key part of counterinsurgency providing security in the population centers? They also are not tuned in at all to who's who in the tribal game. We also aren't going to even come close to stemming the Taliban tide with just two Special Forces battalions spread across the entire country and one U.S. infantry brigade in the east. And we definitely need lots more ANA." Josh sounded exasperated. Sadly, it would be four more violent years and only after General McChrystal requested surge forces that American troops would be dedicated to securing Kandahar City.

"Washington is gripped with what to do about Iraq, Josh," I replied. "We've got what we've got here. From what I can tell from the folks

I'm emailing back at the Pentagon, General Eikenberry is pushing the handoff to NATO sooner than later. Rumsfeld just announced back in December that we are going to a smaller footprint. He wants fewer U.S. troops here, not more."

I still distinctly remember walking out of Josh's office thinking there had been a definite shift in the war. The obvious signs of external support for the insurgency were what had me really concerned. Had Pakistan turned against us? Shia Iran was a natural enemy of the Sunni, extremist Taliban, so the Iranian regime's funneling weapons and training to the insurgency didn't make sense. Were the Chinese secretly funneling new weapons to the Taliban in order to tie us down? As a student of military history, I knew that it was nearly impossible to defeat an insurgency that had an external sanctuary within which to rest and refit in addition to the backing of a state sponsor. Things were looking more and more like what the United States had done to the Russians in Afghanistan in the 1980s.

Later that night Josh knocked on the door of the wood shack where my guys were sitting on cots getting their equipment ready. He asked me to step outside.

"Look Mike, we've known each other since we were eighteen years old with shaved heads at VMI. I love you like a brother, and I'm asking you as a friend and a professional to not go on this mission. You are heading into a buzz saw with only five other Americans with you. An entire French platoon with two platoons of ANA just had their butts kicked outside of Sangin. They still have two of their dead missing. It's bad. You are not under our command, but if you were, I would advise my boss to order you not to go." I was stunned at such a firm request. I could tell he was genuinely afraid for me.

"Josh, I have the opportunity to make a difference here. The UAE are telling me that if they get this base built in northern Helmand, they are going to bring in Chinooks, Apaches, and mechanized infantry, not to mention enough development funds to build the next Dubai. They're Arabs, Josh. I've seen the difference they can make just walking into an Afghan village. They can speak to the Afghans with a level of credibility we will never have. I've been working this for four months, and this mission is it. If I have to fight my way to Musa Qala to get that survey team to select a site for the base, then so be it. Plus, putting on my strategy hat, it's not a bad thing to have one of our best allies build a base with an airstrip on Iran's doorstep. Unless you convince me the Taliban are now running around in tanks, we're going."

"Okay, brother. I know how stubborn you are," Josh replied. "You'll be in my prayers. If something happens to you, your mother is going to kick my butt. I'll be listening for you on the net. Your call sign is Punisher 53, right?"

"Yep. Have the Air Force on standby," I said, giving him a hug.

Falah 2 was a few kilometers behind us with our senior medic, Brian, another operator, and a UAE sergeant in our second GMV. "We're receiving sporadic RPG fire from our left near a grove of trees," Brian said over the radio.

"Roger, try to maneuver so that you hold them in place and we will come back to you and try to flank from the north," I replied.

The next few minutes were a confusing mess of back and forth between me and the UAE platoon commander of Falah 1. His radio net was jammed with Arabic voices yelling. I couldn't get the platoon turned around, but I didn't want to leave my guys in contact.

"The hell with it, Sean. Turn this truck around. We'll flank those Talibs by ourselves if we have to," I yelled over the radio traffic and engine noise.

By the time we made our way back to the ambush, Falah 2 had pushed ahead out of range of the RPGs and out of the kill zone.

"So much for the plan of attack we agreed to with Major Musa," I said sarcastically. Actually, breaking contact with the Taliban harassing fire and moving on was the right thing to do in this situation. We needed to keep the ultimate goal of the mission in mind, and we could have become bogged down clearing the thick mangroves near the river of Taliban fighters. We still had a lot of ground to cover to get to Musa Qala, including crossing the only bridge over the Helmand River at the Kajaki Dam. Sean hit the gas as we turned around and desperately tried to catch up with Falah 1 before hitting the notorious town of Sangin. Sangin was becoming the most dangerous place in Afghanistan, and we had planned to take a road that skirted the east of the town. Instead we rounded a corner and suddenly found ourselves alone in our GMV rolling through the middle of town.

Groups of military-age men with black turbans and black eyeliner stopped what they were doing and lined the dirt road running through the town bazaar. They just stood there, a few feet from our vehicle, and stared us down as we slowly drove by staring back at them. The scene was surreal. In the distance groups of men sped off in the backs of several pickup trucks. Ahead of us we saw two women dart out of their compounds and snatch their children off the street.

"I think they are a little surprised to see us," I said to Sean.

"Yeah, sir. The only reason they aren't kicking our ass right now is they probably think it's some kind of trick," he said back. "We are flappin'. Really just flappin' out here all alone right now."

A few minutes after leaving town I heard a flurry of Arabic on the UAE radio net. Just as we passed a compound and an open field to our left all hell broke loose. It suddenly sounded like I had stuck my head into a popcorn machine as multiple machine guns and a number of AK-47s opened fire on us.

"I got PKMs on the berm to the nine o'clock!" Graham yelled as he swung the .50 caliber machine gun around toward the open field that stood between us and a series of dikes along the Helmand River.

"Punisher 5-3 Alpha this is 5-3 Bravo, we're right behind you," Brian said over the radio. Looking back I saw Brian's GMV roaring up behind us with Falah 2 behind it.

"Hard left, hard left!" I yelled to Sean. "Charge into the ambush!"

Sean swung hard left while Brian's GMV and one of the UAE Panhards pulled up in a line as we swept across the field.

"Stop so I can lay down some fire!" Graham yelled. We stopped, and Graham opened up with the womp, womp, womp of the heavy .50 caliber machine gun. I watched the golf-ball-size rounds fly across the field and hit the earthen berm. The muzzle of the Taliban PKM machine gun and two heads behind it disappeared in a cloud of dust and dirt. Resting my M4 on the door with Gordo standing in the back of the truck firing over my head, we poured as many rounds as we could squeeze into that machine gun position.

"Another one to the left! Left!" As I looked over I saw a stream of tracers flying over Brian's vehicle from another PKM. The Emirati sergeant in the turret returned fire and then dove down into the vehicle as the PKM rounds found their mark, hitting the GMV. The Panhard to the left began firing.

I heard Graham open up again with the .50 cal. as I looked to my right rear. I was amazed to see a blue armored Toyota Land Cruiser with the

Emirati survey team tear off the road and come to a sudden stop. In an instant the passenger door swung open and Major Musa burst forward, M4 in hand. He dove behind a berm and opened up on the Taliban positions in front of him.

"RPGs!" Graham yelled as two trails of black smoke flew over our GMV.

As I turned around I saw puffs of smoke from half a dozen men riding on a motorized barge out in the river. "Are you kidding me? The Taliban's got a navy?" Graham yelled as he swung the gun back to our direct front and toward the barges. The puffs of smoke were from mortars the Taliban were firing from the barges. The rounds began exploding in a line in front of us.

Graham and the Panhard had silenced the second machine gun, but the top floors of two multistory compounds now lit up with muzzle flashes. The glass on the large side mirror next to Sean exploded and the armored side window of his truck splintered at the rounds splashing against the thick glass. Sean threw his massive frame away from the armored glass as the rounds peppered it.

"Shit, more RPGs!" Graham yelled. Some of the rockets exploded in the air as they reached their maximum range. He was desperately trying to load a new box of ammunition into the gun. Gordo and I fired our rifles as fast as we could to try to keep up a volume of fire as Graham reloaded. I saw two men dressed in dark gray *shalwar kameez* run along a stone wall from the direction of the river toward the berm. I could see AK-47 magazines strapped to their chests in green cloth web gear and something in their hands. I peered through the red reticle of my sight to line up a shot. At the last second I saw that they had a small boy running between them. I lowered the barrel of my rifle as they dove behind the berm. I lined up the red dot in the sight of my rifle with the point on the berm where they disappeared. Two men popped up and raised their rifles toward Brian's GMV. I let out a slow breath as I squeezed the trigger twice. One of the heads slumped forward and the other disappeared.

The next volley of mortar rounds exploded behind us. They were ranging us, and the next volley would likely be right on top of us.

"Hey, sir," Sean said, calmly looking over at me with his slow steady drawl. He held up the handset for the radio as he spoke. "The rest of the *falahs* have pushed north. Sounds like it's just us down here. I'm thinkin' it might be time to go."

He was right. We needed to either press the counterattack over the berm and clear the compounds or break contact and get out of there. Either option was better than sitting in the middle of this field. We were in a crossfire from the two machine guns in the mud-walled compounds and about to receive another volley of mortar rounds from the damned Taliban Navy out in the river. To clear the berm and the compounds, everyone would have to leave the vehicles. It would take a whole infantry platoon, not six to nine guys, to clear them out, and I had no idea what we would do about the barge.

"Dammit, all right, let's go," I said to Sean, hopping back into the passenger side of the truck. We signaled the UAE Panhard to go first, and we followed with Brian in the rear.

Graham resumed firing, trying to find the range to the barge while we turned the GMV around to get out of the kill zone. As we exposed the rear of our vehicle to get back on the road, we received another burst of fire.

"Oh shit, I'm hit!" Gordo yelled out.

I looked back and saw him slump down into the bed of the GMV. I crawled between Graham's legs as he stood in the turret. I then had to maneuver over boxes of ammunition and water to get to the back of the vehicle and Gordo. I managed to lift him back into a sitting position on a bench running down the side of the bed of the truck and quickly assessed his condition. The upper portion of his left leg was covered in blood. A chunk of his right forearm was missing, as though a shark had taken a bite out of it. I also saw the pistol holster that he wore on his chest was in shreds, but I figured that the armor plate behind it had stopped the round. Just to be sure, I shoved my hand between the plate and his chest. All seemed normal. Kneeling over Gordo and looking back down, I immediately grabbed his left thigh with both my hands to try to apply pressure to the wound. Blood shot up into my face.

"Oh God, he's got a femoral bleed," I yelled up to Shane. I knew from the medical training I had received from both Brian and Gordo that the femoral artery was one of the largest arteries in the human body. He had only minutes before bleeding out and dying.

I immediately ripped open the first aid kit on his body armor and grabbed the tourniquet. Sliding it up on his thigh, I cranked down on the tightening handle with every bit of strength in my body.

"Damn it, Mike!" Gordo yelled. "That fucking hurts!"

"Sorry, buddy. Suck it up," I said back. "Just doing what you taught me."
I heard Sean on the radio calling for the medevac helicopter.

I looked up and saw a cluster of muzzle flashes on the cliff to our right front. I knew they were higher than Graham could elevate his machine gun, so I grabbed my rifle and flipped the selector switch to automatic. I wasn't going to get off accurate shots from a GMV screaming down a rutted dirt road, so I held the trigger down to fire as many rounds as I could toward them. As we drove by my bolt slammed to the rear, signifying an empty magazine. The muzzle flashes on the ridge stopped.

Lowering my rifle, I grabbed another magazine out of my kit. I typically carried three on the armored plate carrier on my chest, one on the left side of my belt and one in my rifle. I made a mental note that I was loading my fourth magazine and had only one full spare left before I needed to reach into the reserve stash in my backpack.

Turning my attention back to Gordo, I yanked a second tourniquet out of my cargo pocket and strapped it on Gordo's thigh. I pulled the surgical scissors that were part of my gear and cut up the inside of his pants to his belt. Ripping the crotch of his pants open, I lifted his leg and moved his testicles to be able to see better.

"What the hell you doing down there?" Gordo yelled as he tried to look down over his body armor at my head in his crotch.

"Checking for an exit wound, dammit," I said over the noise of the gunfire. I tried to make my voice as calm as possible. Inside I was petrified that I would do something wrong and let him die.

"Oh, okay, good job," he replied as he leaned his head back against the railing. "Glad you listened in class."

By this time we were flying down Highway 611 as fast as we could, trying to catch up with the rest of the element. The road ran along the base of a long series of cliff walls to our right. To our left, farms were interspersed with compounds in the three-hundred-yard stretch between the road and the river. The Taliban had men on both sides of us—up on the cliffs firing down on us and spread out in the compounds and fields to our left. To my absolute shock as I looked out at the river, I saw that the barge with the mortar teams had a motor on the back and was running parallel to us while lobbing rounds to prevent us from driving out of the kill zone.

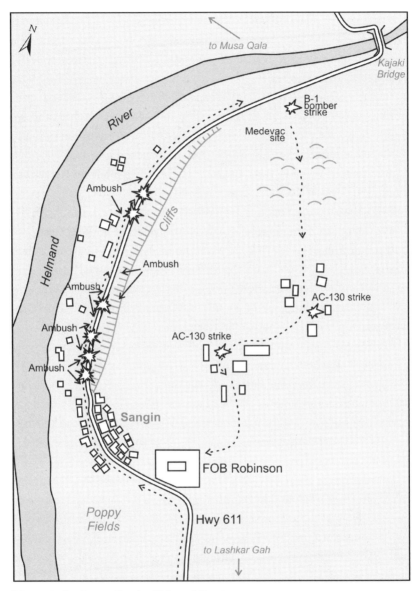

Map 9. Ambush near Sangin, Helmand Province.

"RPG!" Graham screamed as a black streak of smoke arced its way in from our front left and exploded against the rock cliff a few feet from our GMV.

I woke up on the bottom of the bed of the GMV. Sean had violently swerved to avoid the rocket and I smacked my head against the side of the vehicle. My head was pounding, and I looked over to see Gordo slumped over on the bench.

"We're getting off this road!" Sean yelled back as he swerved right onto a trail that cut a break in the cliff. He ascended the hill, and we popped out onto a plateau that led away from the river. Fortunately Falah 1 and 2 had taken the same trail and formed a protective circle a few hundred yards in front of us. I could see the medevac helicopter circling in the distance.

Brian's GMV pulled up, and he jumped into the back of ours with his medical bag. He immediately took over and went to work on Gordo.

It seemed like an hour ticked by and the medevac still had not landed. Graham and Sean were up on the different radio nets, with Sean trying to call in some airstrikes and Graham talking to the medevac. We were still receiving random mortar rounds and sporadic fire, and I heard Graham passing that information on to the pilots.

"Tell them the landing zone is cold!" I yelled up to him. "As long as you are telling them we are receiving fire, he won't land!"

Soon we were loading Gordo onto the helicopter and also an Emirati soldier who had been hit in the head with a bullet that didn't penetrate his helmet but knocked him unconscious. We also put onto the helicopter a scared stiff contractor who was riding in the UAE armored SUV. I couldn't believe our good fortune at not losing anyone else.

I quickly began forming a plan with the ever aggressive Major Musa to make our way to the Kajaki Dam Bridge and on to Musa Qala. Three of our GMV tires were flat from bullet holes. We needed to put on spares and redistribute ammunition. When the satellite phone rang Sean handed it to me. Everyone in theater listened on the SATCOM radio when an element was in contact, and the phone was often used for a more private conversation.

"Mike, this is Dave. What are your plans going forward?"

Dave was the commander from my unit back in Maryland and was serving at the CJSOTF headquarters as the director for Coalition Special

Operations Forces. My various split teams scattered about the country and embedded with coalition units ultimately reported to him.

"We are driving on with the mission," I replied. "We just came up with a plan to counterattack, fight across the bridge if we have to, and then make our way up to Musa Qala."

"Ah, that's not going to work. It's too hot up there. You guys need to abort and start working your way back to base."

I was pissed. Furious. "Dave, we damn near got killed fighting our way up here, and now you want me to just go back?"

"Mike, half the Taliban Army is waiting on the other side of that bridge for you, and they are not carrying pistols in their pockets," he said matter-of-factly. "We're talking Dishkas and recoilless rifles." These were heavy machine guns and small cannons designed to destroy vehicles.

"Sir, you get me some steady air support and I'll punch through whatever they have at the bridge, do the survey, and take the long way back through the desert. I've only taken two casualties, and we have plenty of ammo. I'm tired of running every time we get hit. Gives the bad guys a win and a propaganda victory, dammit!"

"Mike, this is Scott." Maj. Scott Mann was the CJSOTF operations officer responsible for current operations across the entire theater for the Special Forces Task Forces. "I appreciate you wanting to press the fight. That's good Green Beret shit. But you guys have kicked over a supersized can of bad guys out there, and every Taliban commander in the province is getting his boys fired up to come after you. We have Predator over you and we are seeing bad guys in the hundreds trying to converge on you as we speak. You're not going over that bridge, and if I have to be blunt with you, right now I'm worried about how to even get you back to FOB Robinson south of Sangin. If you keep pushing deeper toward Musa Qala they are going to close a steel door behind you so thick it will take a division to punch through. And then you will be surrounded, and you know we don't have shit out there in the entire province but one other ODA and some Brits that just arrived." He paused, talking to someone in the background.

"Okay," he resumed. "In addition to the Pred, I've got an A-10 and a B-1 bomber inbound. You guys get moving south ASAP before the bad guys can mass on you. We will control the close air support through the Predators. When it gets dark, we are trying to get you an AC-130 gunship as well. Your fight is not anywhere close to done yet, Mike."

About thirty minutes after we started moving, a series of huge explosions went off on the other side of a small hill from where we had medevaced Gordo. I found out later that over sixty Taliban fighters had massed there to try to overrun our position. Scott and the CJSOTF staff watched them on Predator feeds as they gathered and prepared to attack before calling in the B-1 bomber to drop multiple two-thousand-pound GPS-guided bombs on them.

Our night movement, with no moon and a bunch of tired men driving under night vision, seemed to drag on forever. Periodically through the night CJSOTF would call, asking us to halt and account for all of our men. Once we had confirmed that no one had wandered off, another series of explosions would crack on either side of us and we'd hear jets scream off into the distance. We spent the next twelve hours picking our way through goat trails, wadis, and villages to make it back to the tiny base south of Sangin.

When it finally arrived overhead, the AC-130 gunship was worth its weight in gold. As had always been my experience in dealing with AC-130s, for some reason the targeting officer was a female. Hearing her soft voice coming over the net after such a long, dusty, adrenaline-rush day was a shock at first, and then quite soothing. Circling overhead, she would periodically turn on the plane's massive infrared spotlight that would make the entire countryside look like green daylight through our night-vision goggles. Twice she called to inform us that a number of men were massing up ahead. Moments later the crack of the 120-millimeter artillery cannon protruding out the back of the AC-130 would ring through the night and obliterate the waiting ambush.

"Target serviced, you're clear to proceed," she would call back coolly.

"Man, she's like the Angel of Death," Sean said.

"I bet she's a smokin' hot blonde," Graham kept saying every time she called. "Probably a tall Swedish-lookin' triathlete."

After every call we had a running debate about what she looked like; it helped keep us awake. Eventually the discussion turned into a bet between Sean and Graham about her hair color. The wager was a bottle of bourbon. Finally, sick of hearing them talk about it, I called the aircraft on the local FM radio so that the rest of theater couldn't hear.

"Brunette," she replied laughing. "Straight dark brown. Half Mexican."

"Oh, no!" Graham yelled in the night.

"Way off target, Graham," Sean said. "I'll take Maker's Mark, thank you."

"That's all right," Graham replied. "I'm just going to have to go thank her next time we are up at Bagram. Yo hablo español!"

Forward Operating Base Robinson was a dusty little outpost on top of a hill just southeast of Sangin. It had only recently been named after a sergeant from my battalion, Chris Robinson. From Madison, Mississippi, where our battalion headquarters unit is based, Chris was one of the funniest and most popular men in the unit. He and his team sergeant were shot while establishing a helicopter landing zone outside of town. Chris died at the scene. The unit had been fortunate in not suffering any deaths during its first deployment to Afghanistan, so Chris's death was a particularly tough blow.

We approached through the desert to avoid going back through the town and bazaar. The British had just taken over FOB Robinson two weeks before we arrived. They were under nightly attack. Also housed at the base was a small team of Tennessee National Guardsmen who were embedded trainers with an ANA company stationed there. The Guardsmen were good guys, but they were artillerymen by training and not too enthusiastic about being embedded with an Afghan Army unit in the "Fallujah of Afghanistan."

The base had not received resupply since the British had arrived. Their helicopters were fired on every time they tried to bring in supplies and often had to leave without landing. Moreover, the Brits' soft-skinned trucks were ambushed whenever they tried to make the trip by ground from Kandahar. As a result, the base was seriously low on basic supplies. It was the first time in my military career that we were in real danger of running out of water. The Guardsmen were rationing one bottle per man and the Brits were nearly out. Finally, we had one of our interpreters approach the ANA and give them some cash to have one of their workers go into town and find a water truck. That night we had one of the ANA's drivers sneak onto the base. The driver told us that he would be beheaded if the Talibs found out. It was a clear indication of how powerful the Taliban had become in the area since we had been there months earlier. It took 10,000 Afghani, or about $200, to get the man to risk finding water for us. The ANA demanded, however, that the water not go to the Brits. The ANA hated the Brits and thought we had come to work directly with them. "You, the Special Forces, you break bread with us. You eat and sleep with us. You ask us our opinion on plans. You share dangers with us," an ANA captain told us. "The British, they just tell me how many men they want for a patrol and will tell us nothing about the mission because they do not trust us. They treat us like they treated my grandfathers. They are going to meet the same fate in Helmand as their grandfathers!" He said as he slapped his leg, reminding everyone listening that the British Army was defeated by Afghan warriors in the epic battle of Maiwand in 1880.

The next night we tried to exfiltrate back to the Ring Road and our base in Kandahar. A few hours into the movement a Humvee broke an axle in an irrigation ditch. The nights were moonless and thus completely dark, which meant that driving with night-vision goggles was harder than usual. At one point, after waiting for nearly three hours for an ANA wrecker that could tow the GMV back to FOB Robinson, I received another call from Scott on the satellite phone.

"Mike, the place is lighting up with pings that you are out there. The bad guys are talking about having you surrounded again. We just had an intercept from a local commander offering a serious cash reward to anyone who can capture one of you."

The hair on the back of my neck was standing up as I scanned the tree line with my goggles. Scott got back on the line. "Mike, I'm about to make your night even worse. There is a bad fight over in the east. All the air assets are tied up. You guys are on your own until we can break some assets free. If you get in some serious shit we will break something free for you, but, until then, you boys are on your own. I'm sorry."

We were halfway between FOB Robinson and the Ring Road and hours from any type of reinforcements. There was simply nothing out there in terms of a coalition base or presence between us and the main base in Kandahar. It was yet another stark reminder of how few assets we had devoted to the massive undertaking of stabilizing Afghanistan.

We prepared the damaged Humvee to be destroyed by pulling off the weapons and other sensitive items and then rigging it with incendiary grenades that would burn it into a useless hulk if we had to abandon it. The wrecker had already been dispatched, but, since it did not have a radio, we had no way of contacting it. We spent the rest of the night staring out along our perimeter, just waiting on the muzzle flashes and

RPGs to start flying at any second. They never came, but it was one of the longest nights of my life. At this point we were approaching forty hours without sleep. The wrecker finally showed up just before dawn, and we made it back to Kandahar.

The idea for the UAE base outside of Musa Qala never regained traction and became caught up in coalition politics. With the British taking security responsibility for Helmand during the transition to NATO, they wanted the UAE Task Force to begin reporting to them if the UAE was going to have a base there. The Emiratis balked. They had a good relationship with the U.S. Special Forces Command in Afghanistan and liked the support they received. I tried to press the case for another survey team, but with the bureaucratic impasse and the survey team getting ambushed, the idea lost momentum and then died. It was a shame, and I was incredibly disappointed. To this day I deeply regret not creating a backchannel to Washington and trying to gain traction for the base from that angle.

The British, prepared for a peacekeeping mission similar to what they had experienced in northern Afghanistan, were quickly overwhelmed with the hornet's nest they ran into in Helmand. In keeping with their counterinsurgency doctrine, they established a series of platoon houses scattered in various village locations throughout the province in order to be able to easily interact with the populace and protect key district centers. The problem was that the houses were too far apart to be mutually supporting, and the British did not have enough residual forces to be able to react to hot spots when they arose. The houses quickly became defensive pillboxes that tied down all British forces in Helmand. FOB Robinson was nicknamed "the Alamo" because it was attacked nearly every day. Eventually the British made the operational decision to close some of the platoon houses and consolidate forces to have the flexibility to surge forces where they needed them. The first house to close was in Musa Qala, and it turned out to be a controversial one. The command decided in October 2006 to broker a truce with the Taliban through some local elders in order to be able to withdraw their men from the house. The elders promised to reject Taliban control if the British withdrew and assured the command that without the contagion of foreign forces in the area, tribal rules would prevail and allow them to control the situation. In reality the elders had no means to uphold their end of the bargain or control the Taliban's actions. In February 2007 a large group of Taliban fighters took the Musa Qala district center by force and raised the white Taliban flag.

By the time this transpired in the fall of 2006 I had redeployed and was back in my civilian position in the Pentagon working Afghan policy. We were very hard on our British counterparts for cutting the deal. The Taliban flag flew over Musa Qala district for the next nine months, resulting in significant humiliation and loss of face for Governor Daoud. In the Pentagon we read reports of strict Sharia law being instituted in the district, along with school closings and a taxation system. Several men were reportedly hanged for being spies, and local Taliban commanders forcibly recruited men to fight for them. The town wasn't retaken until a battalion of the 82nd Airborne, British forces, and several Special Forces teams with their partnered ANA swept up the valley in December 2007. They fought for three days against entrenched Taliban defenses before being able to raise the Afghan flag again over the district.

For everyone serving in Afghanistan in 2006, it was obvious that the insurgency had turned a corner for the worse. Entire swaths of southern Afghanistan were under Taliban control. They had taken advantage of the lack of U.S. troops, the lack of good governance, and a misguided poppy eradication campaign. But this realization had yet to fully hit home in Washington. Back in the Pentagon everyone's attention was turned to the tumultuous debate about the way forward in Iraq. Much of Congress was demanding we get out of Iraq and was attempting to pass resolutions cutting off funding for the war. President Bush's opinion rating was hitting new lows. Central Command and many of the senior leaders on the Joint Staff, as well as Secretary Rumsfeld himself, were still of a mind that standing down while the Iraqis stood up was the correct way forward. Meanwhile, we were hearing constant chatter from our Iraq colleagues in OSD-Policy that the White House was conducting a close-hold series of reviews examining new strategies, including an unthinkable doubling down of our forces into Iraq. In short, there just didn't seem to be enough bandwidth, nor willingness, frankly, among our senior leadership to hear that Afghanistan was starting to go poorly as well.

6 The French in Maruf
A Pawn in a Diplomatic Game

"Sir, wake up," Will said as he poked his head into my shipping container bedroom known as a "man-can." We were at the French Special Forces base outside Spin Boldak in southeast Afghanistan. "Sir, a French recon team has spotted a group of fifteen Talibs in two Hiluxes"—Toyota's overseas equivalent of its Tacoma pickup truck—"traveling down the Maruf Valley and setting up checkpoints." Will was a Special Forces sergeant major attached as a liaison officer to the French Special Forces. He had been working with the French for several months and, in true Green Beret fashion, was stretching the absolute limits of traditional liaison officer headquarters functions. Rather than sitting in the French headquarters and simply ensuring their plans were coordinated with the U.S. Combined Joint Special Operations Task Force command in Bagram, he had operationalized his role by, in the most candid terms, doing what the French refused to do. This was best exemplified by his adopting the Afghan National Army unit co-located with the French and guiding it on operations while also serving as the informal mentor to the local police chief and power broker, Colonel Abdul Razik. While the French focused on conducting unilateral combat operations and calling on the ANA when they were needed, Will and another sergeant mentored the local Afghan Army and police. A tall, lanky Texan police officer, Will was sharp, no-nonsense, and clearly had built a great rapport with the Afghans.

"Okay, do they need our help with air support or something?" I asked, sitting up in my bunk and noticing that the sun was up. The man-can was basically a bedroom in a box; a standard twenty-foot-long shipping container with a bunk bed and desk and wired for electricity. Customizing them with plywood shelves, outdoor sports chairs, and pictures of home became a hobby for most deployed soldiers. The pitch blackness of the metal shipping container completely threw off my internal body clock.

"They want us to take one of the ANA platoons out there and intercept the Talibs," Will replied.

"Why don't they just send a patrol from their forward base in Maruf out to where their recon section saw these guys? They're already out there while we're several hours away."

"Not how the French roll, sir. They do presence patrols and recon missions, but they aren't too keen to get into any fights," he explained. "I've alerted the embedded training team and the ANA. They said they will be ready to go in about twenty minutes, but no rush. As you know, twenty Afghan minutes translates to about an hour in reality."

I had been at the French base a few kilometers to the west of the Afghan border town of Spin Boldak for a few days. The sergeant partnered with Will had to go back to the United States on emergency leave, and my team was currently split between running the new UAE Task Force 7 through their familiarization training outside of Bagram and embedding with Czech Republic Special Forces down in Kandahar. I was told the French Task Force commander had a hard time being told no by American sergeants when we couldn't provide the support they demanded, so Dave, my commander and the Coalition Special Operations director, thought sending an officer down for a few weeks could be helpful.

The French Special Forces Task Group Ares was located on a small base just off Highway 4, the road from the main southern city of Kandahar heading southeast to the border town of Spin Boldak. Spin sat astride the Afghan-Pakistani border across from the Pakistani city of Chaman and was Afghanistan's largest border crossing with Pakistan in the south. The French Task Force consisted of Army and Navy Special Operations Forces and had been in the base since late 2003. The Task Force was led by a Navy captain, Alain, who was, at best, somewhat aloof. A company of about fifty Afghan National Army soldiers also occupied a small compound attached to the base. They were relegated to the back of the base in a row of brick barracks. According to Will, the relationship between Task Group Ares and the ANA was not great. "The commander just uses them to do the things he doesn't want his boys doing, like getting into firefights," Will told me as we walked over to meet the ANA company commander the day I arrived.

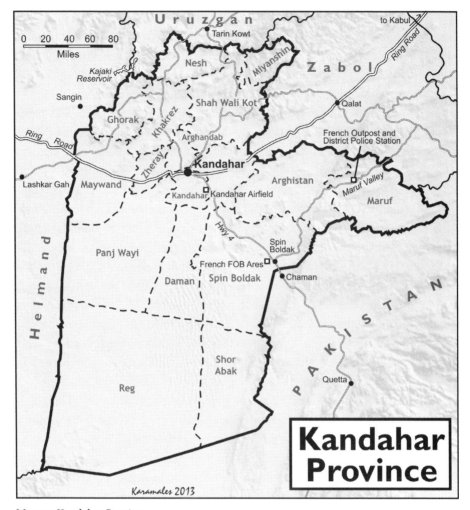

Map 10. Kandahar Province.

"They get reports of Taliban activity in Spin Boldak or spot something in the villages with their recon teams and, rather than investigate themselves, they call the ANA in. What's really pissing the Afghans off is that Captain Alain is constantly keeping them on standby as a QRF [quick-reaction force]. He wants the ANA on QRF duty 24-7 while the French are out patrolling. So they have been constantly on standby just in case the French run into trouble and really haven't been able to get home to visit their families or take their pay home."

I was surprised any of the Afghans were still there.

"Funny you should say that. The ANA chain of command finally intervened about a month ago and granted a pass for the entire company to go home. Man, they were gone!" Will said, smacking his hands together. "All of them. Just poof, gone, back to their homes. The ANA headquarters had to know that would happen. I think they did it just to poke Alain in the eye." Will was half laughing but shaking his head.

"Over the past several weeks only about 50 percent of the Afghans have trickled back in. Finally, Alain made such a stink that the French Ministry of Defense in Paris rang Wardak"—the Afghan defense minister—"and that's why a group of new soldiers just arrived. The ANA general in Kandahar just sent an extra platoon down because the French commander basically shut down his operations until he got more Afghans back here for his QRF. So if the French don't have a QRF, they don't do ops at all. Same thing with medevac or close air support. If the weather gets bad and a medevac helicopter is not available just in case they make contact, then also no operations. If assets are not available to have constant close air support overhead, nope, shut 'em down. They find more reasons not to do operations than to do them. It frustrates the hell out of their men. Their operators and junior officers are damn good. They want to go kick the shit out of the insurgents. But the senior officers are more scared of their bosses in Paris than they are the Taliban!" Will laughed.

"I'm not telling you anything you don't already know, but shouldn't it kind of be the opposite?" I replied incredulously. "Shouldn't the Afghans be out patrolling, interacting with the people, showing them the Afghan government and Army are here and growing, and all the while gathering passive information and intelligence? It's the French who should be sitting back here in their base ready to back the Afghans up if they get in a scuffle."

I had gone to meet the ANA company commander as soon as I arrived. When I knocked on his plywood office door adjacent to his unit barracks, his chai boy, a youngster about twelve who was charged with serving tea and doing menial chores, opened the door, smiled, and waived us in. Captain Assadullah was sitting at his makeshift desk with an ANA major standing next to him looking at a map on the wall. I deliberately walked in and gave a formal salute to the major. He looked surprised for a moment, seeing an American with a full beard and the same camouflage uniform he was wearing standing before him holding a salute. But he quickly stood at attention and returned the salute. Given their problems and apparent disrespect from the French, I instantly decided upon seeing the major to make a bit of a show of giving the Afghans their due.

He smiled broadly as I greeted him with the customary "Salam Aleikum."

"Aleikum salam," Assadullah replied, extending his hand. "You are Captain Mike?"

"I am, sir. May I sit down and visit with you for a moment? If I'm interrupting your meeting, I can come back later."

"Please. Please sit. Sergeant Major Will tells me you are coming, and I am waiting for you." Assadullah motioned to the polyester paisley couch perpendicular to his desk.

The major politely excused himself, telling me his driver was waiting to take him back to Kandahar.

The chai boy appeared with a tray of steaming hot green tea, and Assadullah proceeded to tell me that the major was the supply officer for his *kandak* (the Afghan term for *battalion*) and that they were discussing plans for a delivery of new Ford pickup trucks, as he currently had enough to move only half of his men. Uncharacteristically for an Afghan, Assadullah jumped right to the point.

"The French Task Force does not train us. Many of my men are fresh from basic training. My lieutenants do not have advanced skills. It will be good to have more training. I want my men to be good fighters." Assadullah, who, like many Afghans, used only one name, was a Pashtun from Zabul Province. It was a little unusual to see a southern Pashtun as an ANA officer since a disproportionate number of Army officers were Tajiks from the northern provinces of Afghanistan. The chief of staff of the Army, Bismullah Khan, himself a prominent Tajik with experience fighting the Soviets in the 1980s, had slowly infused much of the Army's officer corps with his fellow Tajiks in command positions. The ANA was generally having a difficult time recruiting in the southern provinces because the area contained many tribes that supported the Taliban or simply opposed the government. A large percentage of the Pashtuns who were recruited were from tribes in the east and northeast. It was the first time I had encountered an Army officer actually from the south.

"Will trains us too much. I am thanking him very much, and I want to tell you he is a good friend of the ANA," Captain Assadullah said as he reached over and touched Will's beard. "Not all of the bearded ones have been so good," he told me candidly. "Some just want to kill Taliban. Sergeant Major Will wants to train the ANA to kill Taliban for him so he can stay back here at the base and cook his steaks!" Assadullah laughed at his own joke. "But that is okay. It is better we go fight. Afghanistan is our country, and it is our responsibility to bring security here."

"That's right, sir," Will replied. "Better to train you to do it so we can all go home and have big meals with our families."

Assadullah went on. "I very much like the mortar and heavy machine gun training. We are a heavy weapons company. The mortar is a very good weapon for hitting the Talibs in the hills. But it is very complicated to learn, and many of my men are uneducated. Will is very patient and a very good teacher. The French, they are not interested in teaching us. The commander still has not even come to my office to have chai. He will always send someone for me when he needs some of my men. This is not how you should treat an Afghan officer in his own country. I think they believe we are still a colony."

I did my best to defend our coalition partner, but, as I'm sure was obvious, my heart wasn't in it. As NATO forces increasingly flowed into southern Afghanistan with the broader strategic shift from the U.S.-led effort to the NATO-led ISAF, tension between the Europeans and the ANA was a problem I was seeing consistently. The Europeans just either didn't care to, or didn't know how to, partner with the Afghans operationally. In their defense, the Europeans were new to the concept, while we had been at it for several years. Admittedly, it was much easier to just go it alone when it came to conducting missions. Most of the Afghan soldiers were illiterate, and, unlike Assadullah, many of the officers were quite content to sit back in the safety of their offices rather than patrol into the hinterlands of Afghanistan. Some Afghans were busier pilfering supplies, selling gasoline on the black market, or using their authority to cut business deals than they were leading their men. But for the coalition to ignore the problem or shunt the problem off to a small group of embedded trainers was not the solution. Most ANA units I encountered were craving to prove their worth and were well aware of their deficiencies. I found that the more they were treated with respect and as equals, and the more that was expected of them, the better they performed.

That chilly morning in April 2006 Assadullah's men were indeed ready in twenty minutes, but they had only four trucks operational.

"Sir, you ready?" Will asked as he threw me a box of French rations. "You want to be on the gun or drive?" Ideally we would have at least three people in the Humvee—a driver, a turret gunner on the heavy machine gun, and someone in the passenger seat to work the radios and be able to dismount when necessary. That day it was just Will and me going with the ANA on patrol.

"If we're lucky we'll roll up on the Taliban checkpoint or set up our own checkpoint at the entrance to the Maruf Valley and they'll hit it" Will said as he started the truck. "Most likely the Taliban are long gone, but regardless, it'll be good to get the ANA out of the base and out in front of the locals."

"You need me to go brief Captain Alain?" I asked as I climbed into the turret with the .50 caliber machine gun.

"Nope, I stopped by and showed him our probable route on a map. The communications center has all of our information and can track us on the blue force tracker." This was a shoe box–size GPS device installed in each vehicle for differentiating friend from foe. "They will pass our information up to CJSOTF. Half the time they forget about us out here because we technically are not an operational ODA. With just two of us running around with a platoon of ANA, we kind of fall off CJSOTF's radar screen. Just the way we like it," Will said smiling.

We were completely unfettered and free to engage the problems of the area as we saw fit. By my later tour in 2009 every team would be required to develop PowerPoint slides to simply leave the wire. Compared to that environment, we had fantastic autonomy.

As we pulled our Humvee up to the gate, we watched the ANA pull up behind us in three tan Ford pickup trucks.

"Thought we were getting four ANA gun trucks," I said.

Will responded, "I'm betting Assadullah decided to keep one back for himself or for emergencies. We are definitely starting to go beyond my threshold for risk, given how far out there we'll be. But I guess we'll be good with three."

The ANA lieutenant came up to greet us. Wearing the ANA's distinctive light green beret, he was clearly Hazaran, with strong Mongolian features that stood out among the other Afghans. The Hazara are a historically oppressed minority, especially by the Taliban, but they tended to be the most educated and hardworking Afghans we encountered, typical of many minorities in developing nations. The lieutenant quickly and professionally described the status of his men and their equipment, and then assured us his men had enough supplies to last three days. The basic math of how much food and water each man needed per day multiplied by the number of days we would be away from the base was a consistent problem for the ANA. I always brought a large amount of Afghan cash just in case we needed to buy food locally.

"It always gives me a chuckle to see how much crap the ANA can pile into the back of a pickup," Will said as the lieutenant walked back to his trucks. Stacked in the back were blankets, boxes of American food rations, water cans, and several old-style American rucksacks. Draped across all of it were a few foam mattresses covered with New England Patriots, Pittsburgh Steelers, and *Star Wars* sheets they obviously obtained from some American unit. The soldiers piled on top of the gear, their legs hanging over the side of the truck bed. Somehow they managed not to bounce out the back as they traversed some of the bumpiest, most pockmarked roads I had ever had the displeasure to experience. Each truck also had a medium or heavy machine gun mounted on a pole just behind the cabin so that someone could stand in the bed of the truck and lay down suppressive fire. The heavy Russian-made machine gun, or Dishka, fired a 12.7 millimeter bullet roughly equivalent to the .50 caliber machine guns found on our armored Humvees and tanks. The womp, womp, womp of the Dishka firing its fist-size shells was very distinctive, and not anything we ever wanted directed at us. The Taliban had the same weapon.

The ANA were impressive during our long movement north from the French base to the notorious Maruf Valley. The trucks kept proper spacing so that, in the event of an ambush, they would not be clustered together. We were second in the convoy, to allow the protective bubble of our IED jammer to extend beyond the first ANA truck. Another sign of Will's training showed in the actions of the ANA whenever the convoy came to a stop. Each time, one of the Afghan soldiers in the back of his truck would hop up in disciplined fashion, unstrap the bungee cords holding the truck's machine gun in place, and point it in opposite sectors of fire in coordination with the other trucks to cover a 360-degree arc. The

Afghan troops also randomly stopped oncoming trucks and cars to do quick searches. Controlling the movement of the population with checkpoints to try to disrupt the movements of the insurgents was a key tactic of counterinsurgency warfare. I liked roving checkpoints better than fixed checkpoints, as they were more difficult to evade and left a sense of uncertainty in the insurgents' minds. With fixed checkpoints, within an hour of setting them up, the traffic would dry to a trickle as the presence of the checkpoint became known. We continued along the dry river bed that served as a road into the Maruf Valley, setting up snap checkpoints for the rest of the day. We never saw any sign of a Taliban patrol.

We finally reached a remote and ramshackle French outpost next to a small bazaar and the Maruf district police station in the center of the valley. A large, mud-walled turret stood to one side of the gate, with sandbags and a machine gun on the top. As we parked our vehicles in the courtyard of the L-shaped mud structure, a French soldier emerged, sporting one of the best combat hairstyles I had seen before or since: a sandy blond afro with dreadlocks that looked as though he had just stuck his hand in a light socket. His long, dirty-blond goatee was also impressive. We gathered around the map on the hood of our Humvee, and the soldier briefed us in heavily accented English on his regular observations of trucks of armed men traversing the valley.

He typically spotted them through his long-range optics from the bluff just north of the town. I asked him why they didn't engage. Clearly frustrated, he answered, "We do not have permission from the Task Group headquarters."

I asked why he didn't call for an airstrike if they were clearly Taliban traveling from Pakistan to the interior of Afghanistan. Growing more frustrated, he explained, "Our rules of engagement do not allow the aircraft to actually drop bombs unless the pilot can see that the men are armed. Even if I tell him I can see their weapons, the pilot is not allowed."

"So," he continued, "the French jets often fly very low through the valley in a 'show of force.'"

I asked if he worked with the police next door, and he complained that they were lazy and corrupt. He also thought the commander had cut a deal with the local Taliban commander because they were from the same Noorzai tribe that straddled the border. He lamented about watching a group of Taliban at a checkpoint hauling two men out of their car and beating them with their rifles and shoes. "I had them in my sights, and just had to watch," the soldier said dryly.

He said that the French command's willingness to let them engage had gone from slim to none since the death of one of their Navy commandos, Loic Le Page. Le Page was killed months earlier as his unit pursued a group of Taliban fighters. Since he was the son of a French general, the incident received a lot of media attention in France. "The less press the better for the officers. Any incident that brings attention to Task Group Ares also brings public inquiries about why we are here in Afghanistan."

I could tell that my questions were only pissing him off, so I backed off and asked if he minded if I went over to introduce myself to the police chief.

"Bonne chance," he snorted as he gladly walked off with the six packs of soda Will had thoughtfully brought for him. Compared to the very well-stocked French mess hall back in Spin Boldak, these guys were roughing it.

I was surprised at the sad state of the camp. The open-top Land Rover vehicles the French commandos used looked old and worn. I sat in one, and the radio looked like a holdover from Vietnam. There was no way it was compatible with ours. I peeked in their small radio room and had the same impression. I thought back to the lamentations I heard in the Pentagon about the paltry defense expenditures of our European and NATO allies.

The police compound was typical of those found in Afghanistan. The main building was white, with peeling paint on walls that consisted of stucco applied over brick. In a number of places bits of brick were exposed. A large dirt courtyard surrounded the building, and the entire area was enclosed by an eight-foot-high mud wall with square turrets on each corner. Sandbags lined each turret, but oddly, only the corner opposing the French outpost was manned. I thought of the French soldier's disgust when I mentioned the police and thought how mutually bad the feelings must have been if the police's only manned guard post was facing the French. I could see a PKM machine gun sitting up on its bipod and two men in *shalwar kameez* staring down at us. Sitting ominously in the courtyard were two flatbed trucks, each with a twin anti-aircraft cannon mounted on a turret on its bed. Even from a distance, I could see that one was so rusted I was sure it was inoperable. But I also knew that these types of heavy weapons served as more of a trophy and an element of stature than an actually useful piece of combat equipment. On one side of the courtyard stood a short, squat building with four small doors; by the stench emanating from it, I knew it was the outhouse. Next to it was a large hole that served as a trash heap. More impressive than the outhouse and trash heap was the distinct smell of hashish being smoked somewhere on the premises.

A man who clearly carried himself as "the boss" walked out the main door, paused at the top of the stairs with his hands on his hips, and walked up to greet us as we entered the steel gate.

"You have got to be kidding me," I distinctly remember thinking. He was right out of a bad Hollywood movie. He must have been five feet tall, but his oversized hat added another foot. The brim was pulled low over his eyes, and he wore dark, aviator-style sunglasses. He was the only man I saw wearing the actual blue Afghan National Police uniform, except that his pants were tucked into black, knee-high riding boots and he was wearing some type of black leather belt over his protruding belly. Set against the ragtag bunch milling around the courtyard and the crumbling building, this mini-Patton cut quite a ridiculous figure. He snapped his fingers and motioned one of his lieutenants inside as we approached the stairs. His face was stern behind the shades as he directed us to enter a bare-bones meeting room.

The room had a number of red and black carpets lining the walls and padded cushions and pillows around its perimeter. There was a window at one end. Along one wall sat a high shelf with rolled-up scroll-like documents stacked to the ceiling. The wall opposite the window held a hand-drawn map of the district, with villages and key mountains noted in Pashtu. It was an indicator of the state of the police's equipment to see a police chief without even a decent map of his district.

We exchanged the usual pleasantries, and I asked about his family. Aside from being the cultural norm in the Middle East and South Asia, asking such personal questions produced a good indication of the true state of security in the area. If the police chief, district governor, or other government official felt comfortable bringing his family to live with him in his district of responsibility, it was a good sign the area was fairly secure. More often than not, unfortunately, the officials' families lived in the provincial capital or as far away as Kabul for their safety.

Not surprisingly, the chief's family lived in Kandahar. After a while he asked me what had brought us there.

"Sir, I have come here from Spin Boldak with the Afghan Army platoon in response to reports of Taliban patrols operating freely and regularly establishing checkpoints in the area," I explained.

The police chief, leaning back against the wall while still wearing the oversized hat, sat up and stiffened. He responded with a twenty-minute speech on the history of the Taliban in Maruf over the past several years. He then spent another ten minutes describing how he and his men killed ten Talibs, including two commanders, just days after he arrived the year prior. Our interpreter was struggling to keep up, as the police chief rarely paused to allow him to gather his thoughts.

I knew from my conversations with Will and from the brief I had received from the French intelligence officer that a steady stream of insurgents had been flowing into Kandahar from Pakistan through a valley that ran east to west and paralleled the main highway into Kandahar City. "This guy is full of crap and he knows it," I thought.

Eventually I cut to the point. "There are rumors in Spin Boldak that the police in Maruf have an understanding, an agreement, with the Talibs to not bother each other. I'm told this police station has never been attacked, but the firebase just down the street has been attacked several times."

The chief stared for a moment, then slowly took off his sunglasses, folded them, and placed them in his pocket, not saying a word. He removed his hat and placed it on the pillow next to him. I saw the interpreter glance at the policeman standing guard at the door and holding his AK-47. I had not worn my body armor as a sign of respect and trust. Plus I hated sitting on the floor while wearing it because it cut into my upper legs. Now I wished I was wearing it as I wondered how badly I had just overstepped and how the hell I was going to shoot my way out of there with just my pistol.

"You don't understand the nature of the conflict here, Captain," the chief said in British-accented English. "I have been speaking in Pashtu for the sake of my men sitting here with us, but let us converse now in English."

"Son of a bitch," I thought. I had obviously underestimated this guy.

"I am Noorzai. The Noorzai held control of Maruf and Spin Boldak during the Taliban's rule. They had control of the border crossing and who and what came and went from Chaman to Kandahar. Most important, they had control of the customs duties. When you Americans came and forced the mujahideen out, you put our biggest rivals, the Achakzai, in charge in the border crossing at Spin Boldak."

"I don't think we were actually choosing one tribe over another," I replied. "I don't think we even understand who is who yet."

"That is your biggest problem, my friend. You are ignorant. You think government good, Taliban bad. This government is not good. In many cases the government is worse than the Talibs. So when you ride into a village with some policemen that hail from a rival tribe that has been robbing from the people in the village, those people are going to view you with hatred. You think you are helping the villagers, but in your ignorance, you are siding with the very people that are abusing them. In Afghanistan the friend of my enemy is most definitely my enemy.

"You put Gul Agha Sherzai in charge of Kandahar, and he, in turn, put his henchman Abdul Razik in charge of Spin Boldak. Razik now has become a very rich man with control of the customs money. He has attacked the Noorzai. He tells you and the French they are Taliban. If any Noorzai were not working with the Taliban before, they are now. You say there are streams of armed Taliban coming from Pakistan into Kandahar down my valley. Who tells you this? Razik? Many of these so-called Taliban are men I know. They are Noorzai. They trade goods back and forth into Pakistan. Why would they come into Afghanistan through Spin Boldak and drive down Highway 4 to Kandahar only to pay Razik's men at their checkpoints? They come this route through the Maruf Valley instead. I know the difference between armed tribesmen and Taliban, but you, my friend, do not."

Will and I had recently met with the notorious, very aggressive and effective Border Police colonel, Abdul Razik. He was surprisingly boyish-looking for a man that had been accused of being a warlord who controlled the area's lucrative border crossings with an iron grip. He had a noticeable widow's peak, and the traditional box cap sat back on his head. Smiling generously as he greeted us, there was coldness in his eyes. He was a member of the Achakzai tribe and was closely aligned with the former provincial governor, the strongman and longtime Karzai family ally, Gul Agha Sherzai. We had heard persistent rumors of his men massacring a group of "Taliban" from the Noorzai tribe. I asked him directly about it and he launched into a thirty-minute speech on the history of the Noorzai tribe and extremism and then quipped that smear campaigns were a national sport in Afghanistan. Over the course of the long conversation I thought about a number of things: how long it would take to either reform or sack men like Razik, how we needed to get out of our fortified bases to know what was really going on, and how the Europeans would not be able to take either the time or the risks necessary to do either one of those things, especially on the difficult Pakistani border.

"Now, to answer your question." the commander continued, clearly irritated. "Any deals I make with my Noorzai brothers is no different than you Americans making a deal with Pakistan. I make deals with my tribe, my clan. Yes, some of them may lean toward the Talibs. This is at a very small, very local level. It is nothing. The deal you have with the Pakistani Army, with the Pakistani intelligence, the ISI, this is where your concern should lie. This is a big, strategic issue. All the time they are sending Punjabis and real Taliban—foreigners—here to cause trouble. The ISI gives them guns, money, training, and helps them plan. And the United States gives the Pakistani Army millions of U.S. dollars. I think your government has a deal with the ISI. Your deal is for Pakistan to deliver you al Qaeda and to not use their nuclear weapons against India. If they do this for you, they can have Afghanistan again."

I started to object, but he continued.

"And what is this with the Europeans? They are not interested in fighting. The French people love food and fashion, not fighting. You have a deal with ISI, and you have handed Afghanistan's future over to the Europeans so you can save face while going after the oil in Iraq. Afghanistan has no oil and no more al Qaeda, so America is not interested anymore.

"You should not come here to lecture me about deals, my friend," he said, pointing his finger at me.

The little Napoleon had just taken my lunch money. My feet and lower legs were completely asleep from multiple hours sitting cross-legged on the floor. My bladder was about to burst from half a dozen cups of chai. I muttered some explanations about the complicated nature of our relationship with Pakistan. His complaints were typical of what I heard from many Afghans. Our relationship with Pakistan did not make sense, so conspiracy theories abounded to explain it.

"I want to show you something," he said as he motioned to the chai boy and pointed to one of the scrolls on the shelf.

The boy cleared the tea cups and bowls of nuts from the center of the carpet as the commander unrolled what appeared to be a hand-drawn map of a city. "You know Quetta?"

"Of course," I replied.

"You know Mullah Omar and Mullah Baradar and Obaidullah?" he asked, referring to the leader of the Taliban movement and two men who were widely believed to be numbers two and three in the organization. "I am showing you where they are living. I know this. I have relatives there. I lived there for years and know this area very well." He pointed to two different intersections and what looked like a dead-end road while telling me where each man lived. "Everyone knows they are there. It is no big secret. But it is like your mafia. They care for the people in their communities, and the Pakistanis look the other way.

"Why cannot America kill these men? You can do anything. You can put people in space. Any educated man must come to the conclusion that America does not want these men dead. If you take that along with your government's cooperation with the Pakistani military, one can only conclude you want to control Afghanistan," he said.

"Sir, I can assure you," I said, choosing my words carefully, "Americans do not want to control Afghanistan. The American people do not want their husbands and sons to be here, thousands of miles from their families. You are right, my friend, there are some difficulties with our relationship with Pakistan. But you must decide how you want to work with us.

"On the one hand," I said, holding my left palm outward, "Afghans say America abandoned Afghanistan after the mujahideen defeat of the Soviet Union in the 1980s. They say that America did not stay here and help Afghanistan rebuild. On the other hand," I said, holding my right palm out, "we are here now to help you, but people say the Americans are here as occupiers and must leave. Personally I believe America's future and Afghanistan's future are like this," I said, bringing both hands together, "and we will be together for the next fifty years. Until Afghanistan is truly strong enough to resist all of these groups and its neighbors working against it, we must be present here in order to be able to help."

The commander and I walked outside. He was clearly very proud of his Russian-made, twin-barrel anti-aircraft cannon and invited me to stand on it for a picture. As I climbed up I could see over the eastern wall that was on the opposite side of the police headquarters from the French base. In the field just over the wall was poppy as far as the eye could see. It was April and nearing time to harvest the poppy bulbs nearly bursting with the white oozing paste from which opium was extracted. I thought back to my time in the Counternarcotics Policy Office, debating what authorities, if any, our troops should have when they came across blatant corruption on the part of Afghan officials. This was clearly an opium field owned and managed by the district police chief. And here I was standing on his cannon surrounded by a dozen smiling Afghan policemen with AK-47s slung over their shoulders. I wasn't about to do a damn thing. It was easy to sit in our offices in the Pentagon and opine about what should be done. It was another thing altogether standing out there with only one other American in the middle of poppy fields as far as the eye could see. The commander seemed to sense my deliberation. He smiled and gently nudged me to turn around for the photo.

One of the great things about the French base at Spin was that each of their platoon houses had its own bar. The Task Group commander was up in Bagram attending a series of meetings, and I ran into his deputy, Lieutenant Colonel Lefebvre, in the wonderfully stocked French mess hall. He invited me back to one of the bars for a nightcap. He was quite proud of a new scotch he had just received from France and insisted I try it. The bar consisted of some plywood shelves holding various bottles of liquor and wine. It was draped with camouflage netting and lined with white Christmas lights. A half dozen camping chairs sat in a circle around a plywood table resting on ration boxes. I wasn't a big scotch fan, so I only sipped the twenty-five-year-old single malt. Lefebvre was curious about my time in the Pentagon before the deployment and seemed quite open and down to earth compared with many of his fellow officers. After a while, the conversation turned to the war and the French Task Group. Eventually he asked me what I thought of their operation thus far, as I was hoping he would. I told him honestly that I thought his men were sharp and well-trained. I also remarked that they probably wished they had more latitude to protect the Afghan people and to be more aggressive in going after known Taliban strongholds.

"Yes, this is the way of the Special Forces soldier, he replied somewhat dismissively. "They want to get into fights with the enemy. "They have trained their entire lives, and I understand this way of thinking and respect it. But we have constraints, and I often have to enforce those constraints on them. The problem is twofold. The first is our defense budget. The men do not have the equipment they deserve. The rifles and basic kit are good, but the more complicated things, like air-to-ground radios and the newest GPS units, are old and in need of updates." He leaned back in his camping chair and pulled out a cigarette. "I think we have also suffered for our years outside of NATO. We are not as compatible as we should be in equipment and training with you Americans or with the Canadians up in Kandahar."

I was shocked at his candor, even if it was scotch-induced, but I certainly didn't mind it. He was confirming a number of my observations that the French Special Operations Forces weren't as prepared as people in Bagram and even Washington assumed. Yet, Washington was begging Paris for more soldiers. I had noticed while on several patrols that not all of the French vehicles had even a local radio. By contrast, nearly every U.S. vehicle had SATCOM giving their occupants the ability to talk to the entire theater and listen to other communications. If they did not have SATCOM, they would certainly have FM radios that would allow communication with other vehicles, dismounted soldiers, and, importantly, aircraft. And whereas every U.S. soldier, particularly Special Forces soldiers, had individual radios, there was often only one per French squad. The French were also borrowing our IED jammers and had older generation night vision. If this was the state of their Special Operations Forces, I could only imagine their regular Army.

"These equipment shortages are not the biggest problem," he continued. "Our issue, to which you are so diplomatically alluding, is not military. It is political. Afghanistan is not a popular war in Europe. People are loudly asking why we are here, and many feel that our very presence in a landlocked, ancient culture actually makes things worse. The Le Page death was a big blow back home. Most Europeans expected we would be conducting lightly armed peacekeeping missions like we did in Bosnia.

"Truthfully, the unwritten instructions from Paris to my headquarters are to take no more casualties. Serious French casualties on the front page of French newspapers will quickly translate to no French presence in Afghanistan. You may disagree, but some activity here, some presence, and at least a show of strength in this area is better than nothing. It's better than France not having a presence at all."

"Actually, as you predict, I do completely disagree!" I said, smiling. "Afghans are making life-and-death decisions every day. Even talking to one of our soldiers can result in death for them from Taliban retribution. If you are going to engage with certain villages and tribes, you must be prepared to take hostile action to protect and support them. Plus, if you are going to truly undermine this insurgency, you must recruit sources within their ranks, encourage defectors, undermine their propaganda, and when necessary, after careful vetting of course, kill the Taliban leadership.

"You also must engage difficult actors such as Colonel Razik. While he is a strong leader and fighter, the rumors of him executing men from rival tribes, even if they are supporting the Taliban, will drive people away from our cause. Your Task Group must decide whether to work with him so that such things do not happen or press Kabul to sack him and deal with the consequences. But we can't just ignore the problem.

"Frankly, sir, having a thorough understanding of the social and tribal dynamics out there is absolutely critical. Admittedly, the American Army has a long way to go toward understanding it ourselves. But you have no operation to recruit human sources and no real ability for signals intelligence. With your national caveat from your government against kill/capture missions, you also have no ability to show the people you are the strong horse and no ability to force men like Razik into line," I continued.

"We have report after report of extremist mullahs traveling across the border from Pakistan to preach in local mosques and point out the fecklessness of the coalition and ANA to provide security. And with Captain Alain holding the ANA back for your reserve, you are retarding their growth as well. That leaves only Razik and his men for the people to see. You do not have a PRT or other types of aid programs to show the Afghan people some positive results of your presence. The people must see something more than French soldiers driving around and corrupt police setting up illegal checkpoints while the Taliban have complete freedom of movement. In my view, very honestly, your restrictions and your presence are causing more harm than good. They are undermining the very basics of counterinsurgency." I realized that I was almost leaning out of the chair. Lefebvre took a long drag on his cigarette, thinking as he exhaled. I sat back and wondered if I had just taken this conversation way too far.

"One thing you must understand, my friend," he replied. "In France, counterinsurgency means a very different thing. It means Algeria, the Guerre d'Algérie. It means millions of locals displaced and killed. It means torture, civil war, and the collapse of France's Fourth Republic. Nearest to my heart, it also means over ninety thousand French military casualties. If any officer here or anyone in the Ministry publicly announces we are conducting a counterinsurgency campaign, we are finished in Afghanistan!" He was starting to get emotional and a little tipsy. I sensed that I clearly needed to dial back the conversation.

"Sir, I deeply appreciate your honesty," I replied. "I knew this about the lingering effects of Algeria on your national conscience but did not fully appreciate it until now. I think honest conversations like these are a good thing among allies. In the end, our intentions are the same, even if our methods are different. One last question, if it's okay with you. Given these strategic downsides, why are you here? Why risk it?"

"The answer is simple," he said, finishing his drink. "We are here for political credit for assisting the American government in the global war on terror. This is certainly the case after my government refused to support you in Iraq. Task Group Ares and the entire French deployment in Afghanistan is a pawn in a much larger diplomatic game."

I just stared at him. It was an extraordinary statement, one I will never forget.

Six months later I was back in the Pentagon working Afghan policy for the Office of the Secretary of Defense and dealing with the issue of NATO's involvement in the war. Every official, from Secretary Gates down to me, was pounding the table for NATO members to commit their fair share of troops to the effort, to drop their caveats preventing them from certain types of operations, and to move their forces from the relatively secure north and west to help the Americans, Brits, and Canadians in the south and east. The problem, in my view, was a matter not just of political will but also of military capability. The bottom line was that most of the NATO militaries, even the supposedly elite units, had seriously atrophied after years of paltry defense spending. The lack of equipment coupled with the lack of sophisticated intelligence operations and the unwritten caveats emanating from European capitals meant that NATO units often did more harm than good when introduced into insurgency-prone areas. This sounds harsh (and I was told often by my NATO policy colleagues that it was way too harsh), but we had to realize that introducing Western troops and money into poverty-stricken areas created huge expectations on the part of the Afghan people. By 2007 many Afghans were growing increasingly disillusioned with both the failures of the Afghan government and the NATO-led coalition to deliver meaningful improvements to their daily lives. Forty-two of the world's wealthiest nations, including the only remaining global superpower, were present in the towns and villages of Afghanistan. My point to my colleagues and my bosses, and it was admittedly a nuanced one, was that it was fine for the Europeans to do more peacekeeping and development-oriented missions in the north. We did not want the Germans, Swedes, or others moving into the buzz saw of fighting that the much more capable British struggled with in places like Helmand Province in the south. There was warranted frustration on our part that a number of NATO countries would not even provide support assets such as fighter aircraft or helicopters. After my experiences on the ground in 2006, I argued that even those critical support pieces were not needed if they came with so many restrictions that they were not useful. What we really needed was U.S. leadership, capabilities, and approaches to counterinsurgency in the south. However, the unspoken bottom line in both the Pentagon and throughout the U.S. national security establishment was that Iraq was the main effort, and to the extent we needed more resources to deal with a declining situation in Afghanistan, they would have to come from Europe.

The other fundamental issue was the bureaucratic shift that occurred within the U.S. national security establishment once responsibility for military operations shifted to NATO's International Security Assistance Force. Whether in the policy offices of the Defense Department, the Joint Staff, the halls of the State Department, or the National Security Council in the White House, Europe-oriented officials suddenly took the lead for our policies in Afghanistan. Afghanistan became just one of a number of issues on NATO's plate, which ranged from missile defense in Eastern Europe to dealing with piracy off the coast of Somalia.

To make matters worse, the United States was now one of twenty-six votes in an organization that needed unanimous consent to make major policy changes. The first ISAF commander, David Richards, was British, and follow-on U.S. commanders reported to the secretary-general and four-star supreme allied commander in Brussels. Many of my colleagues in the Pentagon saw success in Afghanistan as vital to the future of NATO, good for encouraging interoperability among NATO militaries, and important for proving that NATO could operate in an expeditionary fashion outside of Europe. In other words, the war in Afghanistan was a mechanism to make NATO expeditionary, to transform it into a post–cold war alliance, and to keep it relevant in a post-9/11 world. In this worldview Afghanistan had to be successful for NATO to be successful, not the other way around.

The folks working in the South Asia bureaus across our government tended to have very different views. Success in stabilizing Afghanistan and defeating the growing Taliban insurgency was critical to preventing the return of al Qaeda and a fundamental interest to U.S. national security. We fully recognized the tremendous sacrifices of our allied soldiers. But if NATO as an institution turned out to be unwilling or unable to conduct such a complex and costly mission, then so be it. In our view we had an obligation to point out NATO's shortcomings and seek better solutions. It was a constant tug of war that resulted in a sort of policy paralysis from 2006 to 2008 while the situation in Afghanistan continued to worsen.

7 Operation Perth
War by Consensus

In the summer of 2006 my Operational Detachment Alpha and two UAE platoons were dispatched back to FOB Ripley just south of Tarin Kowt in Uruzgan Province to reinforce the half dozen Special Forces ODAs operating in the province along with an Australian Special Air Service (SAS) Task Force.[1] What we found was a hodgepodge of units trying their best to stem the tide of a growing insurgency, each with a separate chain of command, different rules of engagement, and different fundamental approaches to counterinsurgency doctrine.

The situation had changed for the worse in Uruzgan in 2006, just as it had in Helmand, compared to the situation we found when patrolling in Uruzgan the previous winter. A massive security vacuum had been created by a combination of factors: the bitter tribal resentment Governor Jan Mohammad Khan had engendered among several minority tribes in the province; the removal of the soldiers from the U.S. 25th Infantry Division the previous autumn; the removal of strongman and governor Sher Mohammad Akhundzada in neighboring Helmand; and the delayed arrival of the Dutch in Uruzgan and the Brits in Helmand until most of the fighting season had passed. The Taliban quickly exploited this vacuum by infiltrating back into Afghanistan in increasing numbers from their sanctuary in Pakistan and by targeting pro-government mullahs, elders, and officials in Uruzgan.

An Afghan National Army infantry company with its U.S. Army National Guard embedded training team had also been sent to help stem the tide of insecurity in the province. These embedded training teams were made up of twelve to fifteen senior sergeants and officers that somewhat resembled the makeup of the Special Forces ODAs. They were subunits of National Guard brigades that were mobilized and then scattered into small teams aligned with ANA locations. The teams had the primary mission of training and advising the Afghan National Army and embedding with Afghan counterparts from the Ministry of Defense down through its corps headquarters, brigade headquarters, *kandak* (battalion) headquarters, and all the way to company level. Technically, team members were trainers charged with assisting the Afghans at tactical and operational levels with everything from basic planning techniques to fundamentals of leadership and how to maintain and shoot their AK-47s. Often, however, they also served as combat advisors, accompanying the ANA on combat patrols and missions. By doing so they were also a conduit to critical U.S. support assets such as medevac and close air support and provided a U.S. troop presence for nearly every ANA unit spread across Afghanistan. This was particularly important after the transition from U.S. to NATO lead in 2006, when the U.S. conventional forces continued to operate only in Regional Command East. That left Special Forces teams and the embedded training teams accompanying the ANA as the only U.S. presence in the volatile provinces of southern Afghanistan, as well as the semi-stable provinces in the west along the Iranian border. These elements remained under U.S.-led Operation Enduring Freedom with its less restrictive rules of engagement.

The downsides of such an arrangement were significant, as I would see in the summer of 2006 while conducting operations with the UAE Special Operations Task Force in Uruzgan and Helmand. The main problem with the embedded training teams was that they reported through yet another chain of command conducting operations in Afghanistan. The NATO-led coalition itself presented a command-and-control problem, with forty-two nations having military elements on the ground by the beginning of 2007. Each military element reported up to the four-star commander of the ISAF in Kabul. But each unit also had a senior national representative on the ground who reported back to his respective national capital and could object to orders given by ISAF or, in the case of coalition Special Operations Forces, the CJSOTF headquarters. Thus, the ISAF commander maintained only lose control over the operations of these countries, each of which had its own operational restrictions, or national caveats. The ISAF commander did not have the authority, for example, to order the Italians in Regional Command West to shift helicopters or soldiers to support the British in neighboring Regional

Command South. Also the caveats served as constraints on the various nations regarding how and when their forces could be used. They ranged from types of disallowed missions to geographical areas where troops were precluded from conducting operations. In nearly every case, I found that the various coalition Task Forces kept the ISAF or CJSOTF headquarters informed of their activities and requested additional resources when they needed them, but really took orders from their own chains of command under the influence of the national representatives.

The disjointed coalition chain of command was further burdened by a convoluted internal U.S. command-and-control construct. Just within the U.S. military alone we had as many as six independent chains of command, with units from each one often operating right next to each other. For example, the U.S. conventional infantry battalions and brigades reported to their division command at Bagram Airbase in Regional Command East. The embedded training teams also in Regional Command East reported to their operational headquarters, Task Force Phoenix, located on the outskirts of Kabul. The ANA often took its instruction and guidance from embedded training teams that sometimes were not in synch with the conventional maneuver commanders. To make matters more disconcerting, Special Forces teams such as mine reported through a third, special operations chain of command to CJSOTF, also at Bagram. Still worse, our elite special mission units specializing in counterterrorism kill or capture missions did not report to the ISAF commander at all. Add in the activities of our intelligence agencies, and Afghanistan was an international mixing bowl of units operating on their own timelines and agendas.

Just in Uruzgan Province alone, in the late summer of 2006 we had a spaghetti-like line-and-block chart of coalition and U.S. lines of authority. First, we had a Special Forces Company and its five teams reporting to the regional Special Operations Forces Task Force down in Kandahar Airbase, which then reported to CJSOTF at Bagram. Because I was embedded with the UAE, my team reported around the regional Task Force and directly to CJSOTF. Separately there was an Australian Special Air Service Task Force at FOB Ripley that also reported directly to the CJSOTF up north in Bagram. The Australian Task Force also reported to its national military representative, a full Australian colonel, located with the CJSOTF; he could override CJSOTF directives based on national prerogatives.

At FOB Ripley in Uruzgan a recently arrived Dutch PRT and infantry unit reported to the ISAF Regional Command South headed by a Canadian general in Kandahar. Likewise the U.S. Army National Guard training teams embedded with the ANA company stationed at FOB Ripley took instruction from their normal headquarters at Task Force Phoenix. Finally, and perhaps most important, the Afghan National Army company found itself taking guidance from all sides: the embedded training teams living with them, the ISAF Dutch infantry company, and the U.S. Special Forces teams that specialized in working with indigenous forces and wanted an Afghan Army element to accompany it on all missions. Of course the ANA company commander had to pay attention to his Afghan battalion headquarters, also located in Kandahar (but on a separate base from the ISAF regional headquarters).

The irony was that the United States probably had the weight to streamline the command arrangement, but because of the widely varying approaches to dealing with the insurgency and different rules of engagement, we didn't necessarily want a unified chain of command. Under the political agreements between the United States and NATO that gave the Dutch the lead for Uruzgan Province, such a structure would have placed all units operating there under Dutch authority. U.S. and Australian Special Forces would have had to operate under Dutch caveats, which would have meant very limited, if any, offensive operations. Conversely the Dutch and the other European countries didn't want U.S. Special Operations Forces formally associated with their mission because they feared public backlash at home from how American units conducted counterterrorism missions and handled detainees. The result was a system that attempted to work through voluntary cooperation and personalities rather than a unified chain of command. Many times the various personalities came together and worked well. But just as often they did not, leading to strategic misdirection, infighting, confusion, and ultimately lost ground to the insurgency.

To mitigate the command problem in Tarin Kowt, Major Garcia, the Special Forces company commander at FOB Ripley, convened a weekly coordination meeting with all the units. However, this would simply serve to de-conflict operations and ensure everyone was aware of everyone else's planned missions. No one really had the authority to tell anyone else what to do or not to do, or to synchronize operations. At the first coordination meeting I attended after arriving at FOB Ripley the previous winter with two UAE Special Operations Forces platoons, I naïvely asked to see a copy of the campaign plan for the province. The group just stared at me until Major Garcia, a longtime veteran of operations in Colombia, smiled and said sarcastically, "CJSOTF and ISAF are working on it, buddy. It should be out sometime before the end of the war!"

Everyone got a laugh at my expense. I really didn't think it was that funny. No plan. No unified chain of command. We were missing the basic military fundamentals in an incredibly difficult and complex environment.

We even lacked a unified approach on how to deal with the rapidly spreading insurgency. On one end of the spectrum was the Australian SAS Task Force. Doctrinally modeled on the British SAS, they specialized in long-range reconnaissance and direct-action raids. Their operators were impressive, fit, very good at what they did, and not very interested in much else besides finding and killing the Taliban (or who they thought were Taliban). I once asked their operations officer if they were working any development initiatives with local NGOs or a PRT. He laughed and said, "Only if it helps us kill baddies, mate!" I remarked dryly that, actually, it could.

The new Dutch command just establishing itself in Uruzgan was at the other end of the spectrum. They came with firm ideas about stability operations and refused to call the effort in Afghanistan counterinsurgency, using instead a passive, peacekeeping-like approach. One of their national caveats precluded their units from engaging in deliberate offensive operations. They could fire only when fired upon. Even if the Dutch received reliable information that a Taliban commander or bomb maker was at a certain location, they could not launch a deliberate raid to kill or capture him. The caveat particularly frustrated their junior officers. As a workaround, some of the more aggressive Dutch commanders, particularly in their Special Operations Forces, would send a unit to "investigate" a known Taliban location and let itself be fired on first to have the excuse to fire back. It was a hell of a way to fight a war.

In my first meeting with Lt. Col. Nico Tak, the incoming Dutch PRT commander, he made clear that their strategy for the province would differ from the U.S. operational approach. "Instead of having numerous bases and being spread thinly all over the Province, the Dutch Task

Force will take on an ink spot strategy," he explained. "We are choosing to concentrate our efforts on the more populated areas of the capital, Tarin Kowt, and Deh Rawood and then hoping to expand the ink spot as those areas are stabilized.

"With this approach, we seek to reward good behavior," he continued. "Rather than trying to build development projects in insurgency-prone areas, where the projects are difficult to execute and difficult to protect, we will concentrate our resources in those two areas. We will reward the people who are cooperating with us rather than trying to change the minds of people who are against us and the Afghan government. The Afghan people in the outlying rural areas will see the improvement in the lives of the people of those two areas and want the same for themselves. They will work to apply security to their areas outside the ink spot in the hopes that we will then bring the same type of development to them. Afghan tribes have historically been able to control their own villages, and we think they will do so again with the right motivations."

It was one flavor of counterinsurgency theory, and I didn't completely disagree with him. At least it was some type of plan and operational approach. In practice, however, it didn't really apply to the unique dynamics of Afghanistan and would continue to manifest significant flaws until the Dutch left Uruzgan in 2010. First, the carrot had to be paired with a stick, and the Dutch government refused to allow their military to wield the stick. Their approach assumed that strongmen or Taliban commanders would allow ink spots to expand or allow the Afghan people to invite the Dutch into other areas once they observed progress in Tarin Kowt and Deh Rawood. The U.S. Special Forces teams and Australian SAS were certainly willing to be the stick to remove impediments to such progress. But friction quickly arose between both units and the Dutch. Rather than view the Special Operations elements as an adjunct that could help the ink spot to expand, the conventional Dutch military and their diplomatic corps viewed both as a bunch of cowboys beyond their ability to control.

As the Dutch PRT began pouring development funds into the two population centers, another flaw became apparent. Afghans outside of the development zones viewed the effort with disdain. Jealousies and enmity worsened over time as the tribes and communities outside the zones resented what they saw as favoritism toward the tribes inside the ink spots. Now the population of the province saw the Dutch as

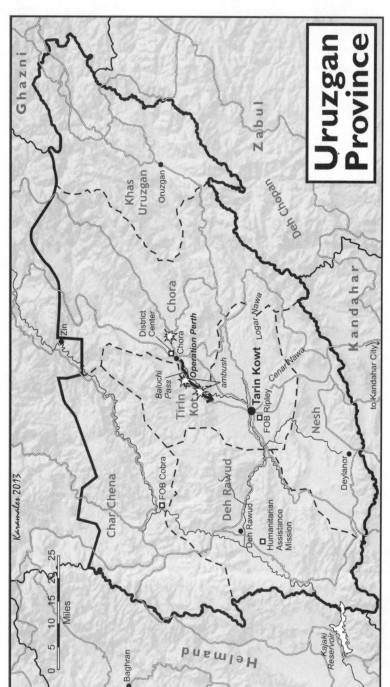

Map 11. Operation Perth, Uruzgan Province.

complicit in Governor Jan Mohammad Khan's nepotism. (He steered almost all reconstruction projects and government positions to his native Popalzai and Barakzai tribes from 2002 to 2005 and continued to have a heavy influence in the province after his removal in early 2006.)

During several of Major Garcia's coordination meetings, an ever-present concern was a local Taliban commander, Mullah Bari, who was regularly attacking and intimidating the district governments of both Deh Rawood and Chora. Mullah Bari was also an explosives expert and was responsible for migrating IED techniques from Iraq to Afghanistan. Everyone was eager to get him off the street, particularly after five U.S. Special Forces soldiers were killed in an IED strike the previous winter.

Bari regularly changed locations within the province, but the Australians thought they had located two of his regular safe houses. The Aussies had committed to a pretty steady rotation of two-man sniper teams with long-range optics to watch the houses. The poor bastards were up in heavily camouflaged hide sites that were scratched out of the hills overlooking both of Bari's compounds with the hope that they would observe him entering one of them and then launch a helicopter assault to kill or capture him. It was a time-honored tactic that required incredible skill and stamina but also put a significant strain on the unit.

Major Garcia and I came up with a plan to complement the Aussies' more traditional approach of using snipers as observers to locate Bari. Garcia tasked one of his Special Forces teams to conduct a medical treatment exercise, known as a MEDCAP, on the outskirts of Chora District to the north of Tarin Kowt. At the same time we agreed that the UAE civil affairs team along with several of my operators would also carry out a MEDCAP, as well as a humanitarian distribution operation, west of Tarin Kowt near Deh Rawood on the Helmand River. A typical MED-CAP involved a team's two highly trained medics, sometimes with the support of coalition or local physicians, bringing a truckload of medical supplies to a village and setting up a clinic. Invariably villagers would appear by the thousands as word rapidly spread that Western medical help was available. The medics would have to employ every bit of their training to treat every conceivable ailment, from dental to intestinal, as well as diseases that are no longer seen in modern hospitals. Many times, however, the instant goodwill and trust garnered by these clinics would yield treasure troves of information on the general goings-on in the area and would sometimes yield tips on insurgent leaders. Our intelligence sergeants often served as aides to the medics and physicians in order to soak up some of this information. In this case we were hopeful the MEDCAPs would have a double benefit: increased goodwill in the Chora and Deh Rawood areas and information on Mullah Bari.

For our portion of the operation the UAE major in charge of his element wanted to take a much more low-profile approach by dressing in garb similar to that worn by NGOs and traveling in civilian vehicles. However, after days of trying, we could not get the package of medical supplies we needed. Helicopter assets were unavailable, and Afghan truck drivers were increasingly afraid to make the trip on the road from Kandahar to Uruzgan. In response, we altered the operation to humanitarian assistance distribution, passing out packages of dates and halal prepackaged meals and initiating the refurbishment of a small village mosque. The PRT commander, a Navy fighter pilot who was on the eve of transitioning responsibility for Uruzgan to the Dutch, told us we were absolutely crazy for traveling to that area in pickup trucks. I told him I felt safer with my men varying and mixing up their mode of travel, that no one would ever expect it, and that we would leave under the cover of early morning darkness so that anyone watching the gate of FOB Ripley would not see us leaving the base. He also had heartburn about the UAE and my men implying we were an NGO, as it could alienate and upset the few real NGOs still operating in the area. I made the point that almost all NGOs had fled and that we might send a positive message to the populace that NGOs had returned. This was a good example of the dichotomy we faced with the issue of multiple chains of command. In this case, had we been consolidated under the PRT or the Dutch, we would have been severely limited in our ability to conduct unconventional operations.

In our combined operations center with the UAE I tracked the progress of our little convoy of three pickup trucks and an Afghan jingle truck bringing up the rear, full of supplies. Hours after sunrise an Australian officer came into our small command center to let us know that two of their sniper teams had observed a group of military-age males traveling in a convoy at high speed toward the villages surrounding Deh Rawood. The Australians were considering engaging if the teams could confirm the suspicious males were armed. However, he wanted to check with us before he gave the go-ahead.

"Whoa! We briefed your ops officer just before our guys left with a full description of our vehicles and numbers of men!" I exclaimed.

Word clearly had not reached the sniper teams. The liaison officer gave me the grid coordinates of the sightings and direction of travel of the vehicles, and, sure enough, it was just east of where my team sergeant, Marc, and the convoy had last checked in. He bolted out the door, jogging back to his command center. Despite his legendary sick sense of humor, Marc was a stickler for operational planning details and an absolute professional. I had no doubt the route was coordinated. It was a close call.

For security reasons, we had not provided advance notice of our MED-CAPs to the village. However, Marc reported that within two hours of their arriving, people were walking in packs down the dirt road that led to the small school where they set up the distribution center. Marc worked with the UAE civil affairs team at the distribution site, while Trip, the ODA's senior weapons sergeant, remained in the pickup truck. Tall, light-skinned, and completely bald, Trip didn't exactly blend in, so he stayed in the truck to monitor the radio and keep close to an M249 SAW light machine gun stashed in the bed of the truck in case of trouble.

Hundreds of villagers lined up. The UAE soldiers distributed dates, meals, and small bags of Tylenol and throat lozenges. The team required every Afghan to sign a name or make a mark as well as pose for a photo, which was taken after each Afghan entered the first room inside the school building. This prevented the people standing in line outside from seeing what we were doing. Sure enough, about midday a middle-aged man with a long black beard entered the room. He stopped, saw the camera, and turned around and walked out, briskly walking back down the road leading out of the village to the north. Not wanting to blow their cover by chasing the man down the road, Marc and our interpreter started asking folks in line the man's name. Several villagers said they did not know who he was, until a young boy blurted out that it was Mullah Bari. His father jerked the boy's arm to be quiet and smiled at us. We couldn't really blame the father. Maybe he sympathized with the Taliban regime. But just as likely he was from a minority tribe that had been brutalized by the police or Jan Mohammad's thugs. Or he was afraid of retribution. Bari had a reputation for mutilating his opponents. Marc called the operations center to inform us that they might have spotted him.

We had coordinated with the police chief in Deh Rawood to have some men available in case the team needed a quick-reaction force nearby. We had hoped to get some useful information on Bari's whereabouts and confirm he was still in the province rather than in Pakistan. We were shocked that he actually walked in the door. In order to protect the humanitarian distribution, we called the police chief, explained that Mullah Bari was walking north down a dirt road from the village, and asked that he be arrested. It was a bit of a risk as we were not completely sure if the police were cooperating with Bari or were too scared to move against him for fear of retaliation. But the Special Forces team based in Deh Rawood had been working with the chief and his men for some time and had vouched for him. There was no way to know for sure, but we made a calculated risk and decided to trust the chief.

Within thirty minutes Marc called back that the police had detained the man and identified him as Mullah Bari. The Deh Rawood police chief was planning to bring Bari to Tarin Kowt late that night; apparently he didn't want to keep Bari at the district headquarters any longer than he had to for fear of the base being attacked. It was a great moment for us and exactly the reason I became a Green Beret. The way we operated was truly unique, compared to that of any other Special Operations Forces service in the United States or the rest of the world. Others, like the U.S. Navy SEALs, the Rangers, or the British and Australian SAS, focused on finding, fixing, and finishing the enemy. We tried to make friends and let them find our enemies for us. We learned local cultures and languages to work by, with, and through local members of host nations. In this case, not only did we take a mafia-style Taliban boss off the street, but word spread quickly through the area that the Deh Rawood police had made the arrest and they received the credit for it. The humanitarian distribution and MEDCAP, which showed the Afghans positive benefits from our presence, made for a double win for Major Garcia and me, and was more effective than killing Bari with a sniper shot or raiding his compound in the dark of night.

Even with the removal of Mullah Bari, by midsummer the Taliban had taken over the district center in Chora, due north of Tarin Kowt and one of the key towns in the province. The Taliban had established a sanctuary in the valley. They were using it as a base of operations to attack the district center in Chora as well as Tarin Kowt and were threatening to turn the entire northern half of the province into a no-go zone for the Afghan government and ISAF. The Australian Task Force cobbled together a coalition force to retake the center and clear the strategic Baluchi Valley, which started in Chora and ran diagonally across the center of the province. The Aussies asked for and received a conventional U.S. infantry company from the 10th Mountain Division because Chora was outside the permitted Dutch zone of operations. So Bravo Company 1/4 Infantry drove its Humvees in from a neighboring province in spite of the Dutch command's being co-located with the Aussies. The Australians also approached the UAE Task Force Command at Bagram to request the presence of UAE platoons and my team as a reserve quick-reaction force. I thought that Operation Perth, as the Australians called it, would be good experience for the UAE platoons, but I questioned the Australian lieutenant colonel commanding the Task Force on the purely kinetic nature of the mission (meaning the purpose was to kill the enemy).

Tall, sandy haired, and with a runner's build, the commander insisted on being called Mark. The SAS was Australia's most elite unit, and Mark had just the touch of well-earned arrogance and aloofness that came with the job. By contrast, most of his staff were incredibly approachable, not to mention being knowledgeable of military operations. During our initial mission briefing, I asked Mark about his plans for the reinsertion of the ANA or police as a "hold" force after clearing the valley of Taliban. I also asked if the PRT would conduct follow-on development projects in the valley.

"No, it's a troops-to-task issue, mate," Mark replied. "It's not our job, nor do we have the resources to hold terrain or do development projects. Our mission is to find and kill baddies. We don't occupy district centers and build schools. I need my men consolidated here, prepared to act as a strike force as we develop intelligence. Candidly, we hope that the Dutch will eventually drop their caveats and work with the Afghans to do more of those types of things outside of Tarin Kowt and Deh Rawood."

I convinced him to agree to my reaching out to the ANA for inclusion in his operation with the thinking that the ANA might be willing to dedicate a platoon to co-locate with the defunct police in Chora.

Again the convoluted command-and-control lines of authority came into play as I tried to coordinate ANA participation in Operation Perth. I approached the embedded training teams, and they thought it was a great idea. They in turn convinced the Afghan company commander that he could rotate a platoon to the district center in Chora after the coalition of Australian, U.S., and UAE forces cleared the Taliban. The Afghan company commander was concerned, however, that the Chora police chief would try to bully the more junior ANA lieutenants, but eventually he relented as he thought it would be good for them to exercise some leadership on their own. The embedded training teams and their chain of command in Kabul were even willing to send an extra team with the ANA platoon to Chora.

Unfortunately, the ANA battalion commander in Kandahar would have none of it. His official reason was that the Ministry of Defense was behind in paying the men and they needed to be in Tarin Kowt when the next payment was being delivered in the coming week. The real reason, we found out from one of the training teams embedded with him, was that he didn't trust the Chora police and was convinced they had cut a deal with the Taliban. We also suspected it had something to do with his being Tajik, from the north, and not trusting Pashtuns in general.

The Dutch commander also had issues with sending the ANA to Chora. He was worried that he would need to send his men as a quick-reaction force so far north should the ANA and handful of Americans be threatened with being overrun. In the end, the ANA didn't send any soldiers to support Operation Perth. The Aussies, as is their tradition, wanted to put a number of two-man reconnaissance/sniper teams along the ridgeline that bordered the eastern side of the Baluchi Valley to have eyes on movement in the valley. Their command requested that the Dutch send a mechanized infantry platoon to position themselves a few kilometers away at the backside of the ridge, where the Australian snipers were to be located. They would simply provide a rear-guard and quick-reaction force should the snipers run into trouble. With no helicopters at FOB Ripley, and being so far from the nearest airbase in Kandahar, help was hours away and we were totally reliant on ourselves for any type of quick support. If those two-man teams were discovered by a large group of insurgents, they could be overrun before support could arrive.

However, because the snipers could potentially participate in deliberate offensive operations, that is, shoot an insurgent fighter after positive identification, the Dutch command team had to ask its national military representative in Kabul if supporting a sniper operation was allowed under Dutch rules of engagement and national caveats. The national military rep, in turn, sent the request to his Ministry of Defense in The Hague, who then apparently consulted the defense committee in the Dutch Parliament for an exception to the rules.

My jaw hit the table when Mark told me during our final coordination brief for Operation Perth that the request for a Dutch platoon had gone to the Dutch Parliament for consideration. "I wish I were kidding you, mate," Mark said. "I don't know how the hell NATO is going to fight a war this way. It's a war by consensus. We have no unity of command." He sounded disgusted. It had been days since the Aussies had made the request. Fortunately the UAE major in charge of the element in Uruzgan stepped up and volunteered to pull the rear-guard duty for the snipers rather than leave the Aussies exposed. When appropriate, we would then move into the valley as the reserve. I was impressed with the Emirati's assertiveness, and the Aussie commander was thrilled with the UAE offer.

A week later, after two days of sitting in the scorching desert at the base of the Baluchi ridge with one of the UAE platoons, I wasn't so thrilled with the UAE major's volunteerism. We had made some good use of our time by conducting random vehicle checkpoint stops on the road running from Tarin Kowt north to Chora, but after a few hours word had gotten around that we were there, and vehicle traffic completely dried up. Finally three Dutch six-wheeled armored vehicles came driving up a dusty trail emerging out of the green valley on the north end of Tarin Kowt. A blond lieutenant jumped out of one of the vehicles as they came to a stop.

"We were denied permission to directly support the sniper teams," he said as he walked up. "But my commander has permitted me to conduct presence patrols in this area over the next two days. I have the sniper teams' radio frequencies and call signs, so, of course, if they come under fire, my rules of engagement allow me to come to the aid of a coalition element. The Aussies are comfortable with it and really want to get you guys in place as their reserve force." The lieutenant was clearly embarrassed at having to come up with such a workaround for a basic combat mission, but he assured us that his "patrol" wasn't actually going anywhere and that he was going to sit right there at the base of the Baluchi ridge, his Parliament be damned.

"God bless you, buddy," I said, shaking his hand while the UAE lieutenant signaled his men to get ready to push up into the mouth of the Baluchi Valley on the outskirts of Chora.

The mortar round hitting to our front made a dull thud, followed by a crack as the sound wave washed over us. My senior medic, Brian, my junior communications sergeant, Graham, our Aussie SAS liaison, Walt, and Trip had pushed north into the green valley around Chora with me in our two GMVs. With us were two platoons of the UAE Task Force that formed a screening line to the east of the district center. Our mission was to prevent Taliban fighters northeast of Chora from pushing into the rear flank of the Australian Task Force as they pushed southwest down the valley. Northeast of Chora, the notorious Gizab District, which had no Afghan government, police, or ISAF presence, was an area of tribal discontent and Taliban support.

The lush green zone ran northeast to southwest following a river that fell from peaks in the center of the country and cut the province in half as it flowed down past Deh Rawood and eventually to the Kajaki Dam on the Helmand River. Weeks before, the Taliban had overrun the district center, set several police trucks on fire, and raised their white flag of purity. The Australian SAS and the local warlord and police chief, Maitullah, along with one of the ODAs from FOB Ripley, had kicked the Taliban out of the center. But it was again under threat of being overrun, and the Chora police chief had begged Governor Monib to convince the coalition to send reinforcements. We had repeatedly received reports of a group of twenty to thirty fighters planning to come down the valley from the northern district of Gizab to retake the district center. They had obviously come, and had brought mortars.

Two rounds hit nearly simultaneously to our right front a little closer than the first one. "They're walking them in, Mike," Brian said, calmly stating the obvious.

"Hey, I see a glint up on the hill!" Graham shouted. He jumped up on top of the vehicle with a set of binoculars to get a better view. "Hey, sir, I see a kid up there. He's looking at us with a set of binos. I bet that little son of a bitch is spotting for the mortars!"

Another ka-thump of a round landed about two hundred meters to our rear. Walt had pulled out his sniper rifle and was making adjustments to the scope. The UAE lieutenant was telling his men over the radio to get ready to reposition the screening line. He was right to prepare to move. But the hill with the kid on it dominated this section of the valley, and even if we moved, we would soon have mortars raining down on us again. I wasn't a fan of being chased around the valley by the Taliban mortar team.

"Hamad," I instructed, "please advise the lieutenant that we assured the Aussie commander we would hold this position and protect his flank." Hamad was the sniper with perfect English who had broken the rules to assist us during the firefight in the Tagab Valley. Since then I had asked to have him with me on every mission. He spoke into the UAE platoon's internal net in Arabic. The lieutenant could easily have ignored both Mark and me, as we had no true authority over him. To his credit, he told his men to hold in place unless the rounds started making impact within a hundred meters.

"Sir, we can't let them walk rounds in on us, but we can't let them push us out of here with a few mortar rounds either," Walt yelled from behind his rifle, propped across the Humvee hood. "We need to take care of this kid. I've got my sights on him."

"The kid just talked into a walkie-talkie. He's definitely the one spotting for the mortar!" Graham yelled down from the roof of the GMV on which he was standing.

This was yet another dilemma like those we constantly faced during our final qualification training to become Green Berets. Again I thought about the cadre instructors during our final exercise, called Robin Sage, saying over and over that we would find ourselves in situations such as this for real one day.

I knew that I couldn't kill this kid. He was a child. For all I knew, the Taliban had a gun to his father's head back in their village. Or they fed him propaganda about the American infidels, such as the story that we regularly took advantage of Afghan women. Or maybe they gave him money. I did know I could justify the shot even though he didn't have a weapon. The act of using the walkie-talkie and binoculars to call in mortars was a hostile act with hostile intent. It was no different from enabling a machine gun by providing boxes of ammunition. I had to decide what to do, quickly.

"Walt, start putting shots at his feet and walk them closer to him until he runs," I yelled. He leaned into his rifle, let out a breath, paused, and squeezed the trigger. A cloud of dust exploded a few feet in front the boy.

The boy jumped back. "He's speaking into his radio again," Graham yelled. Walt squeezed off another shot. This time a rock exploded to the boy's left. He dropped his binos and dove behind a boulder. We then saw him turn and run over the edge of the ridgeline.

The mortar fire stopped. We let out a collective sigh. I wasn't sure whether I was more relieved by the cessation of the mortar fire or that we didn't have to live with hurting the boy.

Once the sun went down we moved into Chora proper and occupied the abandoned police headquarters next to the district center. In the meantime the Australian SAS cleared a series of hills to our south. Bravo Company's infantry swept down the valley toward a small hill that served as a community cemetery. We traveled during the night to move unobserved. The district center was a whitewashed stucco building with a surrounding wall, typical of government buildings in Afghanistan. It had a gleaming blue metal roof. Outside a tin sign read, "Provided by the U.S. Agency for International Development 2005." The sign was full of bullet holes. Inside the police compound walls several burned hulks of vehicles sat in the courtyard. All of the windows were shattered and every room was empty of furniture. The place had been completely looted by either the Taliban or fleeing police.

I climbed up onto a tower on the wall facing the rest of Chora. In the distance the mountain range where the Australian sniper teams were positioned loomed over the entire valley and ran the length of it. Immediately to our southwest was the small roundabout where the road heading due south to Tarin Kowt met the road running southwest down the length of the Baluchi Valley. In the center of the roundabout stood a short two-story tower painted yellow and with a blue roof. Though the writing on the side of the tower indicated it was built and dedicated by the 25th Infantry Division the year before, 2005, the tower already looked as though it had aged several years and been through hell. Part of the problem was the poor quality of concrete and construction materials found in Afghanistan, but part of it was just Afghanistan itself. Whether it was people or buildings, the place had a way of aging things. One-room mud huts surrounded the roundabout and served as the town bazaar. Most had some sort of porch shaded by a thatched roof made with sticks that would allow the owners to get out of the stifling heat of their shops and to get some shade.

I focused on a blue mound lying at the base of the tower and quickly realized it was a body in a light blue police uniform. Two men stood over it for a few seconds, then walked on. We inspected it later, during a patrol through the town. A note pinned to the man's chest said, "Do not touch this man. The same fate will come to any man who cooperates with the Sons of Karzai"—the Taliban's term for the Afghan government—"and the infidel occupiers. Look to Allah and the guardians of His word for your needs."

Needless to say, we had very little interaction with the population of Chora or the Baluchi Valley. The few people who remained would not speak with us out of fear. One retired schoolteacher told us he would have liked to work with us, but he was not confident we would stay around long enough to protect him and his family. I cursed myself for not being able to do a better job of coordinating a follow-on ANA presence.

Mark had kicked off Operation Perth by pushing his commandos and Bravo Company southwest down the valley. In the distance the sound of machine gun fire mixed with periodic explosions rippled down the valley. I listened to the radio in the vehicle in the courtyard below. Bravo Company's infantry had met heavy resistance at the base of what we began calling Cemetery Hill. The soldiers were describing groups of Taliban fighters standing their ground in a network of trenches, stone walls, and fortified compounds. Shortly after the fight began, the infantry had taken casualties and were calling for air support. Within twenty minutes an A-10 ground attack jet swooped overhead, its massive nose-mounted cannon blazing. Meant to destroy Russian tanks during the cold war, the 30 millimeter Gatling-style cannon fired shells the length of a man's arm and sounded like God unzipping the sky. We could see the cluster of compounds at the base of Cemetery Hill explode in a cloud of dust and sparks. Not long afterward a medevac helicopter escorted by two Apache attack helicopters arrived to pick up several wounded infantrymen.

Back at the police station, my guys and several UAE vehicles sat by the gate, engines running and ready to respond to a call for a quick-reaction force. Just as the A-10 disappeared over the horizon, a loud crack that sounded like a cannon shot went off to my left front. Still standing in the turret, I turned to see a large black object fly about five feet over my left shoulder and explode behind our compound. The UAE soldiers pulling security duty up on the wall immediately began firing everything they had at the puff of smoke and dust in a line of trees across a field about four hundred yards to our south.

We had just realized Mark's fear: a two-front fight to our front and rear in the narrow valley. As the Aussies and U.S. infantry were pushing down the Baluchi Valley and encountering heavy resistance, the Taliban had reinforced from Gizab in the northeast in order to pressure us from the rear.

I quickly worked with the UAE lieutenant to send two groups of men to flank either side of the tree line. Several more rounds flew at the compound but thankfully sailed high or landed just short. They sounded like a battleship's cannon firing. We determined the source was a recoilless rifle, something between a bazooka and a small artillery cannon that can fire rounds directly at the target, usually mounted on a tripod or the back of a truck. Their use in Uruzgan marked a significant escalation in the Taliban's capabilities. Clearly the days of hit-and-run tactics with a few AK-47s were long gone. A direct hit from a recoilless rifle round would certainly destroy an armored Humvee or blow a hole in the compound wall.

Our foot patrols reported that they had seen a group of men jump into two Hilux pickup trucks on the other side of the river and speed off when they got close to the tree line. The Talibs had cleverly put the river, still rushing with the spring and summer thaws, between them and us.

"Punisher 5-3 Alpha, this is 5-3 Delta," Brian called up on the net. "We just had a third Hilux come flying out of the trees with a single military-age male in it. We stopped him by firing a few rounds into the Hilux's engine block, and he has a wad of cash, four AKs in the back, a nice bag of dried opium and hash, half a dozen cell phones, and something that is going to really interest you. I'm going to bring them back with us."

"I am just a poor farmer," the man kept saying in Pashtun to my interpreter, Spartacus. (His real name was Rashid, but one of my Roman-legion-obsessed men thought Spartacus sounded better.) "The Talibs came to my home, took my younger brother, and told me to watch these weapons for them or they would kill my brother. I know nothing." Spartacus put his foot on the man's shoulder and shoved until he fell over on his side. A young, short, stocky Tajik from Kabul, Spartacus had no love for anyone cooperating with the Taliban, whom he saw as a bunch of lackeys for Pakistan. He was convinced, as many Tajiks were, that the Pakistanis were using the Taliban to reassert control over his country.

Spartacus interpreted as we asked the man all of the obvious questions: Why was he in the vicinity of men firing a heavy weapon at us?

How many Talibs had come to his house? Why did they come to his house in particular? What tribe was he from? And most important of all, why was there a wooden crate of brand-new recoilless rifle rounds in the back of his truck? He admitted that he was Noorzai from Gizab, a tribe that had broadly aligned itself with the Taliban during their reign, but followed up with, "I know nothing."

Graham called in the cell phone numbers that the man had with him to the Special Forces and Australian SAS headquarters back in FOB Ripley. The name he gave, Haji Lala, didn't immediately register on any of our lists, but we knew it was likely an alias. Our headquarters told us to hold him for at least the night to give them a chance to fully query their databases. The Australians came back and suggested that we hold him for the duration of Perth so that he didn't turn around and help the Taliban attack us. The Dutch, however, who were not participating in Operation Perth but monitored our report on the radio, demanded that we immediately hand him over to the local police or release him. When I politely reminded the Dutch officer on the other end of the satellite phone that I operated under different rules of engagement regarding detainees, he informed me that the Dutch Task Force was responsible for security in Uruzgan and that they would not stand for any coalition member holding detainees while they were in charge. He was especially concerned that we would use "American-style" interrogation methods such as waterboarding. I informed him that I did not have the authority to use such techniques and told him he needed to take the matter up with my higher command. Afterward I stopped answering his calls. It was yet another example of how our convoluted command structure played out on a daily basis on the battlefield.

We walked Haji Lala out to the Chora bazaar. No one claimed to know him. There were no local police anywhere to be found, and we were not very interested in keeping him with us for the entire operation. We also knew that at the end of the day, even if we did keep him with us, we did not have enough information to justify processing him to the internment facility at Bagram Airbase. We would have needed confirmed information from multiple sources that he was at least a midlevel commander to justify sending him there. Even then, it was difficult to get a detention justification past the thresholds set by the Detention Board. I knew that, at best, after guarding the guy for the rest of the operation, we would be able to hand him over to the local police in Tarin Kowt or to the notorious Maitullah, commander of the local quasi-legitimate highway police. The local police in Tarin Kowt were likely to demand a bribe from his family or let him go rather than have to feed him. (The provincial judge for Uruzgan apparently lived in Kandahar and came to the province only a few times a year to check on his property.) Handing him to Maitullah would have been the easy thing to do but not the right thing; I had reason to worry about the guy being tortured or simply disappearing altogether. I told Spartacus to tell him he was going to Guantánamo unless he had more information for us. The man's eyes about popped out of his head as Spartacus translated into Pashtu. I then told Graham and Brian that we would probably just let him go the next morning when we pushed farther into the valley.

We spent the rest of the day running dismounted patrols in and around Chora as the Australians and infantry cleared the compounds and trench networks the U.S. Air Force had leveled in the morning. I lay down on my thin foam pad only to be awakened by Graham, who slept with the satellite phone next to his head.

"Sir, just got a call. Something has popped with our 'innocent farmer' Haji Lala there," he said, pointing to the room where we had locked our detainee along with some water, Afghan bread, and a blanket. "CJSOTF has a helicopter coming to get him. It'll be here in fifteen minutes."

Helicopters were a relatively rare commodity in Afghanistan in 2006. Hell, I could rarely get one to support a mission. So for CJSOTF to dispatch one just to pick up a detainee was significant. "Must have been the cell phones," Graham said.

Brian had been waking up periodically to do medical checks on Haji Lala. We had started keeping a medical log, complete with photos, of any Afghans we detained, so that prisoners could not level false accusations of abuse after they were released or when they appeared before the Detention Board in Bagram.

Brian came over to me. "Sir, the guy is shaking like a leaf. He is soaked in sweat. I'm trying to get him to drink water, but I think he is having massive withdrawals without his opium. I don't mind him suffering a little bit, but I think we should just give him some."

"Fine," I replied. "Give him an IV too, if you have to, but only if you really think he needs it. Get him ready to go out to the landing zone. Be sure to send that crate of rounds with him. The intel guys might be able to trace the serial numbers to their origin. I'll bet you my foam sleeping pad those rounds didn't come from some Soviet-era cave."

When the helicopter arrived, Graham walked our detainee to the landing zone. "Guess you get a trip to visit Bagram after all." Then he muttered to no one in particular, "I wonder if they will let him get some Dairy Queen and see the massage lady."

During the next four days caravans of civilians streamed out of the valley to branching side valleys or caves lining the mountains on either side of us, while the Australians, the U.S. infantry, and my team with accompanying UAE Special Operations platoons found ourselves in rolling, sporadic firefights as we sought to clear clusters of Taliban fighters out of the Baluchi Valley. In nearly every contact the insurgents stood their ground and fought to the death. Thank God they could not shoot worth a damn. For over an hour one morning we traded heavy machine gun fire from our hilltop position, now southeast of Cemetery Hill, puffs of smoke appearing as they fired off another round. They were hitting all around us, but we kept displacing so that they could not fix our position and dial us in. They were using the same ploy, as the next puff of smoke would come from a different tree line or roof. They had apparently caught on to our tactics, something we learned from intercepts of their commander telling his men to set up ambushes and be prepared for dismounted patrols we might send from the hills down into the thick orchard trees lining the river. We continued this cat-and-mouse artillery duel until we finally received air cover. The Taliban team went to ground to find a good place to hide.

Several minutes later the satellite phone rang. It was my team sergeant, Marc, who had taken a cell of our guys and embedded with the Czech Special Forces in northeastern Uruzgan. "Dude, if I hear 'Punisher 5-3, troops in contact,' one more damn time on the net I'm gonna be sick. What the hell are you guys doing down there, taking on the Taliban Army?"

The next night the massive crack of a cannon firing again filled the air. I flew off my pad, thinking it was another volley from Taliban recoilless rifles. I stood there in an exhausted daze trying to untangle myself from the bungee cord on my sleeping bag with Brian chuckling at me. He had been on radio watch and told me that the cannon was ours, from the side of an AC-130 gunship. I ran down the road to the compound housing the Australian commander and his staff. Not thinking, I jogged toward the gate until I heard out of the darkness, "Halt!" and saw the shadow of a figure on the roof with his weapon raised.

"Whoa! American, mate!" I yelled up to him while frozen in place and on the verge of a heart attack. He waved me through, and I walked up to the flatbed truck that held rows of radios and served as the Aussie command post. Mark was yelling into the handset that he had received virtually no warning about the hit from the AC-130. The Canadian Special Operations Forces stationed outside Kandahar City had apparently received intelligence that a high-level Taliban commander had moved into the Baluchi Valley to take over the fight and then helicoptered in to kill or capture him. Even though our higher headquarters and the counterterrorism Task Force (to which the Canadians reported) were both located at Bagram Airbase, word had obviously not reached Mark until the last minute. Not surprisingly, the problem stemmed from the disjointed chains of command in Afghanistan, even between the relatively small numbers of Special Operations Forces.

"That compound is only a kilometer from my position. We could have practically walked there!" Mark yelled into the handset. "Why the hell are the damn Canadians heloing in from Kandahar? What the hell are they going to do that we can't do? I have had to halt all operations tonight because of this mission and this is my operational battle space!"

Mark's commander up at Bagram explained over the radio that intelligence indicated al Qaeda–linked foreign fighters had moved into the area with the Taliban commander to advise them on the battle. As a result the mission was handed off to the separate Task Force command that solely dealt with counterterrorism raids. Mark threw the handset back at the radio and walked away.

I knew something was wrong as I leaned against an Aussie Range Rover and listened to the radio chatter. The Canadians ended up getting pinned down to the point where it was too dangerous for their helicopters to come back in and get them. The fighting in the distance sounded ferocious. In a bit of irony the Aussies were then requested to launch a quick-reaction force to go extract them. Then they too got pinned down by heavy fire. The AC-130 gunship fired round after round from its 120 millimeter cannon and sent streams of shells from its 20 millimeter

Gatling guns that looked like green death lasers coming from the sky in a science fiction movie. I was stunned when I heard the gunship call "Winchester" over the radio. The AC-130 had an entire cargo hull full of ammunition for its cannon and mini-guns. "Winchester" meant the gunship had gone through all of it. None of us had ever heard of that happening. Whoever was still fighting after weathering that onslaught of fire meant business.

By this time the UAE platoons and my operators were sitting in our vehicles, engines running, waiting on the call. For the first time in the deployment I prayed it wouldn't come. Of course we would do anything it took to go help our Aussie and Canadian brothers, but rolling into a vicious firefight in the middle of the night with two other elements already heavily engaged was a disaster waiting to happen. When we added the language barrier, I was exponentially more afraid of fratricide from the Canadians and Aussies than anything the Talibs or al Qaeda could throw at us. It seemed as though half the U.S. Air Force arrived overhead with the withdrawal of the gunship, until both the Aussie and Canadian elements were able to extract themselves on the ground. Somehow they sustained only six wounded and no killed between them. The next morning I saw one of the Australian Bushmaster vehicles, which looked like an armored personnel carrier out of a *Mad Max* movie. We counted forty-nine bullet holes in it. I found out later that the lack of coordination between the Canadian and Australian units in the midst of the fight and conflicting guidance from their separate chains of command had been a huge issue. I thanked God again that we had not been dragged into the mess.

With no rest for the weary, we again came into contact first thing the next morning. Now, however, the previous day's and night's events had apparently made us the priority in theater for close air support. Bravo Company pushed southwest down the valley on the eastern side of the river, with the Aussies pushing down the western side, and the UAE and my team still playing cat and mouse with the Taliban recoilless rifle team and cleaning up pockets of fighters that had been bypassed. At one point we listened as the Aussie sniper teams on the long ridgeline overlooking the entire valley reported four Hilux pickup trucks barreling up the valley in the direction of the infantry. The trucks were too far away for the snipers to engage, so they called in two Dutch Apache attack helicopters.

The pilots reported back that they could not see weapons with the men in the trucks and therefore could not engage under Dutch rules. They could fire only if they saw men with weapons performing a hostile act. I thought the Australian sniper was going to come unglued as he and the pilots debated over the radio whether the men were armed. "I can damn well see the AK-47s hanging out the window!" he was screaming over the radio. In the end the Apaches left the area without firing a shot.

About thirty minutes later the Bravo Company commander called to say that he was in contact with fifteen to twenty insurgents. We heard an explosion of gunfire and the captain quickly began calling in casualties. First, there were several wounded. Minutes later he called up an American KIA. The radio chatter went silent for what seemed like an eternity as the entire Task Force absorbed the news. We later found out the American KIA was Staff Sgt. Robert Chiomento. He was from New Jersey and had two daughters. I remembered meeting him before we left FOB Ripley for Chora and thinking he was the spitting image of an infantry squad leader. The radio burst back to life with an Aussie commando on the net. We could barely hear him as he tried to yell over the gunfire in the background. The commandos had tried to cross the river at a low point to flank the insurgents fighting Bravo Company and ran into a volley of RPGs. A rocket landed at the feet of one of the Aussie commando squads and they were reporting several wounded.

Mark called up and asked that we deploy a quick-reaction force to cover his commandos while they pulled back. The entire Task Force was painfully aware that these Taliban fighters were almost certainly the same group of armed men that the Australian sniper had observed barreling toward us and that the Dutch pilots had refused to engage. In our war of consensus, everyone was ultimately beholden to their national caveats and rules rather than the coalition.

The Aussies had a dozen men wounded from the RPG volley, and Bravo Company was consolidating to evacuate their wounded as well. My two GMVs, followed by three UAE Panhards, charged down the road toward the gunfire. As we rounded a corner to our left and headed downhill into the wadi, a stream of green machine gun tracer fire flew across the front of my windshield, causing Hamad to career off the road and into an irrigation ditch. We slammed to a halt and my head crashed into the truck's metal dashboard. The Panhards pulled up past us on the road and started lighting up the compound that was the source of the machine gun fire. Another burst spat out from the tree line to the left of the compound, and the Panhards shifted fire, seemingly silencing it. Meanwhile Trip, our weapons sergeant who was in the GMV behind us, and Hamad hooked a towline to the back of our truck to get us out of the ditch.

I climbed up onto the roof of a nearby two-story mud hut, which gave me a great view of the valley and the unfolding fight. A Dutch Air Force tactical air controller climbed up the wood ladder behind me and onto the roof. I had no idea where he had come from but assumed he had followed us down the road. He was red-faced and embarrassed at the inaction of his Apache pilots. With our binoculars we could see two men lying behind a PKM machine gun on the roof of a compound across the wadi while men darted among the trees toward the commandos consolidating at the foot of a small concrete bridge. The Aussie snipers on the far ridgeline confirmed the same thing through their long-range optics.

"Do you see that? The Talibs are lying down in a support-by-fire position and are covering their buddies while they are trying to flank the Aussies!" I said to Trip, who had climbed up to the roof with us.

"Yeah, those guys are maneuvering like a well-trained Ranger platoon. These are not your average farmer-turned-Talib. Someone has been training these boys on light infantry tactics," Trip replied.

"All right, brother, that is definitely hostile intent, so let's take them out before they can open up," I told the Dutch air controller.

"I'm not bothering with our Apaches," he snorted. "We have other assets on station."

In a perfect British accent he then worked his magic with the aircraft overhead, identifying the location of the commandos, identifying our location, and vectoring an F-16 onto the enemy machine gun position. About a minute later a big, gray cloud of smoke exploded in the air above the trees where the men were maneuvering, and the house disappeared.

"Got the dismounts with an airburst bomb," he said, looking up from his radio and smiling. By setting the ordnance to airburst, he caused the fragments to rain down like a massive shotgun blast, ideal for attacking enemy soldiers in the open.

After we treated the wounded Australians, we pressed forward down the valley to the sight of the bombing. Slowly and deliberately we crept on foot through the abandoned clusters of compounds and fields leading to the site. It was eerily quiet as the sun dipped below the mountains, casting a long shadow across the valley. My interpreter, Spartacus, about jumped out of his skin on seeing the dead Taliban. "Those are not Pashtuns," he whispered. "They are Pakistanis!"

"How do you know?" I whispered back.

"Look at them! Can't you tell? They are Punjabi." He was referring to the dominant ethnic group comprising the Pakistani Army and intelligence service. "Look at them. All the way here in Uruzgan! We are a thousand kilometers from the border. I bet they are Pakistani ISI intelligence officers. ISI in the center of Afghanistan! I told you they are trying to take us over!" He was shaking his head as he stood in the middle of the group of bodies. "Well, that would explain why they appeared so well trained," I said.

The men did look different. All of them were a little darker, with black mustaches instead of the beards men almost universally sported in this part of Afghanistan. The bodies were dirty but relatively untouched. Each had blood coming from his ears and eyes due to the shock wave from the airburst bomb. I carefully disarmed each of them and searched their pockets for material to hand off to the intelligence teams. One had bandoliers of machine gun ammunition wrapped around his chest in an X pattern, as though he had watched too many *Rambo* movies. Another had an old Russian Makarov 6 millimeter pistol in a chest harness. Another had a small book of doodles and an address book full of phone numbers. We counted seven bodies, and I knew there were at least two more in the pile of rubble that used to be the house with the enemy machine gun team on the roof. I felt reasonably certain that no civilians were in the house, as the entire valley seemed deserted at this point. A pile of RPG rounds was stacked nearby, but we could not find the launcher. The rounds all looked fairly new, with their olive drab paint barely scratched. Each rocket had the safety pin to its warhead pulled, meaning they were armed. They looked almost too perfect, as though left there so that someone would pick them up. Though suspicious, I couldn't leave them for the Taliban to recover and use against us later. I slowly felt around each RPG round for some type of booby trap. Eventually I felt comfortable enough to pick them up and take them back to our patrol base.

I downloaded all of the pictures of the dead insurgents onto the Australian intelligence officer's hard drive after we caught up with Mark's command team. After a few minutes on a secure line, he came back to say he had uploaded them to send to CJSOTF. They later called back to indicate they also believed the men were Pakistani, that several of the phone numbers were of Pakistani origin, and that this was the farthest into Afghanistan that insurgents of Pakistani origin had been identified. He also told me that initial reporting on the new, still-boxed recoilless rifle rounds indicated that their serial numbers were likely of Iranian origin.

"Well, isn't that special, mate," Mark said, smiling. "Iran's showing us the same kind of love they are showing your boys in Iraq."

The fighting around Cemetery Hill, the death the previous night of a second significant Taliban commander, and now the loss of this cluster of men seemed to take the fight out of the Taliban. Several of our interpreters found the channel the Taliban used on their walkie-talkies and heard one man crying as he reported that everyone in his group was dead. Another said he was trapped and was asking what to do. After a while our interpreters started their own psychological campaign and began telling them that they had no hope of winning and should go home. Spartacus launched into a speech on the Taliban net about how the senior Taliban commanders were hiding in Pakistan and were too afraid to come to Afghanistan to fight with them. A number of us, including the Australian intelligence officer and the commander, were convinced that these guys were a long way from home. These were not your average home-grown fighters carrying out the orders of the local mullah. They had not been supplied by the local tribal elder who was forced at gunpoint to send some men with the local Taliban commander. They obviously had small unit tactics training from somewhere, were highly motivated to stand and fight, and were well equipped with new weapons and lots of ammunition.

The next day civilians and villagers started streaming back in to the valley from the mountains. It was as though someone had put up a giant neon billboard announcing, "The Taliban Are Gone!" We had no idea how they got the word. But sure enough, we didn't receive another shot in anger. Though the Aussies and the infantry had, by far, borne the brunt of the fighting in Operation Perth, I felt like I was at the end of my rope. We had encountered no hostile contact the entire winter of 2005 and 2006. But since my machine gun–versus-pistol duel in the Tagab Valley, we had been in contact during nearly every mission in the past four months. I think it was partly the isolation that was getting to me. With the exception of Operation Perth, I rarely had more than two or three other Americans with me, and if something happened to two of us or, worse, if something bad happened to our medic Brian, our chances of surviving were slim to none.

That afternoon I sat on radio watch and listened as the Special Forces team up at FOB Cobra in the northwest of the province pushed up north of the firebase into Char China District in the extreme northwest of the province. Cobra had two teams stationed there, and both had taken over 50 percent casualties and several KIA by this point in the tour. As I sat in the turret getting my night-vision goggles ready for my guard shift, I heard one of the teams call in a frantic "Troops in contact" and that they had a man down. I remember thinking how odd the call was. The sun had just set. We had a tremendous advantage at night, with our night vision and the infrared laser systems on our weapons. Even if the Taliban had initiated an ambush just before dark, the odds of their hitting something were very low unless they had somehow snuck up very close to the team.

Another operator came on the radio. This time I could hear the adrenaline in his voice. He said they were receiving sniper fire and called a second man down. A few minutes later he called in the first man as KIA. The net went silent. He then read out the dead man's battle-roster number, which consisted of the first initial of his last name and the last four of his social security number. The battle-roster system allowed us to identify a casualty without broadcasting the last name all over theater on the SATCOM. One of the team's medics then came up on the net and called in that the unit had sustained head shots to two turret gunners while the vehicles had been stopped and completely blacked out.

"Damn!" Trip said as he walked up to relieve me on guard duty. "Those bastards must have acquired some night vision to be able to make two head shots at night. Maybe that legendary Chechen sniper team isn't a myth after all. That is bad, bad juju if they have that kind of equipment."

A series of sniper attacks around the region had occurred over the summer fighting season. Down in Kandahar two Canadian soldiers had been shot from outside earshot, indicating a truly long-range sniper shot. One man had been hit in the pelvic region, just below his body armor. The other had been hit in the neck. A sort of urban legend had developed that an al Qaeda–affiliated Chechen sniper team was responsible for the shots. At least we thought it was an urban legend.

We both stood there as the team's medic came on the net every few minutes calling in the wounded man's vitals. His pulse and blood pressure were getting lower and lower. We heard the team's captain asking when the hell the medevac helicopter was arriving. He was told it was en route. After about ten minutes the team called up the man as KIA and reported that they were aborting the mission and returning to base. I found out later that there was some confusion back at Kandahar Airfield about a coalition unit that was supposed to send the medevac helicopter. We were certain that neither man would have survived his wounds regardless of how slowly the medevac responded. But the incident was yet one more piece of evidence that fighting in a place as complex and difficult as Afghanistan was hard enough and that trying to do so by coordinating such a large coalition was a recipe for failure.

The next morning we got up to head back to base. We were exhausted. One of my men, who will remain nameless, accidently grabbed a water can instead of a gas can and poured the entire contents into our gas tank. Everyone was ready to return to base and here we were flushing water out of our engine. It was pretty embarrassing, but we finally got the GMV to start. I became worried that, in our tired state, the next mistake would cost us more than our pride.

The UAE platoon and our two vehicles pushed out to the northern flank of the elements moving through the Baluchi pass and angling back toward Tarin Kowt. The ridgelines on both sides of the valley narrowed at the pass, forcing us into a bit of a funnel as the Panhard leading our column dipped down into a wadi. The dry riverbed was very sandy and rocky at the bottom, and the Panhard became stuck for a moment as it attempted to ascend the other side. Hamad slowed our descent into the wadi to maintain our spacing. The turret gunner in the Panhard was hanging over the back of the vehicle to get a look at the back tires while the driver was gunning the engine. I'll never forget the look on the turret gunner's face as he looked up at us wide-eyed while he frantically motioned for us to stop and screamed, "Kef! Kef!" (*stop* in Arabic). Hamad hit the brakes hard. The Panhard's tires had perfectly straddled a large beige antitank mine and the exhaust had blown the sand and gravel off part of it.

"Back up! Back up!" I yelled. I didn't know if it was a standard pressure-activated mine or a remotely wired IED that a triggerman could be attempting to set off. The turret gunner in the Panhard practically flew out of the turret and ran away from the vehicle. Both the driver and the vehicle commander also bailed out the side doors.

"Not too far," I said to Hamad. "Our jammer might be what is preventing a triggerman from sending an ignition signal."

"Commander Mike, we have some chatter," Spartacus said from the backseat, holding his walkie-talkie. He was still scanning the known Taliban frequencies. "They are talking about us. Someone is watching us. He sounds like the triggerman. Another guy is yelling at him to do it!"

We looked at the string of cave openings in the ridge to our right. It was likely the only place he could be while staying within range for an electronic trigger device such as a garage door opener or key fob.

"Graham, open up on that bastard. He has to be up in one of those caves," I yelled. I was pissed, and I wanted him dead.

I heard the turret ring sliding to the right, and the .50 caliber machine gun started thumping in four- to six-round bursts. Pretty soon the whole line of vehicles behind us was firing heavy machine guns and grenade launchers at those caves. The openings exploded in a cloud of dust and sparks. At this point I think everyone was just venting more than actually expecting to hit anything. The chatter on the radio went silent. We weren't sure if we had killed the triggerman and eventually placed explosives on the landmine to blow it in place.

For some reason the close call with the IED really rattled me. I wasn't sure why. The guys in the Panhard sitting on top of the mine had a much closer call than we did. The mine was powerful enough to destroy a tank and would definitely have obliterated either the Panhard or our GMV. For the first time during the entire tour, I was ready to just get back to the base and go home. No more missions. No more cups of tea with elders, convincing them that we were there to help their children see a better future. No more firefights. I wanted to see my family again.

Unfortunately, Operation Perth was typical of many operations ongoing in Afghanistan at the time. We cleared the Taliban out of the Baluchi Valley. We killed a lot of them. Estimates cobbled together from the various units and from the locals put a body count at approximately 150, including two midlevel operational commanders and, apparently, several Pakistanis. The combined coalition operation had one KIA and fourteen wounded. Body count was an obvious loser as a metric for success. And the fact was we never really knew for sure whom we were fighting or why they were fighting us. We were ignorant of the tribal and local sociopolitical dynamics at play. We didn't know if we were fighting insurgents who had commuted into Afghanistan from Pakistani madrassas or homegrown members of the Noorzai tribe who associated the coalition with the abuses of former governor Jan Mohammad Khan. I became convinced that it was a healthy mix of both. At an operational level the total lack of a stay-behind force really frustrated me. I felt strongly about having the Afghan Army in the lead, or at least trailing closely behind us, to hold certain key locations after we left. We were clearing areas the Taliban had controlled, but there was no "hold" at all and therefore few lasting effects from the operation. This was primarily because each member of the coalition had separate chains of command and separate operational approaches to counterinsurgency, ranging from the Australians' mission to find and attack the Taliban to the Dutch focus on protecting their reconstruction efforts in their two "ink spot" areas. The ANA had opted out, and it was still unclear whether the police we had reinstated were doing more harm than good. Fortunately, the United States and UAE had agreed to help. Otherwise the Aussies would have been on their own to deal with the entrenched Taliban in Baluchi.

On the plus side, Operation Perth did take some pressure off Tarin Kowt, and Governor Monib in particular. A technocrat seemingly dedicated to improving governance in the province, he was desperately trying to slowly displace Jan Mohammad's cronies and attract better district governors and line representatives from the various ministries in Kabul to deliver basic services to the people. Striking a blow against the Taliban in Operation Perth bought some time for Monib for the winter of 2006–7. It sent a message that the insurgency could not deny the Afghan government access to entire valleys. The police responsible for Chora reoccupied the district center in the fall. But these were temporary gains. Perth did little to address the underlying problems of longtime tribal discord and disenfranchisement resulting from a lack of security by the Karzai government and the coalition. Unfortunately, operations like Perth were all too common. There were simply not enough foreign and Afghan troops to go around, and the war by consensus made it impossible to make the best use of the troops we did have.

8 Back to Washington
The Pentagon and the White House

In late 2006 I was back in coat and tie at the Pentagon, having been asked to serve as a country director for Afghanistan in the Middle East bureau of the Office of the Secretary of Defense–Policy. I was pleased to find some growing awareness in OSD-Policy of the worsening situation in Afghanistan. However, I also found many of my colleagues increasingly frustrated. Even though our senior leaders recognized the growing problem, the default response was to turn to the Europeans to do more. Washington and the Pentagon were in the depths of the debate over Iraq—namely whether to get our forces completely out or to double down on the war with a surge in troop levels. With Afghanistan we had basically outsourced the war to NATO in order to focus our resources on Iraq.

Still I would spend the next two years in the Pentagon and the White House trying to convince our policymakers that the situation in Afghanistan had taken a turn for the worse and that our European NATO allies were in over their heads despite the brave efforts of their soldiers. I was also determined to make the case that U.S. participation in the war was rudderless, that Pakistan had made a strategic shift against our interests, that Afghan governance was often doing more harm than good, and as a result the United States needed to devote significantly more resources to stabilize the situation. The issue of resources was the crux of the matter. Even if Secretary Rumsfeld, our military commanders, and the White House had fully appreciated the extent of the worsening situation, the prevailing feeling in policy circles was that there was little we could do about it. If Afghanistan needed more international support, NATO would have to provide it. With Iraq dragging on much longer than anticipated and massively straining our military, few wanted to even contemplate having to add more U.S. troops to an effort believed to be already won. Afghanistan needed to remain a success story for the administration.

The departure of Donald Rumsfeld and the arrival of Robert Gates as defense secretary in late 2006 brought an opportunity for new thinking on Afghanistan. The term *counterinsurgency* was controversial in Rumsfeld's Pentagon for a number of reasons, primarily because doctrinally it required significantly more troops and resources to properly execute a counterinsurgency campaign. This was particularly the case in a place as isolated and difficult as Afghanistan. When Gates came on board we immediately sensed a shift toward openness to more troops for Afghanistan. I accompanied Secretary Gates as part of his delegation on his first trip to see the war, in January 2007. The various commanders he visited stressed the tremendous surge in violence during the previous fighting season and NATO's struggle to meet its commitments. They also lamented the peace deal the Pakistani government had recently signed with insurgent groups in their Federally Administered Tribal Areas, which created a huge problem for NATO's efforts in Afghanistan. In fact, one officer reported that attacks in the border provinces on the Afghan side were up 300 percent. An intelligence officer at ISAF headquarters ran through statistics on insurgent attacks in Afghanistan: 139 suicide attacks in 2006, up from twenty-seven in 2005, and the number of attacks with IEDs had more than doubled, from 783 in 2005 to 1,677 in 2006; the number of direct attacks (by insurgents using small arms) spiked from 1,558 in 2005 to 4,542 in 2006.[1]

Maj. Gen. Ben Freakley, the American commander of the Combined Joint Task Force for Regional Command East out of Bagram Airbase, was refreshingly frank with the secretary about the level of violence he was expecting in 2007 and the lack of resources he had to deal with it. He insisted that he needed more troops to have a chance at blunting the expected Taliban spring offensive. The following month Gates authorized an additional combat brigade to be diverted from Iraq to Afghanistan. This doubled the number of conventional combat brigades devoted to the war. I was thrilled. However, the increase was only from one brigade to two.

In Washington the importance of an issue is often reflected by the size of the bureaucracy devoted to it. Afghanistan and Pakistan were no exceptions. While the Iraq team in the Middle East bureau of OSD-

Policy occupied nearly half the bureau's office space with over a dozen personnel, the Afghanistan team consisted of three civil servants. Fortunately, they were some of the sharpest people I've had the pleasure of working with. But none of them had extensive time on the ground in Afghanistan. Even worse, our Pakistan team consisted of one civil servant who was completely overwhelmed by the workload and consistently frustrated with the Pakistanis. Fortunately she had a wonderful sense of humor and a great intellect. This imbalance between policy civilians dedicated to Iraq compared to Afghanistan and Pakistan was consistent throughout our national security bureaucracy, from the State Department to the Joint Staff and the National Security Council.

Making matters worse was the fractured nature of the bureaucracy and the number of offices and organizations that had a piece of our Afghan policy. On a summer afternoon in 2007 the new assistant secretary of defense for Asia, Jim Shinn, who had taken over responsibility for Afghanistan from the Middle East bureau during a reorganization of Policy, called me up to his office. As I walked in Jim was sitting on his office sofa, leaning over a PowerPoint slide that indicated who reported to whom on various topics regarding Afghanistan.

"Mike, try to explain this to me, please," he said with a smirk.

"Well, sir, I hope you have more than a few minutes. Let's start from Afghanistan and work our way back to Washington." I went on to explain the multiple chains of command I had experienced in the field on my recent tour, between the Europeans, the conventional U.S. units, two different Special Operations Forces Task Forces, and the embedded trainers. He was incredulous. He was even more surprised to hear how dysfunctional the policymaking apparatus was back in Washington. I explained that the ISAF commanding general in Kabul reported through a German four-star general in Brunssum (whose headquarters was left over from the cold war and had added little value to the war effort in Afghanistan) to the four-star NATO headquarters in Brussels. Even though NATO was commanded by an American general, he reported to the decision-making body for the alliance, where the United States had just one of twenty-six votes and all major decisions had to be unanimous. Further, Afghanistan often competed for agenda space at the meetings of NATO member nations with a number of items, such as missile defense and antipiracy initiatives.

Separately the U.S. military units (Special Operations Forces and the embedded training teams) still under Operation Enduring Freedom reported back through Central Command to the Joint Staff and our offices in OSD-Policy. Worse still, policy oversight of the major strategic pieces of the war—the Afghan National Security Forces, our Special Operations Forces, NATO, and functional issues like counternarcotics and detainee issues—fell under four different assistant secretaries of defense in the Pentagon.

"It's really problematic because the various aspects of our policy toward Afghanistan and Pakistan don't come together until it reaches the undersecretary, who, as you know, is kind of busy dealing with Iraq, North Korea, Iran, and the rest of the world," I said, exasperated, as I tried to walk through the slides. "The problem is the same in the Joint Staff, and it proves to be maddeningly difficult to be able to get everyone with a policy stake in Afghanistan into the same room inside the Pentagon, much less across the U.S. government."

An accomplished entrepreneur, Princeton professor, and former national intelligence officer for Asia, Jim spent an hour with me trying to grasp the logic behind the series of slides depicting the various reporting chains. Finally he exclaimed, "Who the hell thought to organize a war effort this way, the Taliban? If our enemies were to cook up a command structure for us, this would be it!" We knew we had to attempt to simplify it but also knew that taking on the myriad generals and policy officials with a stake in the war would be an uphill battle. We spent the next two years trying.

The chaotic command situation and lack of U.S. resources was exacerbated by the revolving door of staff and commanders in the field and, with their rotations, the constant loss of institutional knowledge. It wasn't anyone's fault but rather a structural flaw in the makeup of our post–Vietnam-era armed forces. Afghanistan and Iraq were the first wars in American history of significant length to be fought in their entirety with an all-volunteer force. In the past, military-age men were drafted and typically deployed to the combat zone until they were either victorious or became casualties. With the volunteer force, units were rotated for stints, typically six to twelve months, in order to minimize the amount of time soldiers spent away from home and to maintain retention levels.

Unfortunately this resulted in constant rotations to the war zone, re-learning the same lessons, and repeating the same mistakes. By the time a unit truly understood the complicated tribal and geographic dynamics in their assigned areas, they would be getting ready to hand off to a new unit, which would start the learning curve over again. The churn was replicated from platoon leaders up to field commanders and policy staff in the Pentagon. Our structures and rotations meant we maintained little institutional knowledge, while the insurgent, who often spent his entire life in the same area, watched and waited for the next group to arrive.

At my desk in the Pentagon in 2007 I was dismayed to read reports on Operation Troy, a good example of our lack of operational continuity. Troy was a coalition operation to defend the Chora district center in Uruzgan Province against being overrun, the same district center we had liberated in Operation Perth. Since I had left Afghanistan the previous fall, the Dutch battle group had expanded its numbers to approximately 1,400 and now included Chora in its ink-spot strategy, along with Tarin Kowt and Deh Rawood. In June 2007 Taliban fighters overran checkpoints guarding the road between Tarin Kowt and Chora as well as the road in the Baluchi Valley—the very same road we had cleared in 2006. The Taliban mutilated several policemen and killed family members of other policemen who escaped the attack. The Afghan Army company still apparently refused to deploy troops outside of its garrison in Tarin Kowt. During the heavy fighting the Dutch began firing artillery blindly into suspected enemy positions in civilian homes. The resulting civilian deaths caused an uproar in the Dutch Parliament and triggered an ISAF investigation into the incident. It was nearly a year to the day since Operation Perth, and it seemed as though few if any of the lessons learned from the previous year had been captured. I even read a report that a Dutch element struck an IED exactly where I nearly hit one with my UAE platoon. I had passed the grid coordinates up my Special Forces chain, but the information didn't migrate over to the Dutch unit under the separate ISAF chain of command a year later. Plus the Australian, Dutch, and American Special Forces command teams had completely changed since my time there. Operation Troy was nearly a mirror image of Perth.

Rather than fighting a war with cumulative gains and effects that built on previous operations, it was more apparent to me than ever that we were repeating the same operations and the same mistakes year after year, resulting in the growing exhaustion of Afghan, American, and European popular support for the war. By 2007, rather than fighting one six-year war, with efforts that built on each other, it seemed as though we had fought six one-year wars over and over.

Layered on the constant rotations, complicated command-and-control structure, and insufficient resources was the lack of a coherent civil-military plan. In the run-up to the final transition of security responsibility to NATO-ISAF, Mary Beth Long, then the principal deputy assistant secretary of defense with responsibility for the Middle East and NATO, repeatedly asked her staff and every European general that visited the Pentagon when ISAF was going to develop a campaign plan for the war. Gen. David Richards, the first ISAF commander, took charge of the war effort and developed a plan based on classic counterinsurgency theory, which called for Afghan Development Zones. Similar to the Dutch strategy in Uruzgan, it involved an ink-spot approach based around Afghanistan's major urban areas in each region. In theory the Development Zones would allow the coalition to concentrate its efforts, protect the population where it was most concentrated, and provide a somewhat standard conceptual approach to the insurgency across the dozens of troop contributors. The plan quickly ran into the limitations of ISAF's operational control over its members. For the plan to be effective, Richards needed the ISAF contributors to shift their forces and development dollars away from their current efforts and concentrate them on the Development Zones. This never really happened in a meaningful way. To the extent resources were diverted to the Development Zones, the plan ran into the same problems as the Dutch approach in that it created haves and have-nots in the eyes of the Afghans along urban/rural and tribal lines and exacerbated their zero-sum mentality.

The plan reminded me of a story an Afghan elder in Uruzgan had told me about an NGO providing a well to a village. "A well-meaning NGO built a well in a village of the Popalzai tribe," he said. "It was a wonderful well that brought clean water to the entire village. Before this time the villagers carried their drinking water up to the village from the river, and people were often sick. The elders from the village across the river, from the Noorzai tribe, saw this new well and asked the NGO for a well in their village. The NGO apologized and said they could not build it right then, but that they would have more money the next year. Rather than waiting for the several months to see if the NGO would keep its promise, the Noorzai destroyed the Popalzai well! This is the way in Afghanistan sometimes. We cannot have our rivals doing better than us."

The nearest we had come to a comprehensive strategy by the middle of 2007 was Lt. Gen. David Barno's campaign plan that he had crafted as the commander of Combined Forces Command–Afghanistan in 2004. I still had a worn copy on my desk, with its multiple lines of operation across diplomatic, information, military, and economic sectors. History had proven its grossly optimistic timelines, including a prediction that the Afghan National Army would be independently operating by 2008 and that provincial reconstruction teams would transition to Afghan leadership by 2007. But at least it laid out some objectives, a strategy to achieve them, and the needed resources. Barno's dated campaign plan and the Afghan National Development Strategy were the only two strategy documents of which I was aware. There was no overarching U.S. government campaign plan that brought together and focused our defense, intelligence, diplomatic, and development efforts. Certainly nothing of the sort had come from NATO.

Yet, in the policy debates in the Pentagon and Washington, it seemed as though nearly every official between the president and me was determined to affect change in Afghanistan by changing the political will of our NATO allies and strong-arming them to provide the resources they had pledged. In November 2006 NATO held its summit in Riga, Latvia. Heads of state attended, including President Bush, and the top item on the agenda was NATO's assumption of security responsibility for Afghanistan the previous month. President Bush pressed his counterparts to remove their national caveats and start sending their troops into the conflict-ridden southern part of the country. Prior to the summit, Gen. Jim Jones, NATO's supreme allied commander in Europe, British prime minister Tony Blair, and NATO's secretary-general Jaap De Hoop Scheffer called for more reinforcements in the south, but their requests were rebuffed. Germany, France, Turkey, Italy, and Spain politely but firmly rejected calls to send their own soldiers to support British, Canadian, and Dutch forces in the south on the grounds that the situation was too dangerous and that they were "overstretched." Small countries such as Poland and Denmark stepped forward, offering a thousand additional soldiers, including five hundred paratroopers. The rejections seemed to solidify divisions within the ISAF coalition, with the "fighting allies" in the south and east and the "nonfighting allies" in the north and west.[2]

I thought it was a mistake to put the president's credibility on the line after we knew through lower level meetings that there was no way the allies in northern and western Afghanistan were sending their troops to the more volatile areas in the south and east. For the German government to publicly say they were at war in Afghanistan was extremely controversial in Berlin and ran contrary to its post–World War II laws. Personally, I didn't think it was a good idea for the Germans and Italians to go to the south even if they would agree to do so. I had seen firsthand during my previous deployment how much our allies had atrophied militarily after cutting their defense budgets at the end of the cold war. I also witnessed how differently they approached counterinsurgency tactics and strategy. As with the French Special Forces, there was a great deal of frustration among their rank and file, who wanted to get out to the Afghan countryside, engage the enemy, protect the populace, and provide enough security for development and reconstruction projects to flourish. Their hands were tied by political considerations, and they were unable to execute the offensive missions that counterinsurgency sometimes requires. Moving these forces to the south with the heavy national restrictions they had in place would have just led to more unmet expectations and disappointment among the Afghans.

Through the rest of 2007, at several meetings of NATO defense ministers, Secretary Gates pressed again and again for our European allies to provide the number of forces they had pledged, to apply them to the most difficult areas, and to drop their caveats. The requests fell on deaf ears. Eventually fed up with European intransigence, Gates threatened to pull U.S. helicopters out of the peacekeeping mission in Bosnia and Kosovo to satisfy an unfilled helicopter requirement in southern Afghanistan. The NATO office in the Pentagon vehemently disagreed and sent the secretary a lengthy memo on why such a move would be disastrous to our commitment to the Alliance. My office refused to concur with the memo. We thought the secretary's threat was the right course. We even created a policy office solely dedicated to managing the coalition in Afghanistan (and the much smaller one in Iraq). A number of smaller countries, particularly in Eastern Europe, seeking favor with the Bush administration on issues such as missile defense or entry into NATO, committed a handful of support soldiers to get political credit as ISAF. For example, Estonia contributed one hundred, Hungary two hundred, Macedonia 125, and Slovenia seventy.[3] All four countries were relatively recently accepted members of NATO, and several wanted to do more directly with the United States.

At one of the summits I attended as a member of Secretary Gates's delegation, the Slovakian representative announced additional forces to serve in Uruzgan Province. "This will bring Slovakia's troop contribution in Afghanistan to 125 in 2008," the minister said proudly.

"I encourage all allies and partners to contribute as much as they can, especially in support of our efforts in Afghanistan," Gates told the ministers.[4]

My own view differed regarding recruiting as many nations as possible to contribute troops to ISAF, even in very small numbers. The policy placed a tremendous burden on our logistics capability and equipment resources in return for minor operational benefits. The mixing bowl of nations that were providing instruction with little uniformity also confused the Afghans. During one of my visits as a civilian to the Combined Security Transition Command (CSTC-A), a predominantly U.S. organization responsible for the training and equipping of the Afghan National Army, I encountered several American officers and sergeants charged with training the Europeans to train the Afghans. They all complained bitterly that the European embedded trainers for the Afghan Army were arriving with incompatible radios, limited or no night vision, and no real ability to support themselves in the field. I spoke to a group of U.S. Army majors and lieutenant colonels who told me that the time and effort it took for U.S. soldiers to get those teams ready, as well as the logistics requirements for supporting them, was not worth the gain. One pointed out, "We have thirty-six U.S. soldiers tied down here on the base trying to get two NATO embedded training teams of twelve men each ready to go. They showed up here with literally nothing. No vehicles, no jammers, no heavy or light machine guns or radios. We could have the same thirty-six U.S. soldiers out with the Afghans rather than sitting back here training twenty-four Europeans." Another major put things more bluntly: "Sir, this makes no sense. Is our mission in Afghanistan to train the Afghans or the Europeans?"

Eventually Gen. Dan McNeill, the ISAF commander, agreed. During a videoconference with Secretary Gates, he said, "Please, no more flags sir," referring to the map of Afghanistan up on the screen dotted with dozens of flags representing contributors to the ISAF coalition. "Unless it's a critical capability like helicopter support, we don't need every country on the map sending a dozen soldiers on four-month rotations so they can tell you that they have contributed to the war when you visit their capital. Seems as though they often want a concession from the U.S. on some other issue and send a platoon to Afghanistan as a bargaining tool. If I can be frank, Mr. Secretary, it's become more of a burden than it's worth to us out here."

The entire endeavor fed into the overarching narrative that Afghanistan had to be successful for NATO to remain relevant. During a 2007 interagency review of the war effort, an Air Force colonel working in the European bureau of the State Department summed up this view: "Look, though ISAF is facing real challenges in Afghanistan this fighting season, overall the effort has been really good for NATO. It's keeping them relevant. It's forced them to go global and shown them how difficult it is to be expeditionary. It's also shown them that they really are not as interoperable as many nations thought they were. Most important, it's shown the European capitals that they need to increase their defense budgets. I think we need to be careful, however, not to push them too hard diplomatically on not meeting their commitments. Frankly, their governments might just get frustrated and leave Afghanistan, and that would not be good for the Alliance."

The U.S. effort was not without criticism either, from our own convoluted chain of command at every level to how we were measuring success. Secretary Gates held a videoconference every three to five weeks with his senior commanders. The screen at the far end of the conference room in the basement of the Pentagon was split six ways, to accommodate video feeds from the commander of ISAF, Gen. Dan McNeill; the commander of Central Command, Adm. William Fallon; the commander of NATO, Gen. Bantz Craddock; the commander of CSTC-A, Maj. Gen. Robert Cone; and the commander of Regional Command East, who doubled as the senior American in theater, Maj. Gen. David Rodriguez. Each man had a unique role and separate chain of command in theater.

The fact that we had to have multiple American commanders from two regional combatant commands on the screen was an apt visual representation of the command-and-control problem within the U.S. effort. It was a stark contrast to the previous thirty minutes, spent with the Iraq team. In that session there were only two faces on the screen, Gen. David Petraeus's and Admiral Fallon's.

Also in these meetings were the deputy assistant secretary of defense for Afghanistan, Pakistan, and Central Asia, Mitch Shivers; the assistant secretary for Asia, Jim Shinn; the deputy assistant secretary with responsibility for NATO, Dan Fata; the undersecretary for policy, Eric Edelman; and representatives from the Joint Staff. My job was to follow up on any tasks from the secretary.

After reports from each of the generals listing the series of operations ongoing and numbers of Afghan National Army trained, the secretary seemed increasingly frustrated. With his microphone turned off so that only those in the room could hear him, he remarked that, almost a year into the job, he still found it incredible that the ISAF commander, though an American general, didn't technically report to him because he was in a NATO billet reporting to the NATO secretary-general. Just as astonishing, the CSTC-A commander and the Regional Command East commander didn't fully report to the ISAF commander but were "dual-hatted" and reported to both the ISAF commander and to Central Command as the senior American officers in theater. "If I can't make sense of who's reporting to whom, it can't be very clear to the sergeants and captains in the field," he said dryly. "I have to be honest. When we do the Iraq session, I get a clear sense of where we are making progress. When we do Afghanistan, I hear about a tremendous amount of effort, but we shouldn't confuse activity with progress."

I sat in on several of the Iraq videoconferences that sometimes occurred just before or after the secretary's meetings on Afghanistan. One issue was apparent immediately. In discussing Iraq, General Petraeus talked political and reconstruction issues, such as shifts in the Iraqi Parliament, increasing oil flows, and infrastructure improvements. With Afghanistan, a chorus of televised generals emphasized coalition activity, while General McNeill talked about body count and an ongoing list of named tactical operations such as Operation Achilles. At one point Secretary Gates asked, "Dan, I'm trying to get a sense if we are making progress. Are we making gains in quelling the insurgency? If we are winning, by what measure?"

General McNeill replied, "Mr. Secretary, I was sent here to get our NATO partners in the fight. I can tell you, sir, they are in the fight every day. Some may be fighting more than others, but at the end of the day, we are racking and stacking the Taliban in a big way. I think some of our allies and the international media have made the Taliban out to be far more capable than they really are. This really is a ragtag bunch. They cannot pose a strategic threat to Afghanistan."

Sitting in the room with my notebook, I was stunned. Did he just say he was racking and stacking Taliban? The statement smacked of a Westmoreland-like attrition strategy.

The secretary paused for a moment, seeming to digest the general's statement. He looked up at the screen and stated matter-of-factly, "Dan, I recall that, last year about this time, the Taliban were threatening Kandahar City. This sounds to me like they were posing a strategic threat to Afghanistan's second largest city."

After the screens went dark Secretary Gates expressed his frustration to those in the room. "Gentlemen, we have some disconnects here. I'm reading report after report from the CIA saying the situation is worsening in Afghanistan at an alarming rate. Believe me, I know a thing or two about taking the Agency with a grain of salt," he said smiling, clearly referring to his time with the CIA as the deputy director for analysis. "But I'm concerned. CIA's assessments that the situation is dramatically declining doesn't comport with what I'm hearing from General McNeill, Craddock, the ambassador [William Wood, U.S. ambassador to Afghanistan], and others. My sense is that we are not getting this right and that the situation is going sideways on us."[5]

We spent the rest of 2007 in a sort of policy paralysis. Violence continued to rise in every region of Afghanistan, and our response continued to be to ask NATO to do more. Officials across the bureaucracy realized there were serious issues with the chain of command (in NATO-ISAF and the U.S. systems), the lack of continuity, and the lack of an overall strategy. But preventing failure in Iraq dominated every conversation in Washington.

One of my final acts in OSD-Policy was to help prepare the secretary's testimony to the Senate Armed Services Committee in December 2007.

When asked about the overall security situation in Afghanistan, Gates, replied, "Admittedly, it's gotten worse." He added that this appeared to be due to inadequate provision of basic government services and corruption among local Afghan police. He said it did not reflect a lack of U.S. military commitment.

The chairman of the Joint Chiefs, Adm. Mike Mullen, testifying with Gates, had the memorable line of the day: "In Afghanistan, we do what we can. In Iraq, we do what we must."

One day in the summer of 2007 I answered the phone at my desk in the Pentagon. "How would you like to work in the White House?" It was Mary Beth Long, now assistant secretary of defense with responsibility for Africa, the Middle East, and Europe. The Office of the Vice President had called her looking for recommendations for someone to advise Vice President Cheney on counterterrorism and South Asia. "I told them I knew someone that had actually done it and not just studied it. I put your name in the hat, but you will have to take it from there," she said.

That call started a series of interviews spanning several months with key members of Cheney's staff: his national security advisor, John Hannah; his deputy national security advisor, Samantha Ravich; his deputy chief of staff; and his counsel, among others. During one interview, his counsel asked me, "Have you ever written or published anything derogatory toward the president or vice president?"

"No," I answered. "I've been in government and the military my whole career, so I haven't published anything at all."

"Okay. Are there any policies or policy decisions the Bush administration has made with which you have a fundamental disagreement?"

"Oh yes, absolutely!" I blurted out.

"Really?" he said, looking up, surprised. He was clearly used to going down his list of questions and hearing perfunctory answers.

"Sorry. I know that's probably a little too candid for an interview," I said. "But I would be dishonest in saying there haven't been decisions over the past several years that I have disagreed with." There was a long pause. "But that's exactly the reason I'm here," I said. "I believe in having a credible voice at the table and influencing decisions from the inside. It's easy to sit on the outside and throw grenades." Another long pause that started to make me really nervous.

"Good luck. Hope I see you soon," he finally said.

The interviews, vetting, and personnel processing between the Pentagon and the White House went on for months. Samantha invited me back for my fifth interview. "I'm sorry this whole process is taking so long and probably seems a little excessive," she said. "We very much value discretion in this office, and it's important to make sure folks on our little team here supporting the Boss are the right fit. You will have a very broad and very active portfolio with a direct line of information through me or John to the vice president. These positions have a lot of autonomy."

I thanked her for the opportunity and reminded her that I was no graybeard with a PhD in South Asian politics.

"That's a good thing!" she smiled. "You've spent the time most people use collecting graduate degrees out in the field getting your hands dirty. That can be rare in this town. So what do you think so far?"

Through the course of the conversation I candidly explained to her that a number of friends and colleagues advised me not to take the position. They cited the predictable reasons: you can't go work for Darth Vader; you will be radioactive after having "Office of the Vice President" on your résumé; the Democrats are likely to come into office in 2009 and you won't be able to return to the Pentagon; and so on. I explained that I had come to two conclusions. The first was that most of the people giving me that advice were civil servants. I was fairly certain I didn't want to be a career government employee in the Pentagon and therefore wasn't worried about returning. Second, and most important, we were all there to serve, not worry about how things look on our résumé. I told her that, if asked, I would be proud to join the team and advise the vice president as best I could.

After another month of paperwork with the personnel bureaucracies, I parked on the north side of the ellipse and approached the Eisenhower Executive Office Building across from the West Wing. The building is an imposing, bunker-like, massive gray structure that housed the State Department, War Department, and Navy Department prior to World War II. The ornate Victorian interior, with its checkered marble floors, high ceilings, and strong moldings, has some of the most beautiful staircases in all of Washington. It now houses the majority of the president's and vice president's support staff, from speechwriters and travel secretaries to National Security Council (NSC) staff. The vice president's national security staff were in the center of the building in cipher-locked offices.

Fortunately I was able to quickly settle into a routine, as my predecessor, Mark Webber, a well-respected and very smart lawyer who approached issues with a heavy dose of sarcasm, had simply moved upstairs to be the senior director for South Asia at the National Security Council. I was also fortunate to have an existing relationship with the senior director for Afghanistan on the National Security Council staff, Col. John Wood, a steady hand and insightful officer with whom I had worked during his time on the Joint Staff. Thus the only counterpart office where I had to establish relationships was the NSC's Counterterrorism Directorate, headed by former assistant secretary of the treasury Juan Zarate. Juan made it immediately clear that he wanted to be as inclusive as possible, that I had an open invitation to his weekly Counterterrorism Security Group, and that I would be on the cleared list to attend more sensitive small-group meetings on compartmented terrorism-related issues. Right off the bat I was in great shape to plug in to my NSC counterparts and colleagues and hopefully help them guide and shape policy.

Our primary focus was keeping Vice President Cheney informed on our respective parts of the world and weighing in on his behalf at various levels. Since the Office of the Vice President did not have a formal role in the interagency decision-making process, as did State, Defense, and the National Security Council staff, our effectiveness depended greatly on having strong relationships in the interagency. A typical week involved preparing for and attending the various interagency meetings in the White House Situation Room, including the weekly deputies committee meetings on Afghanistan chaired by the president's "war czar," Lt. Gen. Doug Lute. Lute, the former Joint Staff J-3 Operations Office chief who held the same position at Central Command, was brought to the White House as an assistant to the president and deputy national security advisor for Iraq and Afghanistan. The intent for the position was to give more focus to the two wars while the national security advisor focused on the rest of the world. Despite the "deputy" in the title, I quickly learned that it was the first part of the title that mattered in the White House hierarchy more than the second. The title of assistant to the president meant he had direct access to President Bush and had to coordinate with Stephen Hadley, the national security advisor, but not go through him. For example, one could be commissioned as assistant to the president and chief janitor and, technically, would rank higher than deputy assistant to the president and deputy national security advisor. What ultimately mattered was access to the commander in chief.

Lute's position meant the wars were getting extra attention from the White House, but I was initially dubious about what that meant for Afghanistan. Lute had commanded in Iraq and while at Central Command and the Joint Staff focused heavily on the debate about how to turn Iraq around. In contrast, he had never done an operational tour in Afghanistan before he was made war czar. I wasn't sure he had ever been there at all. He was clearly hired to focus on Iraq; nonetheless he expanded his Afghanistan staff at the NSC from two to five and dramatically increased the frequency of meetings on the myriad topics in our Afghan policy that needed high-level attention.

Typically I attended a deputies committee on Afghanistan every week, one on Pakistan about every other week, Juan's Counterterrorism Security Group every Monday, a counterterrorism-related deputies committee on Yemen or Somalia, and various other, lower level meetings. The deputies committees typically involved the number two or three official in each agency, while the principals committees included the cabinet secretaries and was chaired by the national security advisor. While in the Pentagon as the director for Afghanistan policy I had to try to carve out time for Mitch Shivers or Jim Shinn to give me a readout of what occurred at the deputies committees they attended as a "plus one" (the term used for the people who sat in the chairs lining the walls on either side of the Situation Room table and took notes for their principal). Those readouts were critical for our team to effectively do our jobs, which would have been impossible if we didn't have a good sense of what was decided (or, often, not decided) at White House meetings. In my new role I personally attended all of those meetings. Even as a plus one, I was able to keep my finger on the pulse of the interagency on a weekly basis.

I was by no means a member of the vice president's inner circle. I dealt with him directly only when he was dealing with my issues or had a meeting with an official from South Asia. Given his responsibilities with the broad array of domestic issues, political issues, fundraising, his responsibilities in the Senate, and the entire rest of the world, he usually dealt with my part of the world only about two to three times a month. My interaction almost always consisted of pre-briefs before a National Security Council meeting with the president or attending a meeting in the vice president's office with a visiting dignitary such as President Karzai or Pakistan's president Asif Ali Zardari. I did have the opportunity to write a number of white papers and memos, which I hoped would influence his thinking even so late in the administration.

In keeping with his reputation, Vice President Cheney's demeanor was polite but stoic. It was a bit intimidating to think that, in his midthirties, he had sat in the office down the hall as President Gerald Ford's chief of staff, then became minority whip in the House of Representatives, secretary of defense, and CEO of Halliburton on his way to becoming one of the most influential vice presidents in American history. True to form, briefing him was a one-way street with very little feedback. Usually Samantha or John, and sometimes I, would run through our points and receive a curt reply of, "Thank you. Nice work." I once walked him through a white paper titled "We Do Not Have to Get Out of Iraq to Get Back Into Afghanistan," which was my analysis of the U.S. military's footprint outside of Iraq and Afghanistan. It focused on the legacy deployments we had ongoing in the Egyptian Sinai, Bosnia, Kosovo, and Korea and floating aboard ships in case of a crisis. I described the declining security situation in southern and eastern Afghanistan and our current U.S. troop commitments. I also reviewed the military's outstanding requests for additional forces and the unlikelihood that our NATO allies would fill them. I then posited that we did not necessarily have to pull troops from Iraq to bolster Afghanistan, that we could pull from those legacy missions instead. While it would be problematic for our commitments to our allies, I argued that accepting risks in those relationships was far better than continuing to accept a declining situation in Afghanistan by waiting on resources to free up in Iraq. After a few questions I received a "Thanks, Mike. Nice work" from the vice president. I had no idea whether he agreed or thought it was the stupidest thing he had ever heard.

The bottom line was that he held his cards tightly, and his dealings with the president were absolutely confidential. But we would get feedback in other ways, sometimes hearing him repeat in later meetings the key themes of a memo we had crafted. Weeks after my white paper, the vice president accompanied President Bush to a Pentagon meeting in "the Tank" with the chiefs of the armed services and asked for an analysis of what forces were available outside of Iraq for redeployment to Afghanistan. He also asked for a comparative risk analysis of allowing the surging violence in Afghanistan to continue compared to facing other global commitments with fewer U.S. forces. When John told me about the request, I about fell out of my chair. I was encouraged to hear that I might finally be getting the point across that Afghanistan couldn't wait on Iraq.

A mentor in the White House gave me some sage advice not long after I arrived. "Pick just a few things you want to accomplish—no more than three to five," he said over lunch. "Your writ is now all of South Asia and the whole world under Counterterrorism, and there still are some important things for this administration to accomplish." The list for Afghanistan was easy: reintroduce American resources and leadership into southern Afghanistan (civilian and military); fix the command-and-control problems; provide a long-term commitment to building the Afghan Army; and provide our forces the authorities to work alongside tribal militias as a complementary economy-of-force effort. I knew these were military-centric goals, but I was convinced that providing at least some modicum of security was an essential requirement to being able to execute a political or development strategy.

In dealing with Pakistan we had to change the nature of our relationship. As I read reports week after week on Pakistan's support of the insurgency, I became convinced that we were on the wrong track. We had to keep Pakistan as an ally, and they were convinced we needed them more than they needed us. I was ready to push our leadership, to the extent I could, toward the use of bigger sticks. We had tried carrots for years, and it just wasn't working. We had to take a more aggressive stance in our relationship and in our counterterrorism policy. We also had to reduce our dependence on our ground supply routes in Pakistan by diversifying our routes into Afghanistan.

There were a few other key issues for which I tried to lend my support in lower level interagency meetings and keep John and the vice president informed should they decide to weigh in. The president and State Department were determined to cement a significant shift in U.S.-India relations through a civil-nuclear deal. This would allow the United

States to transfer peaceful nuclear technology to India, despite India's failure to sign the Treaty on the Nonproliferation of Nuclear Weapons. I supported this effort by preparing the vice president to request of Pakistan that it not interfere with the deal in the associated Nuclear Suppliers Group. I also closely monitored other issues, such as our campaigns against al Qaeda in Yemen and Somalia, as well as our efforts to quietly assist President Felipe Calderón's government in Mexico in its war against indigenous drug cartels.

One of my deliverables in the office each day was what we called a "night note" to the vice president. Each member of his national security staff wrote a short paragraph on their respective part of the world. It was fantastic to have the latitude to highlight any issue for his focus, such as a key piece of intelligence on which we'd comment or a position on an issue embraced by the Pentagon or State Department that would be presented at the deputies committees. I consciously limited my notes to various aspects of my short list of topics that I wanted to influence.

Before I could begin influencing issues, though, I first had to be given access to a series of compartmented programs. I went through the procedures with the White House security office and the NSC's Directorate for Intelligence Reform, headed by Steve Slick, a longtime CIA operations officer and former aide to Deputy CIA Director John McLaughlin. I sat for hours reading through reams of documents in a small conference room inside a secure space. Much of it dealt with the programs established in the wake of the president's finding signed on September 17, 2001, that set the policy framework for the war on terror. The policies took the gloves off in dealing with al Qaeda and any global extremists associated with them. Some of it was surprising and enlightening. I thought I had fairly high-level access while at the Pentagon, but I now learned that there was a whole series of higher levels of classifications about which I knew nothing. I realized how national security bureaucracies such as Defense, State, and USAID were making decisions and forming opinions partially in the dark. I was surprised to find some highly classified programs were very basic and relatively new, a real disappointment when one considered that the average taxpayer would have assumed we had undertaken such programs years ago!

Still other programs only had their coded name on the nondisclosure statement, with little or no detail. I reached out to the CIA to request a more thorough explanation for one particular program that I sensed was something about which the vice president would want to be informed. I was soon given a taste of what it meant to request a meeting for a member of Vice President Cheney's staff. I naïvely believed I would be having an informal, working-level discussion of the program and its impact, but sitting at the table in the CIA's Counter-terrorism Center were the deputy director, the director for operations, and, significantly, their legal counsel. I asked about leads on al Qaeda's senior leadership, cross-border operations, mechanisms for CIA-military cooperation, and the efficacy of our operations in coordination with the Afghan intelligence agency. To get a more strategic sense of what CIA's contribution was, I asked whether their budget was commensurate to the tremendous tasks they had in front of them in Afghanistan and Pakistan. I knew their funding was minuscule compared to what the military was spending, but, in my view, their mission was just as important and deserved whatever support in the White House I could lend it. After thirty minutes of one-word answers to my questions, I saw the meeting was going nowhere. The few answers they did provide were usually preceded by glances at their lawyers.

I stopped by Samantha's office after returning and told her about the meeting. She smiled. "Welcome to the supposedly apolitical intelligence community!" she said sarcastically. "Do your best to stay on top of that program. It's something the Boss cares about. Juan Zarate and Steve Slick are good guys and will work with you."

Samantha was wonderful to work with. A longtime expert in international finance, Asia, and the Middle East, she had served on the vice president's national security staff since the beginning of the administration. She managed to walk that fine line between being tough as nails and passionate when pushing her views in the interagency, yet gracious and hands off when dealing with our staff. One of my favorite stories about Samantha occurred during one deputies committee meeting on Pakistan chaired by the then deputy national security advisor, James Jeffrey. The meeting lasted over an hour and covered a series of issues, from the U.S. government's anemic public diplomacy budget in Pakistan to the status of aid programs in Pakistan's lawless Federally Administered Tribal Areas. As Jeffrey seemed to be wrapping up the agenda, Samantha, sitting in front of me at the Situation Room conference table, raised her hand slightly.

"I think it's important, as we talk about aid programs in the FATA and military assistance to the Pakistani Army, for us to keep in mind why we are there in such a big way in the first place. We have just spent an hour talking about Pakistan, and I find it surprising there was not even a mention of Osama bin Laden or Ayman al-Zawahiri."

Jeffrey reminded her that we usually covered counterterrorism issues in a separate, parallel policy forum with more limited participation.

"I realize that, Jim," she replied. "But I think it's important for our colleagues here at USAID and State to keep in mind that al Qaeda's senior leadership are still free, and likely in Pakistan, as we pour billions of dollars of assistance into that country in support of their government. I know it's been several years, but I'm really concerned that we have lost sight of our objective here and are providing assistance just for the sake of it."

"I'm not sure what you want," Jeffrey replied.

"I want the status of the hunt for Osama to be number one on the agenda of every meeting dealing with Pakistan. I want Osama's head on a stick on the White House lawn before this president leaves office!" Samantha said, slapping her hand on the table.

"Yes!" I wrote in my notebook. I saw some eyes roll as though to say, "Here go those crude Cheney people again." The bin Laden trail had gone cold, so it just wasn't discussed. Jeffrey concluded by saying that it had been a while since they had an update and that he would get it on the schedule.[6]

The anecdote was emblematic of the fact that we had lost sight of our goals in Afghanistan and the broader South Asia region. In many ways, like the clinic in Achin, our activities were simply perpetuating themselves at a national level and not driving toward specific goals and objectives. As Secretary Gates had lamented during the videoconferences with his generals, it was unclear what success looked like and whether our efforts were making progress toward those ends. The ambiguity was evident from the White House Situation Room all the way down to the military tactical operations centers in the provinces of Afghanistan. What constituted victory, and what was the plan to achieve it?

As violence in Afghanistan continued to escalate in the spring of 2008, momentum was growing in Washington to reform our command-and-control structure. It was finally becoming apparent that NATO forces were unlikely to be able to get the job done in southern Afghanistan. Doug Lute, Jim Shinn, Mary Beth Long, and Eliot Cohen, the much-admired professor from Johns Hopkins University and counselor to the secretary of state, took an extended fact-finding trip across Afghanistan. I loaded Jim and Mary Beth with questions to pose to the command stemming from my experience during my tour in 2006: Was our intelligence apparatus overly focused on targeting? Was our development strategy aligned with our counterinsurgency strategy? What was ISAF's counterinsurgency strategy? Did we have enough resources to execute the strategy if one was articulated?

Among his many impressions, Lute returned particularly incensed at the multiple parallel chains of command, particularly in southern Afghanistan. He ticked off on his fingers the firewalled reporting chains that I had so long lamented during a deputies committee meeting on the issue. "One, ISAF conventional forces to the ISAF commander. Two, Special Forces to CJ-SOTF. Three, our special mission units forces through their counterterrorism Task Force. Four, the embedded training teams to Task Force Phoenix and CSTC-A. Five, the Afghan National Army to the Ministry of Defense." He paused as he switched hands and began using the fingers on his other hand. "Six, the Afghan National Police to the Ministry of Interior. And finally, seven, the one no one in this room has good visibility on, the CIA with their partnered Afghan intelligence units. At best, they coordinate with each other, but no one person is actually in charge of all of them!"

The debate had been brewing for some time about how to make sense of the situation. Consensus was forming at the Defense Department and in NATO circles to make the ISAF commander the overall commander of all American forces as well as NATO forces. This would partially solve the problem by pulling most of the Special Operations Forces and CSTC-A under his command. In a memo to the vice president I made the case that dual hatting was a long-overdue step toward unity of command but was not sufficient to solve the issue of command and control in Afghanistan. The other issue was that the four-star ISAF command had too many strategic issues on its plate and did not have the time to also focus on the operational aspects of fighting the war. ISAF headquarters could not possibly deal with the demands of Washington, the NATO command in Brussels, forty-two other capitals in Europe and Asia that had soldiers in the coalition, the U.S. Embassy in Kabul, the various ministries in the Afghan government, and President Karzai, and still run the war day to day. We needed an intermediate three-star-level command focused on pulling the five regional commands and the training command onto the same page. The Special Forces operator in me hated pushing for yet another layer of management that I would have to deal with on my next tour, but from my perches in the Pentagon and the White House, I could see that the six two-star commands in Afghanistan needed someone to coordinate their efforts. I could also see that Special Forces needed a bigger voice with the ISAF headquarters and began pushing for a one-star Special Operations command in Kabul. Despite my efforts and that of many others, we wouldn't get NATO consensus on the three-star operational command, later named Intermediate Joint Command, until fall 2009—two full fighting seasons later.

While making these adjustments, the fighting in Afghanistan raged. In April, 2008 the Taliban attacked Afghanistan's annual Victory Day Parade in the heart of Kabul, attempting to assassinate President Karzai and successfully killing several high-level officials. That June a series of bombings and attacks in Kandahar culminated with a spectacular prison break at Sarposa Prison, in which hundreds of Taliban fighters were freed. The brutal summer culminated with the Taliban nearly annihilating combat outpost Wanat in Kunar Province, resulting in nine dead American soldiers and twenty-seven wounded. In June I opened my weekly *Army Times* magazine at the office, where I always made myself read the write-ups for that week's KIA before reading any other articles. I was astonished to see that casualties in Afghanistan matched those of Iraq for the first time, despite the fact that U.S. force levels in Iraq were almost three times those in Afghanistan.

At a National Security Council meeting on Afghanistan that fall debate swirled about the causes of the dramatic increase in violence. Gen. David McKiernan, who had replaced General McNeill as commander of ISAF in June 2008, sat alongside William Wood, the U.S. ambassador to Afghanistan, on the videoconference screen on the far wall of the Situation Room. McKiernan cited a series of reasons for the rising violence, but mainly attributed it to the fact that ISAF was aggressively pushing into previously untouched Taliban-controlled areas.

"Eikenberry said same thing in 2006," I wrote in my notebook.

Ambassador Wood chimed in, "This notion that Kabul is surrounded by the Taliban is sensationalizing the issue. We have to work hard to keep a positive message to the international media and to our interlocutors. Things are not progressing as well as we would like, of course, but it's vital that our strategic messaging paint a positive picture."

In fact reports from the field and anecdotal reports I was receiving from a number of Army colleagues confirmed that the much-celebrated Ring Road, championed by the United States years earlier as a symbol of the new Afghanistan, was now regularly hit with IEDs and ambushes right up to the outskirts of Kabul. By the time my ODAs arrived a year later on my next deployment to Afghanistan, the Ring Road was passable only with heavily armored convoys or at night, in blacked-out vehicles with drivers wearing night-vision goggles. "He's conflating giving us an accurate internal assessment and putting a positive public face on things," I noted.

Adm. Mike Mullen, the chairman of the Joint Chiefs, pointed out that President Bush had ordered in additional soldiers over the course of the current year. Secretary Gates expressed his concern that even with the additional troops we were unable to hold terrain that we had cleared of insurgents and wondered at what point the Afghan populace would see the United States as occupiers. "The Soviets deployed 120,000 soldiers and couldn't hold. We want to be careful at crossing the threshold where the Afghan populace sees us as occupiers."

I was alarmed at this line of thinking. The Soviets carpet-bombed the Afghan people, deliberately mined the countryside, and destroyed the agrarian economy while denouncing Islam in favor of atheistic communism. The Afghan popular uprising against the Soviets had nothing to do with an arbitrary number of troops. I felt strongly that current levels of violence and frustration were due to our lack of commitment, not over commitment.

Secretary of State Condoleezza Rice admitted she was attempting a similar increase in civilians, but it was moving slower than she hoped.

President Bush interrupted the back-and-forth commentary. "Regardless of the reasons, it sounds like we are slipping here. I'm not sure we have a clear focus on what victory looks like anymore in Afghanistan."

There was a long pause.

Vice President Cheney, who over the previous hour had not said anything, spoke up. "Mr. President, I think we may have lost sight of our national objectives in Afghanistan, our strategy to achieve them, and who's in charge."[7] This was typical of the vice president: say more with less and cut right to the heart of the issue.

National Security Advisor Stephen Hadley chaired a principals committee a few weeks later and concluded that a thorough review of our Afghan strategy was needed. Though only five months remained in the administration, the president subsequently ordered a full interagency review similar to the one that had eventually led to the troop surge in Iraq.

Lute convened a high-level interagency panel, formed around a nucleus of regular deputies committee attendees, to examine all aspects of "next steps" for U.S. strategy for Afghanistan. Participants included Assistant Secretary of Defense for Asia Jim Shinn; Assistant Secretary of Defense for Special Operations and Low Intensity Conflict Michael Vickers (who had extraordinarily deep ties to the Afghanistan mission, going as far back as the CIA support to the mujahideen fighting of the Soviet Army in the 1980s); the Joint Staff director of operations, Marine Lt. Gen. James "Jay" Paxton; the director of strategic plans and policy, Vice Adm. James "Sandy" Winnefeld; State Department counselor Eliot Cohen; Assistant Secretary of State for South Asia Richard Boucher; senior members of the intelligence community; outside experts; and, of course, the NSC's Afghanistan staff. I represented the Office of the Vice President.

The core group of interagency representatives and outside experts met for the first time on September 22, 2008, and then about twenty times, usually for four hours at a time, and often twice in the same day, in a windowless fourth-floor secure room in the Old Executive Office Building. The group invited Afghan participation and met with Minister of Defense Abdul Rahim Wardak and Director of the Independent Directorate of Local Governance Jelani Popal. Former senior military commanders and ambassadors were brought in throughout the process, primarily to assist the group in understanding the assumptions that formed the underpinnings of our strategy in Afghanistan. The incoming commander of Central Command, Gen. David Petraeus, spent several hours with the group, as did the commander of NATO, General Craddock. The process was a rigorous examination of U.S. interests in, assumptions about, and strategy and plans for Afghanistan. In classic U.S. government fashion, the process culminated in a series of recommendations in a PowerPoint briefing that was reviewed during a principals committee meeting.

Perhaps the most significant of the ten recommendations was that the "whole of government" approach recommended by the review equated to a push for counterinsurgency strategy, with more resources across the board to back it up. The counterinsurgency strategy included increased efforts to train and equip the Afghan National Security Forces, enhance the Afghan government's ability to control its borders and fight the drug economy and corruption, and generally help the Afghans improve governance. Another significant recommendation was the explicit linking of Afghanistan and Pakistan as a related policy issue within a single theater. Progress in one country was inextricably linked to the other, and our policy apparatus needed to reflect that. Not until the Obama administration would offices be renamed Af-Pak and our bureaucracy make meaningful steps toward moving away from treating the two countries as distinct independent relationships. Several principals requested changes and did not think the brief was ready for the president, but Hadley demurred.

"The president is chomping at the bit. He is ready to deflect some of this criticism circulating out there that we have taken our eye off the ball in Afghanistan. I'm going to take some of your suggestions on board, but I'm going to bootleg him a copy this weekend. We need to keep the NSC with him on the schedule for next week."

In a nutshell the review concluded that two overarching attributes best described the campaign in Afghanistan: a lack of coherence and a shortfall in capacity. These two points covered the entire endeavor and neatly bundled what many of us had been saying for years. Coherence was lacking in all sectors—security, governance, and economic development; coherence was also lacking across all major commands and organizations, including ISAF, Operation Enduring Freedom, the UN, and within the U.S. interagency process. Capacity was lacking in the military efforts, in the Afghan National Security Forces, and, most important, in the Afghan government.[8]

I wholeheartedly agreed with all the recommendations. However, I believed that a major factor was missing in the discussion: time. I had participated in five years of interagency briefings on a range of issues for Afghanistan, and nearly all of them had one thing in common: unrealistic timelines or no timeline at all. At the policy level we focused on what needed to be done, while those in the field tended to focus on how to accomplish it. Unfortunately we also tended to defer to the field on how long it would take, and the timelines that were included with the implementation plans tended to coincide with senior leaders' tours of duty. For example, at various points I saw estimates for the Afghan Army to be independently operable by 2005, 2008, and 2011. It just wasn't politically palatable to say that we were committed for a decades-long, or even generational, effort. Though it was in vogue to call the global war on terror the "long war," in reality our planning rarely looked beyond one to three years.

Lute opened the final briefing to President Bush of the strategy review by working through the initial overarching finding: the lack of coherence among the many aspects of our military and civilian efforts. This time he counted up to ten simultaneous wars under different reporting chains—adding the covert war in Pakistan, the Pakistani Army's war, and Operation Enduring Freedom, on top of the seven he had recounted after his trip. Lute also stressed the recommendation to prioritize counterinsurgency with a focus on population security.

Looking down at his copy of the brief, Secretary Gates remarked, "Putting counterinsurgency in front of counterterrorism as a priority is a significant shift. That's an entirely different ball game in terms of resources—military and civilian." He seemed to be hinting at the major increase in civilian expertise that would be needed to implement a counterinsurgency strategy.

Lute replied that counterterrorism should support counterinsurgency and be complementary to it. He went on to say that developing the Afghan Army and police was taking too long and that NATO was not contributing the resources they pledged.

"We need to get State in the game," the president said, taking Gate's cue of the need for more civilians and smiling at the Secretary of State Rice.

"Mr. President, State is looking at increasing resources commensurate with military," she replied. "If we decide to have an Afghanistan surge, we will have a civilian surge too. But what we also really need is for the UN to step up. We were all hoping for the leadership of Paddy Ashdown"—the storied former high commissioner in Bosnia—"but Kai Eide is doing a fine job. He barely has a staff, and we are pushing the UN to provide him the resources he needs. The UN is the best civilian counterpart to the whole military coalition."

"The U.S. must lead," the president said. "We must remain multilateral, but the U.S. needs to run this thing in the south and east. I know that we dual-hatted McKiernan, but he still can't do what he needs. He can't order the Dutch around if he needs them somewhere else, over in Helmand to help the Brits, for example." I was thrilled to hear him imply that we were not going to wait on our international partners in the UN or Europe anymore.

Secretary Gates again raised his concern about our being viewed like the Soviets if we surged the number of U.S. troops necessary for population security. "The Afghan Army must gain the ability and numbers to hold," he said.

"Is that realistic?" President Bush asked. "Are they ready? In Iraq this was a real problem. We relied too much on the locals to do it and things got out of control." He was clearly referring to Gen. William Casey's strategy of handing over security responsibility as quickly as possible.

"The Afghan Army is getting there, it's getting more and more capable, but the police are a long way off," Lute said. "Mr. President, one of our key recommendations is accelerating the building of the Army and police, but that will require more resources."

Admiral Mullen spoke up: "Sir, as you know, McKiernan has a request in for three additional brigades. One of these units would be dedicated to training the Afghans. He also has developed a pilot program for local village defense forces."

I drew a big star in my book and circled it. The topic of training and organizing local tribal militias had provoked heated debate during several of the review sessions. Nonetheless I had pressed my NSC colleagues for a recommendation in the final brief to identify, train, and equip select tribal militias to fill the seams between ISAF forces and the still growing Afghan Army. A watered-down version of the recommendation made it into the final briefing to President Bush, but I was thrilled to hear the field had taken matters into their own hands.

Everyone flipped the page to the slide covering Pakistan.

"Look," the president said, "the bottom line is that al Qaeda still maintains a safe haven in Pakistan. It's no longer intact in Afghanistan, and the Pak Army is still fixated on India. We need to stay focused on al Qaeda."

Mullen replied, "They are getting better in dealing with al Qaeda and the Taliban problem, but yes, sir, they are still largely fixated on India."

"India dominates their procurement and training," the president said, reinforcing his point that Pakistan still wasn't fully addressing the extremist problem on its border with Afghanistan.

Lute said, "One of the things we identified is that the resources we are applying to Afghanistan and Pakistan are disproportionate. We've poured massive resources into Afghanistan, but the main problem is in Pakistan—al Qaeda and the old Taliban regime in the Quetta Shura. However, targeting is ongoing in Waziristan, but Quetta is going untouched."

The Quetta Shura was the the senior leadership of the former Taliban regime that fled southern Afghanistan for the city of Quetta in Baluchistan Province, Pakistan. From speaking to the Afghan border police chief I visited in the Maruf Valley to reading high-level reports in the White House, I knew it was common knowledge in the region that Mullah Omar and his inner circle were running the Taliban insurgency while the Pakistani authorities looked the other way. Targeting individuals in the dense urban environment of Quetta was infinitely more complicated than in individual compounds in the countryside of lawless Waziristan.

Secretary Rice pointed to her brief as she spoke. "This slide gives the impression we've done nothing. We've made incredible efforts in Pakistan. Granted, the government is not responding as we would like, but I don't want to give impression that we've ignored the problem."

"Agreed," said the president. "We haven't exactly been absent on the job here. Billions in military assistance since 2001, and we need to be sure that's captured here."

Turning back to Lute's earlier statement, the president asked, "Is Quetta a realistic goal?"

Gen. Michael Hayden, a four-star Air Force general, former head of the National Security Agency, and now the CIA director, responded, "We will need to get Pakistani concurrence to increase operations in Quetta, Mr. President. As you know, that will be a huge shift for them. Quetta is considered part of Pakistan proper. What goes on in Waziristan and the other tribal areas is much more of a gray area. I make no apologies for them, but for the Pak Army, the Quetta Shura is a strategic hedge against our withdrawal from Afghanistan, and they aren't likely to go after them anytime soon."

"Can't we get at them unilaterally?" the president asked.

"Sir, buildings blowing up in the midst of one of Pakistan's major cities is a lot different than an isolated mud hut getting struck out in the mountains somewhere," Hayden replied. "Unfortunately we will have to look more at arrests, and entering some of these neighborhoods will be like taking on the mafia on their home turf. Everyone will know you're coming, and it won't be pretty. We will just have to balance unilateral action with the assistance the Pakistanis are giving us in pursuing al Qaeda."

I was disappointed in the Pakistan section of the briefing and discussion. Part of the reason it was lacking was that elements of our Pakistan policy that were not directly related to Afghanistan were out of the purview of Lute's review. In my view the recommendations regarding Pakistan equated to more of the same, and I knew that both my men and I were going to acutely feel the impact of our lack of action during my upcoming tour in eastern Afghanistan.

Hadley turned the topic to the possibility of briefing the findings to our allies and to Congress. He reminded everyone that the recommendations were bucketed into what could still be done in this administration and what could wait until the next. "Unless a principal could make the case that something absolutely had to be in place in the spring of 2009, and therefore set in motion now, it should be put into the next administration's bucket," he said. "We do not want to make decisions that could be perceived as attempting to force the new president's hand or box him in."

Tapping on the briefing, the president congratulated the room for putting something together so quickly. "I know you all have taken a hard look at the issues here. And these are very difficult problems with no easy answers. We are finally in a good place with Iraq. And we clearly need to turn our attention and our resources back to helping the Afghans.

"Now, on the rollout strategy, I've been thinking. The results of this review shouldn't be announced by me. If this is what we think is right,

we need to quietly hand this over to the Obama administration. I've decided I don't want to announce these findings publicly at this point. I
will take the hit from history, but I don't want this work discarded out
of hand because it came from me." I was floored. It was a fantastically
selfless position for the president to take.

"Besides, we have to leave a little flexibility for the new Bob Gates!"
the president said with a smile and a chuckle, clearly referring to the announcement by President-elect Obama that he had asked the secretary
to stay on. I could have sworn the secretary actually blushed.[9]

The results of the review were briefed to the Obama transition team,
and many of the ideas found their way into President Obama's early strategic review of the war. I was proud of the NSC team and of any small influence I had on them and on the outcome of the review. We didn't get to
all of the topics I had hoped. There was little in the final white paper and
its recommendations addressing the badly needed political strategy, or a
plan for reconciliation with the insurgent groups. There were no suggestions for transformational economic changes such as the long-pursued
pipeline from Turkmenistan to India that could lift Afghanistan from
being the fourth poorest country in the world. But I was relatively san-
guine about the security-centric recommendations because I was still
convinced that basic security was what the Afghan people most needed
before any other efforts could bear fruit. The results of the review coupled
with the campaign rhetoric of President-elect Obama that Afghanistan
was a war of necessity encouraged me to believe that the war effort was
finally going to get the resources and attention it required.

Alongside dealing with the weekly bureaucratic policy wrangling in Washington, I was able to help arrange one of the more memorable moments
of my tenure with the vice president during his final trip to Afghanistan. In addition to the obligatory briefings with command elements
and his visit with President Karzai, I worked with the 82nd Airborne
Division to have the vice president pin valor medals onto a number of
soldiers. Among them was Specialist Monica Lin Brown, a medic who
had repeatedly run through heavy enemy fire to treat her wounded comrades, shielding several with her body and dragging others to safety. She
became only the second woman since World War II to receive the Sil-
ver Star for her heroic actions in Paktia Province. The staff of the 82nd

and I worked hard for several weeks to ensure that she would be in Bagram Airbase during the visit, and I was even more thrilled when the vice president included a photo of the ceremony in his memoirs and discussed it as one of the more special moments of his time in office.

I was also honored to personally have a similar moment with him. Late in 2008 I was notified by the Army that I would be awarded a second Bronze Star for Valor for my actions during the ambush on our mission to Musa Qala in Helmand. The award had apparently been lost down at Central Command for over a year until a diligent personnel sergeant, determined to clear the "incomplete" line next to my name on her award tracker, flew down to Tampa and searched through a storage trailer until she found a paper copy of the award. Vice President Cheney pinned the award on me in the Indian Treaty Room in front of my family, friends, and members of my ODA. I was thrilled to be able to show off my men in front of so many policymakers, including several assistant and deputy assistant secretaries of defense. I asked my team to stand while I reminded everyone in the room that these were the soldiers who had to live or die with the policies we set forth in that building.

One of my last and more interesting meetings was with Vice President Cheney and President Karzai at the very end of the administration's tenure. The meeting occurred across the street from the West Wing, in Blair House, where foreign dignitaries and heads of state often reside while visiting. Showing flair, President Karzai walked in wearing a gray suit and his traditional green *chapan* cape. He greeted everyone and stopped in front of Samantha and me. Smiling, and to our complete surprise, he said, "I've heard about you two. You are good friends of Afghanistan. Thank you for your efforts on behalf of our relationship with your country." To this day I have no idea where that came from. Perhaps my friends in the Afghan Embassy briefed him about our longtime efforts to get Washington to pay more attention to Afghanistan.

Cheney and Karzai both sat in the front of the narrow colonial-style drawing room and started with small talk. The vice president mentioned the wear and tear the financial crisis was having on everyone.

"Yes, I have been reading about it closely in the news. I must be honest, I was expecting a very different scene when I landed at the airport," Karzai replied.

"How so?" Cheney asked.

"You see, I was expecting to see lines of people waiting in line for food or gasoline. I was wondering if the cities would be dark at night. Instead, we drove by shopping malls with the parking lots full of cars. The streets are clean. Every car has only the driver riding in it. America looks as healthy and beautiful as ever!"

The conversation turned to the recently decided presidential elections in the United States. "It's one of the great things about your democracy, Mr. Vice President. Two hundred years of peaceful transitions. This is something Afghanistan has never had in its entire history. Every transition of power in our history has resulted in the sitting ruler becoming exiled, imprisoned, or killed. I assure you, the point is not lost on me!"

Cheney asked Karzai his feelings about the prospects of the pending elections in Afghanistan in the fall of 2009 and the U.S.-Afghan partnership.

"Let me tell you a story, Mr. Vice President, if you will indulge me. I recently visited the Netherlands for two days of talks with their government. The Dutch foreign minister recounted to me a trip he had made to visit their soldiers in Uruzgan. He described to me how a group of elders hosted the foreign minister for a beautiful, traditional Afghan lunch of lamb and rice. During the lunch, after many pleasantries, the elders thanked the minister for many of the development projects in the province. They also apparently chided him for not providing enough soldiers to secure the road to Kandahar. At the end of the lunch, after several hours of discussion, the elders presented the minister a handmade knife with beautifully inlaid lapis. The minister told me he was very grateful, until the elders asked him to please take it back with him to Washington as a token of their appreciation for American generosity. The minister, a bit shocked, tried to explain that he was not American and that the projects and efforts they had been discussing were sponsored by the Dutch government. The elders smiled and wished him a safe journey back to America!" Karzai laughed.

Cheney chuckled, though he was obviously a bit perplexed at the point of the story.

"You see, Mr. Vice President," Karzai continued, "we have what, some forty to fifty countries as part of this coalition in Afghanistan. They are doing many, many things. Mostly good. But at the end of the day it is only America that matters. I know it is important to the United States to share the burden of helping Afghanistan with other generous nations, but the Afghan people see the coalition's successes and failures as your successes and failures. It is this same way with the elections. When the Afghan people look at me, they see America just behind me. They see my successes as your successes and my failures as your failures."

President Karzai leaned in toward the vice president. "In the Afghan mind," he said, tapping his temple with his forefinger, "America is behind everything." It was a brilliant and not very subtle way to convey that we may as well stick with him in the upcoming elections as every Afghan assumed we were behind him anyway. I would think of this story often in the next year as I dealt with local Afghan officials and tribal elders during my tour in eastern Afghanistan, due to begin just months later. It helped me keep in mind that most Afghans did not see the difference between us and their government. If local officials abused their power, the United States was assumed to be behind it.

People often asked me my impressions of working with Cheney and his team. I typically replied that even though I was there late in the administration, I had a very active portfolio and was able to view our policy apparatus at work at very senior levels. Overall I came away with two distinct impressions. First, the general feeling in the office was as though 9/11 had happened six months earlier, even though it was 2007–8. It was still very much on everyone's mind, and I didn't detect a hint of complacency about the fact that it could happen again. The second was that I didn't detect an ounce of concern regarding politics or legacy in the decision-making process for national security issues. Granted, my time in the office occurred when reelection wasn't a concern, but there was still a sense that the vice president and his staff didn't give a damn about polls or popularity ratings. Their charge was to protect the American people and never letting something like 9/11 happen again, even if it meant doing unpopular things.

On January 19, 2009, I handed in my badge to a Secret Service agent and walked out the south gate on West Executive Avenue. I looked back at the White House and thanked God for my opportunity to serve. I thought about my efforts to bring my experiences from the field back to Washington and use them to help improve our policies in ways I felt were important. I was pleased with the president's decision to order a small increase in U.S. troops and civilians for Afghanistan. I had spent years underscoring the shortcomings of NATO's conduct of a counterinsurgency far from Europe and was pleased for the United States to be reestablishing a leadership role in the war. (Admittedly the increase in U.S. resources had more to do with our success in Iraq than any efforts on my part.) I was especially pleased at the authorization in the strategic review to initiate a tribal engagement program and looked forward to having the opportunity to go out to Afghanistan and actually implement the program. Also encouraging was the increase in the numbers of Afghan National Army soldiers, though I knew they would need our support for years if not decades to come. At the same time, the list of disappointments was long, including not getting a transformative economic project in place and not doing more to tackle corruption. I was also disappointed that we hadn't made significant progress in establishing a more tightly coordinated campaign plan with long-term goals and objectives. Perhaps my biggest regret, however, was not being able to improve our relationship with Pakistan and convince them to take on militant sanctuaries in their borders. Up until the day of President Obama's inauguration we were dealing with the fallout of the Mumbai attacks.

With those thoughts I turned and walked toward my parking spot on the ellipse, looking at the Washington Monument. Months later I would find myself back in uniform, looking across the Afghan border into North Waziristan, Pakistan.

1. A typical ground mobility vehicle (GMV) used by U.S. Army Special Forces teams in Afghanistan for long-range patrols.

2. (*above*) A "green zone" in southern Afghanistan that formed a maze of foot trails, irrigation ditches, and walled compounds.

3. (*opposite top*) The author instructing Afghan National Police in basic tactics in 2006. The police were ill equipped and poorly trained for the isolated paramilitary operations required to combat the Taliban.

4. (*opposite bottom*) A typical Afghan National Police checkpoint. These could inadvertently help the Taliban by alienating average Afghans through bribes and harassment.

5. (*opposite top*) A crater left by an IED hidden in a culvert under the road. Most IEDs were buried in dirt roads and often victim-initiated by trip wires or pressure plates. U.S. and coalition forces became nearly obsessed with defeating the IED through technology rather than addressing the underlying causes of the insurgency.

6. (*opposite bottom*) A combination school and police station that formed our base of operations for patrols around Kora village in the Tagab Valley.

7. (*above*) Sergeant Major Sumar of the Afghan National Army, kneeling (*far right*) while patrolling the cliffs overlooking the Tagab Valley in 2006.

8. Taliban machine gunner's view down the wadi during the ambush in Kora that killed Sumar.

9. An Afghan National Army Ford Ranger pickup truck with mounted PKM machine gun, 2005. Most were later replaced by armored Humvees that offered the Afghan soldiers more protection but raised concerns about the Afghans' ability to maintain them over the long term.

10. (*above*) In the winter of 2005–6 Afghan children mob the author for candy and pencils during a stop to better understand tribal dynamics in Uruzgan.

11. (*opposite top*) UAE-sponsored clinic in Achin District in southern Nangarhar Province.

12. (*opposite bottom*) The ubiquitous Afghan "jingle truck," named for its colorful designs and dangling chains that jingled as the truck bounced down Afghanistan's unpaved roads. They brought supplies to rural Afghanistan and the coalition.

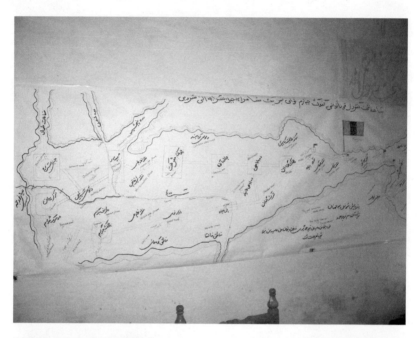

13. (*opposite top*) Hand-drawn operations map of the Tagab Valley, indicating the rudimentary state of the Afghan police. It was found in a woefully ill-equipped Afghan National Police station.

14. (*opposite bottom*) Afghan cooks prepare fresh lamb for a *shura* with village elders in Uruzgan in 2006.

15. (*above*) An all-terrain vehicle scouting for IEDs ahead of a patrol in Helmand Province in early 2006.

16. The French-made Panhard vehicle used by UAE Special Operations Forces. The Panhard was light and heavily armed and had great mobility but could carry a crew of only three, limiting soldiers' ability to conduct foot patrols.

17. Mohammad Daoud, governor of Helmand Province, granting land for the proposed UAE military base outside of Musa Qala. The author's inability to establish the base was a significant missed opportunity to change the complexion of the war in southern Afghanistan.

18. (*opposite top*) The author aboard an Afghan Mi-17 helicopter during a visit to Afghanistan as director for Afghanistan policy in the Office of the Secretary of Defense. The helicopter was provided to the Ministry of the Interior's counternarcotics police for drug interdiction.

19. (*opposite bottom*) The author greeting Vice President Cheney in his White House office before a prebriefing for a National Security Council meeting with President Bush.

20. (*above*) France (*left*) and the author (*right*) agreeing to build a well and furnish desks to a school in a friendly village near FOB Salerno in Khost Province in 2009.

21. The roundabout in Chora, a village in Uruzgan Province, just before the joint U.S., Afghan, Australian, UAE Task Force cleared heavily armed Taliban fighters from the Baluchi Valley during a multiday battle in 2006. Note the white sheet covering the body of a local Afghan policeman lying at the base of the roundabout, left as a warning from the Taliban.

22. A mine-resistant ambush-protected vehicle (MRAP). Though effective at protecting soldiers, the MRAP's excessive size and weight made it ill suited for Afghanistan's rough terrain and forced coalition convoys onto the few roads that could support it. This made their routes very predictable and more susceptible to Taliban IED attacks. Moments after this photo was taken the small stone bridge collapsed.

23. (*top*) The author and Afghan National Army soldiers responding to a Haqqani network suicide bombing of the Khost provincial police headquarters in July 2009.

24. (*bottom*) ODA 21 base in Ghazni Province, dedicated to Sgt. First Class Brian Woods.

25. (*opposite*) Staff Sgt. Matthew Pucino's flag-draped body on the floor of a C-130 just before leaving FOB Salerno in Khost Province for Bagram Airfield and the long flight home.

26. Matt Pucino on his ATV, prepared to scout ahead of his team for IEDs buried in the road. One such pressure-initiated IED would later take his life. The teams refused to allow the threat of IEDs to deter them.

27. This little girl boldly pushed past a group of boys to the front of the line for school supplies we were delivering. Her determination was palpable. Education for girls and women's empowerment are our best weapons to undermine the oppressive, extremist ideology of the Taliban.

28. (*above*) Pakistani Border Post 28 near Shkin, Paktika Province. The Taliban regularly launched rockets at FOB Lilley from the base of this hill, with no response from the Pakistanis.

29. (*opposite top*) Taliban 107 millimeter rockets aimed at FOB Lilley just after the men of ODA 25 disarmed them by cutting the burning fuses.

30. (*opposite bottom*) The blast from the bombing of the Taliban rocket site near Pakistani Border Post 28. Seconds later there was a secondary explosion from destroyed rockets. The bombing was highly controversial due to concerns about civilian casualties.

31. *Arbakai* from the Mangal tribe near Chamkani District, Paktia Province. Well-armed and loyal to their elders, the *arbakai* formed the basis of the Community Defense Initiative, which aimed to organize men like these into pockets of resistance to the Taliban in rural villages.

9 The Mangal Tribe
Protecting People We Can't Access

"You ask us to stand up to the Talibs and the Haqqanis while you hide in your tanks from their bombs," one elderly Afghan man said incredulously as dozens of other wizened elders from the powerful Mangal tribe nodded in agreement. The group was sitting in a semicircle on an oversized rug in front of several bowls of dates and nuts in a concrete community building that tripled as a school, police station, and meeting hall. Most of the men had a mixed allotment of shotguns, old British Enfield rifles, and AK-47s slung over their shoulders. Several were better equipped than the Afghan National Army soldiers who accompanied us. A number of the elders were leaders of the Mangal's *arbakai*, or tribal militia, which protected tribal interests. Rumor and reporting had indicated that the Mangal could mobilize up to 1,500 *arbakai* if they felt the tribe's interests were threatened. Tribal interests ranged from enforcing the decisions of the tribal *shura* to protecting the natural resources found on tribal land. The bottom line was that I wanted those *arbakai* working with us, or at least working against the Haqqani network, one of Afghanistan's three main insurgent groups along with the Hezb-e-Islami Gulbuddin and the Taliban. Led by Siraj Haqqani, the son of the famous anti-Soviet fighter Jalaluddin Haqqani, the group enjoyed a safe haven in North Waziristan, Pakistan, centered on the town of Miram Shah. Since 2004 the Haqqani network had reconstituted its operations in its traditional strongholds of Khost, Paktia, and Paktika provinces and had recently begun executing influence and attacks in the provinces around Kabul. They were widely regarded as the most experienced, sophisticated, and well-funded of the insurgent groups, with decades-long ties to al Qaeda. (Osama bin Laden had volunteered to fight with the Haqqanis during the Soviet resistance in the 1980s.)

It was my job to help thwart their momentum, a job consistently sty-mied by a pervasive sense of risk aversion—in both the military and the State Department—that had gripped the U.S. war effort since my previous deployment in 2006.

The men mostly stood stone-faced as their spokesman, Mullah Gha-foorzai, recounted the long history of the Mangal's support for past monarchies and the current Afghan government and then chastised me for our lack of support for his tribe and lack of presence in their valley. Mullah Ghafoorzai was a big man by American standards, which prac-tically made him a giant by Afghan standards. He had command of the room and sat at one end of the long carpet in his tan *shalwar kameez*, with a gray vest and shawl thrown over his shoulder. He had a full black and gray beard and wore a black turban in the Afghan style. He twirled his prayer beads in his right hand as he spoke in a low, steady tone that slowly began to mesmerize me after a tiring day of travel on dusty, pock-marked roads in the hot Afghan sun.

I had left my position on Vice President Cheney's staff in the White House in January 2009 and immediately donned my uniform to mobi-lize as the commander of the National Guard's B Company, 2nd Battal-ion, 20th Special Forces Group. My unit consisted of over eighty Special Forces operators spread across six ODAs along with several dozen sup-port personnel, such as intelligence analysts and supply sergeants who were attached to my Operational Detachment Bravo (ODB). The ODB was the headquarters element of the unit that typically performed a sup-port role but could also operate autonomously as a team to coordinate the tactical activities of multiple ODAs or conduct higher level meetings with Afghan government or tribal leaders such as Ghafoorzai. For this deployment I had responsibility for my teams' operations across four provinces of Afghanistan's southeast border region in Khost, Paktia, Pak-tika, and Ghazni. Though I had lived and breathed reporting from the field in Afghanistan since my previous tour (along with numerous offi-cial trips as a civilian), three years later I was shocked to see how much security had declined in Afghanistan. I was also dismayed to see how conventionally we were approaching a very unconventional war, con-fining our soldiers to heavily armored vehicles and mandating lengthy PowerPoint briefings for every offensive mission. Though the transition from having input at the highest level of the U.S. government to being

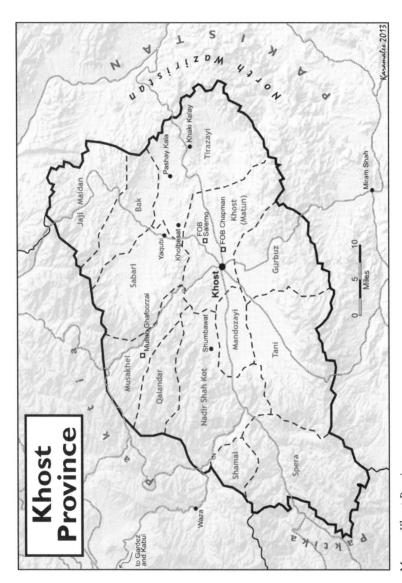

Map 12. Khost Province.

buried in the military bureaucracy as a midlevel officer was difficult at times, I came back to the border region determined to implement some of the policies I had pushed while in Washington—particularly engaging and influencing tribes such as the Mangal.

Mullah Ghafoorzai shifted topics in his diatribe by recalling the "bearded ones" who had come before us, referring to Special Forces teams that used to work closely with him and his men on a regular basis. We were the first he had seen in two years. He lamented that the bearded ones used to bring him supplies and money to pay his men, but more important, he knew they would come to his aid if the Haqqanis came after him. "But now I never see any Americans, and the Mangal are on our own," he said. Bearded ones had come to him one day and informed him that they were forbidden from continuing to support his *arbakai* because the American military command viewed his tribal militia as competing with the growth of the Afghan Army and National Police. I thought back to the debates in 2006–7 within the Pentagon and with the State Department, where many argued that every dollar spent continuing to support tribal militias and other groups was one less dollar spent on growing a legitimate Army and police. They were right in theory, but I had unsuccessfully pushed back on the policy, saying that the timing wasn't right to turn off our support of local militias because the Army and police were taking much longer than expected to develop. We needed some entity to fill the vacuum in the interim and provide the population with security at a local level.

Ghafoorzai went on to explain that his men did not want to join the police because they were too corrupt. One had to "buy" decent positions with the police, often with a loan from higher-ranking officers, and then repay them by passing bribes solicited from local people up the chain of command. Ghafoorzai and his men didn't want to join the Army because soldiers were deployed across the country away from their families in an effort to ethnically mix the Army and reduce cronyism.

As we discovered throughout that fall of 2009 during my unit's patrols into the Mangal areas, the locals in the two most populated Mangal valleys in eastern Afghanistan had not seen *any* coalition or Afghan Army patrol in nearly two years. This was roughly since the introduction of the U.S. military's lumbering mine-resistant ambush-protected vehicles (MRAPs), which were incapable of traversing the mountain passes leading to their lands. As a Special Forces unit, we were one of the last units still allowed to conduct patrols in Humvees and GMVs instead of MRAPs. The ubiquitous Humvee could traverse all but the most restricted mountain roads but lacked the armored, V-shaped underside of the MRAP that deflects the blast of IEDs to the sides. Therefore its occupants were much more likely to be seriously wounded or killed by an IED buried in the road and exploding underneath.

In fact, this particular trip had been an arduous one up into the mountains of Musa Khel District in northwest Khost Province. We had left at 1 a.m. in order to avoid the IEDs that lined the roads north and west of my headquarters at Forward Operating Base Salerno. We knew that only GMVs could traverse the narrow switchback mountain roads that would take us into the mountains that lined the horizon and separated Khost from the rest of Afghanistan.

The few elders brave enough to speak with us explained that many of them had been targeted by the Haqqani network and intimidated into submission over the previous eighteen months, a situation that left their lands a hotbed of insurgent activity replete with large training camps and manufacturing centers for IEDs. The district center in neighboring Qalandar District had been built and then destroyed by the Haqqanis, rebuilt by the local provincial reconstruction team, and then destroyed again. To make matters worse, we received consistent reports of insurgent commanders bragging to Mangal villagers that the Americans were "too scared" to bring their "wheeled tanks" (the Afghan term for the MRAP and other armored vehicles such as the Stryker infantry carrier) up into the mountains, while pressing villagers to provide young men to the insurgency.

Throughout the patrol many of the Mangal were polite but kept their distance. During one stop in a small bazaar, I stepped into a tiny mud hut shop where I was able to get the shopkeeper to open up a bit—after buying a bag full of Pepsis and Afghan candies. He told us that everyone in the village knew we were coming up the valley. I saw my intelligence sergeant, standing at the door, raise an eyebrow. The shopkeeper said he was pleased to see Americans again but repeatedly asked us why we had abandoned his tribe despite their support for the Afghan government. Eventually the conversation turned to a Haqqani training camp that was reported to be near his village. He shrugged his shoulders as though to say, "What can I do about it?"

The Mangal occupied a strategic mountain range that separated Khost, a key eastern province along the Pakistani border, from the rest of Afghanistan. "If we have lost the Mangal, we could lose Khost, just as the Russians did," I said to one of my sergeants as we left another *shura* we visited as we progressed up the valley. My intelligence analysts had been perplexed about why many of the IEDs plaguing the area surrounding the provincial capital were emanating from the Mangal tribal lands. Our rare patrol through these lands taught us why. Part of the reason was simply that we hadn't had nearly enough troops committed to be able to secure areas like the Mangal tribal lands. But I thought the bigger reason was the misuse of the assets and soldiers we did have on the ground in Afghanistan. Our focus on more armor, force protection, and reducing casualties had ceded the initiative and the terrain to the insurgents and cost us our credibility with one of eastern Afghanistan's largest tribes.

The MRAP had undoubtedly proven to be effective at saving American lives while we carried out missions like clearing routes and escorting supply convoys. Secretary Gates made the deployment of the MRAP one of his top priorities in 2008 and 2009, eventually deploying over 7,100 to Afghanistan.[1] It was a necessary and well-intentioned initiative that, unfortunately, had unintended consequences on our counterinsurgency efforts due to mismanagement of the MRAPs once they were in theater.

The problem was that the MRAP was developed for the cities and highways of Iraq, not the mountains and mud trails of Afghanistan. Because the twenty-ton, ten-foot-tall vehicle sometimes rolled over in the rugged terrain and often collapsed its poor mountain roadbeds, the Pentagon worked tirelessly to deploy to Afghanistan the newer MRAP all-terrain vehicle (M-ATV), which had a lower center of gravity, in record numbers and in record time.

Although the rollover problem had been largely resolved by the M-ATV, both vehicles were still too wide, tall, and cumbersome to pass through many Afghan villages or navigate the country's notorious mountain roads and narrow wadis in the heavily forested green zones where most rural Afghans lived. The vehicles could traverse only paved or well-developed roads, which were rare in the fourth-poorest country in the world, and especially in the mountain-lined valleys and villages of eastern Afghanistan.

In my view the fault did not lie with the MRAP, the M-ATV, or any other armored vehicle. The real blame lay with how commanders mandated the use of the vehicles due to their aversion to risk and their attempts to minimize coalition injuries at the expense of the broader counterinsurgency mission. The vehicles' size would not have been a hindrance to that mission if junior Army commanders were also authorized to use other, smaller vehicles to access the difficult areas of Afghanistan when the situation called for it. For example, if a unit needed to access a village that was accessible only by pickup truck or Humvee, then that was what they should have been allowed to use, after an examination of the risk.

Instead what I consistently found was that commanders were *mandating* the use of MRAPs only. If a unit did not have MRAPs or some other type of armored vehicle, its soldiers were not allowed to leave the base at all. This sounds like a minor tactical issue, but its consequences were having strategic effects on how we conducted the war and our ability to access the population. As one frustrated company commander told me in the summer of 2009, "If an MRAP can't get there, we don't go there. I need the flexibility to decide what type of vehicle to use so I can protect the populace and get at the enemy in hard-to-reach places."

Another junior commander, looking up at the hills and mountains surrounding his camp, lamented that he was now unable to access more than 70 percent of his assigned district. "My men can only walk so far with their body armor on," he said as we chatted near the line of Humvees he could no longer use. To make matters worse, there was an additional requirement of a minimum of four vehicles in order to leave the wire. If a unit didn't have enough working MRAPs to meet the requirement, then they didn't leave until the vehicles were repaired.

During our predeployment site visits in the fall of 2008, my key leaders and I visited an outpost in an old fort overlooking Khost City. The fort was on a hill on the edge of the city about a five-minute drive or twenty-minute walk from the provincial governor's office and police headquarters downtown. After sitting in a meeting with the Afghan provincial leadership, I began chatting with one of the American sergeants in the next room, who turned out to be a police mentor. His job was to both train police in various skills critical to effective policing and to work alongside the Afghan police to help them bolster security in the area. Another, unspoken mission was to act as an honest broker or conscience for the notoriously corrupt police. With American soldiers around, the Afghans typically would shy away from or at least have to go out of their way to engage in the bad behavior—bribes, shakedowns, abuses—that they were known for. I asked the sergeant why his mentor team was living up in the fort on the edge of Khost City rather than downtown with the police. He smirked. "Sir, I've been driving my command nuts with that same question this entire tour. The answer always comes back the same: too dangerous. The police HQ down there gets attacked about every six weeks."

"Well, couldn't you help them increase their defenses and their security patrols if you were there instead of here?" I asked.

"Yes sir," the sergeant replied. I asked how often the mentor team was able to get down to the police headquarters. The sergeant shrugged while explaining that they didn't have any MRAPs yet and that his Humvees were for emergency evacuation only now. I asked why his team didn't just walk.

"Sir, we have to have a minimum of twelve men to go on patrol. I've never had more than nine men, so basically we are stuck here. We have to invite the police to come up here. The police chief rarely comes, though, unless we put out a big lunch spread for him."

This cautious approach not only contradicted the principles of counterinsurgency doctrine; it was reckless. Exclusively using these behemoth vehicles prevented U.S. troops from accessing large portions of the populace and allowed insurgent IED cells to flourish in areas relatively easy to reach in vehicles other than MRAPs. The problem was that if a senior commander approved a mission in a Humvee or pickup truck and U.S. soldiers were ambushed or killed by an IED, the resulting inquiry would be a potential career killer. So they defaulted to the safest mode of transportation available to them. The bottom line, however, was that we could not protect and influence a populace we would not allow ourselves to access. Over time I became certain that this force-protection-oriented mentality was causing more American casualties in the long run than it was preventing in the short run.

We were also sending a terrible message to our partnered Afghan security forces, with whom we should have been sharing risks, and to the Afghan people we were trying to win over while peering at them through six inches of plate glass and armor. Further, if the military was not accessing areas of Afghanistan lacking roads that could handle these twenty-ton vehicles, neither were the Afghan National Army. They certainly did not dare to tread where the U.S. military wouldn't.

Later in my tour I realized the extent to which risk aversion had gripped our civilian aid agencies as well. One of my ODA team leaders called me one afternoon to tell me that a U.S. Department of Agriculture civilian advisor had come to him begging for help getting to a local agricultural training center. "What's the problem? Can't he go to the center with the PRT?" I asked.

My team leader explained that the headmaster of the training center was thrilled to have an expert from the U.S. Department of Agriculture assist his students, but after the first day of teaching, the headmaster asked the advisor not to come back. The advisor was naturally surprised and dismayed, and after several cups of chai finally dragged an explanation out of the headmaster. The MRAPs that the provincial reconstruction team used to deliver the advisor drew a lot of attention to the center. The entire area, including any Taliban sympathizers, instantly knew that Americans were present. Plus they made the students nervous, particularly when they took up positions around the center to provide security for the American inside. "The headmaster said the advisor could come back if the military would just come in civilian vehicles, drop him off for the day, and not stand around with guns pointing at everyone," my team leader continued. "The district police chief's son is one of the students at the training center, so there are several ANP there with him. The police chief has assured the advisor that he would be safe there with his policemen if he would return to teach."

"We know how far that went," I said.

"Yep," said my team leader. "Shot right out of the sky by the RSO." The embassy's regional security officer was the official charged with the security of the State Department diplomats and other civilians. He would delegate those responsibilities *if* the civilians in the field were with military protection at all times. Otherwise any trip by a civilian out of the wire without the military had to be approved in Kabul, which meant it typically wasn't approved.

We eventually decided on a workaround that enabled the civilian to help the agriculture center with a reasonable amount of safety. A few times a week he would "sneak" over to my ODA's compound early in the morning and they would drive him, one of our interpreters, and one of the team's civil affairs sergeants over to the school on their four-wheelers. The school was only a few kilometers away in a nearby village. They would go before sunrise and avoid the main road to avoid the risk of IEDs and any potential prying Taliban eyes. It was a risk on all our parts, but we mitigated it in responsible ways. We varied the days the advisor could go so as to avoid a predictable pattern and informed only the center that he was coming. We also made sure we had radio contact with our civil affairs sergeant and that they had a GPS and cell phone with them that we could track if something happened.

I would have been fired on the spot, if not worse, if something had happened to that civilian after we assisted him in getting out there. But I felt strongly that as long as we did it smartly, getting those Afghans in a friendly village the help they needed was a risk worth taking. To me, it was a much bigger risk to have an expert in agriculture sitting on his rear end doing nothing a stone's throw from people who wanted his help. I had attended dozens of meetings in Washington at which the Defense Department hounded the State Department and USAID for more civilians to help the military with these types of key skills. But in this case and many others I witnessed, we couldn't get over our own inflexibility—like surrounding an agriculture school with twenty-ton MRAPs even though the headmaster asked us not to. At the same time, we showed that there were creative and responsible ways to get the job done. But it took all of us accepting a certain level of risk that our civilian agencies, and most military commanders, for that matter, were unwilling to accept.

The regional security office restrictions on civilians and the insistence on our traveling in MRAPs were seemingly minor tactical problems, but they had strategic implications on how we conducted counterinsurgency. Though the restrictions reduced our civilians' exposure to danger and MRAPs saved lives when a vehicle was struck, I questioned whether their misuse actually cost us lives in the long run. One had to wonder why the insurgency more than doubled its use of IEDs despite the introduction of mine-resistant vehicles. If the vehicles were so effective, why did the Taliban, Haqqanis, and other insurgent networks continue to rely on the IED as a key weapon? One reason was that they had simply discovered how to make the bombs large enough to destroy the vehicles. Another was that by limiting ourselves to only armored vehicles, we limited ourselves to the few roads that would support them, thus making it even easier for insurgents to target us. One more reason was that a patrol or mission was usually stopped in its tracks after being struck by an IED and therefore partially defeated, even when all of the soldiers survived in the end.

Ultimately, the real effect of the IED was to prevent us from going where the insurgents didn't want us to go. It astounded me that people failed to realize that causing casualties was only a side benefit of the IED. The true prize for the insurgent leadership was separating the ISAF coalition and Afghan security forces from the populace. Every time we added another layer of armor in response to casualties, we were playing right into the Taliban's and Haqqani's hands.

Over the years I had watched the evolution of how coalition forces traversed the battlefield in Afghanistan, from pickup trucks to Humvees to armored Humvees and GMVs to ever larger MRAPs, while the Taliban escalated their IED campaign by simply building bigger bombs. So I was not surprised when I read a year later that the U.S. Marines were planning to deploy seventy-ton M1A1 Abrams tanks to Helmand Province in southern Afghanistan.

A countryside littered with Russian tanks and armored personnel carriers was evidence enough that this escalation of armor versus explosives was a fool's game. While the Abrams tank was able to deliver precision firepower at great distances, insurgents were easily able to predict the few roads it could travel (unless we decided to demolish farmers' fields and irrigation canals), along with the lightly skinned fuelers and maintenance vehicles the tank required for sustainment.

When I raised such points in planning meetings, my coalition colleagues often asked how I proposed to "defeat" the IED. My initial response was that the question was wrong. We should not be trying to defeat the IED; rather we should be working to defeat the insurgency that plants them. For example, accessing and supporting tribes such as the Mangal were critical for opposing the insurgency. But doing so meant that we would likely take casualties and risk short-term setbacks for longer term gains.

It may have been counterintuitive, but I argued that we actually needed *less* armor and needed to be more flexible and unpredictable. The MRAP should have been one item on a menu of methods to access the population. Instead of dictating that no unit could leave its base unless in an MRAP or M-ATV, we should have allowed units to use Humvees, all-terrain vehicles, ruggedized pickup trucks, and even motorcycles when appropriate. Unpredictability and sometimes keeping a low profile and blending in were the best forms of protection. Knowing their movements were being watched at all times, units needed to use deception, such as varying the time of day and night they moved, their routes of travel, and the types of vehicles in which they traveled, to keep the insurgents constantly guessing. The Taliban could not booby-trap and watch every road, trail, and wadi in Afghanistan, but they could and did hammer us on the few roads that would support armored vehicles.

Throughout the tour, I grew more certain that we might not be able to defeat the IED, but we could make it irrelevant. To do so would require us to rely on the ingenuity and resourcefulness of the junior leaders who were most in tune with the local dynamics and terrain, not on technology or defensive-minded mandates designed to prevent casualties at all costs. Marginalizing the IED would also require higher level commanders to accept greater risk and allow their subordinates to sometimes make mistakes, even deadly ones. They would have to start playing to win instead of trying to avoid losing. It was the only way to start connecting with the Afghan people, who were the ones that would defeat the Taliban in the end. To not do so risked losing key tribes like the Mangal and others, like the headmaster of the agricultural center who became convinced we were not willing to do what it took to stand and fight with them.

10 The Elder in Khost
Risk Aversion and the Cost of Inaction

Our Tactical Operations Center was a much smaller version of what one would see in the typical conventional Army battalion or brigade head-quarters on various coalition bases dotting the Afghan countryside. Situated in a forty-foot-long rectangular room, the focal point consisted of three flat-screen monitors supported by five-foot-tall plywood stands. One monitor typically displayed an electronic map of Afghanistan with a splay of blue symbols indicating the locations of various units generated by shoe-box-size GPS transmitters called "blue force trackers," mandatory in every vehicle leaving a secure coalition base in Afghanistan. Another monitor constantly ran al Jazeera–English, which often reported events occurring in our area of operations before we even knew about them. The third screen usually displayed an electronic version of the PowerPoint mission briefing known as a "concept of operations," or conop, submitted by one of my subordinate ODAs. In its simplest form the conop described the who, what, when, where, and why of the current mission. In its most complicated form, it was a forty- to fifty-slide behemoth with page after page of overhead imagery, detailed schemes of maneuver, and risk assessments.

On some level I had come to resent the Tactical Operations Center. It had become the scene of countless bureaucratic battles over nearly every detail of every operation we wanted to conduct. My staff had derisively come to call our mission "counterbureaucracy" rather than "counterinsurgency." It seemed we spent the majority of our time in an endless series of internal fights and coordination exercises with the myriad chains of command that had veto power over any of my ODAs' missions. The process was exemplified by the conop and its series of mandatory slides for each type of mission. I stared at the current conop up on the screen that was in the midst of staffing and was generating a barrage of questions from our various higher headquarters. Many of us came to deeply resent the conop as a symbol of micromanagement and risk aversion in approving even the most basic mission.

A ceiling-to-floor relief map of my area of operations on the Afghan-Pakistani border hung at one end of the room. It encompassed Khost, Paktia, Paktika, and Ghazni provinces on the Afghan side and North and South Waziristan on the Pakistani side. The map was shaded to show the massive elevation differences of the various mountain ranges. Many nights I just sat and stared at it, awestruck at the magnitude of what we were trying to do. There were tiny markers showing the locations of coalition and Afghan Army posts. It looked as though a dozen Grand Canyons stood between each post, with black dots representing villages sprinkled like pepper in every valley and draw.

Stretched out in front of the monitors were two rows of heavy, wooden, bench-like tables stacked with computer monitors, printers, stacks of intelligence reports, and soda cans. My sergeant major, operations warrant officer, operations NCO, executive officer, and a half dozen other key staff had laptops and small areas for themselves at various points along the tables. Everyone was happy that day. We had just received a shipment of office chairs from the supply officer at the conventional Army brigade a few hundred yards away on FOB Salerno. The chairs would have rivaled anything I'd seen at the White House or Pentagon and were a far cry from the locally purchased, Pakistani-made chairs we usually had. My large, bald operations officer, York, had twice fallen out of his chair when one of the legs snapped. He was leaning back in his new chair, swiveling back and forth, especially pleased.

"Haji Azam's back in Kahki Kalay," Todd said, walking into the room. Todd had been specially trained to handle our human intelligence sources. I could see one of our interpreters hovering by the entrance (he wasn't allowed in the classified area), waiting on instructions for another call from another of Todd's sources. Kahki Kalay was a village due east of Salerno just inside the Pakistani border, where one of my ODAs as well as a nearby infantry unit had put in a considerable amount of effort and support to win over the elders. Haji Azam was a midlevel commander with the Haqqani network known for his brutality and aggressive recruiting tactics. We discussed the mission by phone with ODA 23, which was on the other side of FOB Salerno, embedded with the Afghan National Army commandos. The team quickly began to put together a plan to kill or capture the Haqqani commander. Actually they were dusting off a series of old plans that we simply needed to get reapproved. Azam regularly bounced back and forth across the border with Pakistan. He usually stayed in Afghanistan only about a week at a time, sleeping in different places each night before heading back to safety in Pakistan. He was known for recruiting in the local mosques after Friday prayer. We had one report from an informant in Khaki Kalay that Azam would solicit "donations" from the village during his visits. On one occasion he demanded that the women each bring one piece of their bridal jewelry as a contribution to the jihad being waged by the Haqqanis. He also demanded that a certain number of men return with him to Pakistan for training. If a member of the Afghan Army or someone who worked on the U.S. base happened to be home when Azam and his pack of men rolled into town on their dirt bikes, they had better get out of town very quickly. Azam had no qualms about exercising brutal retribution for rejecting his donation requests. In the district of Mendozai Azam, he and his men had machine-gunned a girls' school while in session after the Mendozai elders had refused to provide recruits. At minimum, I wanted this guy arrested and sitting in a cell in Bagram. Better yet, I wanted to hand him over to the elders of Mendozai; they would take care of things their own way.

The sun was setting and I wanted my team and the commandos to use helicopters so that they had plenty of time to get in and out of the area under the cover of darkness. The road leading to the village was replete with IEDs. If the team went by ground, they would have to return to our base during the day and would surely be hit. Plus Azam was hyper-vigilant, reportedly stationing informants at road intersections and up on Kahki Kalay's nearby hills to warn of any coalition approach. Going in by ground and not tipping him off would be tough, to say the least.

"We'll never get the mission approved this fast, sir," the team leader, Jason, said in the matter-of-fact tone of someone who had been through this drill dozens of times. "We want this guy just as much as anybody, but we won't get it briefed in time, and we definitely won't get helicopters. The helos will just cause us to have to get two more approvals. We'll take our chances and go by ground on the back roads. We'll offset the vehicles and quietly walk in." By "offset" Jason meant the team and their partnered Afghans would drive the vehicles to a location close enough to the target to walk to it, but far enough away that the vehicles would not be heard by Azam or any potential lookouts he had in the village.

I decided to overrule my ODA leadership and go for the helicopters. I understood where Jason was coming from; we had wasted so many days and nights trying to get helicopter support only to have the missions delayed or the helicopters redirected at the last minute that my guys would rather risk their lives to IEDs than have another mission get canceled. I wanted this guy badly, but with the distance they would have to travel, the team would be pressed to get the entire operation completed before sunup. I knew the ODA would have to travel back in their GMVs on roads sown with IEDs during the day through a part of Khost that was completely controlled by the Haqqanis.

Meanwhile, my intelligence and operations shop and staff were furiously putting together the slides that were mandatory for briefings to the numerous higher headquarters that had to provide their approval. A few hours later, after frantic calls and quickly assembled briefs to the aviation unit, two Chinook helicopters at FOB Salerno's airfield spun their blades in the dark in anticipation of the mission's being approved. Thirty Afghan commandos brooded outside my Operations Center, pacing on the gravel.

I was nearby, yelling into a phone. "Who else do we need approvals from? We followed all of the procedures in the emergency conop checklist. We have already had this mission preapproved twice. It's just a different location this time!"

Some key staff couldn't be found. Some liked the plan; others suggested revisions. Still others had questions. The plan evolved as the phone calls and emails flew back and forth. Hours passed. The aviation commander approved the use of his Chinook transport helicopters for the mission, but of course they had to have attack helicopters available to do a combat insertion. Fortunately, the attack aviation operations officer responsible for their mission tasking had been coming to our weekly barbeque for months, and he agreed to get a waiver for the helicopter crews' rest requirements so that they could fly the mission. (In a bid to avoid accidents aviators are required by regulation to get so many hours of sleep commensurate with the number of hours they've flown; these requirements were still in place in the combat zones.) Now, however, the aviation commander's boss back at Bagram Airbase wanted a Predator drone to get "eyes" on the area before he would commit his Chinooks. The Chinook is a cigar-shaped helicopter with rotors on front and back that can hold over thirty soldiers and their gear. They have only defensive machine guns on either side and are vulnerable to ground fire as they flare to land. The Apaches, by contrast, are armored attack helicopters built to kill tanks and ground troops with cannons, rockets, and Hellfire guided missiles. The aviation commander had mandated that all Chinooks conducting air assaults be escorted by Apaches. It was also a standing rule in theater that all medevac flights have an Apache escort. Since we had to have a medevac available in order to go on a mission, the unintended consequence was that we had a number of missions canceled when there were not enough Apaches available to escort the various medevac and air assault missions ongoing across Afghanistan.

York, my operations officer, was also on the phone: "It's already mandatory for Apache attack helicopters to guard his Chinooks! Now he's gotta have Predators to go ahead of the attack helicopters that then go ahead of the Chinooks?"

I knew it was highly unlikely a Predator was going to be available and began to wonder if the aviation commander just didn't want to risk his helicopters and wouldn't outright say so.

The sergeant responsible for Predator support requests at my higher headquarters promised York he would pull some strings, but he didn't sound optimistic. An hour later the sergeant called back and informed him they could get the Predator, but only for an hour due to competing requirements, and only just before dawn, which was after the elder said Azam was likely to be gone. "It's the best I can do," the sergeant explained, "and the only way you'll get the helos."

"Fine," I said. "We have to at least try, or we'll lose any support we have left in this village."

The cell phone in the corner rang. "Where are you?" the elder asked urgently. The Haqqani commander was drinking tea one compound away, he said. "He is suspicious of me and knows my sons have worked as interpreters for Western NGOs. He knows my family supports the government. The police are too afraid to challenge him. He will kill me. I'm afraid," the proud old man said. "You said you were here to protect us."

My interpreter, standing outside my headquarters building, cell phone in hand and relaying the old man's pleas, began to tear up. Todd, my intelligence sergeant, glared at me as though I represented all of the officers standing between him and helping this man. I thought about all of the frustrating times that staff officers, rather than saying yes or no to the mission, expressed a "concern," put one more caveat in place to "mitigate risk," or asked just one more question before sending the conop higher for the next level of approvals.

At this point I was screaming on the secure telephone at my battalion operations officer at the Special Operations Task Force. It wasn't really his fault. He had been on the phone all afternoon and night coordinating all of the mandatory assets, briefings, and approvals that went along with a kill/capture mission. It was a laborious, bureaucratic system for mission approval that had grown over the years with the buildup of rules and requirements. Each one made sense in isolation; it was the accumulation of requirements over time that created a system in which, as a Special Forces officer and commander, I didn't have the authority to go help this man and his village—as if I'd be reckless with my own men's lives. I was livid.

I conferred with Todd, Jason, and Marc. We couldn't get the assets lined up to hit Azam's compound until around 4 a.m., though there was a chance the Predator would free up sooner. Todd and Marc pressed that if we hit Azam's house and he wasn't there, he would suspect that someone in the village had tipped us off and would seek retribution.

"The elder is adamant that we kill the guy when we come, not capture him or let him get away," Todd said.

"You know we can't guarantee that," I said.

"Yeah, sir, of course. But the elder knows that if we capture Azam, he will be released in months and will be back in Kahki Kalay after his head and his family's too," Todd replied.

"Okay, don't stand everyone down until sunup just in case a Pred frees up sooner," I sighed.

By 5 a.m. the Predator still wasn't available. The Afghan commandos gave up on us and went back to their barracks. The helicopters powered down. The sun began to peek over the mountains to the east. Todd walked in and said that the Haqqani commander had moved to another town after morning prayers. The elder would no longer answer our calls.

We received word through the grapevine with our Afghan base workers that the villagers in Khaki Kalay had lost faith in us. The elder survived, but he never spoke to us again. We heard later from another source that the elder sold some of his family's land to Azam at bargain prices. He did so partly to placate the Haqqanis and partly to make up for the income his sons had lost when they quit their jobs as interpreters with the coalition. Their father wouldn't let them work with us any longer. "The Americans won't protect you. We cannot depend on them," he had reportedly told his sons and a group of their friends who worked on a nearby Afghan Army base.

The level of frustration among the junior and midlevel Special Forces officers over the conop process was extreme. Most of my active-duty counterparts had given up trying to change things. The mission approval process had just become a part of the culture, and instead of forcing change, we all found creative ways to game the system. On the one hand, the rhetoric of counterinsurgency espoused flexibility, empowering junior commanders, and maximizing one's time off a firebase and among the populace. On the other, we had an immense and layered military bureaucracy whose instinctive reaction to casualties or operational mistakes was to remedy the situation by requiring that missions undergo progressively higher levels of approval.

Even as the commander of a Special Forces company, I did not have the authority to allow my teams to leave their bases, or even personally leave my own base, for any reason. I first had to ask permission by submitting a conop over email to the Special Operations Task Force in Bagram—even just to walk right outside the front gate of our base to chat with the shop owners in the local bazaar. Granted, we had to send only a few slides for such a mundane mission, but it was beyond frustrating that, as a Special Forces major, I couldn't simply talk to the locals just outside my base on my own accord. For even the most mundane of routine tasks, the Special Operations Task Force would then also have to send the conop up to its higher headquarters, the CJSOTF, for situational awareness (so that our superiors knew where we were at all times we were out of the wire). I received numerous nasty phone calls from my headquarter's operations officer when one of my teams left the base on some short-notice mission before the team's three higher headquarters were aware of it.

There really wasn't any one person or command that could be blamed. The problem was an accumulation of rules over the past decade, usually in response to major events like the four-man Navy SEAL reconnaissance cell that was wiped out in 2005, or a base being overrun by insurgents, such as Combat Outpost Wanat in 2008. The natural response to those types of events was to add another risk-mitigating restriction that made sense at the time but was then applied to everyone and cemented as a steadfast rule. Once they were in place few were ever removed, and they accumulated to the point of absurdity. For example, in response to the SEAL mission, made famous by the book and movie Lone Survivor, all future foot patrols or reconnaissance missions had to have a minimum of nine men. The blanket rule put in place as a result of the Wanat disaster was that there could be no fewer that twelve American soldiers guarding a base at any given time. Years later I actually came across a platoon in a remote outpost with eighteen soldiers; the frustrated platoon leader did not have the twenty-one men necessary to conduct a foot patrol and still meet the minimum requirement to protect his base. The only time he could leave his base was when a squad of soldiers from another unit was flown in for reinforcements. The local Taliban quickly learned that every time a helicopter flew into the base a patrol would soon come down the hill from the outpost. Not surprisingly the patrols were typically met with an ambush. Rather than accepting some risk and relaxing the requirements, the unit's higher headquarters eventually relocated the platoon and demolished the outpost.

In 2005 President Karzai visited the Pentagon to meet with Secretary Rumsfeld. A colleague who attended the meeting told me that Karzai complained vociferously about foreign forces conducting night raids into Afghan homes, sometimes killing civilians. The then commander of U.S. forces in Afghanistan, Lt. Gen. Karl Eikenberry, responded to the complaint by requiring that all night raids be approved at his level, which had the effect of curtailing the number of night raids and also unit flexibility about when to conduct them. Units subsequently had to send in the mission request up to a week in advance to allow it to get staffed for approval up the chain of command. Years later, despite a tremendous increase in the number of missions and a worsening insurgency, Eikenberry's rule had not changed. The result was a systematic and self-inflicted retardation of the most capable military in the world. It felt as though we were defeating ourselves rather than the Taliban defeating us.

In October 2009 Washington came at me in the field in the form of the Assistant Secretary of Defense for Special Operations Mike Vickers. Vickers had previously served as a Green Beret and was renowned from the book *Charlie Wilson's War* as the behind-the-scenes CIA operative who had supplied the Afghan mujahideen in their war against the Soviet occupation. As my team, ODA 22, completed its briefing of the situation around the city of Gardez in Paktia Province, Vickers asked about my overall assessment and any issues we were having. "Our top priority is building the capacity of the team's partnered Afghan National Army unit," I explained. I went on to say that we thought the current estimates for the ANA's capabilities were overly optimistic and that it would be a generational effort for the Afghans to truly be able to operate independently.

"Our second priority is to blunt the growing momentum of the Taliban and Haqqanis in the area as they slowly take control of the districts to the south and east of Gardez," I said. Gardez was just to the west of the mountain range that formed a "C" around Khost to the east and was a key urban center on the roads between the Pakistani border and Kabul to the northwest. It was also the seat of the provincial government of Paktia Province. We were trying to set the conditions for tribal engagement, but we needed to get rid of some bad actors first.

"Okay, what's the issue? Get after them," Vickers said.

I explained that for the more complex missions, such as a mission to search for a weapons cache or to kill or capture a Haqqani commander, my Special Forces teams had to assemble a forty-slide conop for briefing and approval by a dozen higher headquarters if the team wanted to use helicopters.

"A dozen command approvals?" Vickers asked me incredulously. "Name them." The lieutenant colonel who was accompanying him glared at me over Vickers's shoulder.

"Absolutely. Now, assuming that the targeted Taliban commander has gone through all the hoops to verify that he is indeed bad, which is a painstaking process in itself, my ODAs then have to put together a full mission brief and get it approved by"—I ticked them off on my fingers—"one, the Special Forces company commander; two, the Special Operations Task Force commander at Bagram; three, the Special Forces group commander at Bagram; four, the Special Forces general in Kabul in charge of all Special Operations Forces; five, the local battle space owner [conventional battalion commander]; six, the battle space owner's brigade commander [the conventional brigade commander]; and seven, the regional commanding general at Bagram for eastern Afghanistan."

Vickers's brow was furrowed. I continued. "Then, if the mission is using helicopters that belong to the conventional units, as most of them do, we also would have to brief, eight, the aviation battalion commander, and nine, the aviation brigade commander." If the mission was going after Taliban leadership, I said, then the ISAF commander or one of his deputies had to provide his approval. "That's ten briefs.

"Finally, sir, as you know," I continued, "we are proud of the fact that we always conduct our missions with our partnered Afghan Army units. But that also means their leadership should be informed. So we also brief the ANA battalion commander; who in turn needs to brief his boss, the ANA brigade commander. That's numbers eleven and twelve." I had run out of fingers.

The staff at each of these levels *always* had a wide variety of questions, and each of these levels had veto power.

I also explained that before the conop got to step three, some poor staff officer in our headquarters had to make sure it conformed to a 102-item checklist that was focused on the formatting of the Power-Point so that the myriad mission requests coming in from ODAs sprinkled across Afghanistan were uniform in appearance when briefing the various commanders.

For these reasons, the conop had to be submitted over a week in advance in order to get staffed and briefed at all of these levels. The higher the level of mission, the further in advance the conop had to be submitted.

"Keep in mind, sir, this is just to do a search or target *one midlevel Taliban commander.*"

"What the hell are we doing here?" Vickers snapped to the lieutenant colonel. Before he could respond, the ODA's interpreter poked his head in the door to let us know that the ANA colonel and his staff were outside, waiting for us for lunch. The lieutenant colonel took this opportunity to break up what I was sure he viewed as an inappropriate "bitch session" to the assistant secretary, a four-star equivalent who was responsible to the secretary of defense for all Special Forces policy. My guys were smiling at me as we left the room.

I knew the conversation would get back to my headquarters, but I had said my piece. Having escorted numerous officials on these types of trips during my time in the Pentagon, I knew they wanted to hear the unvarnished views of soldiers and civilians closest to the Afghans and the fight. However, I also knew that any questions Vickers asked when he returned to Bagram Airbase would be explained away as isolated, anecdotal, and not representative of what was going on theaterwide. Plus civilian officials had only so much appetite for questioning military officers in the field.

The issue we didn't discuss was the process that had to occur before the conop could even be submitted in the first place. It was essentially a lengthy series of briefings and compilations of intelligence that had to go to a series of evaluation boards at the headquarters in Bagram and in Kabul in order to prove that an Afghan was a member of the insurgency and worthy of targeting for a kill/capture mission. The process was painstaking and thorough, requiring several high-quality sources of multiple types of intelligence before a single person could be placed on a list as "approved" for targeting. It was one of the reasons I cringed back in Washington when uninformed journalists or academics alleged that Special Operations Forces were picking men to target haphazardly or on a single tip from a tribal rival. I completely agreed that there needed to be a methodical vetting procedure in place to provide evidence that an Afghan was indeed supporting the insurgency before he could be deliberately targeted. However, like other issues, the process had grown out of control over time and was now a rigid, exhaustive, and bureaucratic process that took a tremendous amount of staff resources to maintain. Further, because the insurgents we nominated stayed on the list for only a limited period, the entire process had to be repeated for each individual insurgent several times a year and with numerous forms of fresh intelligence from numerous types of sources showing the person in question supported the Taliban. This was especially difficult when most of the higher-level Taliban commanders went across the border to

Pakistan for the winter to rest and refit. By the spring, when these same commanders crossed back into Afghanistan for the start of the spring fighting season, many of them had fallen off the targeting list due to a lack of activity. Though the Afghan Border Police and our informants called in that the Taliban commanders were coming back, there was little we could do about it except begin the nomination process again.

Why was this process allowed to continue? Was our senior leadership out of touch, or were they simply unwilling to change the system? A visit by the commanding general of Special Forces in Afghanistan was illustrative of why the answer was a little of both. When our briefing to the general turned to challenges my teams were having in their provinces, my warrant officer, York, seasoned and never afraid to voice his opinion, lamented the process. He particularly protested how it had ballooned since 2003, when both he and the general (then a lieutenant colonel) had served together. The general was taken aback. He was a charismatic, aggressive leader and wanted us to be successful. He replied that he had denied only a handful of missions in the nine months he had been in command.

"Sir, as we told Mr. Vickers, the reality is that missions are rarely denied outright by any commander along the approval chain," York said. "The problem is that they are questioned to death and delayed until they become irrelevant."

"Or," I added, "one of the commanders in the chain will approve the mission but with a caveat: *only if* a certain asset is available to reduce the risk. As you know, typically those assets aren't available. The problem is that no commander is looked at negatively for delaying or postponing a mission. Security is declining in all of my provinces, often because of our *inaction*. There needs to be some accountability for that. While we avoid being responsible for a mistake, we are going to lose this war." I could see the face of the general's chief of staff contorting and could tell that I was pushing my limits. The general asked me to give some examples of what I had not been allowed to do because of restrictions.

"Sir, a large part of the decline is simply a lack of the necessary resources, military and civilian, to fully implement a counterinsurgency campaign. However, we could do a better job with the resources at hand. The conventional battle space owner has a policy limiting his soldiers to MRAPs, which effectively limits his units to the flat spaces surrounding

Khost City and prevents them from getting into the mountains. Fine. I can work with that, as those areas are the most populated. The problem is that the Haqqanis, with foreign fighter support, have established a string of training camps and IED factories in the valleys and mountains surrounding Khost." I directed my laser pointer to a C-shaped string of mountains surrounding Khost, displayed on the wall-size map. "They are using those camps in these remote areas to stage attacks across Khost and to the interior of Afghanistan toward Gardez and Kabul. I have repeatedly been denied permission to get up there and get at them with my ODAs and their partnered Afghan commandos."

The general asked if the special mission unit operating near us was active. It reported through a separate chain of command that did not include him. I told him about a very successful mission the unit in our area had recently conducted and then asked us to exploit. "Sir, as you know, they don't have to beg for resources and they only go after high-value individuals. But they are in and out. They don't stick around for a longer term security sweep of the area or to project the presence of partnered Afghan Army units like we do. For example, they just hit one of the Haqqani training camps up in Qalandar District when a high-value individual happened to spend the night there. It was brilliant. They got their man and then withdrew while still watching the camp the next day with a Predator. When a bunch of Haqqani fighters came back to the camp to see what happened, the Task Force called in a massive artillery strike and leveled them. The great thing, sir, is that the elders in the area couldn't have been happier. The Haqqanis had put their camp in the middle of a pine nut forest, and the locals were not permitted to harvest their biggest cash crop. Even though the artillery strike destroyed many of their trees, a procession of elders from the Mangal tribe came to thank us for ridding their area of the Haqqani. We are in the process of compensating them for the damages. Since then we have put together several conops for the Afghan commandos to get up into those mountains to do an extended period of patrolling and sweeps through other suspected camp locations. We just had a report yesterday from the CIA base at Chapman that there were two trucks full of Arabs seen driving down the valley."

"What's the problem?" the general asked.

I explained that we couldn't get the conops approved. They never even made it to his level. Because we had to use helicopters at night to get in there, it had to go up through the various approval chains. It was death by a thousand paper cuts. They wanted better or higher quality intelligence reports. The helicopters were down for maintenance. The mission was a low priority because we didn't have a high-value individual targeted. The staff was concerned we would be unable to get a medevac in those tight areas. "So I flew our battalion surgeon down here and stacked an ATV with medical supplies as a mini aid station. It still wasn't enough," I said.

"Eventually we had to shift our staff and the ODAs to other priorities," York added.

The briefing and conversation concluded with us apologizing to the general for complaining. However, we felt we owed it to him to make him aware of the extent of our frustration. I said, "Sir, frankly, my own view is I think we have taken a lot of casualties this rotation. We were guaranteed to get into a fight going after these training camps in some very difficult-to-reach terrain. No one wants to say it, but I think CJSOTF was worried about taking responsibility for approving such a mission. But the sad irony is that not disrupting those camps and IED factories is going to indirectly cause *more* casualties in the long run. Inaction has consequences as well."

"Okay, Mike," the general replied. "As you of all people know, given your background, casualty numbers are a real hot-button issue. You wouldn't believe the questioning and second-guessing that comes pouring in from Washington when an incident like COP Keating occurs." He was referring to another small outpost that had been overrun in 2009. "But it's my job to make sure that a risk-averse command environment doesn't flow down to you. Let me look into this whole issue. I can't promise I can change the conop system. But I am in a position to make it a little more reasonable." We believed the general would make an honest attempt. However, we knew that the more casualties mounted, the more restrictive the command guidance became, the higher the missions had to go for approval, and the more excruciating the detail that had to be provided.

The caution and hand-wringing were another by-product of the fundamental differences we were dealing with in today's wars. Afghanistan was the first extended war in U.S. history that we had fought with an all-volunteer force instead of one built through a compulsory draft. In my view, the draft has been overly criticized by historians because of the stigma of Vietnam. In some important ways, the draft may have been a better system because soldiers were signed up only to serve, win the conflict, and then return home to move on with their other lives. They had family businesses, jobs, and established livelihoods to which they were incredibly motivated to return. It was a powerful incentive to do whatever was necessary to win.

With the institution of the all-volunteer force, the military became a livelihood, and having a successful career therefore became paramount. Soldiers, particularly officers, began to focus on the steps necessary to get promoted in an incredibly competitive environment. While the system created a much higher quality product, it also created an environment where succeeding in one's career became the dominant motivator. A deployment became a one-year slice (albeit an important one) of an otherwise twenty- to thirty-year-long professional career that involved significant personal and family sacrifices. The incentives naturally shifted over time; now one avoided doing anything that would damage one's career rather than taking whatever risks were needed to win the war. The incentive for a commander was to get through the deployment with as few casualties as possible and to avoid an investigation or being reprimanded for a mistake, such as a civilian casualty. The results were a loss of creativity, an emphasis on force protection, and consistent second-guessing from higher headquarters of junior officers when requesting high-risk support such as artillery and close air support. This wasn't a personal indictment of the motives of our officer corps; these were fundamental flaws in our current all-volunteer military system. These flaws were undermining our ability to implement a counterinsurgency strategy that, at its core, required exposing soldiers to the population and taking risks in order to be successful.

All of these requirements had been added over the years for valid reasons. However, the net effect had been that leaving the base became an event rather than an everyday occurrence. Our own requirements for safety, force protection, and 24/7 situational awareness for multiple higher headquarters had become a barrier to interacting with the populace. In a part of the world where relationships and trust were critical to any type of progress, these barriers had become a real liability. In the end the Afghans felt less secure and more exposed to Taliban intimidation and pressure, and our casualties continued to mount.

As the debate in Washington raged in the fall of 2009 about how many troops President Obama should "surge" to Afghanistan, I became convinced that additional troops would help only so much unless we were willing to assume greater risk in the short term, get off our bases and into the villages, and empower decision making down to the junior leaders closest to the Afghan people.

11 Night Raid
The Catch-and-Release Detention System

By November 2009 the security situation in Ghazni had deteriorated to the point that ODA 21 had shifted to almost exclusively conducting raids against Taliban leadership. The Polish battle group with responsibility for broader security and reconstruction activities in the province had limited itself to patrolling the section of the Ring Road that passed through Ghazni to keep it open. The provincial reconstruction team and agricultural development team were regularly attacked every time they tried to engage a village and implement a development project. Entire neighborhoods of Ghazni City were no-go areas for the Afghan National Police. Several districts, including Andar, where Brian Woods was killed, and Qarabagh District in the southern half of the province, were completely under Taliban control, with no coalition or ANA units stationed there. In fact Qarabagh's district governor lived in the relative safety of Ghazni City. Because the area was in such bad shape, I flew out from Khost again with ODA 23, a platoon of ANA commandos, and a small slice from my Operational Detachment Bravo headquarters.

ODA 21's team leader, Grant, and I were frustrated at not being able to do more to better understand the political and tribal dynamics that were fueling the insurgency in Ghazni. We struggled to craft a strategy to turn the situation around with only one ODA and their partnered ANP available for offensive operations. We were certain that part of the reason the area had deteriorated was an influx of senior Taliban and HIG commanders who sensed opportunity given the relatively small numbers of coalition and Afghan troops in the province. We were determined to at least pressure these senior leaders and the locals they recruited with as many raids as possible. We knew that this approach risked alienating the population, but we also knew that leaving these commanders in place to either convince or intimidate tribes into working for them was an even higher risk.

Commanders like Mullah Sadin, the Taliban leader of Qarabagh District, were the type we sought to disrupt. If we couldn't kill or capture him, we would at least make him fear coming back to his own home so he would stay in Pakistan for the winter. Sadin had been captured by ODA 21's predecessors, held at the facility at Bagram Airbase for almost a year, and recently released as a "minimal threat." We had no idea how that determination was made, nor was the team consulted on the potential impacts in Ghazni of his release. In fact, Grant and his team had received a series of reports that Sadin had been preaching in the local mosques around Qarabagh District since his release that the American and Afghan armies couldn't touch him and that anyone who cooperated with us was an enemy of Islam. The catch-and-release detention system that had evolved over the course of the war was another major reason for the decline in Ghazni. Sadin was one of a half-dozen insurgent leaders who had been captured from the province and were now back in their home districts. The U.S. facilities at Bagram were simply too small to permanently detain captured Taliban leaders, especially as the insurgency and number of captures from the coalition grew. To make matters worse, the defunct Afghan court system was years, if not decades, away from functioning effectively. My teams had little to no confidence that captured Taliban leaders would be prosecuted and detained if handed over to the judicial system. The whole situation certainly made us feel as though we were spinning our wheels and was often demoralizing. One bright spot was that a small number of insurgent midlevel commanders had recently tried to seek a truce with coalition forces after they were put under intense pressure by offensive operations. We hoped that the series of raids ODA 21 planned for Sadin and his men could have the same effect of forcing them to the bargaining table.

After several weeks working to get Sadin back on the targeting list by proving he was once again up to no good, ODA 21 submitted a conop to conduct a mission to kill or capture him at one of his homes in Qarabagh. The team's primary source, who was also Sadin's neighbor, had informed us that he was home preparing to leave for Pakistan for the winter. We knew from our vetting process that Sadin's neighbor was motivated by a family blood feud over disputed land. But we also knew from other sources that Sadin had recently killed a policeman by shooting him in front of his village. He also regularly facilitated explosives and weapons shipments from Pakistan. We now simply needed the green light from the various higher headquarters in time for us to get him before he departed.

While we waited for the conop to get fully approved, the ODA thought they had lost him again when the source called and said he had left his home. The source didn't know if Sadin was just spending the night somewhere else or if he had left for the winter.

I told Grant to let the conop for the mission continue processing through the various approval chains. I didn't want to have to start the process over again if he happened to come back. In response he said, "CJSOTF is going to be furious if they take a week to brief this thing all the way up to ISAF, get us the helicopters, and then we don't execute the mission."

"I know. Talk to your intel guys about whether it's worth hitting his house anyway and possibly rolling up the cache he is supposedly keeping. At least he will be afraid to come home at night. Not much else we can do."

While waiting for the conop to be approved, the ODAs conducted their own internal mission briefs, then sat down with their partnered Afghans to discuss the mission. Every detail was discussed: the exact order in which they would get on and off the helicopter; where the helicopter would land; where the interpreters would be located and exactly which commandos or policemen would be partnered with which operator; who would carry which items; and how they would minimize civilian casualties and react if something went wrong.

The method of entering the fortress-like Afghan compounds was always the source of some debate. Many of our conventional brethren and even the elite special mission units were doing what they termed "callouts," where they surrounded a compound, then announced through an interpreter to the suspected Taliban commander inside that he and his men were surrounded, and ordered them to come out. This technique was an effort to reduce possible civilian casualties during forcible entries. Neither my guys nor I were fans of the call-out. Unlike the raids conducted by the special mission units, my ODAs had only a little more than half a dozen American operators embedded with several

Map 13. Ghazni Province.

dozen Afghan Army or police on the missions, and the coordination required for the call-out was too much of a challenge. I preferred the silent entry, where we carried collapsible ladders to the objective and used them to slip someone over the compound's outer wall to unlock from the inside the metal gate found on most compounds' outer walls. Usually one or two operators stood on separate ladders, watching the inside of the compound while everyone else stealthily slipped inside. There was nothing in the world like tapping on a Taliban commander's forehead with the muzzle of your rifle and having him wake up to the shock of a group of American and Afghan soldiers wearing night-vision goggles and standing over him. I loved sending the message that we could literally be standing at the foot of their bed without their knowing it. I also liked that the technique didn't alert the rest of the village in case we entered the wrong compound or if there were other Taliban nearby. The Afghan Army soldiers loved it as well because it wasn't as offensive as blowing in doors with explosives and storming in unannounced. The silent entry was extremely risky, however, for those first few guys up on the ladders, especially the guy who jumped inside, so there were still times we had to place a small explosive charge on the door in order to guarantee we got the thing open and to shock anyone inside long enough for us to get in.

Starting in the summer of 2009 we began to receive regular reports that the Taliban were booby-trapping the doorways of their compounds at night with antipersonnel mines and trip wires. It was clearly a migration of tactics from Iraq. I was with ODA 21 in Ghazni when a report came in that a Ranger had stepped on a pressure-plate IED just inside the door of a Taliban-occupied compound in Kandahar. This news really struck a chord with the team, as they had entered a house rigged to explode earlier that year while searching for the missing U.S. soldier Bowe Bergdahl. After receiving a tip that he might be held in a town on the border with Paktika Province, where he went missing, the team was ordered to assault and search the compound. After finding the home empty, they discovered a vehicle parked in the courtyard with a trunk full of explosives along with several rooms with C4 explosive blocks rigged to collapse the ceiling of the entire house. The Taliban had clearly used Bergdahl as bait for a trap, and we counted our blessings that, for some reason, the house didn't blow.

"Those bastards. I guess we are going to have to start going through the walls rather than through the doors!" Rob, the team's engineer, said as he read the report on the booby-trapped doors. Special Forces engineer sergeants were just as adept at building schools as they were at blowing up bridges behind enemy lines, though most preferred the latter. Rob was as thick as he was tall, had the look of a surfer, and habitually yelled "Good times!" while making a thumbs-up sign. No matter the situation, stranded in a snow storm or firing a rocket from atop an MRAP during an ambush, Rob would respond with "Good times!" A day later I saw him emerge from his workshop at their base with a sheet of plywood ringed with C4 explosives. He had built it to fold in half so that it could be carried to the objective, slapped against the thick mud wall surrounding a compound, and detonated to blow a man-size doorway through the thick wall. "This is definitely going to be a good time!" he smiled as he walked over to the Afghan barracks to show them the new contraption.

Once our initial plan for going after Sadin was set, all of our teams sat down with our partnered Afghan force, laid out as much of the intelligence as we were allowed, and discussed how best to conduct the mission. Each Afghan commander had a different opinion on how the mission should be conducted. Some were content for their men to just go along. My team leaders did their level best to force the Afghans into the planning process, but most days it was an uphill battle. Our more experienced Afghan commanders would absolutely insist on detailed actions their men should take. In contrast, one commander in particular took a strictly hands-off approach to planning. We later learned that his predecessor had been stripped of his rank after his men accidentally shot two young boys as they approached a checkpoint in their family car. The company commander purposely did not want to be included in mission planning so that he had plausible deniability and could point to the Americans should something go wrong.

Late in the afternoon the operations officer from the Special Operations Forces Task Force, our next higher command at Bagram, called with the good news that he had finally shepherded the conop through the approvals. He proudly told us that he was able to get both teams dedicated special operations birds for the mission, the specially outfitted Chinooks and elite pilots who could land us on top of the objective at night.

"Sir, we think Sadin left his house two nights ago," Grant told him.

"You guys damn well better find something to do with those helicopters. We had to move heaven and earth to get them for you," the operations officer shot back. "If we let them go unused, we will never get them again."

By a stroke of luck Sadin's neighbor called later that same day. Apparently Sadin had just returned to his home village for a night before leaving for Pakistan. The mission was a go. We prayed for the weather to hold and for the helicopters to not break down.

Despite how bureaucratically difficult it was to target a single insurgent commander, once we were authorized to go, a part of me truly loved it. No matter how many times I did it, there was nothing in the world like that little jolt of adrenaline I felt when I filed into the black helicopter in the dead of night. The special operations birds didn't have seats, so we could cram in more people. We all sat on the floor and snaplinked into small metal rings running in a column from the cockpit to the back ramp. The whining of the engines was incredibly loud, so everyone shouted to communicate with the door gunners, who instructed us where to sit and where to put our extra equipment. As the ground force commander, I took off my helmet and put on headsets that allowed me to talk to the pilots. I listened to their radio chatter and coordination with the trail helicopter. Importantly, they gave me a periodic countdown for how long we had before landing at our objective, which I passed back to the guys with a hand signal.

An MH-47 Special Operations–equipped Chinook exactly like the one we were in had gone down a few weeks earlier in western Afghanistan, killing seven soldiers and three Drug Enforcement Administration agents. I thought of them as our helicopter thumped along at low altitude, skimming over the scattered clusters of Afghan villages, and then my thoughts wandered to my family, as they always did just before a mission. I genuinely had little fear of death, but I was petrified at the thought of my family having to deal with it. Generally speaking, my rationale was "If I'm dead, I'm dead and it's over." But my wife would have to be a single parent the rest of her life; my daughter would grow up without a father; and my mother would lose her only son. Inevitably, every time I began walking down this mental path, I snapped myself out of it and reminded myself that I was responsible for these guys and had to focus.

I could see through the green filter of my night-vision goggles that some guys were sleeping and some were fidgeting with their gear; most were staring out the open back ramp of the helicopter watching the dim outline of the landscape fly by. Everything was black except for the faint reflection of moonlight on the rocky desert.

The pilot announced, "One minute!" and I made a final check of my GPS to ensure that the helicopter was on the right heading. (They invariably dropped us off facing the opposite way from what was briefed.) I had to hold the GPS out the door gunner's porthole into the freezing air to try to get a signal.

At the "Thirty seconds" call, everyone unhooked their snap link from the floor of the aircraft and awkwardly tried to rise up on one knee with all of their equipment as the helicopter bounced around from the turbulence of trying to land. I was in the very rear of the Chinook, across from the team sergeant, Poppi, and Grant, so that we could be first off when it landed.

Just as I felt the helicopter slow down and lower its back end to land brown dust poured in the open back ramp. When the helicopter slammed down, it felt as though God had reached out and slapped the bird to the ground. I was flung upward into the roof, felt a crunch in my neck, and crashed down on my right knee. Pain shot up my leg as I bounced and slid face first down the back ramp of the helicopter. In the split second that I lay there, I heard a burst of automatic weapons fire somewhere off in the distance.

We hit the ground so hard that I was convinced we had just crash-landed. I was convinced someone behind me was dead. My right knee throbbed in pain. "Go, go, go! Get off the bird!" a voice yelled behind me. Someone grabbed my body armor, picked me up, and shoved me off the back ramp. Pumped up on adrenaline, I ran down the ramp as fast as I could to get clear of the helicopter's blades, took several more steps, and suddenly felt myself in free-fall. A second later my feet hit the ground, my face hit the dirt, and my night-vision goggles bit into my right eye. I had fallen into the mouth of a well, onto a ledge dug into the side. Fortunately the hole was relatively small and I had somehow managed to leap over it in my full stride, to the ledge about four feet below the ground. All I heard behind me was, "Don't follow the Major! Go around the Major!"

During my previous tour I had developed a fear of falling into one of these tunnel-like wells known as a *karez*. They consisted of a row of holes, often hundreds of feet deep, that flowed into an underground aquifer. They were part of an ancient irrigation system that dotted the landscape across Afghanistan and were, of course, completely unmarked.

I was shaken as I looked over my shoulder into the black abyss. I was even more embarrassed when the team's communication sergeant, Tony, extended a hand to pull me up. As I climbed out of my would-be grave, he had a huge grin on his face. "Shut up," I said, "and thank you."

The group moved forward through whirling dust from the prop wash of the departing helicopter. Poppi called for everyone to halt until we could get eyes on the next helicopter coming in. We didn't want the pilot to have to abort the landing because we were in his way or, worse, to land on top of one of us. We spotted the other helicopter to our south, right where it was supposed to be, so Poppi told us to move north to the dirt trail that would take us into the village.

As I looked back I saw most of our partnered Afghan police still in a circle, each on one knee and pulling security. The team sergeant and team leader both yelled for them to get moving, and I saw one of our guys reach down, grab a policeman, and shove him in our direction. Eventually everyone fell in line as we jogged toward the objective compound ahead. Our attached joint tactical air controller, Zeke, called up to the circling AC-130 gunship, asking it to "sparkle" the objective. Seconds later a huge infrared spotlight hit the compound and an even brighter laser pointer shone on the door of the compound we intended to enter.

Minutes into the movement I began breathing hard. We were at 7,500 feet of altitude while wearing fifty pounds of "lightweight" gear. The compound loomed in the distance with its twelve-foot-high mud walls and castle-like turrets. As we jogged directly toward the blinking infrared laser light, I found myself staring at the tops of the walls and slit windows of the compound, just waiting for the flash of an AK-47 or the whoosh of an RPG coming our way. All the U.S. operators were constantly scanning in all directions with the green infrared lasers mounted on their rifles.

Just as we approached the compound, per the plan, two groups of a half-dozen operators and ANP split off to secure the opposite sides of the building. They had two purposes: prevent anyone from escaping and prevent anyone from reinforcing from the neighboring compounds. Simultaneously a three-man element ran to the metal door. One man trained his weapon on the door while the others unfolded Ron's plywood-backed wall charge.

I was at the tail end of the lead assault element for this mission so that I could quickly get to the roof of the building and communicate with our headquarters in case we needed additional support. This would also let Grant and Poppi focus on running the team and the ANP. I also wanted to get into position and listen to radio traffic regarding ODA 23 and their partnered Afghan commandos, who were conducting a raid on a compound in a nearby village that was one of Mullah Sadin's other hideouts. Grant was up front with the assault elements, while Poppi controlled the security elements.

We lined up around the corner from the section of wall Rob intended to take down to avoid any back-blast from the charge. With hushed commands in our interpreter's broken Dari, the team's operators made sure our police assault element was against the wall and away from the blast. Rob called to Grant that the charge was set and ready to fire.

Grant then called a countdown: "On my mark, 3, 2, 1." Boom! Dust and debris flew everywhere, and the police jerked from the shock of the blast. I caught my breath. "Geez, Ron," I thought. "Overkill?" The ANP surged around the corner and began filing awkwardly through the door-size hole in the wall. We followed immediately after them, and the inside of the compound erupted into a cacophony of yelling: "Get down!" and "Hands, hands, hands!" in English, Dari, and Pashtu.

The living spaces were lined up in a long L-shaped building against the outside of the wall to our right. I followed the police into the second room and quickly ran into a dead end. My heart jumped as the Afghan policeman swung his AK-47 around in my face as he was trying to back out of the tiny room. As we left, I broke a green chemlight from a bundle I had hanging off my gear and threw it down in the doorway to mark that the room had been cleared. The team had trained the Afghan police to do this, but they inevitably "forgot" their chemlights, which meant they had probably taken them home or sold them. As we backed out of the room, stepping over blankets and bags of onions, I could see the police gently herding several women and small children into an adjacent room. The women were wailing as they moved from room to room.

The police and the team's operators progressed farther down the long building, escorting men out of the various rooms and placing plastic handcuffs, known as flex cuffs, on them and telling them to squat and face the wall. I finally found what I was looking for: stairs leading to the roof. I bounded up the narrow stairs, so narrow that my shoulders and gear rubbed against both walls, and took a knee on the roof facing toward the rest of the village. Zeke was on my heels, talking to the gunship overhead on his radio as he ascended the stairs. He informed me that the gunship had spotted a "squirter" running from the compound. He was apparently hiding several hundred meters away in a ditch. He had something in his hands, but the helicopter crew couldn't tell if it was a weapon and therefore did not want to engage.

I informed Grant over our internal radios, and rather than cajole and argue with the reticent pilot, he instructed Poppi to send part of the security force in the direction of the ditch to investigate. A few minutes later three of our operators followed by six policemen began making their way toward a line of trees and bushes along an irrigation ditch. Zeke requested a sparkle from the gunship, and again the spotlight shone down, bathing the entire area in green sunlight. The laser-like pointer blinked on the spot where the gunship could see the man hiding in the ditch. As I looked with my naked eye into the pitch-blackness, I reminded myself of the adage that we truly did "own the night." The man had no idea that we were coming for him. I watched our guys cross a field with their green lasers dancing around a dark spot in the bushes. Several shots rang out. The element leader called over the radio that the man had hopped up with a rifle in his hand. I cursed under my breath as I fumbled with my handheld satellite antenna. I had been walking around with my hand in the air like the statue of liberty, trying to get a signal to report what was going on to our higher headquarters. Grant eventually joined me on the roof and began unfolding his backup satellite system.

It was 15 degrees Fahrenheit outside, and the longer I stood still, the more I began to shiver. My toes were already numb, and we had been on the objective for only forty-five minutes. Zeke walked over. "Sir, we are losing the AC-130 to support the infil for ODA 23." The aviation command required that either a gunship or a pair of attack helicopters go ahead of the lightly armed Chinooks and clear the landing zone of any possible enemy fighters before landing the troops. Through my night vision I could see the distinctive black outlines of the two Chinooks on the horizon and said a quick prayer for them.

I heard a commotion and turned around to look into the courtyard. I saw one of the interpreters slap one of the detainees across the back of the head. After a half-second pause the man dramatically fell to the ground, much like a basketball player looking for a foul call. "They so know our rules," I thought. I could see a line of a half dozen men squatting with their arms tied behind their backs, facing the far wall of the compound. The police lieutenant, an interpreter, and two of the team's operators were questioning each of them. Over the wind I could hear the team's intelligence sergeant telling one man to stop lying and asking him to reveal who owned the compound. At the same time, another operator grabbed the interpreter by the arm. I could see the shadow of the operator shaking his head to let him know to knock off the slapping routine.

Weeks later, while in-processing to one of the coalition detention centers, the man who had been slapped pointed to two bruises on his arm and claimed he was beaten while in our custody. This accusation triggered a full-blown investigation from our higher headquarters. After hours of interviews and sworn statements from the team, guided by my executive officer, France, we were fully exonerated. France, a former White House attorney and federal prosecutor, coordinated our response. He tied the investigating major into knots regarding the veracity of the charges and finally got him to admit that these investigations were now mandatory in response to any accusation from a detainee, even if the accusation appeared to be blatantly bogus. Unfortunately, it would not be the last investigation along these lines. Each one took weeks of man-hours and made me wonder how units fared that didn't have someone like France on their side.

France was a colleague from President Bush's White House counsel's office that I had come to like and respect. One afternoon in the fall of 2008, France and I had walked to the President's Library on the ground floor of the White House. He had suggested we meet there and just hang out for a bit as he knew I would find it a fascinating room, complete with Lincoln's personal book collection and a portrait of George Washington by Gilbert Stuart. There, sitting under Lafayette's sword, I had somewhat flippantly asked him to come with me as my executive officer on my next deployment to Afghanistan, scheduled to begin just four months later in February 2009. France, a very intelligent and talented attorney, was a West Point graduate and a Ranger-qualified former military policeman. However, he had been out of the Army for eight years. We both laughed off the suggestion of a deployment as a little ridiculous and probably bureaucratically impossible anyway. Days later he called me at my office and said, "I can't stop thinking about it. I got out of the Army before 9/11 and never had a chance to serve in Iraq or Afghanistan. If you can make it happen, I'm in."

In the next ninety days I was able to get orders issued to him to be admitted into the Maryland National Guard, recognized federally, attached to a Special Forces unit as a military police officer, called to active duty, and mobilized for deployment to Afghanistan. I was quite proud of my bureaucratic jujitsu skills. The move raised some eyebrows, including among my own men. But many of them changed their minds after arriving in theater to find a shockingly litigious environment, where command investigations into every potential wrongdoing were commonplace. From making sure my operators were up to speed on all the variations of the rules of engagement, to building the evidentiary packets required to keep our detainees in custody, to guiding my men through a barrage of investigations, to providing real-time counsel to our officers and NCOs during operations, France was an invaluable asset to the unit. In the end, having a legal counsel who was trained at Georgetown Law and seasoned in the White House and who used the law to help us get things done rather than telling us what we couldn't do was worth its weight in gold. Most of my men more than agreed.

Toward the end of our tour a series of interviews with Taliban prisoners revealed that they trained each other to take advantage of our rules of engagement regarding detainees. The Taliban leadership in Quetta, Pakistan, had instructed their followers to throw down their weapons when confronted with overwhelming force, knowing that we would not shoot unarmed men and that they would then be detained and likely released. The biggest problem was that the Afghan judicial system was

horribly corrupt and ineffective. If we handed detainees over to the local Afghan police, they would almost certainly bribe their way out of
prison or intimidate local officials until they were released. If they were
sent to a U.S. detention facility, their instructions were to automatically
claim abuse (knowing we would have to launch an investigation) and to
take advantage of the clean living conditions while they radicalized less
dedicated recruits and terrorized any inmate who worked with us. The
net effect of our catch-and-release detention system was progressively
less and less support from the populace as released Taliban commanders
exacted retribution on pro-government/coalition villagers and propa-
gated a message that they were untouchable. It was seriously damaging
to our counterinsurgency campaign.

Over the howling wind I could hear two of the men down in the compound courtyard finally admit that they were not from the area and claim
that they were in Qarabagh simply for a wedding. However, when asked
who owned the compound and who they were visiting, both claimed
not to know. Another one of the operators walked up and, through the
translator, told the police to find the men's shoes and some blankets, as
they were starting to shiver violently wearing only their *shalwar kameez*.

"I wonder if we would get the same treatment from them," I said sarcastically.

My interpreter didn't say a word, just drew his finger across his throat
as he shook his head.

Meanwhile several other police officers stepped out of the compound
and engaged in a discussion with the intel sergeant. He then looked up
at Grant and me on the roof, depressed his radio button, and said, "Sir,
we think the women are hiding these guys' cell phones. How do you
want us to search them?"

"Damn," I thought. The Taliban knew we went out of our way to respect Afghan women by not having men search them, so they often hid
contraband in the women's long, flowing robes. Because of space limitations on the helicopters we had not brought a U.S. female soldier with
us, as we normally did, to question and search the women. I had mental
visions of answering to accusations the next day of raping and pillag-
ing the Afghan women—a story that would surely be promulgated by
the Taliban propaganda machine. I could just see, in my mind's eye, the

team leader and me on the phone the entire day with our headquarters, which would in turn be on the phone with their headquarters answering a litany of questions. Grant depressed the switch on his radio, "I want those phones. Have the police search them with our interpreters watching them. No Americans in the room," he said as he went back down the stairs to help deal with the situation. At least it would be Afghan men searching the women and not us. Ten minutes later I saw an interpreter walk out of the room with two cell phones in his hand.

Several minutes earlier we had dispatched the FBI agent who was accompanying us to assist with taking photos of the dead Afghan so that we could identify him later. The agent also carried a machine that electronically recorded fingerprints and other data that would be uploaded into a larger database to help determine if the man was a known insurgent. I knew that we could face accusations of killing an innocent man when the Taliban contacted the local media. The burden of proof was certainly on us rather than the accusers, particularly since this guy had not shot at us first. In general, we went out of our way to collect as much evidence as possible after every contact with the enemy, as though we were on a domestic crime scene. It often exposed us to additional risks, but I felt compelled to do so to protect my men from the investigations that often ensued.

Stepping over the small mud chimneys dotting the roof, Zeke walked up again and informed us that one of the Chinooks that was due to come get us in an hour had damaged its landing gear when it slammed into the ground. "That's just great," I murmured under my breath. This could be a long night. The Special Operations Chinooks conducted missions only under the cover of darkness to avoid risking such valuable assets during the day. If they weren't able to repair the helicopter soon, we would have to remain there throughout the day until the next night. That would make for a long day in a village that supposedly housed Mullah Sadin's extended family and members of his subtribe. Grant had planned to invite the elder of the subtribe to the provincial governor's office after we returned to base to explain the evidence behind why we had seized Sadin. I was afraid of a serious fight breaking out the next day if we were still sitting there in the morning. To make matters worse, a snowstorm was forecast to come the next night and would likely prevent the helicopters from picking us up then as well. Further, the Chinooks would only fly in pairs in case one had a mechanical failure, so asking our headquarters to instruct the fully capable helicopter to make extra trips on its own was also out of the question. The backlash from the "Black Hawk Down" incident in Somalia fifteen years earlier, in which we lost eighteen soldiers trying to react to a series of helicopters getting shot down during the day, was still with us. It was a calculation every headquarters continually had to make. Do you risk a valuable asset like a Special Operations helicopter to extract some men and in turn have to risk significantly more men to recover that asset if it breaks down or gets shot down? I understood the dilemma, but now that I was one of the men for which it wasn't worth risking the asset, it didn't feel so great.

Grant called over the radio to the rest of the guys to tell them about the broken Chinook and to inform them that we would be in the compound for several more hours, if not all night and the next night. I heard several expletives muttered from down below. I noticed that the burning sensation in my feet and hands was gone and that they were now numb. I looked down at my watch thermometer, which said the temperature had dropped to 11 degrees. At least the cold helped my knee to stop throbbing from the hard landing.

As though the ANP were reading my mind, they began pulling wood from a pile in the corner of the compound and started a fire in the middle of the courtyard. Building a fire in the middle of a night raid in Taliban country violated every sense of my military being. Though I wanted the guys to be warm, I knew the fire would turn into an irresistible magnet for everyone on the mission. As I saw the Afghan policemen gravitating toward the fire, I called the team sergeant and reminded him that only the joint tactical air controller, one other ANP officer, and I were on the roof pulling security. He walked across the courtyard with the interpreter to talk to the police commander about sending some of his men up to the roof. He also got into a heated discussion with him about the fire. They compromised, the commander agreeing to build fires only inside the walls of the compound. Soon, however, I saw smaller fires popping up outside the compound out at the security positions. "Perfect target," I thought. I saw Tony wave to one of the policemen standing next to a small burning log with the intent of calling him over to tell him to put out the fire. Absolutely typical of the Afghans, the policeman looked at Tony, looked down at the fire keeping his feet warm, and bent over with his gloved hands to pick up the burning log and carry it with him. He walked with the log over to Tony and dropped it at both of their feet as though to share, now making them both targets. I could see Tony's hands waving wildly as he stomped out the fire as fast as he could, while the policeman looked on confused and a bit bemused, then simply walked over to his buddies standing by another fire.

The element that had chased down the squirter returned from searching the mosque next to Sadin's compound with several more men in custody, who were told to squat and face the wall. One by one, our intel sergeant, the interpreter, and the ANP officer led the men into a room to question them separately. I also saw the silhouettes of two operators walking toward the room beside a man wearing a full facemask to hide his identity. The team had obviously linked up with their source, and he was going to help us identify Mullah Sadin and his men.

We received word that the aviators were flying all the way down to Kandahar to retrieve another helicopter and would hopefully be back in time to pick us up. It would be tight getting both teams out before daylight. Grant and I began discussing contingencies. We decided that if the helos could not pick us up, return to base, and pick up the other team in time, we would all stay put so that we could consolidate and defend ourselves from the compound through the next day, should we have to. Since the roads between this village and the main base in Ghazni were laced with IEDs, we knew it was highly unlikely the Polish battle group stationed at FOB Ghazni would send a ground element to come get us. They would not explicitly say no, of course. Instead they would make an unrealistic series of requests of the American headquarters in Bagram for support, such as route-clearing engineers and overhead aircraft. They would also need to request permission from their headquarters in Warsaw so as to make the mission essentially untenable. Thus, I knew we would be pretty much alone and began wargaming how we would consolidate and best deal with the village the next morning.

The detained men had finally mixed up their stories and identified one of the men as Sadin, the owner of the compound. He was also the Taliban commander we were looking for. I walked over to where he was squatting while facing the wall with a blanket draped over his shoulders. Again I wondered if he would have brought us blankets and shoes, as we had done for him, knowing the answer. I nudged him to stand up.

He turned around and looked at me. He had a well-kept beard, shaved head, and heavily lined face. He glared at me for a moment in the darkness. The Hazaran policeman guarding him hissed and nudged him back down with the butt of his rifle. I stood there staring at him as he squatted, thinking about whether it was even worth taking him, given our broken detention system. Even if we were able to get him back to Bagram, he likely would be released again in less than a year, to terrorize the area again. His neighbor, our informant, would certainly have much to worry about and may stop working with us. I knew my cynicism and frustration was getting the better of my judgment and motioned for the policeman standing nearby to take Sadin to the gate so he would be ready when we departed.

We received word soon afterward that the helicopters were inbound and began pulling in our security perimeter. I gave our interpreter 10,000 Afghanis (about $200) to compensate for the wood we burned, the hole in the wall, and the few windows that were damaged. He gave it to an older man who said he was related to one of the men we were taking. It pained me to give him this money, but I also knew reparations would be important in our efforts to deal with the village elders later on, once Sadin was out of the picture. The money would be part of our message that our issue wasn't with their tribe, their village, or even Sadin's family, but rather with Sadin himself and his support in the killing of Afghan soldiers and policemen who were, after all, fellow countrymen and Muslims.

As we filed out toward the open field where the helicopter's pickup zone was located, one of the women followed us out, wailing at the top of her lungs. "This is a first," I thought. They usually just stayed in the compound as we left. It occurred to me that she had no idea what we were going to do with the men we were taking. We could have been taking them out for execution. I had one of the interpreters go back and tell the woman that we were taking them to the police headquarters in Ghazni City and told him to leave her the police commander's cell phone number. One of the operators walking with me muttered as though he were talking to her, "Here's a tip. Stop letting your husband kill people and this won't happen."

She continued to follow us and wail. I wondered as we made our way to the pickup zone if we had the intelligence wrong. Had we just raided an innocent family and created more insurgents in the process? Was this an effort on the part of our informant to wipe out some tribal competition in the village?

A few minutes later the helicopters came in and the rotor wash blasted us with sand, rocks, and bits of ice as they landed. Poppi counted us on the back ramp, and I slumped down in my seat, lifting up my night-vision goggles and shifting the body armor that had been digging into my shoulders for the past hour. This was how most direct-action missions went for us, with small variations. No heroic firefights or massive bombings causing huge numbers of civilian casualties, as often alleged by the international media. On the contrary, if we did our job right, we would be on top of the target with absolute precision before the enemy had a chance to pick up a gun. Most of these missions came off without a shot.

The next day we called several of our informants to the base to show them pictures of the men we detained. They identified three of the men as Taliban commanders. The man we shot was apparently a mullah who provided Sadin with money collected from the villagers and regularly stored weapons at the mosque. Unfortunately, we couldn't locate the bundles he had been frantically moving that night. France went to work building the evidentiary packets required to submit the men for long-term detention. Again I wondered how a unit without an embedded lawyer ever had anyone accepted by the detention board. These packets were typically twenty-five to thirty pages long and looked like formal briefs prepared for court. His work paid off. By the end of the tour we were responsible for thirty-five of the sixty detainees accepted to the facility in Bagram for all of CJSOTF that year.

Capturing Mullah Sadin was the easy part. The hard part was taking advantage of his absence. The next day Grant visited the Polish commander and pressed him to take advantage of the space created by removing Mullah Sadin by getting his platoons and their provincial reconstruction team down to Qarabagh District to engage with the populace. Despite previous assurances, the Poles hedged, claiming that Qarabagh was still too dangerous. ODA 21 had little choice but to continue to hit the insurgent leadership as hard as we could.

Fortunately, over the next three weeks, for the first time in the tour, we received dedicated surveillance, intelligence, and helicopter assets. A nearby unit of SEALs also began to conduct raids into the area. Finally it seemed the higher commands in Bagram and Kabul realized the gravity of the situation in Ghazni. ODAs 21 and 23 conducted eight more operations like the night raid to capture Mullah Sadin that resulted in the death or detention of most of the key midlevel insurgent leaders across two key districts in the province. We had enough information to conduct fourteen such missions, but several of the conops either did not get approved in time or were canceled due to bad weather or maintenance issues with the helicopters.

The teams also found creative ways to turn rival Taliban and HIG commanders against each other so that each suspected the other was siding with us and causing the raids. A few days after the operations ended, a Taliban commander contacted an Afghan Army general at his base outside of Ghazni City and indicated that he wanted to enter negotiations to reconcile and reintegrate back into Afghan society. He promised to bring several dozen of his fighters with him. It took us some time to determine if the outreach was legitimate. It turned out to be genuine and was an important step forward in Ghazni. How successfully we handled the overture from the Taliban commander was critical; other insurgent commanders who may have been on the fence were watching to see what happened. Notably, every Taliban commander who tried to reintegrate throughout our deployment in 2009 and 2010 did so after a period of successful raids on our part. In this case, the commander said he was coming in because he was tired of being on the run and of fighting other Taliban commanders. In other words, we were realizing a positive reaction to the stick. Now we had to produce some carrots.

After the initial contact I reached back to my colleagues in the Afghanistan policy offices in the Pentagon and the White House because there was no meaningful mechanism or program in place to take care of insurgents who wanted to defect. Or if there was a policy or program, it certainly had not been communicated to us. Several months before this outreach in Ghazni, a midlevel Taliban commander responsible for several districts in Wardak Province to the north of Ghazni had pledged to stop fighting against the Afghan government. However, as part of the agreement, the commander and his men were required to turn in their weapons and forced to disband. Months after doing so and reintegrating, the group's commander was hauled out of his home and brutally beheaded by his former allies.

Needless to say, the Taliban were sending a message to other members of the insurgency through this heinous act, and we had no more reintegration cases in that area for the rest of the year. The reintegration program, as it stood, was analogous to taking on the mafia in New Jersey without a witness protection program. ISAF headquarters disseminated guidance that focused on reintegrating lower-level fighters back into their villages, attempting to find them jobs, and holding local elders responsible for their future conduct, but there was nothing on how to protect these men from Taliban retribution. It seemed to me that providing a protection program was an obvious first step. We should have required them to turn in heavy weaponry but allowed them to keep their AK-47s for basic individual protection. Even better would have been to incentivize them to protect their areas against the insurgency in a type of village defense-force concept similar to the Civilian Irregular Defense Groups program in Vietnam. My sense was that reintegration of fighters was enthusiastically supported by the various military headquarters, Washington, and certainly by our allies in Europe, but the planning on how to actually accomplish reintegration was only paper-deep. The basics, such as the overall purpose of the program, were still unclear to me as an operational commander. Did we want to convince these guys to actively fight along with us and the Afghan government against their former compatriots? Did we at least want them more passively protecting their villages and rejecting Taliban influence? Or was the intent for them to completely disarm and reintegrate back into society?

Operating in the absence of a meaningful reintegration plan, I instructed my guys to take the lead on negotiations with the latest overture in Ghazni. Grant informed me that, prior to our arrival, the State Department officer embedded with the provincial reconstruction team was the coalition point man for any potential negotiations between the local Afghan government and the insurgents. However, previous outreach efforts had apparently led to relatively ambiguous outcomes, such as swearing to follow the precepts of the Afghan Constitution, swearing allegiance to the Afghan government, and turning in a relatively small number of small arms. The bigger problem was that it was unclear within the U.S. government who should have the lead for reintegration efforts. Fortunately, this time the insurgent commander reached out to the Afghan National Army, which was viewed by many in Ghazni as more trustworthy than the local civilian government. This gave Grant the bureaucratic leverage over State to take the lead within the coalition in the negotiations since we were the natural counterpart of the ANA. After several weeks of back and forth the commander balked at coming for face-to-face negotiations. The ODA sent word through its network of informants to the commander assuring him of his safety and that he would not be targeted. This seemed to do the trick, and the commander met with the Afghan Army representative on the outskirts of Ghazni City. The man arrived with two demands: job training and protection. Both seemed reasonable to us. However, the Afghan Army general made the point that jobs were short for everyone in Afghanistan and it would be impossible to explain to the people of Ghazni why men who had supported the Taliban were receiving government support and job training while the people who resisted them and supported the government received nothing. The bigger issue for the Taliban commander was that there was nothing akin to a witness protection program to protect him from retribution. The ANA promised extra patrols in the area around his village, but that wasn't enough. The commander demanded that he be able to keep his group together as a defensive measure for them and their families. Of course he also wanted to keep his weapons, at least their AK-47s and a few light machine guns. After much debate, locally and in dozens of emails back and forth with our various chains of command, the Polish battle group commander was adamant that this not be allowed. The negotiations began to drag on, and our informants let us know that rumors were spreading about the discussions. A week later we received information that the commander had returned to Pakistan. We didn't know if he had returned to the Taliban or had some other legitimate reason for traveling there. We began to wonder if the entire effort was a ploy to cause us to pause operations and reduce pressure. The commander eventually made contact again and the negotiations dragged until we redeployed back to the United States. Grant had to hand the effort off to his successor. We never heard what finally happened.

The main reason we could not close the deal was that we didn't have a coherent policy on our end. Every aspect of the proposal had to be run up the various chains of command: ANA, ISAF, Special Forces, State Department, the Afghan government, and so on. We took weeks to come to a consensus and get back to the Taliban commander with a position, while his life was on the line for reaching out to us.

Thus, we had a negative spiral in Ghazni as we headed into 2010, with the paucity of troops to provide a basic measure of security, our catch-and-release detention policy, and the total lack of a reintegration policy or program. ODA 21 and their ANP, often with ODA 23 and their commandos, conducted raid after raid to beat back the Taliban tide flowing toward Ghazni City from all directions. The teams likened their efforts to mowing the grass: they kept it down as best they could, but it simply kept coming back taller and taller. My only hope was that additional ANA units or the surge of U.S. forces being debated in Washington would find their way to Ghazni quickly so that someone could fill the void when we took men like Sadin off the battlefield. It was clear that when I returned to Washington I would need to raise awareness of the damage our detainee policy was doing to our counterinsurgency campaign and press for better procedures for handling the reintegration of the Taliban into Afghan society.

12 Blackbeard Rising
The Afghan National Army Commandos

"Sir! 2-3 is in a TIC!" the sergeant on night watch at my headquarters yelled to me from the doorway of the headquarters. I was walking back to my man-can after a trip across the gravel walkway between the two-story living containers and the restroom in my main headquarters building. It was 2:30 a.m. on November 23, 2009. I turned around and ran back to the operations center, where my experienced and steady sergeant major, Kevin, and York were hovering over the radio. Our operations sergeant was on the phone with our headquarters at Bagram.

"Arrowhead 2-0, this is Arrowhead 2-3 requesting immediate medevac," the radio squawked. "We have one U.S. WIA [wounded in action] with serious injuries. We've been hit by an IED. We have no additional enemy contact at this time. Stand by for nine-line medevac and vitals."

"How the hell did they get hit by an IED at night?" I asked aloud. I knew that ODA 23 had been conducting a night patrol. I also knew that the patrol was far from routine. The team had ventured into Sabari District, the heart of the Haqqani network in Khost Province. During my first meeting with the conventional battalion commander responsible for Khost he had pointed to a big red circle on his wall-size map and said, "Sabari. Haqqani country. This is their base of tribal support in Khost. You're guaranteed to get hit by an IED here, here, here, and on pretty much any road that can support an MRAP during the day." He had one of his companies co-located with the Sabari district governor and police chief. Though they had a presence, their span of control and influence was limited by the distance they could walk from their combat outpost. They were under constant harassment and attack and didn't dare venture onto the roads unless they were behind a route-clearance package, a full convoy of slow-moving engineering vehicles specially equipped to detect IEDs.

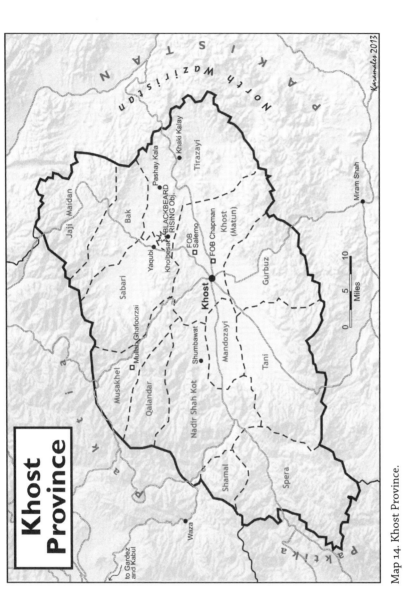

Map 14. Khost Province.

The success of our IED jammers against wireless, remote detonators had caused most insurgent groups to revert back to simply running a wire from the bomb to a nearby hiding place and setting the IED off as their target rolled by a trigger point such as a tree or pile of rocks. The most dangerous IEDs were still those with pressure plates that were victim-initiated. However, insurgents, mindful of not causing civilian casualties that could undermine their support and waste the IED, rarely armed the triggers for victim-initiated IEDs at night. Further, it was too dark for the triggermen to see the markers they used to line up our vehicles with the explosives. So we felt relatively secure in the early morning hours traversing what our conventional brethren had labeled no-go areas.

ODA 23, in an effort to avoid the endless staff questions and scrutiny that came with any type of nighttime offensive action or search, had sent the conop up the chain as a routine vehicle patrol. This meant it only had to be approved by me and my immediate headquarters and could be done within a day. I approved the mission and recommended approval to my boss. I knew the danger; the mission would likely involve the search of a madrassa, which typically housed dozens of young men. But I also knew that Jason, Marc, and the ANA commandos would plan carefully and handle themselves well. It was a calculated risk, but the alternatives were to not go at all or to spend a week fighting for resources they were not likely to get. I had been pushing all of my teams to increase their operational tempo and the frequency that they took their partnered Afghans out on missions. The team didn't even bother asking for helicopter support this time, as they knew they wouldn't receive it unless they had firm information that a specific insurgent commander was present. Instead they elected to take back roads and trails with their GMVs while two men scouted ahead on ATVs.

Months into our deployment we had compiled a stack of reports that a madrassa in a village called Kundi Kalay was a well-known waypoint for Haqqani fighters coming in from Pakistan. We also had reports that packs of men on motorcycles regularly ventured out from this madrassa to harass anyone suspected of working with the Afghan government or ISAF. The team was having a hard time nailing down in advance exactly when the groups of fighters were coming through. With hopes of getting lucky, they decided to pay the madrassa a visit, to at least put the headmaster running the madrassa on notice.

Matt, the ODA's intelligence sergeant, had also compiled a series of reports on two Haqqani facilitators who lived near the madrassa and helped the insurgent groups indirectly by providing supplies, arms, or money. The team and the commandos were not positive the men would be at home that particular evening, but they planned to pay each compound a visit. At best, the men would be found and questioned. At worst, the facilitators would know we were on to them and that life would be a little harder in the future. The team liked to sow paranoia and confusion on these types of missions by whispering just within earshot of the man's family about listening devices in the home and tracking mechanisms on their cars. They would also do things like drop a notebook with names and phone numbers of known Haqqani commanders to try to sow more doubt through the ranks.

I had been sitting up listening to the team's radio transmissions for hours, but all they were calling in were routine checkpoints and code words. So I had decided to try to get a little sleep. They had apparently not discovered anything of note at the madrassa. It was a "dry hole."

Hours later we stood silently in my Tactical Operations Center, staring at the radio and waiting for the battle-roster number to indicate who had been wounded. Our medic let us know he was going down to FOB Salerno's trauma clinic to prepare to help the doctors when the wounded man was brought in.

A voice came over the net. "Arrowhead 2-0, this is 2-3." There was a long pause. "Our, uh, our WIA is now, uh, KIA." The voice was clearly shaky. The hair on the back of my neck stood up and my mouth went dry as the radio squawked again. "Battle-roster number follows, uh, stand by." Another pause. "Papa Uniform 5-4-7-8."

"That's Matt Pucino," York said.

"Oh, God." We all just stood there, frozen in disbelief. Kevin and York looked over at me, and I struggled to maintain my composure.

Apparently, after one of the ANA commandos drove his Humvee into a ditch, the team had decided to skip the vehicle drop-off and drove directly to Kundi Kalay because they were running behind. They tried to surround the first compound of the suspected Haqqani facilitator, but the commandos became disoriented and went to the wrong house. After waiting for over ten minutes to get the commandos in place on the back side of the compound, the team decided to enter without them. The women and children were awake and already gathered in one room. It was obvious that men had recently been there and had left. It was also obvious that the commandos' noisy bumbling around in the dark had cost them the element of surprise. The team was incredibly frustrated with the commandos, especially since they had rehearsed the mission for hours the night before. The team quickly checked another house nearby and moved to the madrassa. They spoke with the headmaster of the madrassa, which was uncharacteristically empty; usually dozens of male students slept there. Jason and the ANA lieutenant sternly told the headmaster that they were watching his school from the sky, looking up as they said it, and that they would be back if they heard any more about his school supporting the Haqqanis. Concerned that they had been compromised, the ODA decided to cut the mission short and return to base. They stuck to back roads that took them through the village of Pasha Kalay. As was their standard procedure, the team and their commandos drove completely blacked out using night-vision goggles. Two operators volunteered to scout ahead for IEDs, each driving an ATV. Their logic was simple and noble: it would be better for a bomb to go off under an ATV and possibly kill one man than for a bomb to go off under a GMV and kill three or four men. That night Matt and Jeff, the team's senior communications sergeant, took turns scouting ahead of the convoy. One rushed ahead of the other as they steadily wound their way through trails and roads barely wide enough for a small car. Just as they came out of a dry wadi, Jeff braked in front of a pile of rocks blocking the right side of the road. Matt accelerated past him and veered to the left side of the road.

The explosion shot Matt's 220-pound frame twenty feet in the air and into the darkness. Everyone slammed on their brakes. Phil, the team's junior but very experienced medic, immediately jumped out of the lead GMV and ran to the smoldering hulk that had been Matt's ATV a few moments before. Jason joined him, and both men began frantically looking for Matt, yelling his call sign, "Blackbeard," over and over. Others jumped out of their GMVs and guided the accompanying Afghan commandos into a secure perimeter to guard against a follow-on ambush. When Jason and Phil found Matt, it was unclear if he was still alive. Phil sprang into action, rapidly but with cool precision, trying to resuscitate him. It soon became obvious that there was no hope. Matt was dead, and the news hit the team like a thunderclap.

While waiting for the medevac helicopter to retrieve Matt's body, the team rigged what remained of Matt's ATV with explosives and thermite grenades. They didn't want to give the Haqqani fighters the pleasure of posing next to it the next day for the propaganda DVDs they sold in the bazaars of Miram Shah, Pakistan.

As the medevac helicopter descended in the open field to the left of the convoy, Marc knelt over Matt's body and held his hand. He made the sign of the cross on his chest and kissed his forehead goodbye.

As the helicopter took off, the team's fury immediately turned to the compound a dozen yards back from the gaping hole in the road and the burning ATV hulk. There was no way in rural Afghanistan, where families have lived in the same homes for hundreds of years and everyone knew everyone, that the inhabitants of the home didn't at least know who dug the hole in the hardscrabble dirt road. This was assuming they didn't do it themselves. Obviously the hole had been dug in the left side of the road, the explosives placed, and the rocks arranged to channel the vehicles right over the bomb. The IED had been initiated by either a trip wire or a pressure plate that was likely remotely armed. The commandos and several operators beat down the gates and doors of the compound with a vengeance and hauled six men outside in flex cuffs for questioning.

By the time the team was able to evacuate Matt's body and clear the compound, the sun was creeping over the eastern mountains due east along the Pakistani border. The morning calls for prayer rang out from mosques across the countryside. Losing the cover of darkness meant the team was now very vulnerable to additional IED strikes. Since the introduction of the MRAP, insurgents had simply responded by employing larger and more powerful IEDs to defeat the additional armor. If a team in a GMV was hit by one of these, it would have meant certain death for the entire crew.

Back at FOB Salerno, Kevin ordered the Operational Detachment Bravo to fire up our vehicles to be prepared to act as a quick-reaction force. ODA 23 was facing a long and even more difficult day, and we feared that every insurgent in Sabari was mobilizing to hit the team again as it tried to maneuver back to base. Fortunately, after several tense hours, they made it back to our base without incident. The looks on the men's faces as they came in the FOB's gate and parked their vehicles were a mix of rage, shock, and exhaustion. Marc immediately began packing his things so that he could escort Matt's remains home. I asked him to stop, take a breath, and think about having someone else go. As the team sergeant, Marc was the backbone of the team, and I needed him to keep his men in the fight. "This team can't shut down while you are gone. The war won't stop while you're gone, and I need this ODA and the commandos out there," I said, pointing over my shoulder toward the gate.

"I need to be there with Matt and his family," Marc replied in a low voice with tears welling in his eyes.

"I need you to focus on the living and to keep the rest of these men alive and combat-effective. We all have to put our grief aside and deal with it later," I said firmly but gently. He eventually relented, and my sergeant major Kevin escorted Matt home. I could tell how much it pained Marc not to be there, but as leaders we had to put our feelings and heartache on hold and focus on the missions ahead.

That night we had a ramp ceremony for Matt at FOB Salerno. The C-130 cargo plane sat in the darkness on the small runway with its propellers turning and ramp down toward the base clinic. A faint blue glow filled its empty interior. Soldiers began pouring out of various buildings to pay their respects by lining the walkway from the clinic to the plane. I was surprised at how many came out. It was a testament to how many people Matt had touched on the base. Because his skills were so broad, he'd regularly dealt with everyone, from aviators to the geospatial imagery analysts who took part in planning missions. He was a leader on the team and in our entire unit. He had combat experience in Iraq and had only recently come to us from an active-duty unit. Though he was relatively new to the Army, having been a Massachusetts patrolman before joining, he was incredibly proficient in nearly every aspect of being a Special Forces operator.

It also hadn't hurt that he epitomized the phrase "tall, dark, and handsome." Built like an Italian Arnold Schwarzenegger, Matt was a bit of a ladies' man. One of the hardest tasks the team had to handle was responding to the steady stream of texts to Matt's phone in the weeks following his death and letting various women, from contractors to pilots across the theater, know about what happened. Of his many exploits one of the best was the story of his rendezvous with the female helicopter pilot. Matt had apparently caught the eye of a Chinook pilot while visiting Bagram Airbase to draw more cash for operations. Weeks later, while flying a routine supply run, she declared a maintenance problem over the radio. She conveniently had to land her helicopter at a forward base where Matt and the ODA just happened to be staging for a mission. After about thirty minutes and a quick rendezvous with Matt, the maintenance problem miraculously cleared up and the pilot was on her way.

As the soldiers of FOB Salerno lined up for the ramp ceremony, the men of ODA 23 stepped into the small morgue attached to the clinic to have a final moment with Matt. They unzipped his body bag to put his Boston Red Sox hat on him along with his favorite sunglasses. They chuckled as they imagined how surprised some young mortuary affairs soldier would be as he or she opened the body bag to prepare Matt for burial. Every team dealt with its losses in different ways. This team masked the heavy burden of its grief with humor. They knew it was what Matt would have wanted.

The men slowly pushed Matt's flag-draped body on a stretcher cart through the cordon of soldiers to the waiting plane. The last group was the Afghan commandos. Each stood ramrod straight at attention in his dark-green camouflage uniform and light-green beret, holding a perfect salute. It was a fitting tribute to a soldier they deeply respected and a sign of the bond Matt had created with them.

The Air Force loadmasters carefully lowered him to the floor of the cargo plane and gently strapped him down. The line of hundreds of soldiers stood at attention in the darkness as the ramp was raised. The team sat on the floor with him, and we each put a hand on him as the plane took off for Bagram and the first leg of Matt's long journey home. I looked over at Kevin and told him how grateful I was to him for volunteering to escort Matt all the way home. It was a grim and difficult task to take on, and it allowed me to continue focusing on the unit.

I sat back on the plane's web seating, thinking about the casualty notification and assistance system that had been developed over the years since the wars in Iraq and Afghanistan began and was now springing into action. The soldiers responsible for our personnel records at my headquarters would have already reviewed Matt's "death form," the unnerving predeployment survey we all filled out. The forms listed every aspect of how we wanted things handled in the event of our death, down to what music we wanted played at our funeral and who we wanted for pallbearers. Kevin and I had to review every one of them to avoid a repeat of the macabre humor of past fallen Green Berets who had listed movie stars for their pallbearers or asked to be buried in their ex-wife's backyard. The wheels were in motion for a chaplain and an Army officer to make that fateful knock on the Pucinos' front door in Florida.

At the same time, the military's intelligence machine was hard at work tracking down the perpetrators of his death. We also had our human intelligence teams and interrogators talking to the Afghan men ODA 23 had pulled from the compound near the blast site. I stopped in at our headquarters at Bagram to see the analysts in the J-2 intelligence shop, where they were sifting through reams of data to connect the dots of who was talking to whom just before and after the blast. They had barely slept since Matt's death two nights before, and I deeply appreciated their dedication. I also appreciated the irony of the situation. For years, while serving in the Pentagon, in the White House, and out in the field, I had complained that our operational intelligence community was too focused on targeting insurgent leadership. It was an important aspect of counterinsurgency, but I had always thought it greatly overshadowed the equally important work of understanding local tribal dynamics, the motivations of warlords, the sources of corruption, and other factors that were causing people to support the insurgency. Now, here I was pushing everyone I could find to devote their time to targeting Matt's killers.

One Haqqani commander in particular was bragging in several mosques around Sabari that his men had implanted the IED that had successfully killed an American. He was also recounting his success to his superiors in Miram Shah, the well-known headquarters of the Haqqani network that was out of our reach, in Pakistan. He told the people in the Sabari mosques that the Americans, much less anyone in the Afghan government, would never be able to touch him. In his view, this was all the more reason why the good people of Sabari should continue to assist the Haqqani network on the way to its inevitable victory. His multiple boasting sessions were his downfall, as we were able to lock onto him and all his associates. A few days later the team at Bagram, working with my guys down at Salerno, had corroborated the information provided by a number of informants. Our people were able to narrow down the locations of the Haqqani commander, his IED bomb maker, and several of his men to a cluster of compounds near the village of Kholbesat. It was surprisingly close to FOB Salerno. In another testament to how highly folks thought of Matt, several other units proposed to conduct the mission for us, also offering us their prized intelligence assets to help pinpoint the men responsible.

Our higher headquarters deployed an experimental vehicle affectionately called the "AssHammer" for its ability to very precisely find and fix insurgent locations. That task was usually carried out by aircraft or drones with specialized sensors, but those airframes were scarce commodities and could stay with us for only a limited amount of time. The AssHammer, however, could stick with us for the duration of the mission.

About ten days later Todd received a call late one afternoon from one of our informants in Sabari District. He reported that the Haqqani commander and his bomb maker were meeting that night in one of the compounds we had identified. Our mission approval process had what we called a "trigger-based conop" that allowed us to prebrief the mission up the multiple chains of command so that the mission location and concept were preapproved and could be quickly initiated once we received a certain type of trigger, such as a call from a source. In reality just tracking down the dozen or so commanders who still had to give their final blessing was incredibly time-consuming. We were certain it couldn't be done in just the few hours between when we received the call from our informant and when we would need to leave that night. Plus we already knew from the planners at the aviation unit that their Apache gunships had been pulled to another mission that evening, so we would not be able to line up Chinooks. Again we decided to take greater risks because of the lack of aviation resources and our self-imposed convoluted mission approval process. We submitted the mission up the chain as a nighttime vehicle patrol. It was not lost on me that this was exactly the type of decision I had made the night before Matt's final mission. We decided to bring in ODA 22 from its base outside of Gardez City in the neighboring province of Paktia to have the forces necessary to search all of the suspected compounds simultaneously. We named the operation "Blackbeard Rising."

The plan was to move in three separate convoys to a vehicle drop-off site in a cluster of hills about eight kilometers from Kholbesat village. We didn't want to risk driving our vehicles anywhere near the village as Sabari was notorious for its network of Haqqani informants who could easily alert a group of fighters and turn the tables on us. ODA 22 and ODA 23, each with a platoon of Afghan commandos, left in two separate convoys, driving with night-vision goggles to the vehicle drop-off site. My small command-and-control cell from Operational Detachment Bravo consisting of France, York, Kevin, me, and several others, trailed behind by approximately thirty minutes. My operations sergeant stayed behind to man the headquarters. We traveled in a mix of MRAPs, GMVs, and ATVs suited to the difficulty of the routes we were planning to take. We knew that the Haqqanis paid villagers who lived in the compounds near our base to alert their IED teams when vehicles left the main gate, so we purposefully left from different exit points and traveled in three different directions to the site. By the time we arrived, all the ODAs and commando platoons were already dismounted and preparing to start the long walk to their targets.

Our element had not made it to the site without incident. One of the GMVs slammed into a shallow ditch as the convoy threaded its way through a narrow canyon. The coupling attaching the axle to the left tire was broken. Kevin and York stayed back with a second vehicle to provide security while a mechanic tried to repair the GMV. We had chosen some pretty nasty off-road trails to maintain the element of surprise, and it was going to be difficult, at best, to tow the GMV through a maze of narrow, tight turns and wadis. Fortunately we had deployed the AssHammer to the top of a nearby hill, where its sensors would have a clear line of site to the targets. As soon as they arrived at the top of the hill, the sensor operators called back with alarming news: "Arrowhead 2-0 this is AssHammer, we have two men talking about a broken-down American vehicle."

If we had lost the element of surprise, these guys could be walking into a trap and would be a long way from any type of support. Since we had nominated the mission as a simple nighttime patrol, we did not have any dedicated assets like Predators or close air support. Now I had to decide whether we were pushing the envelope too far and whether to cancel the mission. As bad as I wanted to take down Matt's killers, I couldn't send over sixty operators and commandos into an ambush in one of the most hostile districts in Afghanistan.

I asked the AssHammer crew if they could determine the two men's location. They replied that it was definitely coming from the direction of

Kholbesat. The men were talking about sending some "friends" to help the vehicle, obviously using a poor choice of code word to cover their intent to send fighters to attack the vehicle.

I asked France to call FOB Salerno and see if there were any other vehicles broken down in Sabari or any of the main roads. I also asked him to be sure to let Kevin, who was still working on the broken GMV, know what was going on and to keep his guard up.

I had a quick conversation with Jason and Marc, who were giving final instructions to their commando platoon leader, Khalid, a short and wiry Pashtun from Nangarhar. ODA 22 had already departed with their commandos, as they had the farthest compounds. "Guys, I know you don't want to hear this, but we may be compromised. We need to make a decision quickly. I'm open to suggestions, but I'm inclined to pull 22 back and fight another day."

"Mike, you know what this mission means to us," Marc replied. "The source just called Todd on his cell and confirmed they are in one of the compounds we identified. The bastards are there!"

The team's interpreter had been translating our conversation to Khalid, and he spoke up. "Sir, we must do this. I know these people. These are my people. Pashtuns. We have been at war for a thousand years. Strength is the only thing these people respect." He clenched his fist. "We must show the people of Khost that we are stronger than the Haqqanis. We must show that the Afghan government will be the winner. It is the only way the Afghan people will follow us instead of them."

We stood there silently in the black, cold night as Khalid's words hung in the air.

France jogged up to the group. "Gents, just got off the radio, and there's another American vehicle down. The unit at Salerno just launched a wrecker out the main gate to recover an MRAP that's broken down on the main road east to the border. It might not be our vehicle that they're talking about."

We didn't know for sure, but I felt there was a much higher probability that the insurgents had been discussing the broken-down MRAP on the main road rather than our GMV in a ditch in a cluster of isolated foothills. My job as commander was to manage risk and make these kinds of decisions. I had to weigh the facts, the costs of action, and the costs of inaction. Whenever possible I defaulted to being as aggressive as I could.

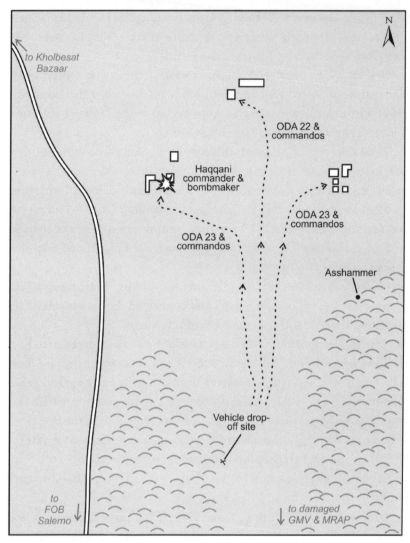

Map 15. Plan for Operation Blackbeard Rising.

"Okay. Go get 'em, guys," I said as I shook the commando lieutenant's hand. He knew what I meant without translation. He turned and barked orders to his men standing around their vehicles.

I stepped back and watched through my night vision as Jason, Marc, and Lieutenant Khalid lined up their men. The commandos' night-vision goggles were older models, and most of the commandos refused to wear them. The ODA tried repeatedly to impart how important it was that they were able to see at night during missions. Nonetheless, I saw many commandos with their goggles in the cargo pockets of their camouflage pants with thin pieces of rope tying them to their belts. Apparently, on the rotation before we arrived, one of the commandos had lost a set of them. This led to the U.S. Training Command coming down hard on the Afghan Ministry of Defense because of legitimate fears that either Afghans were incapable of maintaining accountability for large numbers of goggles or would be tempted to sell them on the black market. The Ministry of Defense sent the commando who lost his goggles to jail in an effort to send a strong message through the ranks. As a result, many of the commandos chose to do without by carrying them securely in their pockets rather than risk losing them and sharing the fate of their comrade. I watched as the line of commandos moved off into the distance, stumbling and tripping over unseen obstacles in the field they were crossing as they moved toward their targets.

Overall, I thought the commando concept was a good one. As is often the case, it was a bottom-up idea that came from the field and had taken years to percolate into reality. The original idea was to take a single battalion from each of the ANA's six brigades, provide them with additional training, equip them with advanced U.S. equipment and arms, and assign a Special Forces ODA to continue their training and accompany them on operations. The goal was to create a structure similar to a Ranger battalion that could continue to pressure insurgent leadership as part of the broader effort to have the ANA gradually take that role away from the coalition.

I thought back to the dozens of meetings in the Pentagon about our policies concerning building and supporting the Afghan National Army. The policy discussions and debates had focused on its size, its capabilities, and its sustainment. My colleagues and I consistently stressed to our leadership that the goal of seventy thousand ANA was nowhere near sufficient for the task of securing the country. That number was somewhat arbitrarily chosen in a complicated formula using inputs from the international community through a joint UN–Afghan government decision-making body called the Joint Coordination Monitoring Board, from the U.S. training command's (CSTC-A) ability to train troops given its limited resources, and from Congress since it authorized the funds.

My office in the Pentagon repeatedly pressed CSTC-A and the Joint Staff to initiate a more strategic assessment to determine the numbers of Afghanistan security forces required to address Afghanistan's short- and long-term security needs.

I kept asking in meeting after meeting, "How do we know seventy thousand is the right number? How do we know we have the right mix of forces? Does that number include enough support personnel—logisticians, training cadre, and procurement officers—or are we planning for the U.S. to provide that type of support in the out years?" In other words, the target size for the ANA was not based on a list of needs developed in coordination with the Afghans but on what we thought we could get from Congress and what the limited number of coalition military trainers could accomplish in Afghanistan. In fact, Minister of Defense Abdul Rahim Wardak pressed us repeatedly during his visits to Washington that he needed a larger and better-equipped force for the daunting tasks facing his Army. The American-educated Wardak was a steady voice of reason in building a professional Army that was loyal to its civilian government and the Afghan Constitution. He was genuinely committed to building a better Afghanistan and truly thankful to the United States. Over the many years he came to Washington his frustration at not being able to turn the tide in Afghanistan grew, but he never lashed out at us. Unfortunately, he didn't help his argument for more Afghan troops by also asking for sophisticated fighter jets and tanks. This led to his appeals being dismissed as coming from a third world defense minister asking for more just for the sake of getting more. Lost in the shuffle was his message that Afghanistan lived in a tough neighborhood and needed a more capable Army than the simple light infantry force equipped for internal security that the Pentagon envisioned.

At the same time, we urged the Joint Staff and the Army to increase the number of trainers available to improve the quality and increase the quantity of the ANA. We pressed our case in the policy and military bureaucracies through Deputy Assistant Secretary Mitch Shivers, a former bond trader and executive who had fallen in love with Afghanistan after he volunteered to go to Kabul as a senior advisor to the Ministry of Finance. Mitch consistently pointed out a major inconsistency in our strategy. The White House's 2007 strategic review of the war in Afghanistan highlighted the ANA as a key pillar for success and eventual withdrawal. Yet CSTC-A was chronically understaffed. Further, the staff they did have was a hodgepodge of National Guard units, contractors, and individual augmentees from the Navy and Air Force. We pressed for the cohesiveness and high level of training found in our best active-duty units, such as the 82nd and 101st Airborne divisions.

I found the quality issue within CSTC-A and the resistance to using our best infantry units in the training role to be institutional within the Army rather than a result of some type of policy disagreement. The bottom line was that colonels and generals commanding brigades and divisions wanted to command those forces in combat, not break them up into small embedded training teams so they could embed with the ANA. Commanding an operational unit in Iraq or Afghanistan was a crucial stepping stone in an officer's career. As a result, the CSTC-A's training and advising mission was relegated to reserve augmentees, while the counterinsurgency mission was handled by active-duty infantry units. I argued to no avail that our best units should be conducting counter-insurgency operations through the ANA, not independent of them.

For all of 2007 and half of 2008 CSTC-A's official Request for Forces, known as RFF 622, to provide additional trainers went unfilled. Of the 2,391 soldiers required to train and mentor the Afghan National Army, only 1,062 were assigned, 44 percent. Our commitment to the Afghan police was worse, with a 39 percent fill. We were still in the midst of the Iraq surge, and, to the extent Afghanistan did receive additional forces, they went to enhancing units conducting combat operations rather than the training and advising mission. Our European allies in NATO were even further behind in fulfilling their commitments for trainers, with only thirty-one of the required seventy-one mentor teams validated to part-ner with the ANA. It was enormously frustrating to have our leadership espouse the development of the Afghan National Army and police as a strategic main effort in the war but then see the request for the critical embedded trainers get systematically denied. The Pentagon's formal re-port to Congress on the Afghan War that year admitted that the train-ing mission was understaffed but simply explained that "Afghanistan de-ployments are being weighed against other global manning priorities."[1]

In February 2008 the United States pushed the international com-munity to grant approval for a top-line increase of the ANA from sev-enty thousand to eighty thousand soldiers, and then another increase to 134,000 later that year. In a series of meetings and briefings in the Pentagon and on Capitol Hill, CSTC-A estimated that eighty thousand troops would be fielded by the end of 2010. I felt at the time that CSTC-A's goals were entirely unrealistic for the amount of time they had allotted themselves, particularly given the chronic lack of trainers provided by the United States and NATO. According to CSTC-A that year, "The long-term goal of the Afghan National Security Forces is to build and develop a force that is nationally respected, professional, ethnically balanced, democratically accountable, organized, trained, and equipped to meet the security needs of the country; and funded from the [Afghan government's] budget."[2]

Everyone who had worked with the ANA in the field knew that most of their soldiers and leaders were genuinely devoted to a better Afghanistan for their children. They also knew that it would take many years (if not generations) of training and mentoring before the ANA hit all of the milestones in the mission description. The most incredible objective was to have the ANA completely supported by the Afghan budget. U.S. funding alone for the ANA in 2008 stood at $1.7 billion, a figure that the Afghans could not expect to match for decades. The entire GDP of Afghanistan in 2008 was a little more than $10 billion.[3]

In fairness to CSTC-A, it had a supremely difficult job on its hands, as the Afghans were starting from a very low point. Perhaps the biggest challenge was that the majority of the recruits were illiterate; some did not even know how to sign their names or count, much less have any sense of the basic mathematics necessary for navigation, fire support, or logistics. Some had cultural issues with being stationed for long periods away from their family or became exhausted from constant combat. Basic systems such as payroll processing took years to put in place, resulting in many units going months without receiving any form of salary. When Afghan soldiers finally did receive payment, they would often disappear for weeks to travel cross-country to take their pay in cash back to their family. As a result AWOL and retention rates across the Army were often abysmal. The Army's basic training center suffered under the handicap of having to pump new Afghan soldiers into units to replace those lost. This drastically lowered the experience levels of the line units.

I argued that the lack of human talent in Afghanistan was a significant issue that would take generations to overcome. We needed to mentor newly minted lieutenants and sergeants as they rose through the ranks and took on increasing levels of responsibility over the span of their twenty- to thirty-year careers. Many of my interagency and military counterparts objected that we had to have the ANA independently operable in years, not decades, and that the long timeline I espoused was not politically feasible. They were right in part. But the issue needed leadership in Washington to set realistic expectations with Congress, the international community, and the American public, about the severity of the challenges we faced and the rationale for taking a long-term approach. Instead, I witnessed leader after leader declare the likelihood of success on his watch. Just months after returning from my 2006 tour and seeing the nascent state of the ANA, I sat in a series of briefings from Maj. Gen. Robert Durbin assuring us at OSD-Policy that the ANA were on a glide path to having a significant percentage of its battalions independently operational in 2008.[4] When it became apparent this was not going to happen, his successor, Maj. Gen. Robert Cone, assured the interagency in 2007 that, even with the higher target numbers, he intended to accelerate the growth of the ANA so that it would be ready to largely operate on its own in late 2011. However, by 2011 only two of 180 Afghan Army battalions were judged able to conduct combat operations independently.[5] It was yet another case of the disconnects that occurred between the realities of what was occurring in the field and expectations in Washington.

The growth and development of the Afghan National Army faced serious long-term challenges, to be sure. But broadly speaking it's important to recognize that, in many ways, the ANA was an overall success story for Afghanistan and the coalition. The Army and the Ministry of Defense were ethnically balanced and were the nation's most respected institutions. Importantly there was rarely, if ever, talk of a coup or other military challenges to civilian rule that is so common in third world countries with messy political situations. At the tactical, small-unit level they often performed well when they were provided proper training and decent leadership. But for a number of reasons, the training, development, and deployment of the ANA was uneven and disjointed for nearly a decade. It was not for lack of effort by many talented and dedicated military professionals from many nations. It was primarily the result of inadequate focus, attention, and resources at the national strategic level. Given those factors, along with the massive challenges facing the Afghans, I thought we had an utterly unrealistic appreciation for how much time it was going to take to enable the Afghan Army to truly stand on its own and be effective.

Standing next to my GMV in Khost, I listened on ODA 22's and 23's internal radio nets as they progressed to the objectives for Blackbeard Rising. It was an exercise in patience and frustration that validated my opinion on how long it was going to take to make the ANA a viable force. Here were the Afghan Army's commandos, their best and brightest, struggling with basic infantry tasks. One of the operators remarked over the net that he had found two commandos asleep behind their machine gun. It was hard not to laugh as another operator remarked, "Good. At least I don't have to worry about getting accidentally shot!" The remark hit home with me personally; a week earlier one of the commandos had accidentally fired his weapon while standing a foot in front of me. The indentation on the wall behind me was an inch to the left of my hip. Someone else on ODA 22 called about not being able to find two commandos. Eventually he found them "resting" by the side of the road. The boots they had been issued were too small and had rubbed massive blisters on their heels. They ended up confiscating sandals from a nearby compound and wore them for the rest of the mission. Lieutenant Khalid, on the other hand, was a bright spot on the mission. I listened to several operators remark that Khalid was cajoling, kicking, and motivating his men to stay alert and perform during the all-night mission. It was leaders like him we needed to nurture and promote over the course of their careers. I thought of Sumar and how much respect he commanded with his recon platoon in Tagab.

"Arrowhead 2-0, this is 2-2," a voice said over the radio. "Target Blue 4 is a dry hole. Progressing to Blue 6."

The teams had decided to use silent entry techniques to avoid alerting insurgents who could be sleeping in neighboring compounds. The teams and commandos carried lightweight, foldable aluminum ladders for scaling the outer walls found in Afghan homes. As ODA 23 approached one of the outer walls to the bomb maker's home, its primary target, they motioned for the commandos to unfold their ladders. Despite hours of practice during training, the commandos struggled to unfold the ladders and lock the legs together. After several minutes of watching them noisily trying to connect the pieces in the dark, Marc took over. They leaned the ladders against the ten-foot mud wall and motioned for the lead commando to go up and over. He refused, standing at the base of the ladder and shaking his head. As an operational philosophy, we had pushed to have Afghans enter Afghan homes first. The commando leadership had wholeheartedly agreed that this was the best approach and believed it would soften some of the criticism about U.S. forces conducting night raids. Unfortunately, Lieutenant Khalid was on a different objective and couldn't be asked to intervene. In a fit of frustration Marc shoved the commando aside, climbed the ladder, and lowered himself down the inside of the wall. Tension-packed seconds passed after he landed inside until he slid open the large bolt locking the gate.

Relieved to get the gate open, Marc stood aside as the line of commandos surged into the compound. Two men sleeping in the courtyard sat up and immediately raised their hands. The commandos rushed into a room behind them. Gunfire erupted. Three commandos flew backward out of the room and ran around the corner of the house. Another commando stumbled out of the room without his rifle and holding his hands to his abdomen. Phil ran up to the door and tossed a flash-bang grenade into the room, intending to stun the occupants inside rather than kill them. He and Todd entered as soon as the grenade exploded. Three two-round bursts from their M4 rifles followed.

"Room clear. Two enemy KIA," Phil called over the net. The men were quickly identified as the Haqqani commander and the IED bomb maker they had been looking for.

Apparently, when the commandos had entered the room, one of the insurgents fired his AK-47, hitting the first commando's rifle and peppering his hand with shrapnel. Shocked by the event, the three commandos behind him fell backward and ran from the room rather than engaging and killing the men as they had been trained. Phil and Todd finished the job.

"Arrowhead 2-0, this is Arrowhead 2-3, jackpot, two enemy KIA," Marc broadcast back to me. "All U.S. personnel green [unharmed]. One commando has minor injuries. No medevac needed at this time. Arrowhead 2-2 primary target is also secure. Both ODAs are progressing to follow-on objectives." Back in the vehicle drop-off site, France and I exchanged solemn looks and nodded. Matt's killers were dead.

"Roger," I answered. "We're going to call up a TIC [troops in contact] and get you some assets overhead to cover your trip back." I was nervous about these guys kicking over a hornet's nest and then making the long walk back to our vehicles. France called the TIC up to our higher headquarters and requested the nearest surveillance aircraft to come overhead.

Meanwhile Kevin was still trying to repair the broken GMV. The front left tire was turned sideways and perpendicular to the vehicle. The part needed was available back at FOB Salerno, but there was no way a wrecker could get from the base to the spot where the GMV was stuck. Our operations sergeant was able to convince the helicopter squadron to send one of their small, two-man, OH-58 scout helicopters to bring the part out to us when they left on their nightly patrols. A few hours later Kevin was swinging an infrared light on a rope in a large circle to vector in the OH-58. The helicopter began hovering directly over him as it lowered between steep cliff-like hillsides, carefully sliding left and right to avoid striking the shrubs and trees extending from the cliffs. As Kevin stood in the blinding dust storm being kicked up from the rotor blades, he tried to keep his eyes on the copilot dangling a large bag with the spare part in it out the helicopter's door. He grew concerned as the helo hovered lower and lower until he finally had to drop flat on his belly with the helicopter skid just a foot over his head. The copilot dropped the bag, and the OH-58 reversed out of the small canyon and accelerated into the night. As Kevin dusted himself off, our mechanic pulled the spare part out of the bag and immediately knew there was a problem.

"Sergeant Major, it's the wrong part," he said. "It's the coupling for the right tire and not the left, dammit."

Eventually York was able to maneuver an MRAP from our vehicle drop-off site into the area. The mechanic strapped the wheel into a semi-upright position and chain the GMV to the back of the much larger MRAP. As the MRAP muscled its way back to us, it created a shallow trench in its wake as it drug the GMV axle along the ground. We weren't sure how the hell we were going to get it back to FOB Salerno, but at least we had everyone together.

"Arrowhead 2-0, this is AssHammer. We have traffic," the speaker box in the GMV squawked. "Looks like the gun shots from the primary objective woke up the bad guys. Several men are talking, have been trying to call the bomb maker, and are putting together a pretty big posse to go investigate."

I was half tempted to have both ODAs try to set up an ambush to attack the incoming Haqqani fighters. I was so sick of constantly reacting to insurgent ambushes; I would have loved to turn the tables on them. But it was going to be daylight in a few hours, and they definitely had home field advantage. Both ODAs and the commandos still had a long walk ahead of them. I called Jason, Marc, and the leadership of ODA 22 and apprised them of the situation. They agreed, aborted the follow-on objectives, and began the trek back to the vehicles.

Our higher headquarters called and asked us if we still had teams in direct contact. All available Predators and other intelligence, surveillance, and reconnaissance assets were committed to other TICs, and they wanted to know the urgency of our situation. As much as I wanted some overhead cover I couldn't in good conscience pull it from others. I replied that we had the situation under control and did not need support.

An hour later, in the distance and coming in from the direction of Kholbesat, I could see several lines of soldiers crossing the fields, their infrared strobe lights blinking in the distance. As they approached our vehicle drop-off site, we could see the commandos guiding several detainees by their arms.

The teams and commandos were exhausted and began loading up the assorted vehicles scattered around our roughly oval perimeter. Six detainees were put in the back of their one flatbed Humvee. The trucks were already crowded with soldiers jammed onto the benches on either side of the bed of the Humvee. I walked up to see the detainees lying on the floor of the truck bed with their hands bound behind their backs and the commandos resting their feet on them.

The only decent road back to Salerno was officially called "Route Alaska" but unofficially dubbed "IED Alley" by the conventional unit responsible for Khost Province. Day or night that unit only traveled Alaska in MRAPs behind a route-clearing package's full complement of specialized engineering vehicles and IED detection sensors. They had guaranteed us that if we traveled down Alaska during the day, there was a 100 percent chance we would be hit by an IED. We devised a plan for most of the force to go back to Salerno through the back trails, try to retrieve another coupling for the GMV, and bring it back out. The

MRAP and broken GMV would stay behind with a second MRAP pulling security. Hours later, as our convoy emerged from the back trails in the cluster of hills near FOB Salerno, I looked up to see our MRAP screaming down Route Alaska as fast as it could, dodging potholes from previously detonated IEDs. It was dragging the GMV with sparks flying out from underneath it as its axle ground against the rocky dirt surface. The strapped-on tire was completely gone. Sometime after we left, Kevin, York, and the group apparently ran out of patience and decided to try their luck with a cannonball run down IED Alley. I thanked God they didn't get hit.

Our informants confirmed the next day that it was indeed the Haqqani commander and his chief bomb maker who had been killed. The district police chief was ecstatic. He had been unable to openly venture around Sabari since arriving in the province, and the next day he drove from Khost City to the Sabari district center. Ghafoorzai, the notable elder from the Mangal tribe, called with his thanks and congratulations. The Mangal were rivals with the Moqbil, one of the tribes that supported the Haqqani in Sabari, so we took his elation with a grain of salt. But his gratitude was still affirming to hear. The commando company commander also received a congratulatory call from his chain of command in Kabul. We were most pleased with the district police chief's willingness to take advantage of the situation by venturing back into his province and working with the conventional unit in Sabari and the Khost provincial reconstruction team to try to fill the void with engagements and, maybe, a quick-impact project in Kholbesat.

We interrogated the six detainees from Kholbesat the next day. The interrogation consisted of basic questioning, and as always, we were sure to have a medic visit every few hours and keep a log of how often we provided them food and water. We also took pictures at regular intervals to have immediate evidence on our side if one of the men later accused us of some type of abuse, as they did in Ghazni.

We knew these guys had a part in Matt's death. But we also knew they did not meet the threshold for acceptance to the detention center in Bagram. Though we had solid reporting that several of them provided the bomb maker with components for his IEDs or helped bury the contraption, the detention center accepted only insurgents we could prove were part of the leadership structure. The lower-level fighters had to be turned over to the local police. We knew that the most likely result was that they'd get out of prison through a bribe or simply receive an outright release. After several days we just released the men back to Sabari ourselves. The provincial police chief declined to take them into custody, citing our lack of evidence. Unfortunately, we could not share our intelligence reporting with him, much less allow it to be admitted to an Afghan courtroom. We also suspected the chief was not keen to offend the Haqqanis over a few low-level fighters.

The day after their release I received a frantic call from the conventional unit based at Salerno. "Khost radio is reporting that yesterday we executed the six men detained in your mission last week," the lieutenant colonel said as soon as I picked up.

"Oh, shit," I said to myself.

"All six were found beside Route Alaska, bound with their hands behind their backs and shot in the back of the head. The radio station is accusing the ANA commandos of executing the men at the orders of the Americans. We have no idea where they are getting this bullshit from. We've sent our public affairs team downtown to the station to try to talk some sense into them."

"Isn't USAID funding that radio station?" I asked.

"Yep. Something like this happened when we first arrived in Khost last year, and AID has a policy of nonintervention. Their line is that they are only providing funding so that the people of Khost can have a radio news service. They are not in the business of dictating content."

"Unless it blatantly runs against U.S. interests! Geez," I shot back.

Hearing the broadcast, I suspected what had happened. Though we had no choice but to release the men we were certain were complicit in setting the IED, we quietly spread word that they sang like canaries about the Haqqani network in Sabari. At a minimum we would sow doubt through the network and cast suspicion on the men. The mafia-like Haqqanis had upped the ante: they executed the men for talking, sent a message to the rest of their supporters, and then blamed the executions on us.

I ran down to the commando camp and spoke with the Afghan company commander. He had already been called by his superiors, who threatened to relieve him of his command. "Commander Mike, I cannot be removed. I have been a soldier for twenty-five years. It is all I know. I could go to prison," he said, his voice shaking.

I told him that he had to immediately go to the radio station and tell his side of the story. "You must tell the people of Khost that the Army is not responsible for these murders and tell them where and when you released those men. The Afghan people respect the Army. When the people hear your voice, they will know you are an honest man and a good soldier."

The commander agreed and broadcast from the station some hours later. He was joined by the Sabari police chief, who confirmed the identities of the men, vowed that they were part of the Haqqani network, and then spoke of the improved situation in the province. Sadly, the police chief was targeted in an ambush weeks later. He survived but was hospitalized for several months and taken out of the picture as he tried to reassert government control in Sabari.

We never found out exactly who ordered the executions. It was a brutal but clever move on the insurgents' part, and one I understood. What I could not understand was the guilty-until-proven-innocent approach by my own chain of command. I spent hours on the phone explaining the exact sequence of events. France also spent hours with the ODA and some of the commandos filling out sworn statements. In fairness, the pressure to explain ourselves was coming from the ISAF command in Kabul and the 82nd Airborne headquarters at Bagram, not my higher headquarters. They particularly questioned why we had the commandos drive the men to the edge of the district and release them. They asked why someone from the ODA hadn't accompanied them. They also asked why we hadn't released the men to the police and why we hadn't photographed the release. The questions were endless and the themes of my responses were the same as when the Afghan police in Ghazni killed the little girl. We can't have it both ways. We can't champion a policy of putting the Afghans in the lead and then constantly question the results when we don't like how things turn out. We encouraged the commando commander to work with the provincial and district police chiefs, which he did. This was the method of release they worked out. Lesson learned. We purchased some digital cameras and requested that the commandos photograph any future detainee releases.

The next day the insurgents struck another blow. The father and son who provided us with the information on when the Haqqani commander and bomb maker were meeting were found hanged on the outskirts of their village. Both had notes pinned to their chests accusing the men of being "Sons of Karzai" and "enemies of Afghanistan."

Todd was livid. "I told them both to leave town," he said, his jaw tightening. "I even gave them money to go stay in Kabul for a while. Obviously they didn't listen. They were both teachers and had families. They just wanted us to get rid of these assholes. I don't understand why they didn't listen."

I walked outside to get some fresh air, thinking about Matt and his family. I thought back to the think tank papers and policy discussions in Washington and Europe about the need for the synchronization of efforts between offensive operations and information operations. I thought about how ignorant we were and the brutal propaganda chess match with the executed prisoners and our murdered sources during the aftermath of the operation. All this was evidence of why counterinsurgency is often called the PhD of modern warfare.

Operation Blackbeard Rising succeeded in avenging Matt's death. It sent a message that the Haqqani network's leadership wasn't untouchable and created some space for the local police chief to reassert his authority. And it was yet another indication of how far the Afghan National Army still had to go. The performance of the commandos, the elite unit of the Afghan National Army, had come a long way tactically, but it would be a very long time before they could independently plan and logistically support their own operations. I was more convinced than ever that we would be partnered with the Afghan Army in some fashion for the next twenty years, at least.

13 On the Border with Pakistan
The Rocket's Red Glare

Standing on the berm wall of a border outpost manned by Afghan Border Police, my team leader, Bobby, and I chatted about the day's patrols with Aziz, the famed local police chief of Shkin in Paktika Province. Suddenly the high-pitched whoosh of rockets screamed from the direction of Pakistan to our right front, arcing through the sky toward the ODA's and Border Police's base, FOB Lilley, at Shkin to our rear. And so began the almost daily ritual of the Taliban launching rockets or shells from their hideouts in Pakistan.

"Incoming!" two of the team's operators yelled as they dove under the nearest vehicles. I barely moved as I didn't recognize the rockets' signature as quickly as they did. I looked off in the distance toward the Pakistani military border post known as Post 28. The white trails of smoke were coming from the base of the outpost that was perched on a small hill several kilometers in the distance. "Son of a bitch," I thought as I realized how near Post 28 was to where the rockets were launching. There was no way they could have missed what was going on, and yet there was no reaction from the Pakistanis. The border posts were manned by members of the border police known as the Frontier Corps that were recruited from the local populace that was often sympathetic to the Taliban. However, the Frontier Corps was led by professional Pakistani military officers. The bottom line was Pakistan may have been an official ally of the United States, but out in the hinterlands we repeatedly saw proof that they were aiding and abetting the Taliban. At best, they were turning a blind eye. Unfortunately, we often made matters worse by dithering in our responses to the attacks, which had the effect of emboldening the attackers and sending a message of weakness to the local populace.

Map 16. Paktika Province.

By the fall of 2009 ODA 25's base on Afghanistan's southeastern border with Pakistan was getting rocketed or shelled, on average, every
two to three days. Many times the rockets were inaccurate and did little damage. But as I looked down at my two men crawling out from under their vehicle, I realized how shell-shocked they had become from
the constant barrage. Over the summer fighting season the rocket fire
had become increasingly accurate as the Taliban honed their aim. Fortunately, the base itself was built with three-foot-thick mud walls and
resembled the Alamo with razor wire. However, one salvo of rockets had
recently struck one of the cannons belonging to the artillery platoon
that was co-located with ODA 25 on FOB Lilley. The explosion destroyed

one of two artillery pieces on the base and ignited an ammunition bunker nearby full of 105 millimeter artillery shells. The massive blast damaged several buildings and wounded the team's junior communications sergeant, Andre, who was nearby. Other rocket attacks had peppered various buildings with shrapnel. The team was just waiting for one of the rockets to score a direct hit. Fortunately, no one from the team had been killed or seriously injured, but with rockets and mortars hitting the base on a weekly basis, everyone felt it was just a matter of time. Needless to say, nerves were frayed.

We knew the insurgents lived and trained in camps just inside of Pakistan, came across the border at night, and set up their rockets on precisely stacked rocks or on elevated metal rails. After each attack they were able to adjust their aim ever so slightly by moving a rock or shifting the medal stands. They then attached the rockets to a timer set to go off the next morning and snuck back across the border. The timer set off a fuse at the designated time, and off went the rockets toward the firebase.

We had consistent and strong evidence that the Pakistani border guards and military stationed in the border outposts not only ignored the attacks but were directly aiding the insurgents. The sad thing about this particular attack was that the night before, we knew it was coming and were not allowed to do anything about it. The previous day, having flown down to FOB Lilley for a visit with the ODA, I stood in the base's operations center with Bobby while we scanned the border through long-distance camera lenses mounted on a tower high above the firebase. We watched as the cameras zoomed across the no-man's land that stretched between the base and the string of Afghan and Pakistani military posts along the border. Several pickup trucks that were clearly not military pulled right up to the base of the hill of Pakistani military Post 28. A dozen men jumped out and hoisted what looked like long tubes onto their shoulders. Leaving their trucks at the foot of the hill, they walked toward one of the launch sites that historically had been used to fire on the base.

We tried to fire on them with the artillery platoon co-located on FOB Lilley with the ODA, but the platoon's higher headquarters, which was different from ours and hundreds of kilometers away in Paktika's provincial capital, replied that the location of the Taliban was too close to the Pakistani post, and therefore they couldn't approve the fire mission.

They couldn't risk collateral damage to the Pakistanis. "Doesn't somebody find something wrong with that statement?" Bobby said sarcastically.

We continued to follow the men with our camera as they popped in and out of wadis and the rolling hills and carried the tubes across the desert. Waiting until the men had added more distance between them and the Pakistani outpost, Bobby asked the artillery platoon leader to again call for permission to fire.

"Now our higher is asking if the men are carrying any weapons," the platoon leader replied as he put down the phone.

"Do long tubes the size of 107 millimeter rockets count?" Bobby replied.

"No, sir, apparently not," the lieutenant said. "Tried that. They want to know if we can clearly ID AKs or RPGs or something."

We all peered at the television screen for several minutes. "There! That guy definitely has an AK." We could see the man struggling to keep it slung on his shoulder as he carried the tube.

The lieutenant walked back over to the phone. "They are concerned that it could be a group of armed locals and won't approve," he said as he came back across the room several minutes later, looking down at the floor and clearly embarrassed.

At this point the sun had set behind the mountains and we could no longer make out anything moving along the ground. "You guys can sit here and wait for the rockets to come ruin your breakfast in the morning, but we are going to be outta here," Bobby said to no one in particular as he left the room.

I felt sorry for the lieutenant. He had already been reprimanded earlier that month for returning fire when the base was receiving effective rocket fire from over the border. Even though it was within the rules of engagement to fire when fired upon, firing into Pakistan was considered especially sensitive. To make matters worse, the Pakistanis had complained that one of their soldiers had been wounded by shrapnel from our artillery. Of course the irony was that the artillery rounds were landing so close to their base because they were allowing the Taliban to fire from such close proximity. Nonetheless, the Pakistanis complained at a national level, and the entire U.S. military approval chain above the poor U.S. lieutenant was investigated. He was eventually exonerated, but the investigation had a chilling effect on him and the entire chain of command. He was not about to take any risks to have that happen again and end his young career before it started. It was yet another example of how risk-averse our war effort had become in Afghanistan. Unfortunately this type of incident was increasingly common in the very litigious environment of the war at that time. The default reaction to any type of gray area became inaction. Junior officers were more afraid of being investigated for making a mistake than they were of the Taliban.

The next morning, after leaving FOB Lilley in the middle of the night for one of the Afghan border outposts, we watched as rockets impacted all around Lilley. Bobby called the coordinates of the launch site back to the artillery platoon and requested that it immediately return fire to destroy any remaining rockets poised to fire on the base. The insurgents sometimes manually lit the fuses for the rockets rather than using a timer, so we always had hope we might kill any insurgents still in the area. The lieutenant back at base responded that he would have to get clearance. "Oh boy. Here we go again with Lieutenant Colonel Michaels," someone muttered, referring to the by-the-book infantry battalion commander who approved each artillery fire mission.

The artillery platoon was operating under different and more restrictive rules of engagement than ours. The rules clearly stated that any soldier or unit had an inherent right to self-defense by returning fire when under effective enemy fire—such as rockets landing on their base. Because the means to return fire was artillery that had a higher chance of causing civilian casualties, Michaels insisted on personally clearing all artillery missions. However, he would do so only after his staff reviewed satellite imagery of each proposed target location to confirm that there were no civilian compounds near the target area. The problem was that the many questions that always flew back and forth between the poor lieutenant and Michaels's staff took too long for the fire to have any effect. Even if permission was given, the Taliban fighters were typically long gone by the time the guns fired.

Of course, the Taliban noticed after a while that every time they launched an attack while close to an Afghan home, they suffered little or no retaliation. Not surprisingly, they began launching their attacks more and more often from next to and even inside of villagers' homes. The unintentional consequence of our policy was to bring fighting even closer to civilians.

Every time they launched rockets against our base and we did not respond, the local Taliban commander responsible for the rocket teams, Haji Zaman, boasted at the mosque during Friday prayers that the Americans were feeble and weak. He taunted the local Waziri and Kharoti tribes about siding with an army that was so soft and afraid to fight. His boasts resonated with the hardened tribal culture, where strength meant survival. Our restraint in not firing back seemed to go unappreciated. We were damned if we fired back and harmed innocent Afghan civilians and damned if we exercised restraint.

In response, ODA 25 began a concerted effort to convince the elders of the Waziri and Kharoti tribes to not allow the insurgents to fire on FOB Lilley from inside their villages. The respected (and feared) police commander, Aziz, led the meetings in close consultation with Bobby; it took a deft mixture of threats, bribes, and appeals to the Pashtun sense of pride to get the elders to act. The threats came in the form of suggestions that American bombers would be forced to respond to the rocket attacks, even if they occurred near the elders' compounds. They also warned that FOB Lilley's clinic, which opened its doors to the locals, would be forced to close soon if the attacks continued. Bribery came in the form of small projects that could be granted to contractors suggested by the elders. Appeals to Pashtun pride came in the form of Aziz subtly questioning who really was in charge of their villages, Haji Zaman and the Taliban or the elders. After weeks of meetings and promises of projects, the local elders finally told Haji Zaman to stop firing from near village homes or face the wrath of local *chelwasti* (regional term for *tribal militia*).

They thought they had outmaneuvered Zaman, but the clever bastard instructed his rocket teams to begin firing from inside ruined and abandoned compounds, hoping we would not be able to tell the difference and would still not return fire. He was right. Michaels and his staff could not tell from satellite imagery whether the building was occupied with people or sheep. Once the Taliban shifted to this tactic the ODA spent weeks patrolling every abandoned compound they could find within artillery range of their base, taking photos and meticulously documenting their grid locations. They were ambushed twice on these missions, and Aziz lost five men, including his deputy in an IED attack.

After Bobby pushed all of this information up to the infantry battalion staff, Michaels finally agreed to allow his artillery platoon to return fire at its own discretion. However, his instructions came with a caveat: the planned impact of the artillery rounds had to be offset several hundred meters from the actual point where the rockets were launched if they were launched in the vicinity of a home. Even if the home was known to be abandoned, the artillery still had to be offset for fear of the possibility that nomads were squatting in the structures. When Bobby called to tell me about this latest restriction, I about fell out of my chair. Our compromise was to return fire but deliberately miss. I knew General McChrystal never intended his civilian casualty directives to be so bastardized and micromanaged. He wanted to establish a culture of restraint and of protecting the populace, but the pendulum had swung too far.

On top of the rules for using artillery in the vicinity of Afghan homes, firing back at the Taliban when they were attacking us from within Pakistan became even more complicated. When the fire came from Pakistan, permission for the artillery to return fire had to come from levels even higher than Lieutenant Colonel Michaels and his staff, which took even longer. This was one of the reasons the insurgents escaped time and again. It was also the reason they had the base "dialed in," or perfectly bracketed. Ultimately, several men from ODA 25 would be wounded from the fire. This was in addition to the propaganda victory we repeatedly handed the Taliban.

Out at the border post Bobby told me the artillery lieutenant was still seeking approval to return fire. "Let's try the Air Force," I suggested. I was seeing firsthand what this team had been putting up with down there for months. The team's communications sergeant called our headquarters on the SATCOM to let them know we were still under fire and were going to bomb the rocket site. Everyone in theater could hear our call over SATCOM, and a few minutes later the communications sergeant yelled up from his vehicle to say that Lieutenant Colonel Michaels was on the satellite phone and wanted to speak to the officer in charge, right now. I told Bobby I would take it.

"Major Waltz, I want to be clear about something right up front," Michaels said sternly. This is my battle space. You do not, I say again, you do not have permission to bomb that site! That launch site is too damn close to the Pakmil, and the other launch site you called up is inside a civilian compound."

"Sir, that's not your call. I'm the ground force commander here, and

we are under direct fire," I retorted, trying to keep a steady voice. I reminded him that I was clearing the actions through my separate chain
of command and that we had confirmed the civilian compound was
abandoned.

"Major, I have not had a single Afghan civilian casualty for the better
part of a year I've been here, and it's not about to start today with you.
This is my battle space, and I have to deal with the consequences of your
mistakes." This was analogous to a quarterback bragging that he had
gone the whole season without suffering an interception, yet he hadn't
thrown any passes. No mistakes had become the metric for success.

I tossed the phone back into the vehicle and nearly jumped out of my
skin as the crack of a mortar tube went off behind me. I looked back at
a group of Afghan Border Police grinning as they loaded another round
into an old Russian mortar tube. Apparently Aziz was fed up with our
dallying while the Taliban rocketed his base, which was adjacent to FOB
Lilley. He had ordered his mortar team to begin firing on the rocket site
next to Post 28. Just as Aziz's men reached for another round we heard
the crack of artillery cannon in the distance coming from the direction
of the Pakistani post. The Pakistani artillery shell sailed high over our
heads, but it was enough for Bobby to run over to Aziz to ask him to
tell his men to stop before the exchange of fire escalated any further.
With an irritated look on his face, Aziz barked an order for his mortar
team to stand down.

We then turned our attention to the ODA's Air Force joint tactical air
controller (JTAC) to call in an airstrike on the site. The pilot of the B-1
bomber circling overhead observed some men running down a wadi away
from the rocket launchers. I authorized the drop and gave the pilot my
initials. On his end the pilot had his cockpit recorder running. Providing my initials as the ground force commander would ostensibly absolve
him of culpability if we accidentally dropped on friendly forces or civilians. The JTAC was grinning from ear to ear; he hadn't been authorized
to call in a single airstrike in the months since General McChrystal's directives came out. "Everyone's overreaction to McChrystal's directives
has cut the balls off the most powerful air force in the world," he said
aloud to no one in particular.

There was a long silence following the JTAC's final instructions to the
bomber, disturbed only by his low whisper as he counted down to im-

pact. This would have turned into a terrible day if he was off target and we hit the Pakmil post. Cracks and thuds, followed immediately by a bright secondary explosion, bellowed across the valley, indicating the bombs must have hit additional rockets or some sort of cache. "Bingo, got more rockets!" Bobby yelled.

The next call was from our higher headquarters. "You know you guys have to get over there and conduct BDA," the operations officer told Bobby over the satellite phone. General McChrystal's tactical directive ordered any unit using artillery or airstrikes to conduct a BDA, or battle damage assessment, "when tactically feasible"; that meant going to the scene of the impact and investigating, taking pictures and documenting the effects of the blasts. This way, when the local Taliban propaganda arm called the international media within hours of the incident and claimed that dozens of civilians were killed as a result of the strike, the coalition would already have evidence to the contrary without having to send a unit back to the scene. The problem was that the "when tactically feasible" part of the directive had become lost in translation in the multiple subordinate commands, and BDA had now become mandatory after every strike regardless of the tactical situation and the danger it posed. Conversely, some units had been denied permission to conduct a strike because of their inability to get to the scene to do BDA. It seemed as though commanders were substituting "when tactically feasible" with "you won't get the support unless."

I could hear Bobby arguing on the satellite phone with the operations officer that his team had been going to the launch sites after each artillery strike and that the Taliban were catching on to their pattern of behavior. "The route to the launch site will likely be laced with IEDs," he was saying. "They will know we are coming."

The operations officer sympathetically told Bobby to send the police with a camera. Bobby informed him that Aziz and his police wouldn't go by themselves because they were petrified the Pakistanis would fire on them with heavy machine guns from their base. The border police regularly exchanged mortar fire and long-range machine gun fire with the Pakistani military outposts on the other side of the valley. There was no love lost between the two. Aziz's police knew that if Americans were with them, the Pakistanis probably wouldn't fire, so they would only have the Taliban to worry about. The rest of the ODA began packing up before Bobby even got off the radio. They knew what the outcome of the conversation would be.

Bobby and I gave each other resigned looks and grabbed our weapons. Aziz was standing next to us now, shaking his head. "I'll go in the first vehicle," I said to both. The first vehicle was the most likely to hit any pressure-plate IEDs waiting on us. "No, I know the route," Bobby replied. "I'll take the lead with one of the MRAPs." Aziz seemed to appreciate our not asking him to go first and nodded solemnly and respectfully to acknowledge that Bobby, as the team commander, would expose himself to the most danger.

This episode reminded me of the controversy over the battle of Ganjgal in northeastern Afghanistan in 2009. We had listened to the fight on the radio in my operations center as a small group of Army and Marine advisors accompanying an Afghan Army patrol was ambushed on the way to meet with elders in Ganjgal village. The room went silent when we heard the call that several Marines were missing in action. Marine Sgt. Dakota Meyer was later awarded the Medal of Honor for finding those missing Marines' bodies and saving others' lives. However, the Army captain who took charge of the firefight as the ground force commander, William Swenson, was repeatedly denied artillery and close air support by his higher headquarters dozens of kilometers away. Swenson, who charged back into the three-sided Taliban ambush with Meyer to find the missing Marines, did not receive his Medal of Honor for another four years due to his angry admonishment of his superior officers in the ensuing investigation. According to documents that described Swenson's interview during the follow-on investigation, he unloaded on the rules of engagement, the leadership of officers who didn't send help, and the questioning he experienced from staff officers while he was under fire and requesting artillery support. "When I'm being second-guessed by higher or somebody that's sitting in an air-conditioned TOC [Tactical Operations Center], why the hell am I even out there in the first place?" Swenson asked investigators. He added that he had been questioned on previous occasions and was frustrated by the complicated process to clear fires, even under duress. "I always get these crazy messages saying that, 'Hey, brigade is saying that you can't see the target,'" Swenson explained. "Brigade, you're in Jalalabad. Fuck you, you know? I am staring at the target. I just get the craziest things on the radio sometimes. Just people second-guessing. If I am willing to put my initials on it, I understand the importance of making sure the rounds hit where they are supposed to hit. I understand the consequences of civilian casualties."

The travesty was that incidents like Ganjgal and what we were experiencing in Shkin were not uncommon. Ganjgal gained notoriety only because there was an embedded journalist, Jonathan Landay of Mc-Clatchy, with the patrol. Ganjgal and the many other battles like it were yet another symptom of the risk aversion that had gripped our effort in Afghanistan. The tragic irony was that the more restrictive we became, the less interaction we had with the Afghan people, and the worse the security situation became.

Pakistani Border Post 28 loomed in the distance as we maneuvered the convoy of vehicles toward the launch site until the terrain became too difficult for the heavy and wide MRAP. We then set out on foot. The trek wasn't easy, requiring us to climb up and down steep wadis and walk through waist-high shrubbery. It was hot, and because our Afghan Border Police were fasting for Ramadan, they were not allowed to drink any water and had not eaten since sunrise. I did my best not to take swigs of water in front of them. Everyone was on edge as the Pakistani border post that had fired artillery at us just hours earlier loomed in the distance, perched on a hill.

As we walked toward the launch site, one of the interpreters excitedly waved for Bobby to come over. I made my way over as well and saw the interpreter jabbing his finger at the walkie-talkie he was carrying. "That's a Pakistani speaking to Taliban!" Haji Zaman and other Taliban often communicated on long-range walkie-talkies. We simply bought one in the local bazaar and had our interpreter scan the channels until he found the one the Taliban were using. We listened as he translated someone from the Pakistani Army post telling the insurgents that the Americans were coming, where to hide, and that we had no air support overhead.

At one point the Pakistanis, in loosely guarded code, seemed to be telling the group where to ambush us. "They are coming to you. Stay where you are. Be ready. We will cover you from here. We will guide you, brothers," the voice said.

"I can tell that is a Punjabi, a Pakistani speaking. I am certain of the accent," the interpreter said, referring to the dominant ethnicity in Pakistan. The other voice replied, "We will be ready for them, inshallah." The interpreter jumped up and excitedly said, "Yes, yes, that voice is definitely Pashtun. He is a Taliban." It was yet another instance of the Pakistani Army directly supporting the Taliban. Providing arms, weapons, and training to the Taliban was bad enough. Directly assisting them in ambushing us was a new low.

One of the operators looked at Bobby and said, "Sir, this is bad news. We're gonna get hit, and we are out here completely exposed." Bobby looked at me as if to say, "Your call." I shrugged.

He nodded at his sergeant and said, "Tell the JTAC to ask one of the planes overhead for a show of force." This was asking the aircraft perpetually patrolling high over Afghanistan to come low over our location to let everyone know they were there and make the Taliban think twice about initiating an ambush.

"Let's go," he said pointing toward the border.

Bobby and I were both opinionated and headstrong and had butted heads over various issues in the deployment, but I loved his aggressiveness. We were far from our armored vehicles and terribly exposed on foot while walking over rolling hills with only scrub brush as cover. Yet he wanted to show the Taliban (and the Pakistanis) that if they initiated an ambush, they would be equally exposed—to the U.S. Air Force.

As we continued our walk toward the rocket launch site, I looked up at the Pakistani border post and thought about the debates in Washington over what to do about our broader relationship with Pakistan and their support for the Taliban. I had attended innumerable meetings in the White House Situation Room with President Bush's Deputy National Security Advisor for Counterterrorism Juan Zarate, the National Security Staff lead for South Asia, Mark Webber, and the war czar, Doug Lute. In those meetings we wrestled with our seemingly contradictory Pakistan policy. On the one hand, we could not have successfully pursued the war in Afghanistan without Pakistan's government allowing us to use their ports, roads, and airspace to move the thousands of tons of men and equipment we needed. They also provided vital counterterrorism cooperation through the capture of several high-level al Qaeda operatives and, in return, received over $20 billion in assistance from the

United States. Yet their national intelligence agency, the Inter-Services Intelligence (ISI), covertly assisted the Taliban and other militant proxy groups that were destabilizing the region. Pakistan had not provided any high-level Taliban to the United States in the years since 9/11. Quite the contrary. From at least 2004 onward, Pakistan had supported the Taliban. Indeed this support was a critical factor in the Taliban's resurgence in 2005–6, the consequences of which the United States, as well as its Afghan and NATO partners, continued to suffer. For years there was a question of whether Pakistan's duplicity was due to rogue elements within its security apparatus, or whether it was a matter of state policy. By 2008 it was clear that Pakistan helped us against al Qaeda and the militant groups that opposed its own government, but aided the Taliban, the Haqqani network, and any other group that helped it control Afghanistan and fight India. It also became clear that the guidance to do so came from the senior-most levels of Pakistan's Army. Support for the Taliban came from the top. The question for the United States was what to do about it.

The elephant in the room while we were wrestling with these issues was Pakistan's nuclear arsenal. Here was a country with five times the population of Iraq or Afghanistan, building nuclear weapons as fast as it could to make up for the shortcomings its conventional army faced against India. At the same time, we had regular reports of al Qaeda and other groups plotting to get their hands on the nukes, either by causing the fall of the Pervez Musharraf government or by co-opting Pakistani scientists with militant sympathies for an inside job. The thought of either happening was a real possibility. If we began to retaliate for Pakistan's support of the Taliban, how far were we prepared to go? Could we really afford to make Pakistan an enemy? Were we prepared to go after insurgent training camps and headquarters in Pakistan and fight the Pakistani Army's tanks and artillery on the way in and out? Were we prepared to shoot down its Air Force, planes that the United States had supplied, to ensure we could fly in supplies that we could no longer send by ground? Whenever we began to contemplate such dark scenarios, we invariably backed away and sought another avenue to convince Pakistan's Army to take on the Taliban itself.

To add a layer of complexity, in the spring of 2008 we received a number of reports that al Qaeda was finalizing plans for another attack on the U.S. homeland. Particularly disturbing was word that al Qaeda was successfully recruiting militants with European or U.S. passports to training camps in Pakistan. I recall reading one threat report in the spring of 2008 that made me question whether I should take my family to the White House Easter Egg Roll despite how excited we were to attend. The threat turned out to be unfounded, but reading those types of reports on a weekly basis will certainly influence one's thinking. We could not afford to be complacent or passive in our policies.

I agreed with those who wanted to expand our counterterrorism operations against al Qaeda's sanctuary in Pakistan's tribal areas. Our primary weapons, the Predator and Reaper drones, were targeting a very narrow set of senior al Qaeda leaders at the time. Many of us felt the list should not only be expanded but the instances in which they were authorized to strike should also be expanded. At that time we were authorized to hit targets only when they were positively identified. Along with Juan, Mark, and others in the CIA and Pentagon, I wanted to expand the aperture to include "signature" strikes. For example, if we intercepted certain types of signals that we could track to a certain location, or if we knew a terrorist leader always traveled in a specific vehicle and that vehicle was parked at a known al Qaeda compound, then that compound could be struck. In addition to the signature strikes, we also wanted to expand the list of al Qaeda leadership authorized for targeting from ten to twenty and to include key Taliban and Haqqani insurgent leaders.

There was reluctance, however, within the president's inner circle to escalate our operations. I wasn't sure if the recalcitrance lay with the president himself or his national security advisor, Stephen Hadley, or whether other pressing issues were simply crowding this one out. Part of the reason was continued assessments by the intelligence community that intensifying our counterterrorism operations in general, and drone strikes in particular, would cause more harm than good over the long run. They asserted that the strikes would further inflame the Pakistani population against the United States and create more radicalized recruits for the militants. Additionally, with President Musharraf's precarious hold on power that spring, the general sense in the White House was that our counterterrorism operations in Pakistan should be conducted judiciously to avoid further destabilizing his government and risk allowing a more militant and less cooperative government to take its place.

A number of us, Juan and Mark included, collectively questioned this assessment. We did not believe there would be as much blowback from intensified strikes as the intelligence community assessed. Fortunately, the International Republican Institute published a poll around that time that reinforced our point. It indicated that many tribes in Pakistan's lawless Federally Administered Tribal Areas were tired of the presence of al Qaeda and other militants and that, surprisingly, the closer the respondents lived to the FATA, the more tolerant of the strikes they were. I made sure to send a summary of the poll in one of the night notes to the vice president with my analysis that there would be less backlash from intensified strikes than the intelligence community was estimating. Regardless, the overwhelming military response against Pakistan that would be demanded from the American public should we suffer another 9/11 would do far more to damage popular perceptions of the United States and Pakistan's political stability than an increased tempo of strikes in the remote FATA.

Three additional events in rapid succession in the spring of 2008 seemed to shift the collective thinking in the White House toward more aggressive action in response to Pakistan's support of militancy. Within weeks of the International Republican Institute poll, a suicide car bomber attacked the Indian Embassy in Kabul, causing the death of several Indian diplomats. All evidence pointed to the Haqqani network with substantial help from the ISI.[1] Days later a damning report came in that answered the long-standing question of how high into the Pakistani government the ISI's support for the insurgency ran. Many in the intelligence community were convinced that the ISI was a nebulous and diffuse organization and that much of its support for the Taliban came from retired or rogue officers acting on the forward envelope of what they were allowed. This reporting indicated that there was no question that Pakistan's support for the various Taliban-related groups was directed by its senior leaders and was extensive and robust. There was no longer doubt that the ISI was ordered to provide funding, equipment, training, and supplies to the Taliban. The Pakistani Army was convinced that the United States was going to leave Afghanistan sooner than later, and they were determined to use these groups to maintain their influence, even at the risk of their relationship with the United States. The final event was President Musharraf's stepping down in August 2008 and the relatively moderate Pakistan People's Party taking power rather than one of the more radical Islamist parties.

All of these events, coupled with the spike in threat reporting on the homeland, prompted President Bush to take more decisive action. In early September a group of Navy SEALs conducted a cross-border raid into South Waziristan, Pakistan, near Shkin and Angoor Adda, resulting in the deaths of several al Qaeda operatives.[2] The Pakistani government reacted by shutting off all ground supplies transiting Pakistan into Afghanistan. I had never seen the Pakistani Army and government respond with such vitriol. On top of the public condemnation for violating Pakistani sovereignty, we also received reliable indications that the Army had ordered its units on the border to fire on any Americans nearing it. The next day a pair of U.S. helicopters on routine border patrol received heavy machine gun fire from a Pakistani border post. Fortunately, no one was hurt, but Pakistan had clearly taken a step down the road to full hostilities with the United States and to transitioning from a difficult ally to an outright enemy. After a series of high-level discussions, we pledged to the Pakistani Army that we would not initiate any additional cross-border raids. However, as a concession, they agreed we no longer had to notify them in advance of any other type of strike, such as those from drones or long-range artillery. Instead we would notify them while they were happening; that way they couldn't tip off the militants. Internally, the president approved the signature strikes and expanded target lists to include more al Qaeda operatives as well as the Taliban and Haqqani leadership. In my view this was a huge step in the right direction toward degrading al Qaeda's ability to plot against the homeland. If they were constantly running for their lives, they would not be able to plan another 9/11.

However, these decisions did little to change Pakistan's overall strategic calculus and its use of militants to achieve its foreign policy aims. In a policy memo I wrote to the vice president I highlighted six steps I felt the United States must take to shift Pakistan's behavior and deal with the militant sanctuary:

1. The United States needed to reinforce its long-term commitment to the war effort in Afghanistan. We needed to show, perhaps through a renewed strategic partnership agreement and more resources, that we were in the region for the long haul. With our focus on Iraq and our outsourcing of the war to NATO, Pakistan was hedging its bets by sup-

porting the Taliban. We needed to show we were going to be the winner and that they should work with us rather than hedge against us.

2. The United States had to deliver consequences for helping militants kill U.S., NATO, and Afghan soldiers. We had to take action in the FATA against insurgent hideouts, even though doing so would put our relationship with Pakistan at risk. We could no longer, in good conscience, provide billions to support the Pakistani Army while they were actively aiding our enemies.

3. The Defense Department had to aggressively begin shifting our ground supply lines away from Pakistan to other routes. There were few good options, with Iran to the west and Russia to the north, so we would likely have to make some concessions to the Russians in other areas of our foreign policy. With approximately 90 percent of our war supplies flowing through Pakistan, we needed them more than they needed us.

4. The United States should continue military assistance only to the extent it would help the Pakistani Army in fighting militant groups, such as purchasing radios, helicopters, and other items focused on combating an insurgency.

5. We should publicize the drone program. It was the nation's worst-kept secret and was even mentioned several times by senators and senior officials. Talking about it openly would give us the ability to influence negative perceptions of the strikes. Because we refused to discuss the program, the Pakistani people and rest of the world received their information from uninformed commentators and Taliban spokesmen, who overstated civilian casualties, minimized terrorist casualties, obfuscated Pakistani involvement in the program, and accused the United States of trampling on Pakistan's (nonexistent) sovereignty in the tribal areas.

6. The United States should dangle the possibility of entering into a civil nuclear agreement, similar to the one ongoing with India at the time, only after Pakistan realized significant progress against militancy. Such an agreement would allow U.S. companies to share nuclear reactor technology with Pakistan in accordance with international regulations. Pakistan was desperate for additional energy sources, and even the potential for such an agreement would have been a powerful incentive for positive change.

Some of the recommendations were eventually adopted. The Pentagon was already quietly expanding our northern supply lines through

Russia and Central Asia to allow us to withstand future shutdowns of our ground supplies through Pakistan. Our military assistance items shifted from what Pakistan needed to fight India to what they needed to fight the Taliban. By the end of 2008 drone strikes against militants in Pakistan's tribal areas had increased nine times over the prior year, with significant effect on al Qaeda's ability to plan attacks on the homeland.[3] However, as the rocket attacks on our base at Shkin showed a year later, little had changed in Pakistan's support for the Taliban.

Out on the border we continued to monitor Pakistani Post 28 as it gave instructions and advice to a group of Taliban that was clearly in the area. Every time a U.S. warplane came overhead the post would call the insurgents and tell them "the weather was turning bad." The insurgents replied that they would "have their party" as soon as the "weather turned good again and their guests arrived."

We finally crested the hill of the launch site, and one of the Afghan Border Police yelled out, "IED!" We initially froze, bracing for the explosion, then slowly walked forward to see an artillery shell shoved under a scrub brush and partially buried with wires coming from it. As we tried to circle around it, we found several more. We gingerly combed the area, hoping to find dead insurgents at the sites of our previous bombing and artillery strikes. It turned out the Taliban had left half a dozen IEDs of various sizes rigged as antipersonnel devices, including a bundle of mortar shells taped together and hanging in a tree about shoulder high. I have no idea why the IEDs didn't explode. Several of us diffused them by simply cutting the wires (which I look back on now as completely insane). The border was marked with a single strand of circular barbed wire stretching as far as the eye could see. As we searched the area right up to the border, and then northward in the direction of Pakistani Post 28, we saw several places where the wire was cut or trampled.

Aziz's border police were very nervous and told us that if we were not with them, the Pakistanis would have fired on them. Through my binoculars I could see several Pakistani soldiers standing on the wall of their compound watching us walk toward them. Suddenly, we crested a low hill and stumbled on a group of seven Russian-made 107 millimeter rockets with fuses burning from a timer toward the back of the rockets. We stepped back, and Bobby radioed FOB Lilley to expect incoming. Bobby and I then looked at each other. No way were we going to let that happen. One of those rockets could have been the Taliban's lottery winner if it scored a direct hit on one of the buildings. We ran up to the back of the rockets with our trauma shears from our medical kits and frantically began trying to cut the burning time fuses. Others ran over and joined in, pulling out pocket knives and anything else that could cut the fuses. With our hands and faces just inches from the backs of the rockets as the burning fuses raced toward them, we managed to cut them in time and prevent the rockets from firing.

Just as we breathed a sigh of relief, the small black box that served as the timer burst into flames just behind the rockets. Suddenly a bunch of Green Berets supposedly with nerves of steel were falling backward and tripping over ourselves while scrambling to get out of the way. But the rockets didn't explode, and we all began laughing hysterically at the entire situation. It was a surreal moment, standing behind those rockets, meters from the Pakistani border, with a group of Taliban somewhere in the vicinity waiting in ambush, while our erstwhile allies looked down on us from their hilltop base.

Our JTAC broke up the party by telling us we were losing our overhead air support (which I'm convinced is the only reason we weren't ambushed that day) because it was getting pulled to another unit in contact. It was time to get out of there. We quickly gathered the defused IEDs, put an explosive charge on them, and blew them in place. We each threw a 107 millimeter rocket onto our shoulders and made our way back to our vehicles and eventually to the base with no other incidents.

Days later, after I had returned to my base in Khost, a single rocket launched from the same area and hit just outside ODA 25's mechanic bay, spewing it with shrapnel. Luckily the mechanics weren't in the building that morning. Bobby ran over to the artillery platoon to begin pressing them for permission to return fire. Again the order came down to do BDA after the artillery platoon was finally allowed to fire. And once again Bobby protested to our chain of command that the insurgents would be waiting on them, but he was ordered to go anyway. As the team neared the launch site, their explosives dog started to sniff around the base of a bush. Andre, the communications sergeant that had been wounded when artillery ammunition exploded after a previous rocket attack, walked over to investigate.

The explosion launched Andre into the air and backward about twenty feet. He landed on his butt and fell back unconscious, his right leg and foot a bloody, smoking mess.

Andre's leg was peppered with shrapnel and dirt, and he had a huge gap in the back of his heel. The ODA's medic was able to stabilize him and prevent the loss of too much blood before a medevac helicopter arrived. I visited Andre in the hospital at my base in Khost. He survived that day and later elected to have his foot amputated rather than face a life of certain immobility and pain.

The constant clashes on the border near Shkin were but one example of the conflicts raging up and down the Afghan-Pakistani border. I had always known it was bad but had no idea it was that bad until experiencing it firsthand. For me, it exposed the magnitude and frequency of Pakistani military support for the Taliban. It also laid bare the futility of trying to defeat an insurgency that enjoyed not only safe harbor but state support. Seeing Andre and, later, Bobby and several other ODA 25 operators come through our hospital in Khost severely wounded brought home to me in a very personal way how muddling along in our Pakistan policy directly affected the lives of our soldiers. It was one thing to have cerebral policy debates in the White House about what to do; it was another to see your soldiers and friends mangled because of the failure of that policy. I couldn't help but feel as though I had failed these men during my time in Washington. Our tepid responses to the cross-border attacks out in the field only made matters worse and exacerbated the situation.

I came away more convinced than ever of my recommendations back in the White House. Given the widespread view in the region that the United States was not serious about a long-term commitment to Afghanistan, Pakistani support for Afghan insurgents was understandable, though not excusable. It was time to move our policy toward using bigger sticks in order to fracture the insurgency's leadership and undermine their sanctuary while we still had significant forces in Afghanistan. We needed to seriously consider cross-border strikes by U.S. forces on the Haqqani and Taliban leadership. The only time I saw the Pakistani Army truly rethink its behavior was after the cross-border raid in 2008. I knew the risks of this approach—risks so dire that heretofore in the face of every incident with Pakistan, U.S. policymakers had defaulted back to trying a different set of carrots. But Andre, Bobby, and thousands of other soldiers as well as the Afghans they supported deserved better. They deserved a change in the U.S.-Pakistan dynamic. We could not just continue more of the same at the expense of more American soldiers' lives and losing the respect and support of the very Afghans we were trying to protect.

14 The Tribes of Chamkani
The Community Defense Initiative

The elders of eastern Paktia Province filed into the large conference room in the governor's mansion in Paktia's capital, Gardez City. The formal regalia of the Pashtun elders, with their traditional black and gray turbans and long tails draped over their right shoulders, never ceased to impress me. Each wore a *shalwar kameez* of various earth tone colors with a suit vest. All had deeply lined faces with long salt-and-pepper beards and, except for the occasional pair of eyeglasses, looked like they had not changed their appearance in hundreds of years. The twenty or so men had endured a full day's travel on rutted, bumpy roads to hear Deputy Governor Abdul Rahman Mangal announce the launch of the Community Defense Initiative (CDI) near eastern Paktia's border town of Chamkani.

CDI was a program sponsored by the U.S. Special Forces Command in Afghanistan to develop community-level self-defense forces in rural and remote locations in Afghanistan, particularly in the Pashtun-dominated south and east, where the insurgency was strongest. Most Pashtun tribes in southern and eastern Afghanistan had a tradition of tribal militias, typically called *arbakai*, dating back centuries. Each tribe called on *arbakai* to either protect tribal interests, such as fertile land, or to enforce the decrees of the elders. On the other side of the border, in the Pashtun areas of Pakistan, they were called *lashkar*. Previous Afghan monarchies had traditionally used a complicated series of alliances with various tribes and their *arbakai* to bring relative stability to Afghanistan's fractious countryside. In fact, during Afghanistan's most recent stable period, that of the Musahiban dynasty (1929–78), the Afghan kings used a combination of centralized and decentralized strategies to provide relative peace and stability. National forces, such as the Afghan Army, established security in urban areas and along key roads, while local communities established security in rural areas with Kabul's support for their militias.

Our meeting in Gardez in the fall of 2008 with Deputy Governor Mangal was an important step toward the resurrection of the *arbakai* concept in eastern Afghanistan. A combination of coalition-backed disarmament programs, President Karzai's desire to keep the Army and police centrally controlled, and Taliban intimidation had marginalized the *arbakai* as well as the tribal *shuras* that governed them over the years since 9/11. But desperation to check the growing insurgency, coupled with a better understanding by 2009 of tribal dynamics in Afghanistan, had led to a new movement within the Special Operations community to leverage and support tribes that were taking the bold step of resisting Taliban influence. By the summer fighting season of 2008 the resurgent Taliban and their allied tribes had overplayed their hand in many areas, attacking schools and clinics, levying taxes, and encroaching on tribal assets such as fertile land and lucrative border crossings. A number of powerful tribes, each for its own reasons, began turning their *arbakai* against the Taliban and Haqqani network in increasing numbers. The coalition command wanted to capitalize on this emergence of anti-Taliban militias acting on their own to protect their communities. Over the next year this type of ad hoc assistance had crystallized into a pilot project in Wardak Province, and then the more formal CDI program.

Deputy Governor Mangal individually welcomed each elder by announcing his name, his tribe, and his district as they took their seat along the long conference table. Mangal then thanked the State Department and USAID representatives from the provincial reconstruction team sitting to his right at the head of the table. Sitting next to me along the back wall was Dr. Seth Jones, a civilian expert on counterinsurgency and counterterrorism at the think tank RAND who was advising the commanding general of Special Operations Forces in Afghanistan on how to implement and expand the CDI program. Seth and I had worked together since my time in the Pentagon and the White House. Along with others, we had pushed the national security establishment in Washington for years for a more thorough understanding and engagement of Afghanistan's tribes. I was thrilled to be sitting there with him as we kicked off the type of tribal engagement and defense program we had only wished for years earlier.

"My friends, my brothers, my fellow tribesmen," the deputy governor began, "our comrades the Americans have joined us today as we announce a new initiative to support us in our fight for a better Afghanistan. They are going to help us organize and train our *arbakai* to better defend our villages and tribal lands. They have also pledged to provide equipment to your men. My brothers, we must take charge of security in our homes and our villages. This insecurity has gone on long enough. We must take responsibility for peace and prosperity in our areas, and that includes stopping the enemies of Afghanistan from using our tribal lands as bases to attack this country. We must stop those doing the work of foreigners from coming across our borders to create trouble in Afghanistan. We are going to begin the CDI program in the districts around Chamkani. It will involve the bearded ones working very closely with your men. Sometimes they must live in your villages." He nodded to me and my team leader, Fitz, who's ODA 26 had responsibility for the areas around Chamkani.

Mangal went on to explain the parameters of the program we had discussed with him in a series of meetings aimed at gaining Afghan government support. He made it clear to the elders that we did not intend to provide weapons to their men, as most Afghan men already had a weapon. We also did not intend to recruit additional men for their forces. The scope of the program was limited to providing existing groups of *arbakai* with supplies and defensive tactical training, preferably in areas that asked for our assistance. Several of the men in the room had been requesting this type of support from Fitz for months to help them defend their lands against Haqqani tactics of intimidation and coercion to support their cause. In exchange for resisting Haqqani cross-border incursions, ODA 26 and the provincial reconstruction team would provide the village and surrounding area with an influx of projects. "The Americans are not going to pay your men," Mangal continued. "Instead your villages will receive additional development projects. This program is intended to benefit the tribe and the village, not one individual. The Americans will also be there to support you if the Haqqanis mount an attack against you. They will be able to bring the jets and bombings."

Several of the elders frowned at the statement that we would not provide salaries, and one elder voiced an objection.

"Your men are volunteers already," Mangal replied. "They are night watchmen at the bazaar or guards for the roads leading to your crops and pine nut trees. You will pay their expenses through collections in the village, as you always have, my friends. But the new projects the Americans are promising will bring more work for your people. You must sit with them and tell them your needs."

The State Department representative, who was new to the provincial reconstruction team and had not participated in many of our earlier discussions, asked Mangal to elaborate on how the *arbakai* would be managed. It was one of the most important points, in my view: how the *arbakai* would be prevented from becoming yet another unruly militia group outside of central government control that preyed on the average Afghan. "The members of the *arbakai* are chosen by the tribal *shuras* representing their communities," Mangal responded. "These men, as the leaders of their tribes, will be responsible and must put their reputation against every man." He repeated the sentence in Pashtu before pausing to let the words sink in. "Their name and honor are tied to the actions of the men they nominate."

I felt strongly that maintaining the tribal *shura* rather than a single individual as the entity responsible for the *arbakai* was important in reestablishing the *shura* as a key governance institution and to prevent us from inadvertently bolstering a local strongman. I had made the point dozens of times in meetings about CDI with NGOs, local United Nations representatives, State Department and USAID officers, and even our own military officers. All of them were concerned that U.S. Special Forces were, in a cowboy-like fashion, returning to a policy of bolstering warlords for short-term security gains. Each time this concern was expressed I explained that the *arbakai* would be governed and controlled by the *shura*, just as they always had been.

An elder from the Jaji tribe stood. "We support this program. We have been needing this for many years. Give us the equipment we need, and we will defeat these dogs, the Haqqani. These sons of Pakistan are no good for our villages and our lands. They threaten to close our schools. They are robbing our children of their futures. They come and force us to give them men for fighting. Our Army is not big enough to protect the border and every valley in Afghanistan. So we must stand and defend our own villages."

I was excited as I heard this and other positive responses like it from the elders as the meeting continued. Each stood and gave a similar speech. Seth was smiling. It had been a long time coming. We had been pushing for this type of program for years in Washington, and now here we were with a hand in actually implementing it.

Just one year prior to this meeting in Gardez, I was vigorously debating the merits of such a program in a very different setting, this time in the ornate Old Executive Office Building next to the White House during President Bush's strategic review of our policies in Afghanistan. The suggestion of a formalized tribal support program was one of the most controversial topics of the fall 2008 review. The main opposition came from the State Department and the representatives to the review from the intelligence community. State's concerns were twofold. The first was that they had tried such a program before. In 2007 the State Department supported a program called the Afghan National Auxiliary Police, which sought to support the regular police by supplementing them with local recruits from some of the most insurgent-prone Pashtun areas. The recruits were put through some abbreviated training and rapidly deployed to serve as a bulwark against the growing insurgency. At first I enthusiastically supported the program from my office in the Pentagon and advised my leadership to do the same. But we soon realized the program was going to suffer from the same issues as the regular police force that State was also charged with developing: a lack of adequate oversight and support. State was not able to deploy enough civilians to the dangerous areas where the auxiliary police were needed, so they hired contractors at enormous expense for training and oversight, and who were limited by their contracts in their ability to partner with the police in the most dangerous areas. Thus once the auxiliary police left the basic training center, we didn't have the ability to know if these newly minted deputies were causing more harm than good by abusing their powers, or even if they were showing up to work at all. It was the same problem State had for years with the national police. By early 2008 we had little idea how many auxiliary police were still working or where. A short time later the program was disbanded.

State's other concern was that President Karzai would object. Karzai, for all his faults, had done a good job in managing the perpetual balancing act among Afghanistan's major ethnic groups, the Pashtun, Tajik, Uzbek, and Hazara. State was certain that Karzai would object to a program that would be seen as favoring the Pashtun over the other groups. He would also object, they argued, to a program that fostered local militias that could compete with the central government's Army and police. They were right that Karzai and his government had to buy into the program, but I pressed that we needed to make a collective decision as part of the review to get him and his key ministers on board.

During the strategic review I argued that a tribal defense program, unlike the auxiliary police program, should be mentored by Special Forces ODAs that were uniquely trained and equipped to live with the tribes. They would provide the oversight that was critical to ensuring the program wasn't abused and a supporting role that was necessary when the inevitable Taliban retaliation materialized. The oversight element was key, in my view, and the major difference from programs we had tried in the past. I raised the example of the successful Campesinos Soldados program in Colombia, where President Álvaro Uribe raised tens of thousands of "peasant soldiers" over the course of a year to participate in an emergency plan implemented by the national government to tamp down the raging insurgency and drug violence gripping Colombia when he came to power. Farmers between eighteen and twenty-four years of age completed their compulsory military service for eighteen months in their home villages in a defensive community watch program. The Colombian Army's practice of placing a cadre of regular Army sergeants in charge of clusters of *campesinos soldados* was vital to the success of the program and provided accountability, supervision, training, and logistical support. After their eighteen months of service the farmers were offered enlistment contracts into the Army or vocational training to assist with their transition back to the civilian workforce. With a similar framework, I was convinced, we could mobilize the *arbakai* in Afghanistan and avoid the pitfalls State was highlighting.

The intelligence community objected that it was very dangerous for the United States to be picking winners and losers among the Afghan tribes. They stressed that we were too ignorant of who was who in the complicated social order of rural Afghanistan and that we would be manipulated to each tribe's advantage over its rivals. By supporting and organizing one tribe we could exacerbate tensions with its rivals and cause instability in areas that had nothing to do with the Taliban. The intelligence representatives were right in that the Afghans were survivors first and foremost and were masters at using us to further their agendas. But I found the argument ironic. Many people had been pressing the intelligence community for years, with little success, to devote more resources to collecting the sociopolitical and cultural information so critical to a counterinsurgency effort. In fact one of the final recommendations of the review was to direct the various intelligence agencies to pool their data into a single tribal database that could be accessed by people who needed it in the field. I also stressed that our ignorance was precisely the reason the teams must live in the village, so that they could have a daily, nuanced understanding of who was doing what to whom.

The two representatives to the review from the National Intelligence Council also reminded the group that the international community had spent years and millions of dollars on a militia disarmament program. It had successfully removed huge numbers of weapons from the militias that had dominated Afghanistan since the withdrawal of the Soviet Union. "You will be opening Pandora's box by rearming these groups," one of the representatives said. "We won't be able to control them, and pretty soon they'll be challenging the legitimate Army and police." Another participant countered that the large militias with tanks and heavy weapons that devastated the country during its civil war were typical of the Uzbek and Tajik warlords found in northern Afghanistan. By comparison, the Pashtun tribal militias were small and fractured and would have oversight from our Special Forces ODAs.

The Defense Department was divided on its views about a potential program. The Special Forces community enthusiastically supported the concept. Many felt it was reminiscent of their greatest historical successes, such as when ODAs embedded with the Montagnard tribes in Vietnam. However, CSTC-A, the training command, objected on the grounds that every resource dedicated to training tribal forces would be one less resource for the Afghan National Army and police. Having fought for years for more and better resources for CSTC-A, I was sympathetic to their concerns. However, I believed that their short timelines were unrealistic and that creating a fully independent military and police force was going to be a decades-long effort. Many tribes in Afghanistan were begging for our help and could be supported in the short term with relatively little diversion of resources while CSTC-A built the Army and police over the longer term.

Dr. Eliot Cohen, the preeminent professor of military affairs and Secretary Condoleezza Rice's counselor at the time, pressed that we needed new thinking to reverse the growing momentum of the insurgency and that what his colleagues at the State Department and intelligence community were suggesting was more of the same. He encouraged the group to take a step back and look at the broader picture: "What's really at stake here is the fundamental nature of our strategic approach. Are we pursuing a 'top-down' or 'bottom-up' strategy?"

Proponents of the top-down strategy believed we would never stabilize and secure Afghanistan without a powerful central government capable of providing services to Afghans in all corners of the country. Bottom-up advocates insisted that Afghanistan was and always had been a quintessentially decentralized society, making it necessary to build local institutions to create security and stability. I felt we needed to pursue both. Creating strong government institutions in a centralized state would help ensure long-term stability, but those efforts were going to take at least a generation. I argued that the top-down state-building and counterinsurgency efforts that were central to our strategy needed to take place alongside localized programs, such as reaching out to legitimate local leaders to enlist them in providing security and services at the village and district levels. If done correctly, the localized programs would buy time for the state building to work and could eventually transition to a state-controlled security force when doing so made sense. Such a strategy would complement a counterinsurgency campaign by tapping thousands of tribal fighters to secure rural populations, allowing international troops and official Afghan forces to focus on large towns and cities. I contended that building strong partnerships with the tribes, whose domains straddled Afghanistan's border with Pakistan, could also prove critical to defeating insurgents entrenched in Pakistan's western tribal areas. For every twelve-man Special Forces ODA in Afghanistan, we could organize and advise hundreds of tribal fighters. The key was how to connect the top-down and bottom-up efforts so that they worked together rather than against each other. I agreed there were significant risks, but I didn't feel we had a choice in terms of options to blunt the Taliban's momentum.

After considerable debate the compromise position in the final draft of the review's recommendations to the president was to authorize the military to start a pilot program. The pilot began in Wardak Province

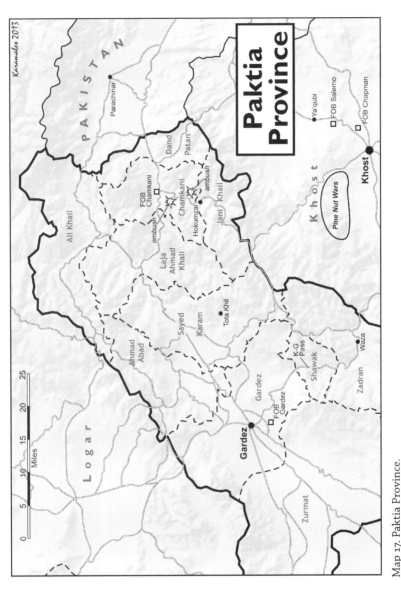

Map 17. Paktia Province.

the following spring, 2009, and by the fall had morphed into the CDI program we were announcing in Paktia Province.

The first CDI site in Paktia Province was Chamkani, the responsibility of ODA 26 and their team leader, Fitz. Chamkani was the first crossroads and bazaar inside the border in an east-west valley running from Pakistan down to the provincial capital of Gardez in the interior of eastern Afghanistan. From a tribal standpoint, the area was even more fractious and complicated than is usually the case in the east. An anthropologist once described to me the differences between the tribes in eastern and southern Afghanistan: "It's like comparing the town halls of colonial New England to the Plantation South. In New England, if you wanted to address a community you addressed an entire assembly. It's the same in eastern Afghanistan. If you want to address a tribe, you speak with a large group of assembled elders and it can be incredibly difficult to reach any type of consensus or decision. In southern Afghanistan, like the Plantation South, if you want to address a tribe, you typically speak with the tribal *malik* or chief. It's much more hierarchical in the south and easier to identify the boss that controls a large swath of territory."

The area around the town of Chamkani had five major Pashtun tribes that formed an intricate web of rivalries and alliances that the Haqqani network repeatedly leveraged to their advantage. The Chamkani tribe, which shared the name of the town and district, occupied most of the area around the ODA's base. To the east on the Pakistani border were the Moqbil and the Jaji tribes. Both were rivals for several lucrative informal border-crossing sites. The Haqqani network in Pakistan had been providing weapons and supplies to the Moqbil in exchange for their support against the government. To the south, west, and north were Mangals. The Mangal lands stretched far to the south and into neighboring Khost Province, where I was dealing with one of their subtribal leaders, Mullah Ghafoorzai. The Mangals had moved onto Chamkani tribal lands over the previous generation and occupied portions of it. This was a huge source of tension that, at times, erupted into protracted firefights. Crossing all boundaries were the nomadic Kuchi, with their herds of camels and sheep.

Everywhere the tribes butted up against each other there were conflicts over resources and land that led to an endless cycle of blood feuds. During one of my visits to the team at Chamkani, Fitz, a down-to-earth

Irish American with a red beard and a Boston accent, was hosting a *shura* to help mediate a dispute between two tribes. The situation was a great example of how a well-meaning development project could actually fuel tribal tensions. It was also an example of how we needed to be very sophisticated in our understanding of and in tune with local dynamics. The issue was that a small NGO funded by USAID planned to pave a road running from a border crossing west to the Chamkani town bazaar. Everyone welcomed the road. However, the Mangal and Moqbil tribes were literally about to kill each other and the road crew because the engineers needed to slightly change the route before the road could be surfaced. This was a critical point to the elders because the roads traditionally marked property boundaries. When the dispute first reared its head, Fitz tried to stay out of it and defer to the district governor to allow the Afghan government to resolve the issue. Unfortunately, as is often the case in Afghanistan, the district governor was from the Mangal tribe, as was his police chief, and therefore was not trusted by their rivals the Moqbil. Fitz had to become personally involved when the Haqqanis began intervening on the side of the Moqbil by attacking the road crews. A few days after an attack, several Mangal elders and the police chief came to the ODA base claiming to have information on the "insurgent" group conducting the attacks. Not surprisingly the men they were accusing happened to be Moqbil tribal leaders. Fortunately Fitz and his team had developed relationships with the Moqbil elders and were confident they were not the ones attacking the road crew. At the *shura* each delegation presented deeds and papers signed by former government officials, each claiming rights to the lands. After the marathon session, Fitz ended up splitting the difference and buying off the leaders on either side with a small project each. The road was allowed to proceed.

Other disputes didn't end as peacefully. South of Chamkani, in the mountains that divided the provinces of Paktia and Khost, the local government tried to mediate a dispute between different factions of the Mangal and Moqbil over a disputed tract of forest rich with pine nut trees. The pine nut harvest was a significant cash crop for both tribes, but unclear boundaries were a constant source of hostility. As tensions boiled over, the Haqqanis armed the smaller Moqbil tribe with heavy machine guns and mortars to attack several Mangal villages and seize the disputed land. We watched from my headquarters as both sides exchanged heavy volumes of fire, killing several dozen men on both sides. The local district government tried to negotiate a resolution, but to no avail. The Haqqanis, however, then cleverly sent a delegation to help resolve the issue. In a stroke they had exacerbated tensions, indebted the Moqbil tribe by providing them weapons, made the government look weak, and enhanced their legitimacy as the arbiter of problems. We found out later the Moqbil repaid their debt by allowing the Haqqanis to set up insurgent training camps and a bomb-making facility on their lands.

Fitz and his team met daily with the leaders from most of the tribes around Chamkani, trying to maintain status as a neutral arbiter. I was convinced we had to take a different strategy. We were being neutral, but the Taliban and Haqqanis were coercing or intimidating tribes into working with them. We had to start supporting the tribes that were asking for our support. I sympathized with those critical of American forces siding with one side or the other in these types of messes, but the Taliban and Haqqanis were employing a sophisticated tribal engagement and manipulation strategy to meet their agenda, and I felt strongly that we had no choice but to start doing the same or continue to get outmaneuvered.

ODA 26 had a tough time getting the CDI program up and running despite the elders' initial enthusiasm during the meeting in Gardez. Fitz initially chose the village of Hokumzai, to the south of Chamkani, for a number of reasons. First, it was a known key stop for insurgents infiltrating from Pakistan into the interior of Afghanistan. If Fitz moved the ODA there and began training and organizing the Chamkani tribal *arbakai*, he could disrupt a major route Haqqani fighters used on their way from Pakistan to conduct attacks in Khost Province to the south and deeper into Afghanistan to the west. Second, three tribes butted up against each other in Hokumzai. Fitz hoped that, by being physically present, he could better influence the tribal leadership and broker a series of disputes that were constant sources of tension. The initiative quickly fell apart, however, as word spread that the ODA was planning to move into the village. Twice the team tried to relocate to Hokumzai but came into heavy contact with dozens of fighters launching attacks from the hills lining the road to the village. On one occasion the team called in Apache gunships to beat off the attacks and killed over twenty insurgents. The Haqqanis clearly didn't want ODA 26 in the village. Before the team could make a third try, the Haqqanis resorted to their typically brutal tactics by kidnapping the son of one of the Chamkani tribal elders that supported locating the CDI in Hokumzai. They then proceeded to torture him while broadcasting live over a pirate radio station they had set up in the mountains. It was a brutal and callous act. The next day a delegation from Hokumzai, who were already waffling due to intense Haqqani pressure, arrived at the team's base to withdraw the offer.

To assist ODA 26 in establishing the program, I was ordered to move one of its sister teams, ODA 24, from FOB Chapman in Khost Province, north to Chamkani.

As a tragic aside, just a month after ODA 24 vacated their portion of Chapman, a double agent for al Qaeda, Hammam Khalil al-Balawi, detonated his suicide vest in the courtyard of the team's former living quarters, killing seven CIA employees. The dead included Chief of Base Jennifer Matthews, her logistics officer, Liz Hanson, and a case officer, Harold Brown, all of whom had worked closely with us. ODA 24's compound had adjoined the CIA compound on Chapman, so when it came time to meet and debrief al-Balawi, who had claimed to know the whereabouts of al Qaeda's number two, Ayman al-Zawahiri, the CIA decided to have the meeting on the then vacant Special Forces compound. Jen stood out from the other chiefs of base we worked with when she made a point to come see me the day after she took charge at Chapman and wanted to cooperate with us on a number of initiatives. This wasn't always the case with our CIA colleagues; many had a "we will call you when we need you" attitude.

I was visiting a village near our base at FOB Salerno when we heard the blast and saw the small mushroom cloud from the explosion just down the road at Chapman. We sped to the site to try to assist with the casualties. The aviation unit based at Salerno landed a Chinook helicopter just outside the compound to evacuate the wounded. The scenes at Chapman and back at the trauma hospital at Salerno, where the casualties were treated, were horrific. Sadly Jen was later blamed in the media and in the Agency's internal investigation for allowing al-Balawi to enter the compound without being searched. She made the judgment that he was such a valuable source she wanted to create an air of trust from the outset of the meeting. She felt that searching a man who was supposedly risking his life to help us could ruin that dynamic. Plus Jordanian intelligence had vouched for him. But because she was an analyst (albeit one of the Agency's most talented on al Qaeda) and was not an operational case officer, many armchair quarterbacks opined in the aftermath that she was in over her head as chief of base in a combat zone. I sensed a good bit of misogyny in the aftermath of the bombing. My own experience was that she was knowledgeable, tough as nails, and worked well with us for the broader mission. Her memory deserved better.

In Chamkani, with ODA 24 in support, ODA 26 next attempted to work with the Moqbil tribe to the east of their base near the Pakistani border. The team knew the Moqbil was a small tribe often marginalized by their larger Mangal neighbors. They were constantly complaining that key government posts such as the district governorship, the police chief, and several provincial positions, including the deputy governorship, were always controlled by their rivals. Even though we knew several Moqbil elders had close relationships with key insurgent leaders in Pakistan, they seemed very receptive to the team's overtures to provide projects and training to their small *arbakai* force. The Moqbil also controlled several unofficial border-crossing sites that made them of even more interest to us. A series of *shuras* with various elders from the cluster of villages in the Moqbil areas seemed to bring consensus that the area was ready to accept the ODA in their midst. The team found a large compound that it could rent for a base of operations while training the *arbakai* and began discussions on the types of development projects that best suited the area. However, just as the ODA was preparing to move into place, a group of Moqbil elders came to the base and absolutely refused to allow the team to rent the compound it had identified. After several weeks of negotiation the Moqbil elders suggested a compromise. They would send *arbakai* to our base for training rather than the team living in the village and working directly with them. They also still wanted, of course, several development projects in their area. We considered their offer but, in the end, insisted on the team living in the village. Living in the midst of the Afghans was critical to the design of CDI as it was the only way we could provide proper oversight and mitigate all of the concerns that the program's detractors had raised. We simply could not have our finger on the pulse of the nuances of ever-shifting tribal rivalries from inside the team's fortified base on a hill. In my view, "commuting" back and forth to the battlefield was one of the biggest reasons we were struggling to understand and contain the insurgency.

Eventually I was able to sit down one-on-one with one of the elders during a visit to the base at Chamkani. He summed up his change of heart: "We do not believe you will stay with us. Many of us do not like the Haqqanis and their brutal ways, but our tribe is small. They are backed by the Pakistani Army. The Afghan Army is not in this area. When we agreed to accept your support, we believed you would support us, protect us, and defeat the Haqqanis with your airplanes when they attack us. But your president says you are leaving Afghanistan. We cannot trust our lives to you if you will leave us."

This was in December 2009. President Obama had announced the surge of U.S. forces at a speech at West Point. However, the show of strength and commitment delivered by the surge announcement was immediately undercut by the president also announcing a date for its withdrawal. I distinctly remember being horrified as I watched the speech in my headquarters. "He's just told the world we are leaving," York exclaimed. "Who the hell is going to risk their life to work with us now?" Another officer watching with us compared the announced surge and then withdrawal to President Roosevelt announcing D-Day in June 1944 but then telling the Germans that the invasion force would leave a year later. "What do you think the Germans would have done? Wait us out?" he asked rhetorically. We could not have sent a worse message to the Taliban, the region, and the Afghan people.

And we immediately felt the impact in the field. Out on one of the most remote borders in the world the Moqbil elder had somehow heard of the speech. He didn't even acknowledge the surge. He heard only "America is leaving."

Sadly I had experienced a nearly identical encounter with Mullah Ghafoorzai of the Mangal tribe in Khost just a few days earlier. I had developed a relationship with him over the latter half of 2009 after the so-called pine nut wars with the Moqbil. He was a respected leader of a large Mangal subtribe and had several hundred very well-equipped *arbakai* reporting to him. By December 2009, after dozens of cups of tea and hours of discussions with me, Ghafoorzai was ready to commit his men to be nominated for the CDI program and to openly oppose the Haqqanis. I hoped it would be one of the key achievements of my tour. But in our final meeting to secure his cooperation, Ghafoorzai went cold on me. He normally greeted me with a large bear hug and an animated discussion about our families and the goings-on in the valley his tribe inhabited. But this time he remained seated on the pillows lining the far end of the wall as I entered. After some awkward pleasantries, I found out why. "We always suspected you would abandon us. Now your president has said it," he said sternly. "I am sorry, Commander Mike, but my men cannot work with you now. The Haqqanis will target us daily. They already have a bounty on me. Without your support, they will eventually get to every one of us and our families."

I responded that the president's announcement was really focused on sending additional U.S. soldiers. "He is planning to only eventually withdraw the reinforcements he is now sending," I pleaded. "Our troop levels will simply return to what they are now. That will be several years in the future."

The nuances of the strategy were lost on him. "I am sorry, my friend. Several years is nothing in this part of the world. Until America is ready to pledge its grandchildren to stand shoulder to shoulder with my grandchildren in this war, I cannot work with you." It was a stunning example of how a policy announcement had immediate impacts on the ground.

We learned several lessons in the process of trying to establish those initial sites in the early days of CDI. The first was that we had to move very quickly when elders gave us the green light to come and work with them. If we waited, the insurgents or even other local leaders who disagreed with the move would quickly put significant pressure on the elders to back away from us. We also learned that we had to strike a balance between choosing locations based on how we wanted to affect the enemy versus where we had the most tribal support. We had to follow the support. Most of all, in a strategic sense, we had to send the signal of America's resolve and commitment to stand with these people. Back in Washington the national security bureaucracy was fighting over troop numbers. The numbers were important, but more important was providing long-term assurances to the people we were supposed to protect.

Despite the challenges with establishing CDI in my areas of responsibility, eventually the program gained traction and enjoyed increasing success. Part of the reason was that the Special Operations Command in Afghanistan, to its credit, was adaptive in its approach and adopted the lessons learned from the field. Critically, they grew a local security program that focused solely on using tribal militias to enhance security into a full-fledged stability program that focused on addressing the local causes of conflict. Accordingly, the name of the program evolved into Village Stability Operations (VSO). This more mature and robust version heavily augmented the ODAs with civil affairs teams, psyop teams, infantry squads, and healthy development budgets. The ODA became an orchestrator of governance, development, and security while living with the Afghans to be able to easily interact with them and have a strong sense of what was going on in their communities. The tribal *shuras* still nominated men, usually from their *arbakai*, to participate in the VSO program, but those men now became Afghan local police and officially worked for the district Afghan police chief. This meant the men were paid and had an official tie to the government. Importantly, groups of Special Forces officers were sent to liaise with local Afghan officials in the districts and provinces that had VSO programs. These officers had the critical task of helping to tie the tribes and villages to the formal Afghan government apparatus and, in turn, ensure that local officials supported the local police. They were the critical link between the bottom-up and top-down strategies.

In the south the program enjoyed increasing success due to the more hierarchical nature of the tribes and their physical distance from the Taliban and Haqqani sanctuaries in Pakistan. For example, Khakrez, once a booming local economic hub in Kandahar Province, had fallen prey to a growing Taliban insurgency that used the district as a safe haven for staging attacks on Kandahar City. After the establishment of VSO, however, local villages were empowered to protect themselves and resist Taliban intimidation. As 2009 progressed, Taliban control of the district was reversed by local defense, development projects, and strengthened ties to the Afghan government. Within six months every shop in the once-shuttered bazaar had reopened, resulting in a resurgent local economy. The additional jobs then fed into a greater desire for local security. In addition local *shuras* once again became important in settling tribal disputes, which helped counter the Taliban's intervening as an arbiter.

Out in western Afghanistan, Zerkho Valley in Herat Province became another example of the VSO program's potential. The valley was a known enemy safe haven and transit point for the Taliban. The Special Forces firebase at the entrance to the valley was constantly attacked, mainly because the tribes in the valley turned a blind eye to the Taliban's activities. Those individuals who did resist or worked with the ODA were silenced. Taliban commanders often recruited from the tribes whose elders had little incentive to resist them. Rather than responding to the insurgent attacks by fortifying and reinforcing the base, as had been our practice in the past, the two ODAs stationed there managed to convince the two main tribes in the valley to allow them to move into a village on the border of their lands. Within months of the teams moving in they had established strong relationships with the local tribal leadership. After meeting the needs of the villages with localized projects and physically protecting the elders, IED attacks completely ceased and locals began pointing out arms caches that the insurgents had stored for future operations. By the time of my redeployment in early 2010, I was reading reports of elders who hadn't spoken to each other in years meeting in *shuras* and local men working in the Zerkho Valley rather than seeking work in Iran. "The security situation since Special Forces moved into Zerkho Valley is getting much better," District Governor Lal Mohammed was quoted as saying in an article in *Army Times.* "I appreciate their presence in the valley—it's a very dangerous area."[1] The article also mentioned that a half dozen other nearby villages had asked to be included in the program after seeing its benefits. I was also thrilled to read of progress in my former areas of responsibility. The ODAs in Chamkani, Khost, and Shkin had growing VSO programs. Most heartening was the series of reports, including the National Intelligence Estimate on Afghanistan, which cited the Taliban and Haqqani leadership as viewing the VSO program as a strategic threat to their insurgency.

The success of the program moved the Army Special Forces community and leadership away from focusing on targeting Taliban commanders and back toward a combination of rural stability and training the elite portions of the Afghan Army. An article in *Army Times* in 2011 quoted one of the most aggressive Green Beret colonels, Donald Bolduc: "The Village Stability [Operations] program and the efforts to establish ANA Commando units together form CJSOTF's highest priorities." He acknowledged that this was a far cry from a few years earlier, when CJSOTF was "more focused on 'kinetic' operations to capture and kill insurgents." He admitted, "Special Operations Forces had an enemy-focused approach to how we conducted operations. . . . As a battalion commander for two rotations, did we do population-centric operations? We sure did. But I was focused on the enemy. The enemy was a viable threat that operated in the rural areas very effectively and we went after them. My theory at the time was pressure, pursue, punish. My three Ps now: presence, patience and persistence."[2]

The enthusiastic support for VSO ran from the operational level back to Washington. I was thrilled to see this level of buy-in and that General Petraeus made getting President Karzai's full support for the program one of his top priorities when he took command of ISAF in the summer of 2010. On July 14, 2010, the Pentagon's press secretary Geoff Morrell said at a news conference, "While we are simultaneously operating at a far higher tempo and degrading the Taliban so they are less of a threat to these local communities, we can utilize a willing, local, armed population to do community policing."

The local police forces are not militias, Morrell explained. Karzai approved a plan to put up to ten thousand community police in place, to be paid by the government and to operate under the control of Afghanistan's Interior Ministry.

"This is about putting locals to work, so that they can be on watch in their communities for people who shouldn't be there, and then work with the established security organizations—the [Afghan] Army, the police, the coalition—to make sure they don't menace their communities," Morrell said.

Other officials said examples of Afghan villagers banding together to deny the Taliban access to their towns had been encouraging. "We clearly have seen examples of local communities repelling attempts by the Taliban to infiltrate and intimidate their communities," Morrell said. "We have also, though, seen examples where there are communities that may not have stepped up in that demonstrable a way, but clearly want to and are looking for help in doing so."[3]

Karzai's formal endorsement was great news, but placing the program under the notoriously corrupt and ineffective Ministry of Interior concerned me. During debates in the White House in 2008, I argued that such a program should be more of a national guard than an auxiliary police. I felt that putting the highly sensitive program under one of the least functioning and most challenged ministries was a mistake. It made more sense to have community defense units reporting to the much more capable Army and Ministry of Defense, which could better support them logistically.

Over the next year a number of think tanks and embedded journalists in Afghanistan reported on the growing success of the program. In October 2011 Adm. Bill McRaven, commander of Special Operations Command, testified before the House Armed Services Committee. "Our greatest success in Afghanistan has come from the Special Forces officers and [noncommissioned officers] who have been on the ground trying to change the landscape, if you will, in terms of our relationships with the Afghans," he said. "The village stability operations, developing the Afghan local police, this is the most promising effort we have in Afghanistan right now."[4] By mid-2012 the VSO program had spread to over eighty districts with nearly seventeen thousand local police in every region in Afghanistan. I attended a predeployment training session called "Academic Week" hosted by Special Operations Command where ODAs on the verge of deploying to Afghanistan spent several days attending courses on everything from negotiations to tribal dynamics. Many people were saying that the Green Berets had finally returned to their historical roots by using their language and cultural training to undermine the insurgency by denying them tribal support. One ODA commander had flown back from Afghanistan to share lessons learned with the group and presented a slide show of his experiences. His initial entry into a valley was met with multiple IED strikes and two casualties. The opening slides were photos of heavily armored vehicles, men in full body armor, and weekly firefights. However, after he and his team worked closely with the elders, recruited Afghan local police, established checkpoints, and arrested a Taliban commander, the valley began to stabilize. His slides from the end of the tour showed his men driving around the area in Hilux pickup trucks with no body armor and wearing nothing but *shalwar kameez* shirts over their camouflage pants. He didn't have a single firefight the last two months of the tour and had expanded the bubble of stability to the next valley. Importantly, the ODA had reestablished the local *shura* as the authority that then arbitrated a long-standing dispute over water rights among three tribes and the district governor.

This is not to deny that the program was fraught with peril. I was very concerned at the same conference to hear that the interior minister, a Tajik from northern Afghanistan, was not allowing the expansion of the VSO program in the Pashtun south unless there was the same level of expansion in the Tajik-dominated north. Even though the VSO program was needed to a far greater extent in the south and east, where the Taliban insurgency was obviously the strongest, the minister insisted the same level of attention and support be provided to his ethnic brethren in the north. I became even more disturbed after finding out that the minister had further insisted that the militias in the north be provided organization, training, and weapons but that the ODAs did not need to live with the Tajik local police. Instead they could just visit from time to time and provide over watch from a distance. This was clearly a strategy to use the VSO program to reconstitute and organize the former Northern Alliance militias as they prepared for a resurgent Pashtun Taliban movement in the wake of the U.S. withdrawal. Having the program manipulated to prepare for a potential return to civil war was a nightmare scenario for all of us who supported the program.

Overall, however, I was convinced that we were finally getting it right on a number of levels. I felt I had truly contributed to nudging the war effort in a positive direction by pushing for a program like VSO from the Pentagon and White House and then overseeing its implementation in several areas in the field. The program required our ODAs to permanently get out of their bases and into the villages. We were taking on the Taliban at their own game of leveraging fault lines in Afghan society. As more villagers joined the local police, not only were the Taliban physically pushed out of the villages, but a psychological barrier was created between the people and the insurgency. Afghans could travel more freely, attend school without fear, engage in greater commerce, and use traditional justice systems to address disputes. Further, the VSO program was sustainable over the long term with relatively small numbers of U.S. troops and could be used to secure the villages while the Afghan Army and police secured the cities and major roads. However, despite its initial successes, the program was still ripe for abuse and would require sustained engagement by our Special Forces. Given the Obama administration's mantra of withdrawal of U.S. combat forces, did we have enough time to make the good results of VSO permanent? Was VSO the right strategy implemented too late? Most disturbing, would the precipitous withdrawal of oversight of the local police by our Special Forces result in the program doing more harm than good in the long run?

15 Washington Again
Wishing the Problem Away

When I left the White House on January 19, 2009, Afghanistan was widely perceived by much of President Obama's national security team as the "good war," in contrast to the "bad war" in Iraq. Indeed candidate Obama had called Afghanistan the "war of necessity" and one he was determined to win. When I arrived back in Washington in the spring of 2010 I was surprised at how much the national discussion on Afghanistan had changed in the previous year. The debate in Washington had changed from "How do we succeed?" to "How quickly do we leave?" After two contentious reviews of U.S. strategy toward Afghanistan in 2009, officials in the Obama administration had discovered how difficult success in Afghanistan was going to be and how much of the nation's treasure it was going to take to get it right. The president appeared to have acquiesced to the military in agreeing to the troop surge but now clearly desired to focus his efforts on domestic issues. Despite thousands of American troops pouring into Afghanistan in 2010, I soon discovered that the president's newfound desire to end America's participation in the war underscored every aspect of his administration's approach, from pressing the military for drawdown schedules to negotiating with the Taliban and stating that al Qaeda was essentially defeated.

I returned to the secretary of defense's Afghanistan-Pakistan policy office. Having worked for Vice President Cheney, I wasn't expecting a warm welcome from the new Democratic leadership in the Pentagon, even though I was technically a nonpolitical civil servant. I was pleasantly surprised at the gracious welcome of the new deputy assistant secretary of defense David Sedney, who immediately assigned me to a sensitive issue: representing the Pentagon in the establishment of a policy framework for negotiating with the Taliban. However, after several meetings in the White House with the small group handling the reconciliation strategy I quickly became disenchanted. The underlying theme of everything we were discussing seemed to be how to end the war rather than how to win it.

In my view, establishing parameters for negotiations with the Taliban had previously been lacking in the war effort and was sorely needed. However, the timing of the effort and the administration's motivations behind the proposed talks were problematic. My experience the previous year in Afghanistan had shown that the war in 2010 was, at best, a stalemate. We were pushing for the reconciliation talks too soon; we should have waited until we were negotiating from a position of strength. And the outreach was viewed by many Afghans as the first major step toward abandonment. I tried to weigh in with my experiences from the field, pointing out that the Taliban were winning in many parts of the country and that reaching out to negotiate at this point was viewed as desperation.

I quickly sensed that there was another agenda at play, particularly within the State Department and Ambassador Richard Holbrooke's Office of the Special Representative for Afghanistan and Pakistan. Officials seemed to be pushing for reconciliation as an end to be achieved for its own sake. Further, there was little effort to incorporate Afghanistan's ethnic minorities into the potential negotiations, leaving them dangerously suspicious that the United States, President Karzai, the Taliban, and Pakistan were cutting a deal that was against their interests. As the year progressed, State's agenda to charge ahead and use the reconciliation talks as a mechanism to quickly end the war seemed to intensify.

At the same time I was participating in debates in the White House and State Department about whether the time was right to cut a deal with the Taliban, I was also attending a series of remembrances for the fallen from my unit. The services were respectful and heartfelt, of course, but also emotionally exhausting. They culminated with Memorial Day at Arlington National Cemetery. As we walked among the newest rows of headstones in Arlington's Section 60, I contemplated how we had lost our way in Afghanistan. Between my time in the Pentagon and the White House and my multiple tours in the field, my thinking had crystallized. I was more convinced than ever that historians would look back on the war and contribute its malaise to a handful of key strategic flaws.

Perhaps the most significant error was that the Bush administration (including me in my minor role) never really set clear goals and objectives for why we were in Afghanistan once the Taliban and al Qaeda were defeated in late 2001. The U.S. military focused on a pure counterterrorism mission by mopping up remaining elements of the Taliban regime and was very slow to adopt a strategy for how to ensure they remained defeated. The Bush administration's initial reluctance to do nation building along with the shift in our national focus to Iraq only exacerbated the situation by delaying the adoption of an end state that defined success in Afghanistan. In the vacuum of our strategic drift, the Taliban reassembled in the safety of their sanctuary in Pakistan and forcefully reasserted itself. It wasn't until the U.S. government's strategic review in 2006 that we finally used the term *counterinsurgency* and thereby implicitly admitted we had an insurgency on our hands. Eventually we found ourselves half-heartedly backing into a nation-building campaign as we realized how much effort it would take to get the Afghan government and security forces back on their feet and that the "lead nation" strategy wasn't working. However, by that time, the effort had been turned over to NATO, whose members could not agree on the definition of counterinsurgency, much less an operational plan to conduct it.

As a result of this lack of strategic focus, we had a perennially underresourced war effort. The insurgency intensified, year after year, and we reacted with perfunctory attempts to match the escalation the following year. But we found ourselves chasing the violence and could never get ahead of it to tamp it down. In Afghanistan we had a country with a larger population than Iraq's that was sprawled across some of the most difficult terrain on earth, with little infrastructure, no natural resources or tax base, no access to seaports, an insurgent sanctuary next door in Pakistan, extreme poverty, and a horrid 75 percent illiteracy rate. Yet we devoted a fraction of the resources to the effort compared with Iraq.

We tried to compensate for the lack of U.S. resources by leaning on NATO to provide them. As I experienced with the Dutch, Polish, and French forces, we grossly underestimated how much the European militaries had atrophied in the years since the end of the Cold War. They simply were not ready to conduct an extended campaign thousands of miles from Europe in one of the most difficult places in the world. They arrived ready for Bosnia-style peacekeeping, not a complex and violent counterinsurgency campaign alongside a quasi-functional partner in the Afghan National Army and police. Once on the ground, NATO found itself incapable of conducting counterinsurgency because of member states' radically different approaches to dealing with it and the restrictions their home governments placed on them. Moreover, the move from U.S. to NATO lead in 2006 sent the signal to the region that it was the beginning of the end for the United States in Afghanistan. Ultimately, that shift resulted in unmet promises to the Afghan people, frustration, and a security vacuum for the Taliban to exploit.

Another crucial mistake was our inability to effectively dissuade Pakistan from supporting the Taliban, the Haqqani network, and other groups that served their strategic ends. Having served in four provinces along their border and experienced Pakistan's duplicity firsthand, I returned to Washington more convinced than ever that the Pakistani Army was not going to change its ways unless it believed cutting ties with militants would be useful in achieving its goals. So long as we publicly announced our withdrawal (which left Pakistan to deal with the mess in Afghanistan) but continued to provide billions to support the Pakistani Army, there was going to be little incentive for them to change.

Finally, I'm convinced that history will look back on President Obama's announcement of a troop surge at the same time he announced a timetable for its withdrawal as a critical strategic miscalculation in our policy toward the war. Just as the president declared he was sending our military and civilians the resources they had so long deserved, he pulled the rug out from under the positive effect they would have before they even arrived. As promised, eighteen months after his December 2009 West Point speech announcing the surge, President Obama gave a follow-on speech in June 2011 outlining his strategy to begin the withdrawal of not only the surge forces but all combat forces by 2014. He spoke of focusing on "ending the war" and "nation-building at home" rather than abroad.[1] It was the final piece of evidence that the administration was simply wishing the problem away and had no intention of making the long-term commitment necessary to stabilize the region and prevent the resurgence of terrorist sanctuaries that could be used to attack America again. As a result, I decided to leave government for the private sector, where I hoped to continue to serve in a different capacity.

Once the president announced his intent to eliminate all combat forces by the end of 2014, the debate in Washington became limited to the numbers of supporting troops that would remain and the timeline for the rest to leave. The issue was finally settled when the president announced that all military forces, regardless of function, would be withdrawn by the end of 2016. These debates over troop numbers and timelines were important but missed the bigger point. The larger strategic issue was the signal Obama had sent to our allies, our enemies, and the region: America was leaving, period. This signal presented a host of fundamental problems to the war effort going forward.

First, the entire region began to maneuver for a post-American Afghanistan, mostly in ways that ran counter to U.S. interests. That maneuvering is ongoing today. What the Obama administration didn't and still doesn't fully appreciate is that the Afghan people, the Afghan government, the Pakistanis, the Indians, the Iranians, and the rest of Central Asia weren't listening to the policy nuances of how many and what type of U.S. forces will remain. All they heard was U.S. withdrawal and abandonment. Disturbingly, all the Taliban and al Qaeda heard from the 2011 speech was that they had survived our surge and they only needed to outlast us a few more years, until the final U.S. pullout in 2016. The entire region was, and still is, hedging against the United States rather than siding with it.

Second, as Defense Secretary Robert Gates very bluntly warned on his way out of office (around the same time as Obama's 2011 speech), our European allies would use the gradual withdrawal of U.S. forces as the green light to head for the exits. Despite the bombings in Madrid and London, Europeans had been agitating over their involvement in "America's war" in Afghanistan for years. Hearing the president confirm that we were leaving served to quickly disintegrate any remaining allied resolve. A number of European governments actually accelerated their own withdrawal timelines. Declining troop numbers also greatly reduced the ability of U.S. government civilians—who operated under military protection—to go out into the provinces and provide assistance to the Afghans on agriculture, rule of law, and economic development. After the president's announcement, the civilian agencies quickly developed their own withdrawal schedules, pulled back their already meager presence from forward bases, and cut funding. During a visit to Kandahar that year, one senior U.S. military commander described USAID as a source of instability rather than stability due to its continued lack of a meaningful presence in the provinces and its resultant inability to fulfill its promises to Afghans.

Third, every Afghan I spoke to in the years following my return to Washington, from cabinet ministers to my former interpreters, was increasingly concerned about the prospect of a renewed civil war in the wake of the American withdrawal. My Tajik, Uzbek, and Hazaran friends believed the United States was cutting a deal with Karzai and the Taliban that was going to leave them in the cold. A multitude of notable Tajik leaders—Deputy Interior Minister Mohammad Daoud (since assassinated by the Taliban), former intelligence chief Amrullah Saleh, former minister for reconstruction Mohammad Ehsan Zia, and others—increasingly began to spend time away from Kabul and back in their home turf reconstituting old alliances and networks. It became clear to me that the former Northern Alliance, which had resisted the Pashtun Taliban during their brutal regime, was getting the band back together. Unfortunately for the United States, that included outreach to its old allies in Iran, Russia, and India—all of whom were increasingly viewed as more reliable than the United States.

This has left our Afghanistan policy going forward a policy of hope and assumptions. We are assuming the Afghan National Army and police are going to be able to stand on their own after we leave. As of this writing we still have advisors at the higher headquarters level of the Afghan Army. However, the advisors' knowledge of how the Army is performing out in the mountains and border regions comes from self-reporting from the platoons and companies with no foreign advisors. We have little means of knowing how they are actually doing, and once all advisors are withdrawn in 2016 we will be completely blind regarding their performance against the Taliban and al Qaeda. If our assumptions about the security forces are wrong and they can't stand on their own, we may not know it until it's too late.

We are also assuming the Afghans will be able to manage a successful political transition to a successor for President Karzai. We are hoping that the outcome will be viewed as relatively legitimate by all of Afghanistan's ethnic groups, particularly the Tajik-dominated Afghan National Army and that Afghanistan's neighbors will give the new government a chance to succeed. As President Karzai aptly reminded Vice President Cheney during their final visit in 2008, no Afghan leader in the country's history has peacefully transitioned; all have either eventually been exiled or executed. This seems to be the very worst time for us to significantly draw down our forces.

Finally, the current policy is based on the assumption that al Qaeda can't stage a comeback after we withdraw. I find this a very dangerous assumption, given an increasingly unstable Pakistan, a diminished U.S. and coalition presence, growing ethnic tension, and Afghan Army and police forces that are years away from independent operations. A counterterrorism strategy must be nested within a broader counterinsurgency strategy, as a populace that faces retribution from extremists won't be very inclined to continue to provide us the intelligence we need. Additionally, in my experience, the CIA and the military are dependent on each other for supplies and protection at their various bases near the Pakistani border. With the military leaving, I'm certain the CIA will have great difficulty maintaining the same intensity of counterterrorism operations against al Qaeda in Pakistan that have been so successful in keeping their leadership on the run. Given these dynamics, I have yet to find someone who supports the administration's drawdown strategy who can tell me what we are going to do if all of these assumptions are wrong and al Qaeda stages a comeback after we leave. Al Qaeda's resurgence in Syria and Iraq, along with groups like the Islamic State of Syria and al-Sham (ISIS), shows the folly of this strategy of hope. Except, in the case of Pakistan, should things go wrong and al Qaeda once again become ascendant, even more is at stake: nuclear weapons.

The bottom line is that our policy going forward is underlined by ambiguity. The uncertainty of whether our assumptions will hold true has everyone guessing and hedging in unconstructive ways. As one Afghan businessman recently remarked to me, "I feel as though my entire country is speeding toward a cliff. No one, from government officials to the lowest villager, knows what is going to happen. I do not want to make any investments in my business. I don't even want to leave money in an Afghan bank until I have some idea of how this will turn out." He and many of his colleagues in a national business association have moved their money out of Afghanistan to Dubai and other neighboring countries. Similarly, an agriculture professor at the University of Kabul told me that numerous grants from international organizations have been put on hold, causing him to lay off several research assistants and to cancel an agriculture extension program. "The entire international community is reevaluating their investment in the Afghan people because America has decided to walk out. We do not need billions of dollars from the United States. We just need America to tell everyone to stop packing up to leave!"

In late 2012 I was asked to give a talk to a group of congressional staffers on what I thought should be the long-term way forward in Afghanistan since I had come to so strongly disagree with the U.S. withdrawal strategy. I began the talk with a historic reflection on an allied country in East Asia whose infrastructure and agricultural economy were in shambles after decades of war and occupation. This country's political system was corrupt and dysfunctional, and its populace was deeply impoverished. In fact its literacy rate in 1945 was lower than Afghanistan's literacy rate today.[2] However, over a period of fifty years the United States made long-term investments to partner with the Army, stabilize the economy, and build human capital until the country was able to transition into an industrial powerhouse, a technology leader, and a functioning democracy. That country is South Korea.

Though not a perfect analogy, it was worth reminding the young staffers of what was possible when the United States decided that stabilizing a country was important to its long-term national interests. Of course it would have been political suicide for President Eisenhower to announce in the 1950s that the United States planned to have forces in South Korea for the next five to six decades, just as it would be difficult for President Obama to face the American people with a similar message today. But Eisenhower steadfastly made the case for why it was critical to our national security to blunt the spreading ideology of communism in Korea, and he quietly put the pieces in place to remain engaged on the Korean Peninsula until we had a thriving ally contributing to global stability. I made the case that we should be doing the same for Afghanistan today. Preventing extremism from regaining a foothold in Afghanistan and once again threatening the region and possibly our homeland is as much in the interest of the United States now as it was to stop communism decades ago. In fact we know from the treasure trove of internal communications seized from the Osama bin Laden raid that al Qaeda senior leaders and the Taliban discussed taking advantage of the post-American vacuum in Afghanistan to quietly reestablish themselves in the ungoverned spaces of the border region and eventually turn their sights back on Pakistan and its nuclear arsenal.

In response to a staffer's skepticism about whether such a strategy was sustainable over the long term, I explained that by 2010 we seemed to have finally had the makings of a winning formula in Afghanistan after learning from nearly a decade of mistakes. Despite all of our previous blunders, I felt we had several key ingredients in place to establish a degree of security for the private sector and development to flourish. We had Special Forces teams partnering in rural areas alongside key tribes that were increasingly denying the Taliban access to recruits and support. We also had in place ongoing tactical advising of the Afghan National Army and police at a low enough level that, if sustained for the long term, could have helped a new generation of Afghan leaders protect their nation.

I did not advocate, then or now, leaving a massive foreign footprint in Afghanistan indefinitely, but I do firmly believe the drawdown needed to be much more gradual and needed to be dependent on security conditions and not an arbitrary timeline. To be sure, a more measured drawdown of support staff and infrastructure while still having troops and civilians embedded in rural Afghan villages and Afghan security forces would have required the military's leadership to drastically change its tolerance for risk. The bases may not be as comfortable, medevac may not be as readily available, and every level of headquarters may not have full visibility on every mission. But I'm convinced our men and women, military and civilian, in harm's way would accept the higher risk, if only our leadership would let them.

Had we continued the strategy of tribal engagement that was just starting to show signs of success while continuing the tough work of improving the Army and police, we could have solidified our gains realized during the surge. Further, in 2010 multinational corporations and investors had just started to realize the potential of Afghanistan's promising mining, agribusiness, and telecommunications sectors. Especially in the mining sector there were real possibilities for Afghanistan's untapped marble, gemstones, and rare earth minerals such as lithium to transform the world's fourth-poorest economy. But the Afghan Parliament and ministries needed substantial long-term mentoring to put laws and regulations in place that would attract outside investment. Instead, many experts were withdrawn and mentoring programs cut by 2013 as part of the broader withdrawal strategy.

I concluded my talk to the staffers by reinforcing the point that we must take the same long-term view with Afghanistan in order to blunt the ideology of extremism as we did in Korea against communism. What Afghanistan most needed was a positive and consistent strategic message from the United States that said, "We are with you for the long haul because supporting you against instability and extremism is in our national interest." Even if our troop numbers gradually diminished in the background (as they did in Korea, from fifty thousand in the 1960s to twenty-five thousand today), such a message could have had profoundly positive effects. If the Afghan people, the Afghan government, and the Pakistani Army heard that message of commitment from the United States, they would be much more inclined to work with us instead of hedging against us.

Many experts argue that most Americans, and by extension the Congress, are not prepared to commit to such a sustained obligation in South Asia. I contend that our leadership in Washington has never explained to the American people what we are going to do if Afghanistan once again descends into chaos and al Qaeda realizes its plan to move back into Taliban-controlled areas to rebuild itself. They have never explained the real possibility of those same forces then destabilizing a nuclear-armed Pakistan and that a stable South Asia is directly connected to our national interests and the protection of our homeland. Instead, all the American people have heard is how difficult the war has been and therefore that we need to leave. Supporting Afghanistan as we did Germany, Japan, and South Korea after World War II would absolutely be tough and expensive. But the cost would pale in comparison to trying to regain the trust of the Afghan people after we have abandoned them for a third time. In the end, I have come to firmly believe that, as the Mangal elder Ghafoorzai told me over chai in Khost, we must be prepared to commit our grandchildren to stand shoulder to shoulder with his grandchildren.

NOTES

1. STATE OF THE WAR

1. Gall, "Cheney and Afghan Milestone."
2. Franks and McConnell, *American Soldier*, 324.
3. "Rumsfeld Declares the End to Combat Operations in Afghanistan."
4. Author's notes, B/2/20th Special Forces Group, July 2003.
5. Author's notes, weekly videoconference with Joint Staff and Central Command, October 2004.
6. Radio Free Europe/Radio Liberty, "Afghanistan."
7. Author's notes, U.S. Counternarcotics Strategy in Afghanistan, 2004.
8. Author's notes, Afghan Interagency Operations Group meeting, State Department, September 2004.
9. United Nations Office of Drug Control, "World Drug Report," 180.
10. Author's notes, Joint Staff Afghan Desk, Office of the Secretary of Defense–Policy, Stability, and Regional Office meeting, April 2005.
11. Jones, *In the Graveyard of Empires*, 243.
12. Author's notes, Central Command and Joint Staff briefings, June 2005.
13. Author's notes, meetings with Lieutenant General Eikenberry, Joint Staff and Office of the Secretary of Defense–Policy offices, July 2005.
14. Author's notes, Afghan Interagency Operations Group meeting, State Department, December 2004.
15. Author's notes, NATO military delegation meeting, 2005.
16. Aldinger, "U.S. to Cut Troop Level in Afghanistan."
17. Jones, *In the Graveyard of Empires, 204.*

4. THE CLINIC IN ACHIN

1. United Nations, *The Situation in Afghanistan and Its Implications for Peace and Security*, 1.
2. Luehrs, "Provincial Reconstruction Teams."
3. Baron, "Gates: 'Congress Is Part of the Problem' in State, USAID Shortfalls."
4. "ISAF Fact Sheet," 2006.
5. "USAID Fact Sheet," 2006.

5. THE ROAD TO MUSA QALA

1. Phillips, "U.S. Takes Over Fight in Helmand."

7. OPERATION PERTH

1. FOB Ripley was named after the legendary Vietnam-era Marine Col. John Ripley, the father of one of my VMI classmates and the subject of the book *The Bridge at Dong Ha*. The base was just south of Tarin Kowt, the capital of Uruzgan Province. "'He's a hero to the Marine Corps,' said Colonel Kenneth F. McKenzie, Jr., commanding officer of the Marine Expeditionary Unit (Special Operations Capable), referring to Col. John W. Ripley, the new FOB's namesake. 'He's a true warrior and an honorable man.'" Milks, "22d MEU (SOC)'s FOB in Afghanistan Pays Homage to Marine Hero." McKenzie includes Colonel Ripley in the small group of Marine leaders mentioned prominently in the Corps' proud history.

8. BACK TO WASHINGTON

1. Author's notes, Secretary Gates trip to Afghanistan, 2007.
2. Author's notes, Interagency meetings before and after Riga Summit, 2007.
3. Author's notes, ISAF troop numbers briefing, 2007.
4. Author's notes, NATO Defense Ministerial, NATO HQ, 2007.
5. Author's notes, Secretary of Defense videoconference, 2007.
6. Author's notes, Pakistan Deputies Committee, 2008.
7. Author's notes, NSC meeting, 2008.
8. Ballard, Lamm, and Wood, *From Kabul to Baghdad and Back*, 221.
9. Author's notes, NSC meeting, 2008.

9. THE MANGAL TRIBE

1. Feickert, *Mine-Resistant, Ambush-Protected (MRAP) Vehicles*.

12. BLACKBEARD RISING

1. *Report on Progress towards Security and Stability in Afghanistan*, 17.
2. *Report on Progress Towards Security and Stability in Afghanistan*, 14.
3. *Report on Progress Towards Security and Stability in Afghanistan*, 58.
4. Maj. Gen. Robert Durbin and First Deputy Minister of the Interior for Security Abdul Khalid, Department of Defense news briefing with Maj. Gen. Robert Durbin and Minister Abdul Hadir Khalid from the Pentagon, January 2007.
5. Mora, "Only 2 of 180 Afghan Battalions Can Operate Independently of U.S. Forces."

13. ON THE BORDER WITH PAKISTAN

1. Mazzetti and Schmitt, "Pakistanis Aided Attack in Kabul, U.S. Officials Say."
2. Mazzetti and Schmitt, "Bush Said to Give Orders Allowing Raids in Pakistan."

3. New America Foundation, Drone Database, http://natsec.newamerica.net /drones/pakistan/analysis.

14. THE TRIBES OF CHAMKANI

1. Naylor, "Program Has Afghans as First Line of Defense."
2. Naylor, "Program Has Afghans as First Line of Defense."
3. Garamone, "Karzai Approves Plan to Keep Taliban Out of Villages."
4. McRaven, "Testimony before House Armed Services Sub-Committee on Capabilities and Emerging Threats."

15. WASHINGTON AGAIN

1. Obama, "Transcript: Obama's Speech on Afghanistan War Withdrawal."
2. Savada and Shaw, *South Korea: A Country Study.*

BIBLIOGRAPHY

Afghanistan National Independent Peace and Reconciliation Commission. "40 Armed Taliban from Ghazni Province Along with Their Weapons Joined the Reconciliation Program." Press release. May 2009.

Aldinger, Charles. "U.S. to Cut Troop Level in Afghanistan." Reuters, December 20, 2005. Web.

Allen, John R., Michele Flournoy, and Michael O'Hanlon. *Toward a Successful Outcome in Afghanistan*. Washington DC: Center for New American Security, May 2013.

Associated Press. "Commanding Generals of NATO-Led International Security Assistance Force in Afghanistan." November 20, 2012. http://www.foxnews.com/world/2012/11/20/commanding-generals-nato-led-international-security-assistance-force-in/.

Bajer, Justyna. "Top Polish Officials Visit Troops in Ghazni Province." Afghanistan International Security Assistance Force. Press release. N.d. http://www.isaf.nato.int/article/isaf-releases/top-polish-officials-visit-troops-in-ghazni-province.html.

Ballard, John R., David W. Lamm, and John K. Wood. *From Kabul to Baghdad and Back: The U.S. at War in Afghanistan and Iraq*. Annapolis MD: Naval Institute Press, 2012.

Barno, David W. "Fighting the Other War." *Military Review*, September–October 2007, 32–44.

Baron, Kevin. "Gates: 'Congress Is Part of the Problem' in State, USAID Shortfalls." *Stripes Blank RSS Test*. Stripes Central, August 23, 2010. Web.

Belasco, Amy. *Troop Levels in Afghan and Iraq Wars, FY2001–FY2012: Cost and Other Potential Issues*. Report R40682. Washington DC: Congressional Research Service, July 2, 2009.

Bergen, Peter. "The Battle for Tora Bora: How Osama bin Laden Slipped from Our Grasp—The Definitive Account." *New Republic*, December 22, 2009. http://www.newrepublic.com/article/the-battle-tora-bora.

———. *Holy War, Inc.* New York: Free Press, 2001.

Bergen, Peter, and Katherine Tiedemann. "The Drone War." *New Republic*, June 3, 2009.

Brennan, John O. "The Ethics and Efficacy of the President's Counterterrorism Strategy." Remarks presented at the Woodrow Wilson International Center for Scholars, April 30, 2012. http://www.wilsoncenter.org/event/the-efficacy -and-ethics-us-counterterrorism-strategy/.

Cerami, Joseph R., and Jay W. Boggs, eds. *The Interagency and Counterinsurgency Warfare: Stability, Security, Transition, and Reconstruction Roles*. Carlisle PA: Strategic Studies Institute, U.S. Army War College, December 2007.

Chandrasekaran, Rajiv. *Little America: The War within the War for Afghanistan*. New York: Knopf, 2012.

Cheney, Dick. *In My Time*. New York: Threshold, 2011.

Coll, Steve. *Ghost Wars: The Secret History of the CIA, Afghanistan, and Bin Laden, from the Soviet Invasion to September 10, 2001*. New York: Penguin, 2004.

Connable, Ben, and Martin C. Libicki. *How Insurgencies End*. Santa Monica CA: RAND Corporation, 2010.

Dobbins, James F. *After the Taliban: Nation-Building in Afghanistan*. Washington DC: Potomac Books, 2008.

Fair, Christine. "Pakistani Power Play." *Foreign Policy*, November 5, 2012. Web.

Feickert, Andrew. *Mine-Resistant, Ambush-Protected (MRAP) Vehicles: Background and Issues for Congress*. Fort Belvoir VA: Defense Technical Information Center, 2009. Fas.org. Congressional Research Service, January 18, 2011. Web.

Feith, Douglas J. *War and Decision: Inside the Pentagon at the Dawn of the War on Terrorism*. New York: Harper, 2008.

Fishstein, Paul, and Andrew Wilder. *Winning Hearts and Minds? Examining the Relationship between Aid and Security in Afghanistan*. Boston: Feinstein International Center, 2011.

Flynn, Michael T., Matt Pottinger, and Paul D. Batchelor. *Fixing Intel: A Blueprint for Making Intelligence Relevant in Afghanistan*. Washington DC: Center for New American Security, 2010.

Franks, Tommy, with Malcolm McConnell. *American Soldier*. New York: Regan Books, 2004.

Gall, Carlotta. "Cheney and Afghan Milestone." *New York Times*, December 20, 2005. http://www.nytimes.com/2005/12/20/international/asia/20afghan .html?_r=0.

Galula, David. *Counterinsurgency Warfare: Theory and Practice*. Westport CT: Praeger Security International, 2006.

Garamone, Jim. "Karzai Approves Plan to Keep Taliban Out of Villages." American Foreign Press Service, July 14, 2010.

Grau, Lester W., and Michael A. Gress. *The Soviet-Afghan War: How a Superpower Fought and Lost*. Lawrence: University Press of Kansas, 2002.

Green, Daniel R. *The Valley's Edge: A Year with the Pashtuns in the Heartland of the Taliban*. Washington DC: Potomac Books, 2012.

Hopkins, Nancy, ed. *Afghanistan in 2012: A Survey of the Afghan People*. Washington DC: Asia Foundation, 2012.

International Crisis Group. *Afghanistan: The Long, Hard Road to the 2014 Transition.* Asia Report No. 236, October 8, 2012.

"ISAF Fact Sheet." ISAF Headquarters, NATO, 2006. Web.

Jalali, Ali Ahmad, and Lester W. Grau. *The Other Side of the Mountain: Mujahideen Tactics in the Soviet-Afghan War.* Quantico VA: U.S. Marine Corps, Studies and Analysis Division, 1999.

Jones, Seth G. *In the Graveyard of Empires: America's War in Afghanistan.* New York: Norton, 2009.

Kaplan, Robert D. *Soldiers of God: With Islamic Warriors in Afghanistan and Pakistan.* New York: Vintage Departures, 2001.

Lawrence, T. E. *The Evolutions of a Revolt.* Ft. Leavenworth KS: Combat Studies Institute Studies Press, 1920.

Luehrs, Christoff. "Provincial Reconstruction Teams: A Literature Review." *Prism* 1, no. 1 (2009): 95–102.

Mazzetti, Mark, and Eric Schmitt. "Bush Said to Give Orders Allowing Raids in Pakistan." *New York Times*, September 10, 2008. Web.

———. "Pakistanis Aided Attack in Kabul, U.S. Officials Say." *New York Times*, August 1, 2008. Web.

McRaven, William. "Testimony before House Armed Services Sub-Committee on Capabilities and Emerging Threats." September, 22, 2011. http://armed services.house.gov/index.cfm/2011/9/the-future-of-u-s-special-operations -forces-ten-years-after-9-11-and-twenty-five-years-after-goldwater-nichols.

Milks, Keith A. "22d MEU (SOC)'s FOB in Afghanistan Pays Homage to Marine Hero." Official Website of the United States Marine Corps, May 10, 2004. Web.

Mora, Edwin, "Only 2 of 180 Afghan Battalions Can Operate Independently of U.S. Forces." CNSNews.com, September 27, 2011. http://cnsnews.com /news/article/only-2-180-afghan-battalions-can-operate-independently-us -forces.

Naylor, Sean D. *Not a Good Day to Die.* New York: Penguin, 2005.

———. "Program Has Afghans as First Line of Defense." *Army Times*, July 20, 2010. http://www.armytimes.com/article/20100720/news/7200336 /Program-has-Afghans-first-line-defense.

Neumann, Ronald E. *The Other War: Winning and Losing in Afghanistan.* Washington DC: Potomac Books, 2009.

Obama, Barack H. "Transcript: Obama's Speech on Afghanistan War Withdrawal." CNN, June 22, 2011. Web.

Phillips, Michael M. "U.S. Takes Over Flight in Helmand." *Wall Street Journal*, September 13, 2010. Web.

Program for Culture and Conflict Studies. *Provincial Overview: Paktya Province.* Monterey CA: Naval Postgraduate School, November 15, 2011.

Radio Free Europe/Radio Liberty. "Afghanistan: A Chronology of Suicide At-
    tacks Since 2001." January 17, 2006. http://www.rferl.org/content/article
    /1064789.html.
Rashid, Ahmed. *Descent into Chaos: The United States and the Failure of Nation
    Building in Pakistan, Afghanistan, and Central Asia*. New York: Viking, 2008.
*Report on Progress toward Security and Stability in Afghanistan: Report to Con-
    gress*. Washington DC: Department of Defense, June 2008. Web.
"Rumsfeld Declares the End to Combat Operations in Afghanistan." Fox News,
    May 1, 2003. http://www.foxnews.com/story/2003/05/01/rumsfeld-declares
    -major-combat-over-in-afghanistan/.
Saum-Manning, Lisa. "Comparing Past and Current Challenges to Afghan Lo-
    cal Defense." *Small Wars Journal*, December 27, 2012.
Savada, Andrea M., and William Shaw. *South Korea: A Country Study*. Washing-
    ton DC: Government Printing Office for the Library of Congress, 1990. Web.
Shreckengast, Seth A. "The Only Game in Town: Assessing the Effectiveness of
    Village Stability Operations and the Afghan Local Police." *Small Wars Jour-
    nal*, March 27, 2012.
Tanner, Stephen. *Afghanistan: A Military History from Alexander the Great to the
    War against the Taliban*. Philadelphia: Da Capo, 2009.
Tariq, Mohammed Osman. *The Tribal Security System (Arbakai) in Southeast Afghan-
    istan*. Crisis States Research Centre Occasional Paper No. 7, December 2008.
Tyson, Ann S. "Afghan Supply Chain a Weak Point." Afghanistan Mission to
    the UN in New York, March 6, 2009. Web.
United Nations, General Assembly, Security Council (SC). *The Situation in
    Afghanistan and Its Implications for Peace and Security*. Report A/61/326-
    S/2006/727, September 11, 2006.
United Nations, Office of Drug Control (UNODC). "World Drug Report, 2005."
USAID/Afghanistan. "Performance Monitoring Plan." December 16, 2012.
    http://afghanistan.usaid.gov/en/about/performance_monitoring.
"USAID Fact Sheet." Washington DC: U.S. Agency for International Develop-
    ment, January 27, 2006. http://2001-2009.state.gov/p/sca/rls/fs/2006
    /60029.htm.
U.S. Embassy in France. "U.S. Bronze Star Medal of Valor Posthumously
    Awarded to French Navy Commando Loic Le Page Recognizing Heroic Com-
    bat Action in Maruf Valley, Afghanistan." Press release. November 22, 2006.
Vanden Brook, Tom. "IED Attacks Keep Rising, U.S. adjusting." *USA Today*, Sep-
    tember 7, 2006. http://usatoday30.usatoday.com/news/world/iraq/2006
    -09-07-ied-us_x.htm.
Wyler, Liana Sun, and Kenneth Katzman. *Afghanistan: U.S. Rule of Law and Jus-
    tice Sector Assistance*. Report R41484. Washington DC: Congressional Re-
    search Service, November 9, 2010.

INDEX

Special Operations Task Force
(SOTF), 14, 247–48
Spin Boldak, 142, 152–53
strategy: Afghan reconstruction,
30–32, 34, 39–40; author's suggestions on, 210–12; coalition
development, 103–5; counterinsurgency, 34–35, 219–23, 337, 354;
counternarcotics, 28–29, 35–39;
counterterrorism, 31–34; flaws in,
350–57; NSC interagency review
panel and, 218–24
Strmecki, Marin, 34
Sumar, 75–77, 78–80, 83–91
supply lines, 322, 323
support in Afghanistan: from Can-
ada, 126, 165, 184–85, 200; from
Czech Republic, 125, 142; from
Denmark, 200; from Estonia, 202;
from France, 52, 141–46, 149–
50, 156–59, 200; from Germany,
30–31, 40, 45, 46, 200–201; from
Hungary, 202; from Italy, 30–31,
45, 46, 200–201; from Macedonia,
202; from Netherlands, 46–47, 165,
166–69, 173, 181, 185–87, 198, 226;
from Norway, 123; from Poland,
24, 200, 257, 273, 275; from Slovenia, 202; from Spain, 46–47, 200;
from Turkey, 46–47, 200; from
United Kingdom, 30–31, 37, 123,
125, 137–38, 139–40, 200
SUVs, 94–96, 107
Swenson, William, 315–16

Tactical Operations Centers, 241–43
Tagab Valley, 64, 65–67, 70, 89
Tajiks, 46, 75, 145, 180, 331, 347, 353
Tak, Nico, 166–67
Taliban: about, 5–6; Andar tribe and,
19–20, 22, 24–25; Border Post 28

and, 306–17, 323, 324; Dan Mc-
Neill's views on, 205; drug trade
and, 39, 58–59; in Ghazni City,
257; in Herat Province, 343–44; in
Kandahar Province, 343; in Kapisa
Province, 75; in Musa Qala, 138–
40; Operation Perth and, 176–81,
183–88, 189, 193; Pakistan and,
154–55, 222–23; Pakistani Army
and, 48, 318, 320, 325; propaganda
campaign of, 13, 15, 17, 59–60, 314;
reconciliation talks and, 348–49,
353; reintegration of, into Afghan
society, 276–78; Sarposa Prison
break and, 216; strategic flaws in
dealing with, 350; tribal manipulation of, 338; tribal militias and,
328, 345; in Uruzgan Province, 55,
58, 198
tariff revenue, 102
Tarin Kowt, 162, 167, 172, 175, 182,
193, 198
Tarin Kowt PRT, 57, 165, 174
TIC. See troops in contact (TIC)
timelines, 219–20, 294, 352
Todd, 92, 242, 246, 289, 291, 299, 305
Tony, 7–10, 265, 272–73
Tora Bora Mountains, 75, 93, 112
training teams, embedded, 137, 162–
64, 173–74, 197, 202
tribal militias, 76, 221, 229, 232; CDI
and, 327–31, 334–36, 339–42; debate in Washington on, 331–33;
VSO and, 343–47
tribes, differences in, 336–37
Trip, 171, 187, 190
troop numbers, 32, 43, 47, 123. See
also troop surge; withdrawal from
Afghanistan
troops in contact (TIC), 12–13
troop surge, 341–42, 351–52